MILTON PLESUR

AMERICA'S

APPROACHE

OUTWARD THRUST

O FOREIGN AFFAIRS, 1865-1890

 Northern Illinois University Press / DeKalb

Preface

To COMPREHEND the significance of an era, one must use a broad spectrum of sources. The diplomatic history of a particular time must be understood in terms of more than accomplishments of the top decision makers and the provisions of international agreements. Viewed in this light, the foreign policy of a country is much wider than the record of its diplomacy.

This book is a study of our nation's outward thrust in the Gilded Age, defined here as stretching from the conclusion of the Civil War to, as the nineteenth century approached its end, the aggressive diplomacy of the Harrison administration (1889–1893), which forecast the expansionism of the Spanish-American War.

In the first seven chapters, this compilation treats such dynamics of overseas interests as trade and the commercial need for foreign outlets, concern over the role and prestige of Washington's formal diplomatic and consular establishments, its stepped-up participation in a spate of international conferences, and the perennial problem of protecting American citizens abroad. This segment of the book also includes the naval and merchant marine renaissance of the time and various missionary, literary, and travel interests that increasingly captivated American attention in the late Victorian Age.

The remainder of the book is devoted to more specific interests of the United States in several areas of the globe: Europe, sub-Saharan Africa (particularly the Congo), Latin America, Canada, Hawaii, Samoa, and parts of the Orient. Certain other areas, such as the Middle East, are discussed, but generally only incidentally and in connection with the items treated in the earlier chapters.

My aim is not merely to retell the familiar diplomatic relationships covered by the textbooks and monographs. I have, therefore, purposely omitted, or merely mentioned, some items of importance. For example, little is said about the Fenian issue or Grant's abortive Dominican coup. Instead, I have selected certain subjects which highlight America's mounting concern with the wider world and which illustrate our expanding economic, political, and cultural interests overseas. All this prepared the ferment of the nineties over expansion and the overriding problem of international commitment during the century then dawning.

Methodologically speaking, this study is attitudinal: it explores public thought in the United States toward foreign affairs in the Gilded Age. The pitfalls of such a task are obvious. Cumulative thought is awkward to describe, hard to gauge, impossible to concretize, and embarrassingly contradictory and divided. Frequently, it is impossible to determine whether a given expression mirrors public thought or was meant only to stir interest. Newspapers, periodicals, an occasional "find" among manuscripts, and official governmental publications must serve as barometers. Although they do not necessarily reflect dominant opinions, they shed light upon an epoch in American history which only recently has received the attention it deserves.

I am indebted to the Committee on Research and Creative Activity at the State University of New York at Buffalo and to the Research Foundation of the State University of New York for grants which allowed me to make the necessary travel arrangements and which provided research assistance. In addition, I extend sincere thanks to the secretarial staff of my department and to the personnel of the following libraries and institutions: the Lockwood Memorial Library (State University of New York at Buffalo), the University of Rochester, the Buffalo and Erie County Public Library, the Library of Congress, and the National Archives.

A great debt is due my former teacher, my friend and colleague

Professor Selig Adler, Samuel Paul Capen Professor of American History at the State University of New York at Buffalo. His concern with this project, his unselfish devotion of time, and his suggestions are most gratefully acknowledged.

I also wish to thank the following people, who aided me with patience, intelligence, and sincere interest during their careers as doctoral students at the State University of New York at Buffalo: Professors James J. Horn of the State University College at Brockport, New York, and Carmen A. Notaro of Hilbert College, Hamburg, New York; and Mrs. Myra S. Goldstein and Mrs. Joanne Wheeler. They assisted in improving the original draft and checking bibliographic details. This work also reflects the interest and encouragement of others far too numerous to pay adequate tribute to here.

Lastly, my appreciation goes to my father and mother, Matthew and Sophie Plesur, who show typical parental concern and pride in all my projects.

Contents

Preface / v
1. Setting the Stage / 3
2. Early Economic Imperialism / 14
3. Stirrings in the State Department / 35
4. The Literati Cross the Sea / 51
5. The Eagle's Protective Wing / 67
6. The Nation's Right Arm / 87
7. The Overseas Americans: Travelers, Scholars, Technicians, Explorers / 103
8. American Ambivalence: Attitudes toward Europe / 126
9. Spotlight on Darkest Africa / 144
10. The Persistent Monroe Doctrine: Increasing Involvement in Latin America / 157
11. The Quest for a Canadian-American Consensus / 182
12. Across the Pacific / 198
13. Epilogue: Out of the Doldrums / 226
Bibliography / 237
Index / 265

America's Outward Thrust

Approaches to Foreign Affairs, 1865–1890

CHAPTER 1

Setting
the
Stage

DIPLOMATIC historians have given scant attention
to the period known as the Gilded Age (1865–1890). They have
generally contended that expansionism and interest in foreign policy
were in a state of slumber: the post-bellum years were a quiet inter-
lude before the hectic expansionism of the 1890s. The conventional
explanation for this apparent lethargy in foreign affairs has been
that America was preoccupied with internal developments. As one
writer puts it, the sap of manifest destiny ran out of the national
veins on the battlefields of Bull Run, Antietam, Fredericksburg,
Gettysburg, and the Wilderness. During these "doldrum decades,"
a preoccupation with industrialization and the westward push precluded a vigorous interest in overseas affairs. As the editor of the
New York Herald curtly declared in 1881: "Our foreign policy is
a domestic policy." [1]

Historians have agreed for the most part on the factors which

---

[1] Thomas A. Bailey, *The Man in the Street: The Impact of American
Public Opinion on Foreign Policy* (New York, 1948), p. 273; "America Is
Not England," *New York Herald*, Dec. 19, 1881.

prevented a vigorous foreign policy. Writing in 1901, Theodore Clarke Smith listed several of these obstacles: the mountainous national debt, which reduced enthusiasm for further expenditures; preoccupation with Reconstruction policies; and the development of the New South and the West. Later historical research has generally reaffirmed Smith's findings. Samuel Flagg Bemis points out in his survey of diplomatic history that the attention of the United States, "a nation of happy beings" little concerned with foreign affairs, was concentrated upon the great economic and political activities of Western settlement and railroad completion. Thomas A. Bailey observes that Americans were so busy with their own affairs that, in the absence of compelling foreign-policy issues, they had little time to give to their relations with other powers. Julius W. Pratt, exploring the explosion of the neoexpansionist forces of the 1890s, also explains the disinterest of the earlier period in terms of national absorption in domestic problems. This thesis also finds a place in Dexter Perkins' provocative interpretation of American diplomatic history. Professor Perkins describes the years 1870 to 1895 as a quiet component in the diplomatic cycle, a period in which diplomacy remained static in the absence of momentous foreign crises.[2]

While Perkins and most other historians have not judged this quiet period as necessary or desirable, Professor Allan Nevins has praised Hamilton Fish, President Grant's Secretary of State, for preventing the time table of American expansionism from being set ahead by twenty years. Nevins believes (as did Grant's contemporaries of the Gilded Age) that Fish opposed a policy which, if

---

[2] Theodore Clarke Smith, "Expansion after the Civil War, 1865–1871," *Political Science Quarterly* 16 (1901): 412–436. See also Donald M. Dozer, "Anti-Expansionism during the Johnson Administration," *Pacific Historical Review* 12 (1943): 253–275. For a sampling of textbook accounts of the traditional interpretation, see Samuel F. Bemis, *A Diplomatic History of the United States*, 5th ed. (New York, 1965), p. 432; Thomas A. Bailey, *A Diplomatic History of the American People*, 8th ed. (New York, 1969), p. 391; Julius W. Pratt, *America's Colonial Experiment* (New York, 1950), p. 11; Dexter Perkins, *The Evolution of American Foreign Policy* (New York, 1948), p. 54; Perkins, *The American Approach to Foreign Policy* (Cambridge, Mass., 1952), p. 119. See also L. Ethan Ellis, *A Short History of American Diplomacy* (New York, 1951), p. 255 and J. Fred Rippy, *America and the Strife of Europe* (Chicago, 1938), p. 77.

accepted, would have added to the national postwar confusion, strained federal finances, saddled a weak administration with crushing burdens, and unfavorably altered the temper and ideals of the people.[3]

Even the ardent expansionist Secretary of State, William H. Seward, recognized the power of isolationism, and in 1868 observed that American attention "continues to be fastened upon the domestic questions which have grown out of the late Civil War. The public mind refuses to dismiss these questions even so far as to entertain the higher but more remote questions of national expansion and aggrandizement." [4]

Contemporary sources substantiate, for the most part, the historian's picture of "little America." State papers are filled with warnings against foreign entanglement. In 1878, President Rutherford B. Hayes congratulated the country (and himself) for steering clear of European problems. Grover Cleveland declared unequivocally, in 1885, that he opposed territorial acquisitions: "The genius of our institutions, the needs of our people in their home life, and the attention which is demanded for the settlement and development of our vast territory, dictate the scrupulous avoidance of any departure from that foreign policy commended by the history, the traditions, and the prosperity of our Republic." [5]

---

[3] Allan Nevins, *Hamilton Fish: The Inner History of the Grant Administration* (New York, 1936), p. 910.

[4] Seward to Z. S. Spalding, July 5, 1868, quoted in *Papers Relating to the Foreign Relations of the United States*, 1894, app. 2, p. 144 (hereafter cited as *Foreign Relations*).

[5] Message of Dec. 2, 1878, *Foreign Relations*, 1878; James D. Richardson, ed., *A Compilation of the Messages and Papers of the Presidents*, 20 vols. (New York, 1897–1916), 11: 4886; message of Dec. 8, 1885, *Foreign Relations*, 1885. Cleveland went on to state that "our duty . . . instructs us to address ourselves mainly to the development of the vast resources of the great area committed to our charge, and to the cultivation of the arts of peace within our own borders, though jealously alert in preventing the American hemisphere from being involved in the political problems and complications of distant governments" (p. vi). For a full treatment of the basis for Cleveland's diplomatic conservatism, see George R. Dulebohn, *Principles of Foreign Policy under the Cleveland Administration* (Philadelphia, 1941), esp. pp. 1–7, 89–92. Dulebohn stresses the fact that Cleveland's fundamental ideas regarding foreign policy originated in the general concept of the national interest: that a policy of peace was especially adapted to our interest.

Congress also was dominated by the anti-expansionists. Representative Randall L. Gibson of Louisiana, for example, sympathized with the idea of a "grand Republic" on the Roman model of *urbis et orbis*. He maintained, however, that the first policy of America should be to build up its own resources. In the Senate, Carl Schurz, a liberal Republican from Missouri, voiced all the anti-expansionist arguments of his day: the sacred ideals of George Washington, the maintenance of a prosperity based upon a nonintervention policy, the harmful effects of a possible expansionism on our hemispheric position, and the invulnerability of the United States from foreign attack. Schurz rejected the notion of an American mission; the United States needed to clean its own house before spreading its "superior civilization" to the rest of the world.[6]

Foreign events seemed to count for little in the humdrum platforms of the major parties. On the whole, the politicos appeared oblivious to external problems. They routinely reaffirmed the necessity of protecting the rights of Americans abroad, emphasized the need to cultivate friendly relations with all nations, and urged attention to the new demands arising from an expanded American commerce.[7] Yet, in the time-tested manner of party platforms, these planks meant nothing; they offended no potential voters and marked no new milestones on the road to world leadership.

The press affords an additional barometer to prevailing opinion. In general, it recommended that the country limit its activity in the realm of foreign policy. The *New York Herald* cautioned the incoming Garfield administration that noninvolvement was the wisest course in foreign affairs. And Frederick T. Frelinghuysen, the competent Secretary of State in the Arthur administration, was praised for his statement that "the American eagle should not strain his naturally fine voice by shrill and prolonged screaming on small occasions." The *Catholic World* contended that the dullness of the

---

[6] *Congressional Record,* 47th Cong., 1st sess. (Mar. 10, 1882), 13, pt. 7, A33: Edward McNall Burns, *The American Idea of Mission: Concepts of National Purpose and Destiny* (New Brunswick, 1957), p. 280.

[7] See Thomas H. McKee, ed., *The National Conventions and Platforms of All Political Parties, 1789–1900* (Baltimore, 1901), pp. 133, 138–139, 147, 150–151, 165, 172, 177, 184, 189, 204, 207–208, 213, 234, 236, 240, 244, 251, 255; Kirk H. Porter and Donald B. Johnson, eds., *National Party Platforms, 1840–1956* (Urbana, Ill., 1956), pp. 37–85.

dispatches incorporated in a volume of *Foreign Relations* proved that our quiet, commercial people disdained the glory and glamor of overseas adventure.[8]

With Congress and the press opposed to foreign involvement, it is not surprising that—aside from the purchase of Alaska—all postwar Republican expansionist projects were stillborn. President Grant's scheme to annex Santo Domingo only contributed to the 1872 GOP schism, and a dozen years later the Mugwump malcontents forced both parties to abandon an outward display of expansionism. As the crusade for civil service reform replaced the expansionist plank, the exposé of public and private corruption captured the press. Discussions of reciprocity with Hawaii in the 1870s were crowded out of the news by press coverage of such events as the Beecher-Tilton affair. This scandal, involving the renowned Congregationalist minister of Brooklyn's Plymouth Church, who was accused of adultery with a member of his choir, proved more dramatic (and sold more papers!) than reports on the potentials of Pearl Harbor or Pago Pago.[9] If the membership card to the great powers' club was a "real estate complex" consisting of land and political control in less-developed regions, America did not seem ready to join.

Despite the preoccupation with internal problems and the general aversion to overseas expansion, America in the Gilded Age was never totally inactive in the realm of foreign affairs. The traditional picture of the Spanish-American War as the dividing line between nineteenth-century isolationism and twentieth-century involvement presents, as Professor Bailey suggests, an example of the dangerous use of "watersheds" in the study of American diplomacy. Indeed, Bailey contends that while the United States eschewed foreign involvement in the years after the Civil War, the nation was nevertheless a world power and had been since 1776. With independence,

---

[8] *New York Herald,* Feb. 8, 1881, June 1, 1884; *Springfield (Mass.) Daily Republican,* Dec. 12, 1881; "Among Our Diplomats," *Catholic World* 36 (Feb. 1883): 599–611.

[9] See *Atlantic Monthly* 30 (Sept. 1872): 382–383; Donald M. Dozer, "Anti-Imperialism in the United States, 1865–1895" (Ph.D. dissertation, Harvard University, 1936), pp. 76, 82–114; Joe Patterson Smith, *The Republican Expansionists of the Early Reconstruction Era* (Chicago, 1933), pp. 117–124.

America had acquired the ingredients of world power: more land than all of the continental European states save Russia, a population which outranked that of many other nations, a liberal atmosphere which made the country a mecca for the masses of the world, an adequate militia, leadership in mercantile shipping, and abundant natural resources.[10]

Other historians, studying the American position on the international level, have reached no consensus. Ernest R. May, for example, disagrees with Professor Bailey's conclusions. He contends that the physical assets of a nation do not necessarily determine its status; a country must think of itself as a great power before it can become one, and this the United States did not do until after the Venezuela boundary dispute in the mid-1890s. Europe regarded the United States as a second-rate nation, a country that was not yet included in the same category with Great Britain, Austria-Hungary, Germany, France, Russia, and Italy. May dismisses the naval buildup and "flagwaving" over Samoa in the 1880s as motivated more by domestic pressures than by increased foreign concern. May also rejects our business expansionism as proof that America was ready to abandon isolationism and assume the responsibilities of a world power.[11]

On the other hand, Walter LaFeber maintains that business expansion before 1898 played a primary role in the decision to embark upon colonialism and the assumption of world power status. He believes that the decision for empire rested upon a complex of factors: a consensus for expansion among business and political leaders (including the State Department); the ultimate results of steady economic growth, which led to more and more political entanglements; the military responsibility related to the sudden acquisition of overseas real estate; and the rationalization of a commercial empire that resulted from these territorial gains. LaFeber has placed the whole question of America's emergence on the world stage into proper perspective by demonstrating the con-

---

[10] Thomas A. Bailey, "America's Emergence as a World Power: The Myth and the Verity," *Pacific Historical Review* 30 (Feb. 1961): 1–16.

[11] Ernest R. May, *Imperial Democracy: The Emergence of America as a Great Power* (New York, 1961), chap. 1. See also May, *American Imperialism: A Speculative Essay* (New York, 1968).

tinuum of history. While great power status came in 1898, the preceding years formed the incubation period: vigorous commercial expansion eventually necessitated political dominion overseas.[12]

Other scholars who are currently working in the field of diplomatic history have devoted increasing attention to the Lincoln-to-McKinley period. In the first editions of his popular textbook, Thomas A. Bailey titled the chapter dealing with this period "The Nadir of American Diplomacy." Interestingly, he modified his thesis in later revisions, merely stating that the American people were far more occupied at that time with domestic affairs than with foreign developments. Although Robert H. Ferrell is in general agreement with this traditional view, he notes a change in popular and official sentiment that occurred as early as the first Cleveland administration. Richard W. Leopold also refers to the period 1867–1889 as a low point in American activity, yet his textbook traces the roots of imperialism much earlier than 1898. Alexander De Conde cites a number of minor foreign problems of the "quiet years," which, when linked with the material presented by Bailey, Ferrell, and Leopold, reveal a new picture of diplomacy in the Gilded Age. Significantly, Selig Adler, in his history of American isolationism, describes the 1880s as the period when diplomacy began to pull clear of the postwar doldrums.[13]

Whether great power status came in the 1890s or earlier, it is certain that the United States did not make the decision for colonialism and world involvement in a sudden movement which caught the

---

[12] Walter LaFeber, *The New Empire: An Interpretation of American Expansion, 1860–1898* (Ithaca, 1963), pp. vii–viii, chap. 1 passim, pp. 407–417.

[13] Bailey, *A Diplomatic History of the American People,* 4th ed. (New York, 1950), p. 427; ibid., 8th ed. (New York, 1969), p. 291; Robert H. Ferrell, *American Diplomacy: A History* (New York, 1969), pp. 322 ff., 357; Richard W. Leopold, *The Growth of American Foreign Policy: A History* (New York, 1962), pp. 13 ff., 105 ff.; Alexander DeConde, *A History of American Foreign Policy* (New York, 1963), p. 292; Selig Adler, *The Isolationist Impulse: Its Twentieth-Century Reaction* (New York, 1957), p. 18. See also LaFeber, *The New Empire,* chap. 1; David M. Pletcher, *The Awkward Years: American Foreign Relations under Garfield and Arthur* (Columbia, Mo., 1962), introduction and passim; Wayne S. Cole, *An Interpretive History of American Foreign Relations* (Homewood, Ill., 1968), chap. 18–19, 21–22. Foster R. Dulles's *Prelude to World Power* (New York, 1965) is a brief account of the era 1865–1900.

national psyche off guard. The new departure had its roots in the quiet years of the Gilded Age. Appetite for new territory, quiescent rather than entirely nonexistent, was emerging, along with many other portents of the "New America." The transition from an agrarian to an industrial economy brought a never ending demand for markets. And as the mainland was riveted together with bonds of steel rails, the vision of continental development gave way to the seductive thoughts of overseas empire. Need and desire thus compelled our diplomats to devote more and more of their attention to the Pacific and all the rest of the outside world. Acquisition of new markets brought further necessities: an adequate navy, an isthmian canal to join the oceans, and (as Admiral Alfred T. Mahan would soon point out) the establishment of bases at which our ships could refuel. These outposts would also protect American overseas interests and stimulate foreign commerce. In other words, the sequence followed naturally: from industrial expansion to markets, thence to a bigger navy to protect them, and thence to bases to make such naval strength possible.

In addition to markets and security, there was the ever increasing concern for American prestige. To allege that this change came with the suddenness of a revolution is to disregard the significant events of the Gilded Age. The new urban industrialism stimulated a new variety of "spread-eagleism" which would eventually manifest itself in Theodore Roosevelt's "big stick policy" in the Western Hemisphere and Taft's concept of "dollar diplomacy" in eastern Asia.

The press sometimes recognized the forces of this transition. The *New York Times*, while never sanctioning a "spirited" foreign policy, observed that many "second class statesmen" wished the United States had more influence in world politics. Even this conservative journal recognized that the United States had entered upon a new epoch of national vigor, a period in which the Republic could look beyond its own borders to wield a larger and more wholesome influence on world affairs. By the 1880s, a few editors were even recommending an activist diplomacy as indispensable to American prosperity and honor. In 1889 the *New York Daily Tribune* warned Europe that, while America had no territorial ambitions, the nation was beginning to realize its lost opportunities and future necessities. The United States was bent upon regaining commercial supremacy, attracting Canada into political union, and wielding a more direct influence in the affairs of the American continent.[14]

While the press was interpreting the changes in American sentiment, two Secretaries of State, William H. Seward and Hamilton Fish, were attempting to speed up the process of change. In retrospect, Seward can best be described as the harbinger of a new variant of expansionism. His predictions about future territorial acquisitions blended realism with idealism, and were startlingly prescient. Seward grasped the impact of the closing frontier on overseas expansion and mapped out a theoretical plan for American empire. The future struggle for world power, he reasoned, would center in Asia, and therefore increased American commerce with the Orient would enhance our status. The decline of Spain's American empire, presaged by Seward, would eventually place additional territory in American hands: Mexico would be absorbed and her capital city would become a center for wider Yankee penetration. Canada would be annexed and, together with the Caribbean, would form part of a continental base.[15]

Secretary Seward rationalized his dream of an American empire by envisioning the benefits of exporting the American brand of freedom, the bountiful profits of trade, and the removal of the peril of a europeanized Caribbean and Pacific. An open door policy in the Orient, a transcontinental railroad, and domestic protective tariffs were essential parts of his master plan. Initially, he failed in the implementation of his blueprint because of abolitionist fears of adding land to the pre–Civil War slavocracy, and, later, because domestic problems precluded a vigorous foreign policy. But his plans for the insular strength that would come with the acquisition of Cuba, the Danish West Indies, and Hawaii foreshadowed the imperialistic impulse of a future generation.[16]

---

[14] "Minding Our Own Business," *New York Times,* Feb. 13, 1881; "Our Future Foreign Policy," ibid., July 16, 1881; "American Foreign Policy," *New York Daily Tribune,* Sept. 10, 1889.

[15] Joseph G. Whelan, "William Henry Seward, Expansionist" (Ph.D. dissertation, University of Rochester, 1959), pp. 221–233 passim; also LaFeber, *The New Empire,* pp. 25–28; Frederic Bancroft, "Seward's Ideas of Territorial Expansion," *North American Review* 147 (July 1898): 79–89; Frederick Merk, *Manifest Destiny and Mission in American History: A Reinterpretation* (New York, 1963), pp. 228, 250.

[16] Whelan, *William Henry Seward,* pp. 222–223; LaFeber, *The New*

Seward's spiritual heirs were President Ulysses S. Grant and Secretary of State Hamilton Fish. This team was an important link connecting the expansionist chain of thought from the time of William Seward to Theodore Roosevelt. As President, Grant hoped to extend American interests into Latin America and the Pacific—plans that were always welcomed by the leading expansionists. In addition, border squabbles, fishery problems, a persistent anglophobia, the need to court the Irish vote, and a desire to round out the American empire made Grant's talk of annexing Canada a very seductive political lure. Undoubtedly, his most nefarious scheme was the proposed annexation of Santo Domingo. Grant's Civil War experiences had pointed up what he felt was the need for Caribbean bases, and, as President, he recommended such a policy so often in his annual messages that the theme could almost be referred to as annexation-by-White House-resolution. Disappointments and discouragement occurred after 1869, when the President's interest in the island was first whetted, and until 1871, when formidable congressional opposition killed the scheme. Although their annexation schemes failed, Grant and his secretary, Fish, succeeded in other areas. They were responsible for the "nontransfer principle" of the Monroe Doctrine, the proposition that territories in the New World are not to be transferred from one European power to another, or from an American to a European country, for focusing attention on the West Indies, and for establishing the first formal grasp on Hawaii and Samoa.[17]

The urge for empire accelerated under the aegis of the Harrison administration. Damning the small state as a relic of the past, the American imperialist looked toward the concentration of people and territory into one great dominion under the control or protection of the United States. On the practical level, this new spirit manifested itself in the search for what became known as a "large policy": an American-owned isthmian canal, an American Hawaii and Cuba, and the maintenance of American influence in Samoa. On the theoretical level, the dreams of empire can be seen in the political rhetoric

---

Empire, pp. 27, 30–32. For a complete treatment of Seward's foreign policy, see Glyndon G. Van Deusen, *William Henry Seward* (New York, 1967), chap. 35–37.

[17] LaFeber, *The New Empire,* pp. 32–39; Richardson, *Messages and Papers* (Dec. 5, 1870), 10: 4053–4055.

of the period. For example, when George E. Seney addressed the 1887 Democratic convention in his home state of Ohio, he expressed the belief held by many Americans of that decade: "The spectacle of the continent, from the Arctic Ocean to the equator, subsisting as one nation under a common constitution . . . with one flag . . . would be the grandest moral and political sight possible on the face of the globe." [18]

By 1890, the reluctance to engage in further expansion had been partially overcome by economic and psychological changes in a nation that was inherently adventurous and speculative. America began to demand a place in the sun. The "trivial chatter and sterile inaction" of the postwar decades had been accompanied by subterranean forces of change. Although historians have generally assumed that expansion was scarcely an issue for several decades after Grant's Santo Domingo fiasco, and that the exploitation of the United States' natural resources and the erection of its industrial and transportation complex were of overriding concern, this view needs serious qualification. The concern for internal matters serves only to veil the significant developments in the area of diplomacy, but these developments must be explored before the complete story can be told.

---

[18] A. T. Volwiler, "Harrison, Blaine, and American Foreign Policy, 1889–1893," *American Philosophical Society Proceedings* 59 (1938): 637–648; *Congressional Record,* 50th Cong., 1st sess. (Sept. 5, 1888), 19, pt. 10, A481.

CHAPTER 2

Early
Economic
Imperialism

IN 1900, BROOKS ADAMS recorded his impressions of the phase into which the United States had entered some thirty years before. America, like other industrial nations glutted with products, had required new markets, and the increased competition among the powers resulted in an international scramble for resources. In this struggle, Adams argued in *America's Economic Supremacy* (1900), the United States had a special advantage. Wealth and power were moving westward, and this historical movement of exchange gave this country the opportunity to enhance its national interest. The key to international status was the ever changing location of the hub of commercial interchange, and by 1890 New York City figured prominently as one of these new junctions. Adams warned, however, that unless America continued to capitalize on this natural movement, the center of commerce could conceivably move eastward toward Germany or Russia, reversing the historic Western tradition of exchanges that formed the basis of world power. American expansion into Asia was one means of counteracting the march of Germany and Russia; the other was a continuing rapprochement with Great

Britain and the creation of a common front of Anglo-Saxon nations.[1]

Even more crucial than American expansion was the attitude of business toward expansion. The failure of the business community to act intelligently and aggressively in this time of crisis was, for Adams, a source of constant concern. This class, he lamented, was mainly concerned with the "privatized" needs and pleasures of a highly efficient, materialistic civilization. Indeed, the reluctance of business moguls and their political vassals to think in terms of expansion led Adams to his conception of the "Law of Civilization and Decay." Late nineteenth-century America, rapidly exhausting its productive energy, was disintegrating under the pressure of internal economic competition. In this situation, the country had two choices: to remain inert until it was supplied with fresh, energetic material by the infusion of "barbarian" blood, or to grow by expanding into new areas. Adams, and many other Americans, did not wish to remain inert.[2]

The United States, in spite of claims to self-sufficiency, had never been economically isolated from the rest of the world. American products and commerce had played a considerable global role in colonial times, and as a leading producer of cotton and wheat the country was deeply involved in the world economy long before the shelling of Fort Sumter. After the interruption of the Civil War, moreover, the country's economic growth gathered speed. This acceleration, partly the result of the postwar shift of political power from the Southern planters to the Northern industrialists and financiers, was reflected in the international market. Indeed, the increased volume and variety of exportable finished goods accounts for the chief difference between ante- and post-bellum commerce. By the time Harrison entered the White House in 1889, any dream of commercial isolation was permanently buried. America's industrial might

---

[1] Brooks Adams, *America's Economic Supremacy* (New York, 1900), pp. 12–13, 25–26, 84–85, 190; John P. Mallan, "Roosevelt, Brooks Adams, and Lea: The Warrior Critique of the Business Civilization," *American Quarterly* 8 (Feb. 1956): 216–230. See also William A. Williams, "Brooks Adams and American Expansion," *New England Quarterly* 15 (June 1952): 217–232.

[2] See Mallan, "Roosevelt, Brooks Adams, and Lea," loc. cit.

had reached a point where supply exceeded domestic demands and its need for foreign markets was sharply increasing.[3]

Despite the need for new markets, certain inherent weaknesses in our trade projections persisted. The most important factor undoubtedly was, as Brooks Adams pointed out, the preoccupation of American businessmen with domestic pursuits. The large profits available from our own untapped economic resources monopolized attention. Although the need for foreign markets compelled certain elements within the United States to think in expansionist terms, the business community as a whole did not conspire for foreign annexations or for investment opportunities for our surplus capital. Surprisingly, the promotion of American export trade in the early postwar period came from governmental offices. American businessmen seemed so indifferent to foreign markets that one consul wished the energy and enthusiasm manifested in behalf of businessmen by the State Department would prove contagious. Only when events called attention to the potential profit in the Far Eastern market did Wall Street jump, belatedly, on the 1898 expansionist bandwagon.[4]

The size of congressional subsidies proved a further disappointment to those interested in the development of foreign trade. The *New York Herald* commented that even if the $800,000 appropriated for this purpose were $800 million, our overseas commerce would not grow while there were still laws on the statute books that "crushed" it. Congress thought of subsidies in terms of protective

---

[3] Between 1870 and 1900 foreign trade jumped from $13,305,000 to $2,429,233,000 (Bureau of the Census, *Historical Statistics of the United States, 1789–1945* [Washington, 1949], p. 244). "The Export Commerce of Today," *Bradstreet's* 2 (July 10, 1880): 4; Thomas C. Cochran, "Did the Civil War Retard Industrialization?" *Mississippi Valley Historical Review* (hereafter *MVHA*) 48 (Sept. 1961): 197–210. Beginning in 1874, America's exports began to exceed its imports in value. The value of manufactured goods in terms of constant dollar purchasing power rose 82 percent in the decade 1869–1879 and 112 percent after 1879 (LaFeber, *New Empire*, p. 6). See also David E. Novack and Matthew Simon, "Commercial Responses to the American Export Invasion, 1871–1914: An Essay in Attitudinal History," *Explorations in Entrepreneurial History* (Winter 1966): 121–147.

[4] Consul George C. Tanner, Verviers, Belgium, Oct. 5, 1880, in *Consular Reports*, vol. 1 (Nov. 1880), no. 2; Consul Frank H. Mason, Marseilles, June 16, 1884, ibid., 15 (Feb. 1885), no. 50.

tariffs, designed to build up internal resources, rather than in terms of grants to encourage foreign trade.[5]

Those who *did* look overseas for trade opportunities often failed to plan for the realization of their aims or to cooperate with their competitors to advance common interests. The old spirit of frontier individualism was still too strong to permit participation in "trade associations." American businessmen often paid little attention to the law of supply and demand. American cheese, gin, herring, furniture, and stoves were sent to Holland even though the Dutch produced these goods more cheaply and efficiently. American exports were sometimes of too high a quality to meet local requirements, and consequently were undersold by their less expensive English and German equivalents. Too often, Americans then compensated for this by exporting large quantities of inferior goods. Such a policy, again, was both shortsighted and foolish; inferior goods closed rather than expanded markets. For example, when chemical analysis of American celluloid collars and cuffs revealed that the ingredients used in their production were dangerous to health, these products were banned. American leather goods were also blackballed in the German market because the peculiar red dye of hemlock leather was injurious to health and made the products difficult to dry when they became wet. The same lack of foresight contributed to unsatisfactory trade relations with Canada. American products, more often than not, reached the Canadian market out of season. Fur coats did not sell well in Quebec in the middle of July.[6]

American business representatives abroad contributed to this confusion; they were, for the most part, inefficient and poorly trained. In contrast to their German and English competitors, American business agents rarely spoke the language of their customers. Consuls continually pointed out the necessity for overcoming this handicap. Our Manila consul felt that American merchants would never establish successful contacts with the islanders until they had mastered the Spanish language. Another consul advised that the large sums of money invested by such companies as Montgomery Ward in mak-

---

[5] *New York Herald,* May 19, 1886, Dec. 12, 1883.

[6] "The Mistakes of 1880," *New York Daily Tribune,* Dec. 31, 1880; *Consular Despatches, Berlin,* no. 10, Oct. 8, 1881; Consul General Frederick Raine, ibid., no. 11, June 26, 1885; *Commercial Relations,* 1879, pp. 53–54; ibid., 1884–1885, 1: 254–255.

ing illustrated catalogs available in Europe would be wasted unless the overseas representatives of these firms were thoroughly prepared for their tasks.[7]

While the government seemed at times more cognizant of the foreign market situation than the business community itself, the stream of communications that flooded consular and State Department bureaus is proof that some businessmen and industrialists were not apathetic to the potentialities of overseas commercial enterprise. In 1878, New York businessmen urged Congress to increase telegraphic communications between the United States and foreign nations. In the 1880s an American fishing concern, anxious to establish a caviar market in Germany, requested the assistance of the consulate; and the American Machinist Publication Company asked our officials in Germany to locate the proper agency for increasing its circulation. By 1880, American Exchange was acting as the European agent for the Pennsylvania Railroad, the Great Western Steamship Company, the Globe Express Company, the Pittsburgh Folding Chair Company, Rand McNally and Company, the New York Life Insurance Company, the *New York Times*, the *American Exporter*, and the *Chicago Tribune*.[8]

American expansion into the world economy pushed in many directions. Standard Oil began foreign distribution of its products in 1879, and other American oil companies developed production

---

[7] H. H. Leavitt to John Davis, n.d. (received Dec. 15, 1884), *Consular Despatches, Managua*, no. 10; *Commercial Relations*, 1885–1886, 1: 823; ibid., 1886–1887, pp. 657 ff.; ibid., 1887–1888, pp. 179 ff. Linus P. Brockett's *The Commercial Traveller's Guide Book* (New York, 1871) has a section on the need for language training (pp. 73–75). Consul General Raine, June 26, 1885, *Consular Despatches, Berlin*, no. 11.

[8] *Senate Journal*, 45th Cong., 2d sess. (May 1, 1878), p. 456; William Hooker, Importing and Fish Preserving House, New York, Dec. 1883 (received Dec. 21, 1883), *Miscellaneous Letters to the Consul, Berlin*, no. 741; L. B. Moore to Mark S. Brewer, Feb. 5, 1883, ibid., no. 109; Henry F. Billing to Evarts, Jan. 23, 1880, *Miscellaneous Letters, Department of State*.

See the following articles for excellent case study analyses of overseas business concern: R. A. Church, "The Effect of the American Export Invasion on the British Boot and Shoe Industry, 1885–1914," *Journal of Economic History* 28 (June 1968): 223–254, and Robert B. Davies, " 'Peacefully Working to Conquer the World': The Singer Manufacturing Company in Foreign Markets, 1854–1889," *Business History Review* 43 (Autumn 1969): 299–325.

in Russia, Austria, and Latin America. Several firms, following the Pullman example in England and Canada, established foreign branches; and other Americans invested in foreign utilities (especially ocean and land telegraph cables) and agricultural enterprises. Foreign loans were floated as early as the 1860s by Dabney, Morgan and Company, and repayments on its loan to Peru were begun in 1871. By 1869, American investments abroad amounted to between $50 million and $100 million. Although the United States had not yet entered the stage where outlets for surplus capital and goods were recognized necessities, the outward thrust in finance had begun.[9]

Latin America attracted much of our surplus capital—that which was not invested in Europe. Mexico, politically weak, offered many special possibilities to Americans, and its natural resources were easily exploited by American skill, capital, and managerial energy. After the Civil War, American promoters rediscovered the ancient Spanish gold and silver mines, investing in them as well as in Mexican railroads, factories, oil wells, and refineries. In 1880, under the congenial Díaz, Mexico began the "give-away policy," which by 1884 brought more Americans to Mexico City than had been there since the Mexican War (1846–1848).[10]

The Latin American market, prized and guarded by the United States because of proximity and the Monroe Doctrine, was also a subject of extended discussion. Our "legitimate influence" south of the border, some argued, could be maintained only through closer commercial contacts. Because increased trade would counteract foreign penetration south of the Rio Grande, reciprocity legislation was often considered the panacea. Central American union, long envisioned by the State Department, was another plan designed in part to facilitate our commerce with that region. Although Blaine's pan-American idea, perhaps the climax of the reciprocity talk, was pictured by its critics as transforming South America into commer-

---

[9] Cleona Lewis, *America's Stake in International Investment* (Washington, 1939), pp. 1–2, 34–36, 75–78, 181–182, 201, 202, 219, 290, 293–294, 315–316, 323–324, 334–335, 440. See also Paul D. Dickens, *American Direct Investment in Foreign Countries* (Washington, 1930), p. 37.

[10] *Commercial and Financial Chronicle* 41 (July 18, 1885): 62–63; David M. Pletcher, *Rails, Mines, and Progress: Seven American Promoters in Mexico, 1867–1911* (Ithaca, 1958), p. 28 and passim.

cial vassalage, most contemporary opinion saw it as a mutually beneficial idea. Secretary William M. Evarts viewed reciprocity merely as a boon to honest business transactions. In a circular to our consuls in South American cities, he asserted "the United States are in a condition to supply cheaply and easily many products and manufactured articles . . . to all or nearly all of the Spanish American republics . . . receiving in return natural products." The secretary recommended that products be adapted to Latin American tastes, and urged the establishment of better steamship and market connections, the founding of mercantile houses and banks, and the extension of more liberal credits by American merchants to our southern neighbors.[11]

Canada, a traditional area of commercial expansion, became a concern of those enthusiasts whose target for American expansion extended to the North Pole. Canada, many predicted, would have to become part of a North American union—much like the one projected by Blaine for Latin America. Although the advocates of political union made considerable noise, the most feasible plan for closer relations lay in the commercial field. Canadian liberals desired closer ties with the United States as a means of pulling out of the disastrous depression of the 1880s. On this side of the border, representative businessmen and politicians favored tariff reciprocity. The leader of the movement, S. J. Ritchie, an Akron, Ohio, capitalist who was also president of the Central Ontario Railroad, lobbied in Congress, and local booster organizations discussed the reciprocity question. Congress debated the issue and committees reported it favorably, but reciprocity lacked universal popularity. The idea that Canadians in general, and French-Canadians in particular, did not possess the educational, religious, political, or general business acumen of the Yankees prejudiced tariff reciprocity, as well as the fear that such a course would harm American farmers and lumbermen. Zealous advocates of such a program could not dispel the notion

---

[11] *Cleveland Leader,* July 6, 1889; *American Economist* 4 (July 12, 1889): 25–26; LaFeber, *New Empire,* p. 9; "Commercial Interests Sacrificed," *New York Daily Tribune,* May 2, 1882; Consul H. C. C. Astwood, San Domingo, *Consular Reports,* 6 (June 1882), 161–162; quotation from Evarts in Chester L. Barrows, *William M. Evarts: Lawyer, Diplomat, Statesman* (Chapel Hill, N.C., 1941), p. 376.

that reciprocity was but a veiled attempt to seduce our northern neighbors into full *Anschluss*.[12]

Fishing rights off the Newfoundland coast, a subject of conflict since the Revolution, continued to provide another obstacle to Canadian-American cooperation. Even after the fisheries settlement of 1871, Canada continued its retaliation. American protests reached fever pitch in 1887, when the House of Representatives authorized President Cleveland to bar Canadian ships from our ports. The following February, the abortive Bayard-Chamberlain pact, which attempted to end the century-long problem, provided the Senate Republicans with a powerful weapon. Jingoism assisted election-minded conservatives in blocking Democratic chances in 1888 by defeating this proposed compromise.[13]

American commercial interest was not restricted to this continent. Nineteenth-century Russia, for example, was a new and important area of American economic expansion. While trade with the domain of the Czars was not extensive, American businessmen were beginning to show definite interest. The United States consul in Odessa continually emphasized the need for trade depots where American wares could be displayed. American "reaper kings" invaded the Russian grain lands in the late 1870s, and late in the next decade Cyrus McCormick sent a wire binder to Russia for exhibition and trial and established a branch office in the Ukraine at Odessa. At the same time, Wharton Barker, a Philadelphia banker, devised a plan to develop Russian coal mines; and the Equitable Life Insurance Company extended its services into Russia. Despite the belief of some businessmen that American industrialism and Russian backwardness were essentially incompatible,[14] American machinery and

---

[12] Benjamin F. Butler, "Defenseless Canada," *North American Review* 147 (Oct. 1888): 441–452; Donald F. Warner, *The Idea of Continental Union: Agitation for the Annexation of Canada to the United States, 1849–1893* (Lexington, Ky., 1960), pp. 155–156.

[13] "The Fisheries Question," *Public Opinion* 1 (May 22, 1886): 106; H. C. Lodge, "The Fisheries Question," *North American Review* 146 (Feb. 1888): 121–130.

[14] See George S. Queen, "The United States and the Material Advance in Russia, 1887–1906" (Ph.D. dissertation, University of Illinois, 1941); Consul Leander M. Dyer, Odessa, Sept. 25, 1880, *Consular Reports,* 1 (Nov. 1880), 174–177. See also Edward J. Carroll, "The Foreign Relations of the United States with Tsarist Russia, 1867–1900" (Ph.D. dissertation, Georgetown University, 1953).

technological skill contributed to the material advancement of Russia.

The vast Pacific continued to stir the American imagination, as it had since New Englanders began sending ginseng to the Orient in Confederation days. The fishery resources of Alaska and the northern Pacific spelled great opportunity to many, including Secretary Blaine. Pacific merchants and Western farmers were aware of Samoa's potentialities, and some viewed Pago Pago as the commercial focal point of Polynesia. Commercial dreams were reinforced by political concerns, and the fear of foreign influence dominated our Hawaiian policy. The Hawaiian reciprocity treaty of 1875, roundly debated when introduced, was eventually renewed in 1884, but only after we had secured Pearl Harbor as a naval station. Reciprocity was the momentary substitute for political annexation.[15]

Although the Far Eastern trade figures were not impressive, some merchants were already envisioning brighter developments on that horizon. In response to a congressional resolution, the Navy Department commissioned Commodore Robert W. Shufeldt to open Korea to world commerce—an assignment he completed in May 1882. While Shufeldt's mission attracted little attention at home, the persistent sailor-diplomat predicted that the Pacific would soon become America's commercial domain. His treaty with the Land of the Morning Calm would form another link in the chain uniting East and West.[16]

---

[15] Draft of undated speech by Blaine on Alaska, in Blaine MSS, Library of Congress, "Speeches, 1860–1888"; *Consular Despatches, Apia,* vol. 96, no. 60 (July 1, 1880); ibid., vol. 109, no. 37 (Dec. 8, 1883); *Samoan Times,* Sept. 21, 1878; *Reports of the Diplomatic Bureau,* vol. 7, no. 1010 (Mar. 30, 1880). In 1886, George H. Bates investigated the problem of power rivalry in Samoa and concluded that either we renounce our interest or step up our commercial policy (*Special Missions, Department of State,* 3, no. 1 [July 22, 1886], 451–464), Blaine to Minister James M. Comly, Nov. 19, 1881, *Instructions, Hawaii,* vol. 2, no. 111 and Dec. 1, 1881, ibid., no. 113; "Reciprocity in Congress," *Bradstreet's* 5 (Mar. 18, 1882): 162–163; *San Francisco Journal of Commerce* (Oct. 14, 1880).

[16] *Congressional Record,* 45th Cong., 2d sess. (Apr. 8 and 17, 1878), 7, pt. 3, 2323 and 2599–2601; Charles O. Paullin, *Diplomatic Negotiations of American Naval Officers, 1778–1883* (Baltimore, 1912), p. 309; Shufeldt to Secretary of Navy Thompson, Oct. 13, 1880, in "Letters from Commodore R. W. Shufeldt, *Ticonderoga,* October, 1878–November, 1880," 2 vols. (Department of Navy Archives, National Archives), vol. 1. See also Paullin's *The Opening of Korea by Commodore Shufeldt* (Boston, 1910).

Africa proved more than a realm of romance to many Americans in the Gilded Age. In 1878 Commodore Shufeldt, on the first leg of his eventful voyage to the Orient, visited West Africa and recommended the establishment of a consular service in that "great commercial prize of the world." President Arthur also recognized the importance of Africa to America's economic destiny. In his 1883 annual message, he suggested cooperation with other powers in opening the door to the Congo. Congress was not immune to the "African fever," and was continually petitioned to authorize land surveys, railroad establishments, and trading posts. Senator John Tyler Morgan of Alabama, a well-known expansionist who introduced a far-reaching African resolution in 1884, recommended that the President provide protection for American traders and missionaries in the Congo and formally deny the right of any one nation to exclusive sovereignty in that region.[17]

Although interest in Africa was great, the "fever" never got out of control; the United States moved very slowly from its traditional isolation toward African affairs. At the 1884 Berlin conference on Congo affairs, for example, our delegate, John A. Kasson, was instructed to confine his attention to commercial topics and not to enter what seemed like the eternal wrangling over Africa's political future. But in spite of the limitations in Kasson's instructions, the United States participated in an international conference on Africa that was called for both political and economic reasons.[18]

Even the virgin Arctic commanded attention, and one congressman, in pleading for funds for its exploration, felt that we should not hesitate in establishing polar stations in what men called a "race for glory." Part of this interest was scientific, but there was the usual commercial motivation as well.[19]

---

[17] Shufeldt to Thompson, Aug. 2, 1879, in "Letters from Commodore Shufeldt"; Frelinghuysen to Tisdel, Sept. 8, 1884, *Special Missions, Department of State,* vol. 3, no. 1; Frelinghuysen to Kasson, Oct. 14, 1884, *Instructions, Germany,* vol. 17, no. 345; U.S. Congress, Senate Committee on Foreign Relations, *Report* 393, 48th Cong., 1st sess. (Mar. 26, 1884).

[18] John A. Kasson, "The Congo Conference and the President's Message," *North American Review* 142 (Feb. 1886): 119–133.

[19] "Arctic Exploration," *New York Daily Tribune,* Mar. 10 and Dec. 27, 1877; *Congressional Record,* 45th Cong., 2d sess., 7, pt. 5, A393 (Rep. Benjamin A. Willis, June 13, 1878); *Senate Report* 512, 46th Cong., 2d

The multiplication of American commercial journals was another sign of the mounting interest in foreign trade. A sample of these new trade magazines, which undoubtedly influenced the extent and variety of American exports, includes *American Investments, Dry Goods Chronicle and Fancy Goods Review, Manufacturer and Builder, Railroad Gazette, Railway Age, Manufacturers' Gazette, American Exporter, Manufacturers' Record,* and *Iron Age.* These publications, so often opposed to governmental regulation in domestic industry, were quite willing to allow the government to interfere on the international scene. In 1885, for example, *Age of Steel* felt that merchants and manufacturers needed a "spirited" policy and that the government should encourage markets for business, even if by force.[20] The "have gun, will travel" concept of the day was not confined to gunfighters or ex-cowboys.

Local commerce organizations, especially those in New York, spoke out boldly at annual conventions, issuing reports, petitions, and resolutions in favor of promoting trade. The New York State Chamber of Commerce, worried about British competition in the international carrying trade, voiced special concern over British monopolization of the South American trade, which it claimed rightfully belonged to the United States. The chamber also opposed the Chinese Exclusion Act because it jeopardized American business interests in the Far East. At its 1884–1885 meeting, the Board of Trade and Transportation of New York suggested that the Atlantic seaboard cities unite to discuss common commercial problems. The national issues of union with Canada, an isthmian canal, tariff reciprocity, and broadened Hawaiian trade united the New York chamber and its sister organizations in favor of bolder policies to widen the national horizon.[21]

Christian missionaries were also interested in expanding America's economic horizon and, in the Gilded Age, began to take up "the white man's burden" with increasing zeal. Despite the fact that their credo was religious propagation, their activities also encompassed

---

sess. (Apr. 21, 1880); "Commerce and the Arctic Seas," *New York Herald,* Nov. 20, 1878.

[20] *Age of Steel* 57 (May 23, 1885): 9.

[21] See for example, *Annual Reports of the Corporation of the Chamber of Commerce of the State of New York,* 8th–32nd Meetings, 1865–1890 (New York, 1865–1890).

the dollar nexus. Missionaries served as economic pioneers, furnishing valuable information to both government and businessmen. In the backward regions, they proved so important to commercial expansion that one missionary stated that commerce owed "everything" to the missions. So great were the possibilities for trade that arose out of missionary work that it was even suggested that commercial circles invest in such religious work. Missions would enlighten and morally transform people about to receive the benefits of Western economic penetration. The commercial work of the missions would be only incidental, neither aggressive nor conspicuous. The task of missions was not to drum up trade; this function characterized the "outer court of the temple of missions" and should not penetrate the "inner shrine" of missionary devotion. Whatever was to be accomplished had to be by way of indirection, but there was certainly an affinity between the portable altar and the salesman's sample case.[22]

But the businessman was not always viewed as a responsible partner in missionary endeavors. Although commerce was a great factor in the development of civilization and the progress of the Gospel, its agents too often wrecked the work of the missionary. And the tendency to measure missions by mercantile and monetary standards—Do missions pay?—was not always appreciated by the devout.[23]

Most successful in combining the two goals of religious conversion and economic expansion was Josiah Strong, the general secretary of the Evangelical Alliance for the United States. In the preface to

---

[22] Especially noteworthy was the increased missionary work in Hawaii and Korea. In the Sandwich Islands, as Hawaii was called, the first whites were missionaries and, more often than not, their sons entered the business world. The founder of the Dole enterprises is a case in point. Korea's diplomatic relations with the United States were facilitated by Dr. Horace N. Allen, the first American missionary to the Hermit Kingdom.
See "The Opening of Africa," *Missionary Herald* 74 (Mar. 1878): 88; Kenneth S. LaTourette, *A History of Christian Missions in China* (New York, 1929), pp. 842–843; Rev. James Johnston, ed., *Report of the Centenary Conference on the Protestant Missions of the World,* 2 vols. (New York, 1888), 1: 112; Rev. James S. Dennis, *Christian Missions and Social Progress,* 3 vols. (Chicago, Toronto, New York, 1897–1906), 3 (1906): 457–460, 470–474; Augustus Charles Thompson, *Future Probation and Foreign Missions* (Boston, 1886), p. 5.
[23] Rev. F. F. Elinwood, "The Relations of Missions and Commerce," *Missionary Review of the World* 11 (Dec. 1888): 881–887, 964.

his best-selling *Our Country* (1885), the Reverend Strong succinctly stated his formula:

> Success in the world of the World's conversion has, with rare exceptions, followed the lines of human growth and prospective greatness. . . . The principles of such a strategic wisdom should lead us to look on these United States as first and foremost the chosen seat of enterprise for the World's conversion. Forecasting the future of Christianity . . . we must believe that it will be what the future of this country is to be. As America goes, so goes the world.

Since the United States, the greatest of all Anglo-Saxon domains, held in its hands the destiny of mankind, this country must reach out and reshape the world in its own image. Merchant and missionary must work together. Anglo-Saxons should colonize and convert Mexico, Central and South America, the islands of the South Seas, Africa, and beyond. Merchants had an almost sacred obligation to extend the fruits of American capitalism to Africa and Asia. Commercial expansion into these two continents (Strong's favorite sites) not only helped strengthen civilization in these regions but also made America strong. New markets reduced labor unrest, which, Strong contended, was caused by industrial overproduction.[24]

 Just as the activities of the American missionary pulled him into a kind of foreign service, so the agricultural surpluses of the American farmer forced the latter to concern himself about the international market. Northern agricultural and cereal goods accounted for the bulk of American export and trade. By 1880, agricultural staples comprised 84.3 percent of all the products shipped abroad; and the years 1873 to 1882 were the most remarkably productive period in the history of American wheat growing. Acreage increased from 29 to 41 million acres, production from 368 to 555 million

---

[24] Josiah Strong, *Our Country: Its Possible Future and Its Present Crisis* (New York, 1885), pp. vii (preface written by Austin Phelps, D.D.), 7–15, 29, 153–158, 159–180, 218; LaFeber, *The New Empire*, pp. 72–80; see also Strong, *Expansion under New World Conditions* (New York, 1900), pp. 255, 258, 264, 271–275, 302, and Dorothea R. Muller, "Josiah Strong and American Nationalism: A Reevaluation," *Journal of American History* 53 (Dec. 1966): 487–503. Muller asserts that Strong was an internationalist in the sense that Americans, as Christians, had an obligation to fulfill the missionary charges of world evangelization.

bushels, and exports from 40 to 150 million bushels. The wheat growers depended upon the export market for about 30 to 40 percent of their gross annual income, relying especially upon British consumption. Small wonder that the increased exportation of cereal goods from the Northern states to Europe was viewed with alarm by the European landholding aristocracy. Because our economic stability rested upon the ability of European markets to absorb our agricultural surplus, these markets were jealously guarded. American farm journals regularly reported on foreign agricultural developments, urging increased American aggressiveness in capturing markets. In describing the faltering Italian wheat production, for example, one source suggested that our millers could supply all Italian needs; was not the United States the "granary of the world"? Indeed, the United States replaced Russia, preoccupied with Near East tensions, as the chief supplier of wheat for Europe.[25]

Live cattle, another agricultural export spawned by the post–Civil War frontier, created a profitable trade, 97 percent of which was with Great Britain. The first recorded live cattle shipment (because of the excessive spoilage and expensive carriage of dressed meats) occurred in 1868. Between 1868 and 1885, over 800,000 cattle on the hoof, valued at over $80 million, crossed the seas. By 1885, however, fear of diseased cattle, losses in transit, the short shipping season, and the development of refrigeration led to the replacement of the live cattle export trade with dressed beef.[26]

Despite successes in the export trade, the farmer maintained a precarious financial existence. Agricultural journals reflected his anxiety over mounting overseas harvests, which depressed American farm prices. The demand for agricultural products overseas fluctuated with foreign war scares and droughts, forcing the farmer to

---

[25] Hjalmar H. Boyensen, "America as a Civilizer," *Christian Union* 31 (May 28, 1885): 8–9; *Northwest Miller* 10 (July 30, 1880): 67; Richard E. Edmonds, "Our Exports of Breadstuffs," *International Review* 11 (Nov. 1881): 450–462; Morton Rothstein, "America in the International Rivalry for the British Wheat Market, 1860–1914," *MVHR* 67 (Dec. 1960): 401–418.

[26] Joseph Nimmo, Jr., *Report in Regard to the Range and Ranch Cattle Business of the United States* (Washington, 1885), pp. 53–68; William D. Zimmerman, "Live Cattle Export Trade between the United States and Great Britain, 1868–1885," *Agricultural History* 36 (Jan. 1962): 46–52; LaFeber, *The New Empire,* p. 10.

produce for a "blind" market. In the 1880s, a sharp price decline in the grain trade compelled American farmers to sell at lower prices in order to retain a share of the British market. The English leverage on American prices, and increased competition from Russia, Egypt, and India, stimulated American wheat growers to search for new markets in South America and the Far East. Out of desperation, the farmer joined the expansionist camp.

Although the farmer, the missionary, and a segment of the business community assumed a substantial role in expanding American economic interests overseas, the government played an even greater part. The marvelous growth of America's export trade was due in great part to Secretary of State William M. Evarts's revitalization of the consular services. Evarts believed that the federal government, rather than the self-appointed captains of industry, should stimulate our overseas trade. Long associated with the great New York City merchants and shippers, he sought out consuls with business experience, investigated the corps, and tried to present American products to foreign consumers in the most favorable light. He observed, for example, that many of our goods glutted foreign markets simply because the natives could not read the labels and therefore were unaware of the uses of the products. Perhaps Evarts's most valuable contribution to overseas trade was his inauguration of monthly consular reports to assist in the extension and encouragement of American industry and commerce. These reports, dealing with regional details (labor conditions, competing manufacturers, movements of trade, finance, banking, taxes, communications, exhibitions, and conferences), were hailed by trade journals, industrialists, and local chambers of commerce.[27]

Consuls and their reports provided the businessman with a wealth of specific information on commercial affairs. Consul V. V. Smith, for example, felt that one of his major tasks in the West Indies was to communicate directly with manufacturers and request samples of their goods, together with price lists. The consul in Japan promoted the British technique of establishing local newspapers to advertise

---

[27] Brainerd Dyer, *The Public Career of William M. Evarts* (Berkeley, 1933), pp. 234–237; Sherman Evarts, ed., *Arguments and Speeches of William Maxwell Evarts*, 3 vols. (New York, 1919), 3: 20; "Secretary Evarts' New Trade Circular," *Bradstreet's* 2 (Aug. 7, 1880): 3.

products more widely. While consulates frequently advised American businessmen to establish overseas branch houses that were well stocked with staples, a consul in Berlin advised that it would be advantageous for our manufacturers and exporters to work together in opening a permanent exhibit of American wares in Germany. Our man in Buenos Aires urged the establishment of an American bank in the Argentine capital to facilitate monetary exchanges. Such agencies would foster trade with the United States by better serving the demands of the foreign market.[28]

Another manifestation of the government's role in economic expansion was "pork diplomacy," which pertained to western European discrimination against American hog products. By 1880, the United States produced a great percentage of the world's hogs and its pork products. When coupled with the contracting European production of livestock, the unprecedented supply ratio gave American producers 95 percent of the export trade in hog meats. In February 1879, Italy became the first of three European nations to pass exclusion acts that limited the importation of American pork; but the Italian, and later the French, acts proved much less severe than their German counterpart. In 1880, cases of trichinosis developed in Berlin and the Reich charged that the infection had been caused by American meats. On June 25, 1880, the German government prohibited the importation of American pork, except ham and sides of bacon, and followed this decree with a series of regulations for the inspection of American meats—and, subsequently, a ban against all of our meat products. These measures created an uproar among American exporters, who now recognized the magnitude of the meat export trade.[29]

---

[28] V. V. Smith to Seward, Nov. 1, 1877, *Consular Despatches, St. Thomas,* no. 93; Consul T. R. Jernigan, Osaka and Hiogo, Japan, Feb. 27, 1889, *Consular Reports,* 30, no. 105 (May 1889), 183–186; Consul General Edmund Jussen, Vienna, Apr. 23, 1886, ibid., 19, no. 65 (July 1886), 212; Consul Frederick Raine, Berlin, Jan. 22, 1880, ibid., *Berlin,* no. 320; Consul E. L. Baker, Buenos Aires, Sept. 30, 1887, *Commercial Relations,* 1886–1887, pp. 657 ff.

[29] See Louis L. Snyder, "The American-German Pork Dispute, 1879–1891," *Journal of Modern History* 17 (1945): 16–28; John L. Gignilliat, "Pigs, Politics, and Protection: The European Boycott of American Pork, 1879–1891," *Agricultural History* 25 (Jan. 1961): 3–12; Robert M. Packard, "The French Pork Prohibition in American Diplomacy, 1881–1891"

German officials justified the exclusion of American meat as a health precaution but, as our consul in Berlin pointed out, this was undoubtedly a pretext, disguising Germany's real aim of protecting its home markets. The *Chicago Tribune* declared that the "rule-or-ruin policy of the most selfish landlordism and the most necessitous aristocracy in Europe" was the cause for discrimination against the American hog. The *New York Times* wondered if American pork consumers were congenitally immune to trichinosis. The major meat exporters, such as Armour and Company of Chicago, rallied to support Secretary Blaine's denial of the German accusation. The *Atlanta Daily Constitution* pictured Blaine carrying a "full-grown bald-headed Eagle under his arm, prepared to turn him loose in all his native ferocity upon the slightest provocation." But because Blaine's tenure in the State Department was cut short by President Garfield's assassination, retaliatory steps against Germany were not immediately taken. The new secretary, Frederick T. Frelinghuysen, was less aggressive, and he instructed Minister Aaron A. Sargent merely to protest the legislation on the grounds that it was erroneous and unjust. President Arthur, who appointed a commission to examine the issue, invited Berlin to send livestock experts to the United States to inspect the raising of hogs and the packaging of hog meats, but Germany declined the offer.[30]

The move for retaliatory legislation gained new momentum in the Senate when the Committee on Foreign Relations recommended a bill to avenge the American hog raisers. This reprisal, embodied in the Meat Inspection Act of 1890, gave the President the power to exclude products of foreign countries that discriminated against American goods. The meat issue was finally settled on August 22, 1891, with the Saratoga (New York) agreement, whereby Germany agreed to admit American pork and extend to American agricultural products the same tariff concessions granted to other countries. In

---

(Ph.D. dissertation, Harvard University, 1954); "American Pork in Europe," *New York Times,* Jan. 31, 1884.

[30] "The American Hog vs. the German Empire," *Chicago Tribune,* Apr. 27, 1883; *New York Times,* Feb. 23, 1881; "The Pork Picnic," *Atlanta Daily Constitution,* Mar. 26, 1881; Armour and Company to Blaine, May 18, 1881, *Miscellaneous Letters, Department of State;* Frelinghuysen to Sargent, Nov. 28, 1882, *Instructions, Germany,* vol. 17, no. 66; telegram, Feb. 15, 1883, ibid.

return, the United States promised not to put the meat inspection
law of 1890 into effect, which would have invoked further retaliation
and reprisal.

The "hog crisis" was but one step in the path that led toward
the eventful day of April 6, 1917. It also manifested what would
become an even deeper cause of German hostility: the penetration
of our products into the Reich and Berlin's aggravation at its increased economic reliance upon the United States. At home, the pork
question became part of the larger controversy involving the role of
the federal government in food inspection and sanitation. Washington's reluctance to assume responsibility for public health illustrates
the strength of the "laissez faire state" on the domestic front, yet
the hog crisis pointed out the necessity for federal controls on this
important segment of American business activity. It also provides
an excellent example of the growing economic emphasis in our foreign relations. As Mr. Dooley put it:

> If all thim gr-reat powers . . . was . . . to attack us
> . . . I'd blockade the Armour an' Company an' th' wheat
> ilivators iv Minnysoty. I tell ye, th' hand that rocks th'
> scales in th' grocery store is th' hand that rules th'
> wurruld.[31]

The perennial tariff debate also reflected the growing concern
with commerce and industry, and its outcome was bound to affect
foreign economic commitments. While the high rates of the post–
Civil War era spelled increased prosperity to those producing for
the domestic and export markets, importers, middlemen, and transportation moguls felt the tariff should be reduced in order to stimulate a two-way foreign trade. Those who favored higher rates usually
painted a rosier picture of our home markets than was justified by
the facts. The way to increase foreign trade, they argued, was not
to disturb the existing tariff wall but to open up direct communications, using our own steamers, carrying our own mail, and maintaining a more efficient consular service.

Appeals for tariff reduction usually fell on deaf ears. The
American Economist, for example, attributed America's higher

---

[31] Finley P. Dunne, *Mr. Dooley at His Best*, ed. Elmer Ellis (New York,
1938), p. 125.

standard of wages and labor's better living conditions to our protectionist policies. Interestingly enough, labor generally skirted the issue of tariffs, seeming to be in doubt about the proposition that high rates underlay a high level of wages. While some unions recommended high rates to protect American industry, there were others, like the International Typographical Union, which championed the cause of free trade.[32]

Part of the agitation against free trade was the fact that the term seemed to connote foreign hostility to American economic growth, or that it usually implied free trade with Great Britain. Opponents reasoned that lower rates would crush the American producer by flooding the domestic market with cheap British goods. Sectional conflict also figured in the tariff cleavage. The Midwest was portrayed as being in mortal battle with Eastern centers of free trade agitation. Certainly the *New York Herald* displayed free trade sympathies, as it continually pointed out the danger of retaliation against our high tariff policies. But the *Springfield* (Mass.) *Daily Republican* exhibited the same leanings when it suggested that a revised and modified tariff would give added impulse to trade. Seen as a whole, the tariff battle was neither a class nor a sectional conflict.[33]

No resolution to this seemingly endless debate appeared in the Gilded Age, but some enlightened protectionists favored reciprocity as a compromise measure. In 1880, a Boston Board of Trade delegation appeared before the House Committee on Foreign Affairs to support a resolution for appointing commissioners to investigate reciprocity possibilities between the United States and certain Brit-

---

[32] *American Economist,* 4 (July 5, 1889), p. 8; see *Proceedings of the General Assembly of the Knights of Labor, 1878–1890* (Philadelphia, 1878–1890); *Report of the Annual Session of the Federation of Organized Trade and Labor Unions of the United States and Canada* (after 1886 the title is *Report of Proceedings of the Annual Convention of the American Federation of Labor,* 1881–1890 (Cincinnati, etc., 1882–1890).

[33] *New York Herald,* Dec. 6, 1884; *Springfield (Mass.) Daily Republican,* May 3, 1875.

According to Paul S. Holbo ("Economics, Emotion, and Expansion: An Emerging Foreign Policy," in H. Wayne Morgan, ed., *The Gilded Age* [revised and enlarged ed., Syracuse, 1970], p. 210), the story of tariffs—a complicated subject involving partisanship, special economic interests, and emotional and political ideology—was by no means largely the "revelation of a depression-driven search for foreign markets."

ish provinces, especially Canada. Over the cries of opponents, who contended that reciprocity improved trade by lowering duties, thus reducing the Treasury surplus and promising to create a deficit, Secretary of State Frelinghuysen negotiated such treaties with a number of Latin American countries. The Department of State felt that these agreements represented progress in the right direction. Effective economic applications of the Monroe Doctrine, they were designed to help dispose of our dollar surplus and, at the same time, counter European influence in an area vital to America's security.[34]

From one point of view, then, the irrepressible conflict of the latter part of the nineteenth century was not over the nature of the Union; it was, instead, a tug-of-war between the United States and Europe for commercial supremacy. After the Franco-Prussian War, the new commercial thrusts from the Continent caused many Americans to question our hesitancy and apathy. One commercial journal felt that, while our foreign trade was "good," that of Britain, France, and Germany was even better. Why should we lag behind, possessed as we were of the advantages of fertile soil, a beneficial climate, an energetic population, and the best transportation system on earth? American industry, finance, and agriculture were making such enormous strides in the closing decades of the nineteenth century that the United States could well become the workshop and financial center of the world, as well as its granary. By 1890, America's economic growth threatened to upset England's control of world finances and her role as the self-proclaimed custodian of civilization and the harbinger of commerce to distant regions. British and continental newspapers recognized this trend and frequently warned against the American "invasion."[35]

The humming assembly lines of American factories no longer turned out products designed only for a home market. The revitalized consular service, the worldwide economic activities of the mis-

---

[34] Pletcher, *The Awkward Years*, chap. 10, 16, and passim; LaFeber, *The New Empire*, pp. 47 ff.; "Reciprocity, Subsidies and the Tariff," *Atlanta Constitution*, Feb. 14, 1880.

[35] "Relative Foreign Commerce of the United States and Other Nations," *Commercial and Financial Chronicle* 41 (Aug. 1, 1885): 114–115; Frank A. Vanderlip, *The American "Commercial Invasion" of Europe* (New York, 1902), p. 93; Consul E. P. Brooks, Cork, Oct. 27, 1881, *Consular Reports* 5 (Jan. 1882), 4–6.

sionaries, the beginnings of overseas financial investment, and the search for foreign business opportunities all attest to a developing, if somewhat immature, interest in overseas economic affairs.[36]

---

[36] For a different interpretation, see John A. Garraty, *The New Commonwealth, 1877–1890* (New York, 1968). Professor Garraty feels that historians have overemphasized economic pressures, especially the drive for markets, in the determination of foreign policy. He feels that the inconsistency, opportunism, and partisanship of our politicians suggest that economic factors exerted, at most, a "peripheral influence on the formulation of policy" (p. 282). A different point of view is that of Howard B. Schonberger, who in his forthcoming volume, *Transportation to the Seaboard: A Study in the "Communication Revolution" and American Foreign Policy, 1860–1900,* maintains that conscious efforts were made after the Civil War to develop the foreign market.

CHAPTER 3

Stirrings
in the State
Department

Today the foreign service is respected as an essential arm of government. On the judgments of the diplomats, on their reading of men's minds and moods, Washington makes decisions that evolve into diplomatic policy. During the Gilded Age, however, America retained the archaic, early republican belief that the diplomatic corps was an unnecessary and costly luxury, a "humbug," a "nurse of snobs," and a "relic of mediaeval, monarchical trumpery." [1] Such beliefs reinforced the seeming lack of interest in diplomatic matters and buttressed the popular conviction that the United States did not wish to play a leading role in the struggles of the great powers. Yet this active, sometimes abusive criticism of the foreign service was in itself a form and symptom of a new interest in foreign affairs. The mounting concern over the quality of our diplomatic and consular services and the increasing American participation in international exhibitions and conferences reflected these changing attitudes.

---

[1] *Public Opinion* 6 (Feb. 9, 1889): 367; "The Diplomatic and Consular Service," *New York Herald,* Apr. 10, 1880.

One of the many charges leveled against the diplomatic corps in the post–Civil War years was that of financial frivolity. Economy had been a persistent goal since the time of Jefferson's "wise and frugal Government." As the Indian problem waned in the 1870s and the apparent need for military appropriations lessened, the armed services and the diplomatic corps became the favorite targets of the "friends of retrenchment and reform." Representative William McKendree Springer of Illinois, chairman of the House Committee on Expenditures of the State Department, concluded in 1876 that the annual cost of conducting foreign affairs could be reduced by a million dollars. This reduction, he estimated, could be realized by reducing salaries, cutting appropriations for contingent expenses, eliminating the position of chargé d'affaires ad interim, and closing some of the less important missions in Central America, Uruguay, Haiti, and Liberia. Representative Abram S. Hewitt of New York, a chief "watchdog" of the budget, reasoned that we needed only two overseas ministers, one in London and the other in Berlin. Hewitt believed, for example, that our political relations with Greece had been reduced to a "nullity" and thus required "no center of political intelligence." [2]

Still another report suggested that lowering the diplomats' salaries would eliminate the "spoils system" within the foreign service: nominal remuneration would not only repel fortune seekers but, somehow, attract diplomats of quality. Economy in government, rarely practiced on the domestic scene, was the guiding concept behind diplomatic expenditures, but it seldom enjoyed a favored position in the perennial pork barrels of those pre-budget years. [3]

Behind the push for financial reform within the foreign service was the widely held argument that the United States had fewer diplomatic concerns than most other nations. American diplomacy was "a good deal of simulacrum" or just so much "fol-de-rol." Questions between Washington and foreign capitals which called for diplomatic negotiations were few in number, trivial in nature, and easily dismissed. If a serious crisis arose, it was argued, lawyers

---

[2] *New York Daily Tribune,* Jan. 10, 17, 1876; *Congressional Record,* 45th Cong., 2d sess. (Mar. 11, 1878) 7, pt. 2, 1649; ibid., 3d sess. (Dec. 10, 1878) 8, pt. 1, 76–77.

[3] *New York Daily Tribune,* Jan. 24, 1876; *Congressional Record,* 49th Cong., 2d sess. (Feb. 12, 1887) 18, pt. 3, A80.

and special commissions could handle the situation. Some critics even contended that the foreign service was inferior to the press as a source of reliable information. The perfection of steam transportation and the laying of the transatlantic cable also made personal diplomatic contacts unnecessary. E. L. Godkin of *The Nation* suggested that the telegraph would allow one minister, stationed in Paris, to do the work of the entire continental mission.[4]

American pride also played a major part in debunking the foreign service. Diplomacy per se was a vestige of autocracy—a rejection of the simplicity and purity of the American republic. For one representative, the language of the diplomat was "meaningless mummery, which [had] ceased even to amuse." Secretary James G. Blaine even suggested that President Harrison refrain from employing such words as *gracious, very gracious*, and *gratefully* because they were peculiarly English and hence might offend American ears. Our envoys not only failed to represent the American yeoman, but these "flunkeys and lord lovers" brought back to this country the habits and characteristics of foreigners. Critics of American ministers stationed in London felt that the latter were subject to a de-americanizing, almost hypnotic influence which took effect within thirty days of their arrival at the British capital. The *Washington Post* wondered whether such influence was due to the Thames water or the celebrated London fog! The worship of all things Western, and the equating of the wide-open American West with the symbols of democracy and simple republicanism, helped stimulate such criticism. It was commonly asserted that such men as the famous Indian fighter and rodeo entrepreneur, Buffalo Bill Cody, were the real American representatives abroad, if for no other reason than that they returned home just as American as the day they sailed away.[5]

---

[4] "Our Diplomatists," *The Nation* 26 (Mar. 28, 1878): 209–210; "Our Foreign Legations," ibid. 42 (Jan. 14, 1886): 26–27; "An American Diplomat," *The Chautauquan* 5 (June 1885): 549; *Congressional Record*, 49th Cong., 2d sess. (Feb. 10, 1887) 18, pt. 3, A93; "The Diplomatic and Consular Service," *New York Herald*, Apr. 10, 1880; *The Nation* 30 (Jan. 22, 1880): 51.

[5] *Congressional Record*, 50th Cong., 2d sess. (Jan. 12, 1889) 20, pt. 1, 718; Blaine to Halford, Mar. or Apr. 1889, Benjamin Harrison MSS, Library of Congress, vol. 73; *Congressional Record*, 48th Cong., 1st sess. (May 14, 1884) 15, pt. 4, 4164; *Washington Post*, Jan. 14, 1889; *St. Paul Daily Gazette*, July 17, 1887.

The work performed by the diplomatic corps was also brought under attack, and the press lamented that our foreign ministers abroad seemed to fulfill a wholly ornamental role. The *New York Times* suggested that the most important skill of a minister was his mastery of the art of presiding at formal banquets, and it reported that a manual on this subject, written by our London minister, was available at State Department expense. The *New York Herald* felt that the most pressing duties of ministers—attendance at coronations and royal weddings—might well be assumed by poets, and it proposed that when humor was desired, Mark Twain could be dispatched overseas to save the expense of a permanent minister.[6]

The caliber of the foreign-service personnel also received frequent unfavorable comment. Our representatives overseas were portrayed either as nonentities or as types reminiscent of corrupt politicians, such as New York's Boss Tweed. They were, for the most part, ill at ease in the elite social circles, culturally ignorant, and possessed nothing but an aptitude for excessive lounging in foreign capitals. According to one tale, an envoy spent his whole term abroad in a vain endeavor to be sober enough to be presented at court. The *New York Daily Tribune* sarcastically proposed the establishment of a scientific commission to ascertain, by a balloon experiment, the altitude above sea level at which American representatives could be employed without disgracing themselves and their country. More constructive suggestions came from *The Nation*, which consistently supported a more professional service, schooled in European traditions, and from the *New York Times*, which predicted that such choices as James Russell Lowell as minister to Britain could best end the "flunkeyism" which all too often characterized our diplomatic corps.[7]

Ironically, part of the problem stemmed from the success of civil service reform. While the Pendleton Act of 1883 led to the decline

---

[6] *Congressional Record,* 48th Cong., 1st sess. (Rep. William E. Robinson, May 14, 1884) 15, pt. 6, A432; *New York Times,* Apr. 1, 1885; "Our Diplomatists," *New York Herald,* Dec. 11, 1884.

[7] "Our Diplomatists," *The Nation* 26 (Mar. 28, 1878): 209–210; "An American Diplomat of the Old School," ibid. 11 (Aug. 18, 1870): 102–103; *New York Daily Tribune,* Sept. 1, 1886; "American Ministers Abroad," *The Nation* 4 (Feb. 14, 1867): 132–134; *New York Times,* Jan. 26, 1880.

of the spoils system on the domestic front, it did not apply to appointments made directly by the executive with the consent of the Senate. The foreign service thus became a favorite resort for those seeking patronage. Not only were positions in both the foreign and consular departments notorious political plums, but, with few exceptions, their terms were not longer than that of the administration in power. Secretary of State Thomas F. Bayard, for instance, made twenty-seven new appointments in only four months, and the Cleveland administration was lauded for its restraint in making hasty replacements. It was precisely these conditions, political patronage and lack of tenure, that caused a small group of liberal reformers to advocate abolition of the foreign service.[8]

Despite the rash of adverse criticism, from time to time the press and various periodicals published feature articles that defended the diplomatic service. A persistent minority realized that the United States was inadequately represented in the diplomatic world and argued that reform, not abolition, was the answer to the problem. America's new industrial position and the examples of some able diplomats buttressed this group's demand for an improved foreign service. Capable ministers, such as Charles Francis Adams, George Bancroft, and Andrew D. White, brightened the diplomatic roster. And it was argued that appointments of the caliber of James Russell Lowell, a man of taste and culture, would cancel out such hacks as General Robert Schenck, who introduced draw poker at the Court of St. James's. Some sources unequivocally denied that the service was corrupt or incompetent. The *Omaha Bee*, for example, contended that our foreign service had never received the fair and generous consideration its importance merited. Other statements were even stronger. The *Chautauquan* described our overseas establishments as a positive good, shedding a respectable "luster" on the United States, and William Henry Trescot, who had served on

---

[8] William Barnes and John Heath Morgan, *The Foreign Service of the United States* (Washington, 1961), p. 133; *New York Daily Tribune,* July 17, 1885; "The Diplomatic Service," *The Nation* 60 (June 11, 1885): 476.

Although Cleveland favored civil service, he appointed Anthony M. Keiley to Rome in 1885 to placate Virginia Democrats, the Irish, and Catholics. See Joseph P. O'Grady, "Politics and Diplomacy: The Appointment of Anthony M. Keiley to Rome in 1885," *Virginia Magazine of History and Biography* 81 (Apr. 1968): 191–209.

diplomatic missions, maintained that Americans took "a just pride in the administration of their foreign affairs." [9]

Although most critics refused to consider the abolition of the foreign service, the majority did not take "a just pride" in its administration, and they were anxious to remedy its weaknesses. John A. Kasson, one of the more outstanding American diplomats of the period, was seriously concerned about the prevailing American indifference to global affairs and the baneful intrusion of the spoils system in the foreign service. During the Arthur administration, he wrote dispatches from Vienna emphasizing the importance of trained personnel who could speak the language of the country of their assignment. Kasson believed the time had come when the United States needed a distinctive and consistent policy in international relations. To escape from what he deemed America's "condition of inferiority," Kasson recommended the establishment of a foreign-service school in Washington. Knowledge of international law, which this school would provide, was the first step toward a revitalization of the diplomatic corps. [10]

Other Americans were also concerned over the efficiency of the foreign service. Former diplomat James B. Angell, in his presidential address before the 1893 meeting of the American Historical Association, told his audience that, as historians, it was their duty to foster friendly relations between nations by placing the council table and arbitration tribunal on the same pedestal as the battlefield and the warrior. Other critics believed that the salvation of the foreign service lay in adopting the British system. That service, with its assured tenure and system of internal promotions, provided the best model for an American corps of career diplomats. The instrumentation of this plan, *The Nation* contended, would present little difficulty, and its editor proposed that the law forbidding the cashiering of army and naval officers on grounds other than court-

---

[9] "American Diplomacy," *New York Daily Tribune,* June 5, 1882; "Mr. Lowell," *The Nation* 40 (May 28, 1885): 436; "Our Foreign Service," *Public Opinion* 2 (Mar. 26, 1887): 517; "Foreign Relations of the United States," *The Chautauquan* 8 (Nov. 1887): 102–104; William H. Trescot, "The Administration of Our Foreign Affairs," *International Review* 8 (Mar. 1880): 308–322.

[10] Edward L. Younger, *John A. Kasson: Politics and Diplomacy from Lincoln to McKinley* (Iowa City, 1955), p. 284; Barnes and Morgan, *The Foreign Service of the United States,* p. 193.

martial be extended to the diplomatic corps. The executive branch, under President Cleveland, supported more extensive changes. Among other proposals, Cleveland asked for a system of personnel evaluation which rewarded efficiency and penalized inefficiency.[11]

In spite of the activity of some crusaders, the concept of a professional career in the diplomatic corps was slow in developing in the United States. As early as 1868, a select joint committee of Congress proposed that the foreign service be established on a merit system, but it was only in the late 1880s that external forces began to push the service in the direction of professionalization. The increasing number of men entering the service with the intent of making it a full-time career, American travel abroad, and the ever growing tide of immigration all enhanced the need for competent agents abroad.[12]

This new demand for a professional foreign service can best be seen in the pressure exerted for the creation of the rank of ambassador. Secretary of State Thomas Bayard made such a suggestion in the late 1880s, arguing that this step would enhance the status of our overseas representatives. The secretary deplored the humiliation American ministers endured when outranked by representatives of second- or third-rate powers. Robert Todd Lincoln, minister to Great Britain in the early 1890s, complained that his inferior title involved him in constant embarrassments and delays. Nicholas Fish, writing from his post in Bern, Switzerland, complained that, by seniority of arrival, he should have ranked fourth, yet his title made him inferior to all other foreign representatives. The White House eventually joined those who sought to raise the rank of our major diplomats. In his annual message in 1889, Benjamin Harrison noted that, in view of the importance of our relations with Latin America, our diplomatic agents in those countries should be raised to a uniform rank of envoy extraordinary and minister plenipotentiary. It

---

[11] James B. Angell, "The Inadequate Recognition of Diplomatists by Historians," *Annual Report of the American Historical Association* (1893), pp. 15–23; "Diplomatic Appointments," *New York Times,* June 14, 1887; "Wanton Removal of Diplomatic Agents," *The Nation* 48 (May 23, 1889): 420; Richardson, *Messages and Papers,* 11: 5091.

[12] Barnes and Morgan, *The Foreign Service of the United States,* pp. 147, 148. See also Warren Ilchman, *Professional Diplomacy in the United States* (Chicago, 1961), pp. 49–52.

was inevitable that a country of 56 million would be drawn into the international vortex, at least to the extent of having suitable representation abroad. On the initiative of Senator George F. Hoar of Massachusetts, Congress created the ambassadorial rank in 1893, elevating many legations to embassy status.[13]

American financial niggardliness with respect to the diplomatic service also came under occasional sharp rebuke. In 1878, Senator George F. Edmunds of Vermont urged that the President be given funds he could use at his discretion to employ agents to promote American interests in foreign countries. Commenting sardonically on ministerial salaries, the *New York Times* felt that a diplomat should at least receive the equivalent salary of a mediocre lawyer or United States judge. Even E. L. Godkin, a renowned champion of economy, came to favor additional appropriations for the diplomatic service. The executive branch also was awakening to the financial needs of American agents overseas. For example, President Chester A. Arthur called for expenditures to meet the expanded duties of our overseas establishment; and his Democratic successor, Grover Cleveland, referred to this need in the annual message of 1886:

> I trust that in considering the submitted schedules no mistaken theory of economy will perpetuate a system which in the past has virtually closed to deserving talent many offices where capacity and attainments of high order are indispensable.[14]

Whatever financial antipathy congressional leaders had for the diplomatic service, it was conspicuously absent in their dealing with consular appropriations. In their opinion, a consul deserved financial support because he, unlike the diplomat, performed a practical

---

[13] *New York Times*, Dec. 6, 1887; Frederick H. Gillett, *George Frisbie Hoar* (Boston and New York, 1934), p. 149; Fish to J. C. Bancroft Davis, Mar. 22, 1881, Davis MSS, Library of Congress, vol. 29; Richardson, *Messages and Papers*, 12: 5468; *Congressional Record*, 52d Cong., 2d sess. (Feb. 23, 1893), 14, pt. 3, 2039.

[14] *Congressional Record*, 45th Cong., 2d sess. (Mar. 27, 1878), 7, pt. 3, 2072; *New York Times*, Aug. 6, 1879; William N. Armstrong, *E. L. Godkin and American Foreign Policy, 1865–1900* (New York, 1957), p. 47; Richardson, *Messages and Papers*, 11: 4829, 5091.

function. He reported on the economic conditions in his territory, watched for possible openings for American products, forwarded information on the best forms of advertising, and advised on the best methods of shipping and packing. The consul was an essential official—the business agent of the government. The diplomat, on the other hand, was too often an unnecessary and costly ornament.[15]

Certain defects in our consular services were consistently the object of the reformer's zeal. Among the weaknesses most commonly attacked were the appointment of foreigners, who owed first allegiance to the countries in which they were stationed; the consular privilege of trading for profit; the appointment of political hacks who were rewarded for party service; and the inadequate salaries which forced most consuls to depend upon a second income. Little wonder that most members of this cumbersome and inefficient organization spoke only English, were deficient in business and administrative experience, and totally ignorant of international law and comity.[16]

During the 1880s, reform of the consular service became the prime objective of various groups. The National Civil Service Reform League, interested in perfecting not only domestic agencies but the entire governmental structure, began to question the efficiency of the consular service. The growing strength of these and other reformers fortified the executive branch in its efforts to improve the consular machinery. In 1884, Secretary of State Frelinghuysen submitted a comprehensive report that contained suggestions for improving the consular system. Two years later, when the House

---

[15] "The Diplomatic and Consular Service," *New York Herald,* Apr. 10, 1880.

[16] The first three defects were noted by Secretary of State Edward Livingstone as early as 1833, and more than fifty years later were still unremedied ("Our Consular Service," *New York Times,* Dec. 28, 1887). See also the following: Perry Belmont (chairman of the House Committee on Foreign Affairs), "Defects in our Consular Service," *Forum* 4 (Jan. 1888): 519–526; "The Consular and Diplomatic Service," *New York Herald,* Jan. 2, 1879; "Our Consuls and Commerce," *New York Times,* Dec. 21, 1880; "An Unholy Alliance," *New York Times,* Apr. 29, 1882; "Consuls," *The Nation* 4 (Jan. 25, 1886): 104–106; "Defects in the Consular Service," *Bradstreet's* 14 (Aug. 7, 1886): 82–83; "The Useless Foreign Missions," *Des Moines Iowa State Register,* Jan. 6, 1880; Pletcher, *The Awkward Years,* pp. 17–21.

again failed to approve another consular reform bill, Grover Cleveland spoke out in favor of the proposed changes.[17]

The business community added its support to the agitation of the civil service reformers. While general apathy and the refusal of Congress to relinquish this reservoir of patronage had been sufficient to block reform measures, pressure from business gradually counteracted this resistance. The Standard Oil Company, for example, which exported three-fourths of its production, was vitally interested in increasing the world demand for petroleum. When foreign competition increased markedly in the 1880s, the Rockefeller interests made special efforts to obtain information on foreign markets, and some American consuls were even placed on Standard Oil's payroll.[18] Indeed, this concern, and constructive criticism directed by the business community at the consular service, mark the transfer of interest from the political aspects of diplomacy to what would later be termed dollar diplomacy.

Increasing interest in the diplomatic and consular services was not the only manifestation of a quickening concern for foreign affairs. The dissipation of American provincialism can be further measured by American policy toward the transatlantic cable. The first such cable was laid in the 1850s, but the greatest development in this means of communication did not occur until later. Yet, by the early 1860s, the federal government was strongly encouraging the installation of telegraphic facilities between the Old and the New World. In 1867, Congress granted the American Atlantic Cable Telegraph Company of New York the right to build and operate a submarine cable across the Atlantic. In 1873, it authorized the Secretary of the Navy to determine whether a cable linking the Pacific coast and Japan could be completed by 1876. And in 1879, Secretary of State Evarts informed a French cable company that its proposed transatlantic project would receive federal money. America's concern for low-cost cable tolls was fostering closer commercial relations with the outside world, which in time would lead to stronger diplomatic ties.[19]

---

[17] Ilchman, *Professional Diplomacy*, p. 44; House Executive Document 121, 48th Cong., 1st sess., pp. 1–148.

[18] Harold F. Williamson and Arnold R. Daum, *The American Petroleum Industry*, 2 vols. (Evanston, 1959), 1: 488, 497, 635–644.

[19] Act of Mar. 29, 1867, 75 U.S., *Statutes at Large*, vol. 10; George A. Schreiner, *Cables and Wireless and Their Role in the Foreign Relations of*

The expositions of the late nineteenth century, which President McKinley termed the "timekeepers of progress," are another example of the growing participation of the United States in world affairs. The support of these international exhibitions by the government and the business community indicate the extent to which America was concerned with creating new markets and expanding old ones.

Beginning with the Crystal Palace Exhibition in London (1851), at which Europe was able to view such American products as McCormick's reaper, Colt's six shooter, Goodyear's vulcanized rubber, false teeth, artificial legs, and improved coffins, a routine and a rationale emerged vis-à-vis exhibitions. Congress would pass a bill approving our participation, appropriate the necessary funds, and appoint a commissioner general who, under the direction of the Department of State, would make the necessary regulations, publicize the fair, and contact interested participants. American entry in these exhibitions, which was justified as a demonstration of our industrial strength, would advertise our goods to the world and dramatize our economic self-sufficiency. Some even looked upon our participation as a more than symbolic contest between the products of democracy and those of monarchical despotism. American involvement in these events grew steadily.[20]

At the 1867 Paris Exposition, the United States was represented by a thirty-seven-man commission and 356 displays, ranging from furniture to forestry and from art to livestock. By 1873, the American exhibits at Vienna were supervised by a 654-man commission, and Congress had appropriated $200,000 for our participation. Americans were urged to attend this event. Various directives and handbooks were published containing descriptions of sea routes, ship schedules, information on European cities, tables of monetary exchange, hotel etiquette, railroad schedules, and even the exact location of Vienna's forty-seven beerhalls. Although the poor organi-

---

the United States (Boston, 1924), pp. 23–25, 29–50, 60–63, 190–192. *The American Economist,* in an article titled "A Pacific Cable" (4 [Aug. 30, 1889], 137), reported that a committee had been appointed by the San Francisco Chamber of Commerce to investigate a cable to Australia via Hawaii and Samoa.

[20] Joseph M. Rogers, "Lessons from International Exhibitions," *Forum* 32 (Dec. 1901): 500–510; Merle Curti, "America at the World Fairs, 1841–1893," *American Historical Review* 55 (July 1950): 833–856.

zation and political scandals which surrounded the appointment of personnel marred the United States' participation in the Vienna Fair, the displays of American machinery impressed European observers.[21]

At the next fair, held in Paris in 1878, American exhibitors sponsored 1,229 of the 52,800 displays. In spite of congressional delay in accepting the invitation (in the midst of a depression) and authorizing the appropriations, the United States made a remarkable showing. The American exhibit won 140 gold medals and 8 special prizes—compared to only 18 gold medals in 1867. Abram S. Hewitt, a cynic about diplomatic endeavors, endorsed the exposition and predicted that our showing at Paris would greatly increase American exports. Others reasoned that our participation would attract skilled European immigrants and foreign capital. While the United States could learn from the industrial and artistic displays of the Old World, the *New York Times* thought that the American exhibits at Paris would demonstrate to our manufacturers that they could produce better products than many of their transatlantic rivals.[22]

The United States also participated in the smaller international fairs. Exhibitions held in Sydney and Melbourne, Australia, in 1879 and 1880, and subsidized only to the extent of $28,000, attracted over 300 American representatives. In 1880, the United States was represented at the International Fishery Exhibition in Berlin, and our minister reported that the American display was one of the largest. The next year, Edison's incandescent lamp was the central attraction of the International Exposition of Electricity at Paris.[23]

---

[21] *Official Papers Relating to the Conduct of the Legation of the United States at Paris with regard to the Commissioners for the International Exposition of 1867* (Paris, 1867); C. W. DeBernardy, *The American's Hand-Book to Vienna and the Exhibition* (Philadelphia, 1873); *Report of Guido Kustel, Commissioner to the Vienna Exposition of 1873* (San Francisco, 1874).

[22] Curti, "America at the World Fairs," loc. cit.; *Congressional Record,* 45th Cong., 1st sess. (Nov. 19, 1877), 6: 528, 536 ff.; Richard C. McCormick, "Our Success at Paris in 1878," *North American Review* 129 (July 1879): 1–22; "The Exportation of American Wares," *New York Times,* Dec. 24, 1877.

[23] Curti, "America at the World Fairs," loc. cit. See also National Archives, *Preliminary Inventories, Number 76, Records of United States Participation in International Conferences, Commissions, and Expositions* (Washington,

These expositions not only displayed America's new technological image but, more important, provided an outlet for the growing commercial and social relations between the New World and the Old.

Another illustration of the interaction between the United States and Europe can be seen in the role America played in a number of international conferences. These meetings, opposed by some as inconsistent with American tradition, were indeed innovations. They were the product of an increased awareness of the benefits of cooperation in nonpolitical areas, as well as the logical conclusion of a new national self-consciousness.

American participation in these international conferences began in the 1860s, but, as in other areas of foreign involvement, progress was slow. In 1863, American diplomat John Kasson attended such a meeting in Paris—but the attempt to establish uniform postal regulations was unsuccessful. Failure also marked two other attempts at world cooperation in the 1860s. Washington did not choose to attend the convention dealing with uniform merchant marine signals; and the Paris conference of 1867, for standardizing weights, measurements, and coinage, revealed that the United States was not the only nation unwilling to modify its monetary system and adopt a uniform metric or decimal system. Although we sent a representative, George G. Fogg, to the Geneva convention of 1864, at which the major European nations approved the formation of the International Red Cross, isolationist sentiment was still strong enough to impede American cooperation in the humanitarian endeavor to draft rules for the treatment of wartime wounded. Ironically, it was Secretary Seward, who was usually ahead of his time on international measures, who was most responsible for blocking American acceptance of the International Red Cross. Finally, in 1882, the Senate agreed to participate in the Red Cross convention.[24]

American cooperation in world projects made more headway in the 1870s and 1880s. The United States was represented at the Bern conference of 1874, and agreed to the establishment of the

---

1955), pp. 93–109, for a general description of all National Archives holdings on the expositions described in this chapter.

[24] Clark E. Persinger, "Internationalism in the '60s," *Historical Outlook* 20 (Nov. 1929): 324–327; Foster R. Dulles, *The American Red Cross* (New York, 1950), pp. 2, 8–11, 15; *Congressional Record,* 47th Cong., 1st sess. (May 12, 1882), 12, pt. 4, 3859.

International Postal Union and a uniform rate (5 cents or the equivalent) for the transmission of global mail. The Postmaster General enthusiastically reported that the changes brought about by the Bern conference and by a similar meeting in Paris in 1878 would contribute greatly to "the dissemination of truth" and "the advance of civilization." [25]

Other matters were also settled by international congresses. In 1882, Washington cooperated with several European countries in providing for the protection of submarine communication cables. That same year the United States took the initiative in fixing a prime meridian for standardizing navigation charts and delineating international time zones. The maritime conference of 1889 adopted marine signals and marked out collision-free ship routes. The United States and other nations represented at the Brussels conference of 1886 agreed on the exchange of public documents and the establishment of bureaus in their countries to print lists of publications that would be sent abroad. [26]

Monetary issues, which were intimately bound up with the social and economic unrest of the period, also had international ramifications. Unless the United States was prepared to adopt a free silver policy at a higher ratio than the existing values (which was strongly opposed by the Republican Party), the only alternative was an international agreement on the silver issue. Fearing unilateral action by Europe, the State Department arranged for a conference in Paris in 1881. While this country could not convince the other Atlantic powers that she intended to suspend the silver coinage allowed by the Bland-Allison Act (1878) unless an international agreement

[25] Clyde Kelly, *United States Postal Policy* (New York and London, 1931), pp. 218, 221; Daniel C. Roper, *The United States Post Office: Its Past Record, Present Condition, and Potential Relation to the New World Era* (New York and London, 1917), pp. 74, 246, 250–253; John F. Sly, "The Genesis of the Universal Postal Union," *International Conciliation*, no. 233 (Oct. 1927), pp. 393–443; Persinger, "Internationalism in the '60s," loc. cit. See also Budd Gambee, "The Great Junket: American Participation in the Conference of Librarians, London, 1877," *Journal of Library History* 2 (Jan. 1967): 9–44.

[26] Norman L. Hill, *The Public International Conferences* (Stanford, 1929), p. 229; James B. Childs, *International Exchange of Government Publications* (Washington, 1927), pp. 4–5; "The Marine Conference," *Washington Post*, Oct. 10, 1889.

was reached, the overriding fact is that the Senate approved our participation. In addition to taking part in full-fledged conferences, the United States, beginning in 1879, sent confidential "silver missions" overseas. During the first Cleveland administration, for example, Boston's sound-money businessman, inventor, and reformer, Edward Atkinson, was dispatched on a fact-finding mission. He told the European powers that the United States desired the joint use of both silver and gold in its monetary system. Bimetallic fervor in Congress, linked to the domestic pressures of the day, ruined any chance for worldwide agreement. And, of course, such diplomacy was permeated with the baneful influence of party politics.[27]

After the interruption of the Civil War, the American Peace Society resumed its international work by exchanging correspondence with similar groups. The Universal Peace Union preached immediate disarmament and regularly urged Congress to oppose action that smacked of an aping of European imperialism. Peace advocates arrived from Europe to lecture and lobby in the United States and lend an aura of solidarity to a worldwide crusade. The press uniformly hailed these congresses, calling international arbitration the key to world peace.[28]

For a country supposedly preoccupied by intense political and economic strife and crippled by isolationism, the number of conferences in which the United States participated—and sometimes even initiated—and the various international obligations it incurred in this age testify to the changes in American attitudes toward foreign relations. Such stirrings in the State Department were accompanied

---

[27] Jeannette P. Nichols, "A Painful Lesson in Silver Diplomacy," *South Atlantic Quarterly* 35 (July 1936): 251–273; Nichols, "Silver Diplomacy," *Political Science Quarterly* 48 (Dec. 1933): 565–588; George B. Young, "The Influence of Politics on American Diplomacy During Cleveland's Administrations, 1885–1889, 1893–1897" (Ph.D. dissertation, Yale University, 1939), pp. 14–15, 44, 48–49, 278, 287; *House Miscellaneous Documents* 396, 49th Cong., 1st sess. (1881 conference), pt. 3. See also Henry B. Russell, *International Monetary Conferences* (New York and London, 1898).

[28] Merle Curti, *Peace or War: The American Struggle, 1636–1936* (New York, 1936), pp. 75–77, 138; Margaret Shaw Herring, "The World Peace Movement, 1889–1914" (M.A. thesis, Cornell University, 1932), p. 10; "International Arbitration," *Boston Congregationalist* 39 (Oct. 27, 1887): 368.

by similar movements among various elements within American society, elements that strongly promoted interest in world affairs. Agitation for reform in the diplomatic service, the growing recognition of consular contributions, and our participation in international expositions and conferences were symptomatic of a new century of world involvement. The United States did not emerge upon the stage of international politics without persistent, if undramatic, preparation.

CHAPTER 4

The "Literati" Cross the Sea

Fʀᴏᴍ ɪᴛs ʙᴇɢɪɴɴɪɴɢ, American literature was deeply influenced by European models. The Continent so intrigued American writers that, despite the pleas of the Revolutionary generation for a national literature, the great American *literati* of the early nineteenth century continued to cross the seas in search of themes and inspiration. Washington Irving recorded his impressions of English life in his *Sketchbook* and described his travels in Spain in *The Alhambra*. Nathaniel Hawthorne placed *The Marble Faun* in Italy. In *Redburn* and *Israel Potter*, Herman Melville exposed the misery of slum life in Liverpool and London. This tendency of American writers to look toward Europe for ideas as well as models, which accelerated in the late nineteenth century, played an increasingly important role in shaping American attitudes toward the Old World.

American literary journals illustrate the increased foreign orientation of Gilded Age America. *Galaxy* and *Harper's* gained reputations as "faithful purveyors of English and French literature." The *International Review* and the *Literary World* employed French and German correspondents to furnish firsthand views of European developments. *Scribner's Monthly* could only conclude that if an American magazine wished to "keep its hold on the public attention at home, [it must] satisfy the appetite of its readers for knowledge of the past and present of the Old World." Americans were by nature "passionate pilgrims" to whom Europe was a "lodestone," a magnetic force that attracted them to its shores.[1]

James Russell Lowell (1819–1891) was one of these pilgrims, and his literary and diplomatic career succeeded in breaking down some of the provincialism of Gilded Age America. As minister to the Court of St. James's, Lowell found the "differences between the American of English descent and an Englishman . . . mostly superficial." He was encouraged by the signs that America and England were beginning to think increasingly along common lines. In a speech before the Liverpool Philomathic Society, Lowell applauded the "enormous extension of the race which speaks English." He considered England's colonization efforts a "remarkable fact," a "great distinction [which] ennobles a nation," and he looked to the near future "when the good understanding among all . . . English-speaking people [might] have great weight in deciding the destinies of mankind." Lowell's mission to London helped in no small measure to improve Anglo-American relations, which had been strained by England's actions during the Civil War.[2]

Just as Lowell's appreciation of English culture strengthened Anglo-American friendship, his love of French literature helped to transplant French aspects of European culture to American soil. Having traveled extensively on the Continent, he was deeply impressed by the French people, their literature, and their history. He insisted that "France had something that may fairly be called

---

[1] Frank L. Mott, *A History of American Magazines,* 5 vols. (Cambridge, Mass., 1938–1968), 3: 248, 254, 257, 258; Matthew Josephson, *Portraits of the Artist as American* (New York, 1930), p. 289.

[2] See Lowell's *Writings,* 10 vols. (Boston, 1890) and *The Complete Writings of James Russell Lowell,* 16 vols. (Boston, 1904); Walter F. Taylor, *A History of American Letters* (Boston, 1947), p. 206; Richard Croom Beatty, *James Russell Lowell* (Nashville, 1942), pp. 250–252; Mark A. DeWolfe Howe, ed., *New Letters of James Russell Lowell* (New York, 1932), p. 252; Beckles Willson, *America's Ambassadors to England (1785–1929)* (New York, 1929), p. 383; James Russell Lowell, *American Ideas for English Readers* (Boston, 1892), pp. 59–62, 86–88, 92–93; Charles Oran Stewart, *Lowell and France* (Nashville, 1951), p. 14.

literature before any other country in Europe." "Loving precision, grace, and finesse," the French mind "had brought wit and fancy and the elegant arts of society to a great perfection." As professor of modern languages at Harvard (1855–1886) and editor of the *Atlantic Monthly* (1857–1861) and *North American Review* (1864–1872), Lowell communicated his own enthusiasm to many Americans.[3]

Henry James (1843–1916) was another American who found in Europe what Henry Wadsworth Longfellow had called a "holy land." But, unlike Longfellow, James could not return to what he termed the cultural barrenness of the New World after having breathed the atmosphere of the Old. Too much the individualist (like his renowned psychologist brother William James), Henry could not play the reformer. Rather than work directly to improve American society or its literature, he achieved an analytic perspective as the "lonely cosmopolitan of letters," and he became the most famous literary expatriate of his day.[4]

James's first trip to Europe was made during the first year of his life. He spent three years of his schooling abroad, and by the time he was twenty-six had crossed the ocean many times. Thereafter, James lived alternately in London, which eventually became his permanent residence, in Paris, the city from which he profited most, and in Italy, a country he especially loved. His travel writings were marked by acuteness of observation and brilliant detail and expression. Unconcerned with the purely physical and aesthetic aspects of Europe, James interpreted his mission as one of fusing the monuments of the past with the daily life and politics of the present. Having studied the English mind as expressed in English customs,

---

[3] Stewart, *Lowell and France*, pp. 17, 95, 126; Robert E. Spiller et al., *Literary History of the United States*, 3 vols. (New York, 1948), 1: 606.

[4] Spiller, *Literary History*, 2: 1041. See also Henry James, *Foreign Parts* (Leipzig, 1883), *The Diary of a Man of Fifty and a Bundle of Letters* (New York, 1880), *Notes of a Son and Brother* (New York, 1914); and Percy Lubbock, ed., *The Letters of Henry James* (New York, 1920); Van Wyck Brooks, *The Pilgrimage of Henry James* (London, 1928); F. O. Matthiessen and Kenneth B. Murdock, *The Notebooks of Henry James* (New York, 1947); George A. Finch, *The Development of the Fiction of Henry James from 1879 to 1886* (New York, 1949); R. B. Mowat, *Americans in England* (Cambridge, Mass., 1935), pp. 213–226; Leon Edel, *Henry James*, 4 vols. (Philadelphia and New York, 1953–1969).

mores, and codes of human relationship, he filled his *Transatlantic Sketches* with a colorful appreciation of England's cultural evolution. The greatest charm of *A Little Tour in France* lay in its sense of warm comradeship with the French people. Italy, and the people of this land of art and the picturesque, figured in many of his short stories and novels. In 1869 he wrote to his brother William of his invigorating emotional response to the Old World: "At last—for the first time—I live! It beats everything . . . the effect is . . . indescribable." Later he was to exclaim: "My choice is the old world— my choice, my need, my life." [5] Such travel works as *Transatlantic Sketches*, "Paris Revisited," *A Little Tour in France*, "Italy Revisited," *Portraits of Places*,[6] and the articles that appeared with clocklike regularity in *Lippincott's*, *Galaxy*, and *The Nation*, established Henry James as the chief representative of a new school of writers who were deeply absorbed with foreign themes.

James was repelled by the encroaching materialism of America. He expressed this feeling in a letter to Charles Eliot Norton, a friend of many artistic and literary figures of the day: "It behooves me, as a luckless American, diabolically tempted of the shallow and superficial, really to catch the flavour of an old civilization (it hardly matters which) and to strive to raise myself, for one brief moment at least, in the attitude of observation." [7]

The novelist required "manners, customs, usages, habits, forms . . . things matured and established"; but in the United States these necessities were only "developing." He told his friend and fellow writer William Dean Howells that he had abandoned the "uniform, monotonous American scene" in order to "feast his eyes

---

[5] Morton D. Zabel, ed., *The Art of Travel: Scenes and Journeys in America, England, France and Italy from the Travel Writings of Henry James* (Garden City, 1958), pp. 23, 48, 313; Spiller, *Literary History*, 2: 839, 841; Christof Wegelin, *The Image of Europe in Henry James* (Dallas, 1958), pp. 25, 36–37; *Overland Monthly* 5 (Jan. 1885): 112; Robert L. Gale, "Henry James and Italy," *Studi Americani* 3 (Rome, 1957): 189–203.

[6] *Transatlantic Sketches* (Boston, 1875); "Paris Revisited," *New York Tribune*, Dec. 11, 1875; "Italy Revisited," *Atlantic Monthly* 41 (Apr. 1878): 437–444; *Portraits of Places* (London, 1883); *A Little Tour in France* (Boston, 1885).

[7] Van Wyck Brooks, *New England: Indian Summer, 1865–1915* (New York, 1940), pp. 286–287; Merle Curti, *The Growth of American Thought*, 3d ed. (New York, 1964), pp. 508–509.

upon the more graceful arrangements of Europe." The United States was too "thin" for him—the antithesis of that "density" of culture on which literature must draw. Intellectually sensitive Americans, according to James, turned to Europe, "dying for a breath of 'culture.' " The Old World presented him with a rich complex of good and evil shaped by the inheritance of centuries. Roderick Hudson, in an early James novel, articulates the frustration of Americans longing for self-definition through a deeply rooted cultural tradition: "It's a wretched business, this virtual quarrel of ours over our own country, this everlasting impatience that so many of us feel to get out of it." [8]

James's fascination with Europe led to the development of the "international" novel, in which his restless Americans struggled to understand their experiences abroad. Americans, following their impulse to explore a culture which promised a maturity yet to be reached in their homeland, are immersed in a sometimes enlightening, sometimes cruelly destructive sophistication. Energetic and naive, Americans are intrigued, baffled, and occasionally suffocated by the rigidity and subtlety of convention. Throughout his career, James's works were to bring European and American points of view into confrontation. His characters were usually involved in the merger, or clash, of Old and New World types. A major theme was the contrast between American innocence and European sophistication, or the possibilities for good and evil in a life of superior cultivation.[9]

James was well known for his clever and witty stories of young American girls touring Europe, who were often his medium for presenting the American's first experience of Europe. Indeed, they

---

[8] Robert C. LeClair, *Three American Travellers in Europe: James Russell Lowell, Henry Adams, Henry James* (Philadelphia, 1945), pp. 181, 208; Vernon L. Parrington, *Main Currents of American Thought,* 3 vols. (New York, 1927, 1930), 3:239; Josephson, *Portraits of the Artist as American,* pp. 162–163; Henry S. Canby, *Turn West, Turn East: Mark Twain and Henry James* (Boston, 1951), p. 78; Stephen Spender, "The School of Experience in the Early Novels," *Hound and Horn* 7 (Apr.–May 1934): 417–433; Elizabeth Stevenson, *The Crooked Corridor: A Study of Henry James* (New York, 1949), pp. 8, 57; quote from *Roderick Hudson* in Van Wyck Brooks, *The Pilgrimage of Henry James,* p. 48.

[9] F. O. Matthiessen, ed., *The American Novels and Stories of Henry James* (New York, 1947), p. vii; Spiller, *Literary History,* 2:1049.

acted out a morality tale. Christopher Newman, the perplexed American millionaire of *The American*, is rejected by an old French royalist family whose daughter he wishes to marry. In *The Europeans*, James depicted two Americans who return from their assimilative experience of European sophistication to reencounter life in staid New England. *Roderick Hudson* tells of an American student of sculpture whose discovery that Italy affords him the chance to develop his art leads to his final deterioration. *Daisy Miller*, *Washington Square*, and *The Portrait of a Lady* explore the theme of the innocent, loyal, candid American spirit exposed to the sterility behind the genteel facade of European culture. *Daisy Miller* became a classic example of the ordeal of an American girl at the mercy of her europeanized compatriots. In recording his impressions of Paris in 1877, James put it this way: "It is hard to say exactly what is the profit of comparing one race with another . . . but it is certain . . . we constantly indulge in this exercise." Even late in life, James worked the same subject over and over, but in such later works as *The Ambassadors* and *The Golden Bowl* a new, less tortured sense of sympathetic mutual understanding emerges.[10]

Because he never relinquished his concern for America, James contributed greatly toward establishing an expanded national consciousness. He found in Europe an excellent vantage point from which to study America in its clash with the Old World. In the international novel, James took an ironic pride in the "americanism" of many of his Yankee travelers. His approach to the cultured European was influenced by a puritan morality that reached deeply into his American roots. In his novels, Americans of varying sophistication (Daisy Miller, Christopher Newman in *The American*, Isabelle Archer in *The Portrait of a Lady*, and Lambert Strether in *The Ambassadors*) demonstrate a moral strength superior to the Europeans. Despite popular assumptions that James was a genuine expatriate, the United States fared best in his works. However, his

---

[10] Wegelin, *The Image of Europe in Henry James*, pp. 61, 69. The most famous "international" novels are *The American* (New York and Toronto, 1877), *The Europeans* (London, 1878), *Roderick Hudson* (London, 1880; New York, 1882), *Daisy Miller* (Boston, 1879), *Washington Square* (London, 1881), *The Ambassadors* (New York and London, 1903), and *The Golden Bowl* (New York, 1904). The quote is from Zabel, *The Art of Travel*, p. 213.

use of complex but controlled perspectives makes it impossible to say whether he was an American writing about England or an Englishman writing about America; his artistry bridges the two countries. As one of his biographers puts it, James belongs in the cosmopolitan pasture but when he recorded the history of the Daisy Millers and Christopher Newmans, he was also reaching into his own authentic experiences.[11]

In 1916, to protest America's reluctance to enter World War I, James capped his long residence in England by becoming a British subject. Nevertheless, he felt that he was merely a competent novelist, not a great one (contemporary critics would not agree), because he had not remained at home and cultivated his roots in American life. He revered Europe and its intellectual stimulation, but his American ties were never deeply submerged. To him, the great story of the Western world, the Old World's discovery of the New, was fulfilled by the New World's discovery of the Old. At the heart of James's vision was the reflective American, looking simultaneously outward in the direction of Europe and inward at himself.[12]

Although James and Lowell were perhaps the most famous American writers who found audiences across the Atlantic, other writers made American perspectives on Europe a vital part of their art. William Dean Howells (1837–1920), the "father of realism" in American literature, shared Henry James's cosmopolitanism. Howells, while serving as American consul in Venice during the Civil War, fell under the spell of Italian civilization. At a New York City celebration held to promote Italian unification, Howells exclaimed: "The citizen of every free country loves Italy next to his

---

[11] Stephen Spender, "A World Where the Victor Belonged to the Spoils," *New York Times Book Review,* Mar. 12, 1944; Osborn Andreas, *Henry James and the Expanding Horizon* (Seattle, 1948), p. 171; Josephson, *Portraits of the Artist as American,* p. 92; LeClair, *Three American Travellers in Europe,* p. 207; Henry S. Commager, *The American Mind* (New York, 1950), p. 65; Edmund Wilson, "The Ambiguity of Henry James," in F. W. Dupee, ed., *The Question of Henry James* (New York, 1945), p. 184; Edna Kenton, "Henry James in the World," *Hound and Horn* 7 (Apr.–May 1934): 506–513; Leon Edel, "The Enduring Fame of Henry James," *New York Times Book Review,* Sept. 3, 1961; Edel, *Henry James,* 1:15.

[12] Edel, *Henry James,* 1:15; Richard Grozier, Jr., "Henry James and American Moral Attitudes" (M.A. thesis, Georgetown University, 1954), p. 144; Wegelin, *The Image of Europe in Henry James,* pp. 145, 151, 163.

own land, and feels her prosperous fortune to be the advantage of civilization." [13]

Of Howells's more than 200 books, at least fifty have Italian backgrounds, and four of his ten travel accounts record his impressions of Italy. The sketches he submitted to the *Atlantic Monthly* in 1863, which were published as *Venetian Life* three years later, are a work of social analysis which James Russell Lowell described as the best book ever written about Italy. *Italian Journeys* (1867) was primarily a guidebook for tourists, but the more ambitious *Tuscan Cities* (1886) was hailed as the apotheosis of all travel books. In the manner of Henry James, Howells elevated travel literature to a level which combined colorful local history with vivid contemporary observation.[14]

A Foregone Conclusion (1875), a novel derived from Howells's Italian experiences, was so successful that it warranted fourteen printings in as many years. Howells depicted a Venetian consul as the protector of Florida Vervain, who saved her from the fruitless love of an Italian cleric. *A Fearful Responsibility*, *The Lady of the Aroostock*, and *Indian Summer* are among his other novels that have an Italian background.[15] Howells attacked idealized conceptions of the Old World in these novels of social realism, which often placed, in the manner of Henry James, a naive American in conflict with sophisticated, perhaps amoral, Europeans.[16]

As the editor of the *Atlantic Monthly* magazine from 1871 to 1881, Howells kept his readers abreast of striking new developments

---

[13] Van Wyck Brooks, *Howells: His Life and World* (New York, 1959), p. 26; Edwin H. Cady, *The Road to Realism; The Early Years, 1837–1885, of William Dean Howells* (Syracuse, 1956), pp. 92, 95; James L. Woodress, Jr., *Howells and Italy* (Durham, N.C., 1952), pp. vii, 186, 199, 200. Quotation from Howells, *The Unity of Italy* (New York, 1871), in Woodress, p. 199.

[14] See Howells, *Tuscan Cities* (Boston, 1886), *Venetian Life* (New York, 1866), *Italian Journeys* (New York, 1867); Woodress, *Howells and Italy*, pp. 27, 50, 62, 73, 180, 200; Clara M. Kirk and Rudolph Kirk, *William Dean Howells* (New York, 1960), p. lxxviii.

[15] See *A Foregone Conclusion* (Boston, 1875), *A Fearful Responsibility* (Boston, 1881), *Indian Summer* (Boston, 1886), and *The Lady of the Aroostock* (Boston, 1879). See also Woodress, *Howells and Italy*, p. 73.

[16] Everett Carter, *Howells and the Age of Realism* (New York, 1950), pp. 50, 51; Albert Mordell, ed., *Discovery of a Genius: William Dean Howells and Henry James* (New York, 1961), pp. 12–13.

in foreign literature. Having had little formal education, Howells developed broad interests in German, Russian, Spanish, and French literature. The Turgenev vogue in this country, for example, derived its impetus from Howells. So absorbing were Howells's Old World interests that Van Wyck Brooks believes he was bored and repelled by all that was not European. Howells, who made ten visits to Europe between 1861 and 1913, felt that a European experience was essential to the sensitive American who yearned for freedom from a business culture. But the "dictator of literary Boston" did not find it contradictory to regard Europe as a "chateau to be rented for a season of self-indulgence." Perhaps it was Howells's growing sense of American cultural independence that enabled him to sketch what Henry James said was the most authentic picture both of the American abroad and European curiosity about the United States.[17]

Bret Harte (1836–1902), famous in American literature as a Western, regional writer, left for Europe in 1878—never to return. While overseas he served as American consul in Crefeld (Rhenish Prussia) and in Glasgow. Harte became so popular in England, which he came to regard as home, that the *London Daily News* remarked: "The East and West contend for the reflected rays of his celebrity." Treated more kindly by English than by American critics, Harte recognized that his chances for success and acceptance were better overseas than at home. He was superstitiously opposed to visiting America, but such sentiments about the United States as he voiced in later life reflected a persistent if somewhat ambivalent patriotism.[18]

Lafcadio Hearn (1850–1904), who was born in the Ionian Isles and educated in Ireland, England, and France, came to America in 1869. After he visited New Orleans in 1877, he began to write Creole

---

[17] Brooks, *New England: Indian Summer,* pp. 232, 249; Woodress, *Howells and Italy,* p. vii; Howells, "Recent Fiction," *Overland Monthly* 9 (Feb. 1887): 214–220; Kenneth E. Eble, ed., *Howells: A Century of Criticism* (Dallas, 1962), pp. 19, 232. See also Robert L. Hough, *The Quiet Rebel: William Dean Howells as Social Commentator* (Lincoln, Neb., 1959), passim.

[18] George R. Stewart, Jr., *Bret Harte: Argonaut and Exile* (Boston, 1931), pp. 198, 264, 271, 289; Geoffrey Bret Harte, ed., *The Letters of Bret Harte* (Boston and New York, 1926), p. 285.

sketches which drew on the Latin flavor of his days in Paris. But
instead of returning to Europe in the manner of James, Hearn was
driven by the hypocrisy and moral climate of Western civilization
to search for more remote traditions. El Dorado and the conquista-
dor heritage of primitive Spanish America entranced him, and in
1889 Hearn set down his memories of a West Indies sojourn in
Chita: A Memory of Last Island.[19]

Hearn's chief preoccupation, however, was Japan, and his reputation rests largely upon his interpretation of that country, which
became very popular in the West. His interest in Japan was first
stimulated by the Japanese exhibit at the New Orleans Exposition,
which he described as a small oasis of quiet in a large wilderness of
bustle. His response to Japan itself was both ecstatic and reflective.
"What I love in Japan is the Japanese . . . the poor simple humanity of the country. It is divine." "The first charm of Japan is
intangible and volatile as a perfume." "There is some charm un-
utterable in the morning air." "Impressions so multitudinous and
so sharply novel come to me every day that the mind refuses to digest
them. Everything seems enchanted now." "What an education the
Orient is!" "How it opens a man's eyes and mind about his own
country." Within Japan's "rarified, highly oxygenated atmosphere," Hearn was drawn to "the poor simple humanity of the
country." [20]

Charmed and delighted with Oriental life, and married to a
Japanese, Hearn produced at least a dozen books on Japanese life
and culture. His *Glimpse of Unfamiliar Japan* (1894), the chief
record of Hearn's intoxication with that country, is the first account
to portray its people and institutions sympathetically to the West.
While Hearn always felt Japan to be a beautifully ordered society,
and always championed Japan against the West, he spoke propheti-

[19] Sidonia C. Rosenbaum, "The Utopia of Lafcadio Hearn: Spanish America," *American Quarterly* 6 (Spring 1954): 76–78.

[20] Elizabeth Bisland, ed., *The Life and Letters of Lafcadio Hearn,* 2
vols. (Boston and New York, 1906), 2: 3; Elizabeth Stevenson, *Lafcadio
Hearn* (New York, 1961), pp. 144, 200; Henry Goodman, ed., *The Selected
Writings of Lafcadio Hearn* (New York, 1949), p. 399; Bisland, *The Japa-
nese Letters of Lafcadio Hearn* (Boston and New York, 1910), pp. 5, 97;
Vera McWilliams, *Lafcadio Hearn* (Boston, 1946), pp. 270, 301; Daniel
Stempel, "Lafcadio Hearn: Interpreter of Japan," *American Literature* 20
(Mar. 1958): 1–19.

cally of the difficulty of grasping the strange nuances of the Japanese mind. The driving power of Shinto, with its implications of militarism and regimentation, disturbed Lafcadio Hearn. Although he was the first Caucasian to reveal the beauty of Japan's customs, traditions, and folklore, he glimpsed the possible danger of a modernized Japan, and he recognized the potential power of China as well.[21]

The American poet Joaquin Miller (Cincinnatus Heine [Hiner]) (1841?–1913), another of the literary pilgrims entranced by foreign lands and culture, journeyed to Britain in 1870, where he worshiped at the shrines of Burns and Byron. He seemed to thrive on English drawing-room life, and steadily mounted the social ladder. Miller then spent two years in Italy, writing poems that would appear in his *Songs of Italy* (1878). Miller's poetry exhibits the same international perspective that his more lasting contemporaries set forth in prose.[22]

Profound and restless, discontent with both his own life and the age in which he lived, Henry Adams (1838–1918) traveled to Mexico, the West Indies, Europe, Egypt, Japan, and the Pacific islands. Watching the "New America" take shape after the Civil War was a source of deep distress for Adams's painfully ironic self-consciousness. In *The Autobiography of Henry Adams*, Adams stated that "society in America was always trying, almost as blindly as an earthworm, to realize and understand itself; to catch up with its own head, and to twist about in search of its tail." [23]

Adams's travels overseas began at the age of twenty, when he became a student at the University of Berlin. Later, he rambled about Europe as a tourist, and spent the Civil War years in London as secretary to his father, the American minister. In 1886, a year

---

[21] Stevenson, *Lafcadio Hearn*, p. xiv; McWilliams, *Lafcadio Hearn*, pp. li, lii; William W. Clary, "Japan: The Warnings and Prophecies of Lafcadio Hearn," *Claremont Oriental Studies*, no. 5 (Apr. 1943), pp. 1–17; Charles W. Hutson, ed., *Editorials by Lafcadio Hearn* (Boston and New York, 1926). See also Nina H. Kennard, *Lafcadio Hearn* (London, 1911), and Yone Noguchi, *Lafcadio Hearn in Japan* (New York, 1911).

[22] Martin S. Peterson, *Joaquin Miller: Literary Frontiersman* (Stanford, 1937), p. 79; M. M. Marberry, *Splendid Poseur: Joaquin Miller, American Poet* (New York, 1953), p. 119.

[23] Henry Adams, *The Education of Henry Adams* (New York, 1931), p. 237.

after his wife's suicide, Adams began twenty years of intensive travel
that took him around the globe. Unfortunately, Europe did not
completely answer his lifelong quest. Adams described Italy, for
example, as "mostly an emotion," while London "had become his
vice." The vital society he longingly sought was most nearly found
among the natives of Samoa and Tahiti. Adams's comments on
France were pure rhapsody, however, especially when he described
the majestic cathedrals and the organic unity of Western culture
which they represented. When asked in 1886 why he was going to
Japan, he responded that he was seeking Nirvana. Despite his seemingly fruitless personal quest, Adams was successful in popularizing
faraway places among the American intelligentsia.[24]

Mark Twain (1835–1910) gave a different twist to American
ambivalence toward Europe. *The Innocents Abroad* (1869) was a
travel book—perhaps the most famous one of the generation—that
did not worship the shrines of antiquity; instead, it satirized them.
As Matthew Josephson commented, Sam Clemens threw brickbats
at the stained glass. While chuckling at the "old world fraud" by
which Europe tried to hide from reality behind archaic mythologies
of aristocracy and monarchy, Mark Twain delighted in his Americanism.

> Wherever we went, in Europe, Asia, or Africa, we made a
> sensation. . . . We always took care to make it under-
> stood that we were Americans—Americans! When we
> found that a good many foreigners had hardly ever heard
> of America, and that a good many more knew it only as a
> barbarous province away off somewhere . . . we pitied
> the ignorance of the Old World, but abated no jot of our
> importance.

The Innocents Abroad was valuable for "pricking many of the
bubbles and exploding the humbugs of travel." [25]

---

[24] Adams, *Education of Henry Adams,* pp. 89, 92; Elizabeth Stevenson,
Henry Adams: A Biography (New York, 1955), pp. 187, 345, 346, 352.

[25] Josephson, *Portraits of the Artist as American,* p. 156; Carter, *Howells
and the Age of Realism,* p. 58; Philip S. Foner, *Mark Twain, Social Critic*
(New York, 1958), pp. 117–118; Spiller, *Literary History,* 2: 837; Mark
Twain, *The Innocents Abroad, or the New Pilgrim's Progress* (Hartford,
1886), p. 645; Henry Nash Smith, *Mark Twain: The Development of a
Writer* (Cambridge, Mass., 1962), pp. 31, 37.

At the heart of Mark Twain's view of other lands was his allegiance to the democratic ideals of his own. In *A Connecticut Yankee in King Arthur's Court* (1889), the basis of Hank Morgan's authority was his passionate commitment to the cause of the masses, as opposed to the nobility, the monarchy, and the established church. Morgan was the protagonist of the American-style industrial revolution—the projection of an affluent United States contrasted with an indigent Great Britain. For Mark Twain, baseball was symbolic of the American pulse. When Morgan taught the knights an American game and demonstrated his Buffalo Bill–type skill with the lariat, he was also exhibiting Twain's chauvinism. Mark Twain's indictments of the social, political, and religious practices of the Hawaiian Islands were similar to his attacks on these practices in King Arthur's England. The missionaries who attempted to destroy the old order of the islands were performing the same role as the Connecticut Yankee, who sought to liberate Arthur's serfs. Twain's vision, shaped almost entirely by his experiences west of the Mississippi, is an essential part of America's literary emancipation from Europe; it fed and strengthened America's emergent nationalism.[26]

However, as Robert E. Spiller points out, if the Westerner developed apart from the Old World, he secretly longed to glance back at it over his shoulder. Indeed, Mark Twain's thoroughgoing Americanism did not confine him within America. Realizing that "travel is fatal to prejudice, bigotry, and narrow-mindedness," he was surprisingly open to the virtues both of European traditions and attempts to alter them. He vacillated between admiration for middle-class Gladstonian reform and respect for Victorian stability. Twain even admired the British blend of elitism and democracy, and once asserted that he preferred to live in England.[27] His political views

---

[26] Mark Twain, *A Connecticut Yankee in King Arthur's Court* (New York, 1889); Smith, *Mark Twain*, pp. 144, 158; Louis J. Budd, *Mark Twain: Social Philosopher* (Bloomington, Ind., 1962), pp. 118, 135; Frederick W. Lorch, "Hawaiian Federalism and Mark Twain's 'A Connecticut Yankee in King Arthur's Court,'" *American Literature* 30 (Mar. 1958): 50–66; Spiller, *Literary History*, 2: 921.

[27] Henry Nash Smith, "Origins of a Native American Literary Tradition," in Margaret Denny and William H. Gilman, eds., *The American Writer and the European Tradition* (Minneapolis, 1950), p. 70; Spiller, *Literary History*, 2: 838; Twain, *Innocents Abroad*, p. 650; Budd, *Mark Twain: Social Philosopher*, pp. 56, 58; Foster R. Dulles, *Americans Abroad:*

were expressed in the accents of those who are eager for knowledge of more than their own land. While never an expansionist in the classic sense, Twain celebrated America's advance into the Pacific, prophesied that San Francisco would become the golden gate to commerce with the Orient, and pressed for a trade reciprocity treaty with Hawaii—and eventually demanded its annexation. He even asked President Grant to encourage Chinese educational contacts with the United States, so that their youth could be steeped in Western culture.[28]

As social discontent grew to a boil in the Age of the Brownstone, the utopian novel made a place for itself on the American literary scene.[29] Because these works reinforced the contrast between domestic inequalities. and an imagined life of social perfectibility,

---

Two Centuries of European Travel (Ann Arbor, 1964), p. 117; John C. McCloskey, "Mark Twain as Critic in 'The Innocents Abroad,' " *American Literature* 25 (May 1953): 139–151; Howard G. Baetzhold, "Mark Twain: England's Advocate," ibid. 28 (Nov. 1956): 328–346.

Justin Kaplan's analysis of Twain (*Mr. Clemens and Mark Twain* [New York, 1966]) very clearly points out the celebrated author's feelings toward Europe. He spoke of breathing the "free air of Europe," and eventually the skepticism of *The Innocents Abroad* disappeared. England lionized him, according to Kaplan, because he epitomized the American's Western qualities, which they admired, and Twain used the English as a gauge by which he could measure the discontent with Gilded Age America. England satisfied his zest for the romantic past and the orderly present. For Twain, Germany, too, meant Protestant rectitude, industriousness, orderliness, and thrift, and the contrast with the disorderly United States was obvious. It should be noted that Twain spent a sixth of his life in Europe, and even referred to himself as a "self-exile" while making his grand tour in 1878 (see Kaplan, pp. 46, 50, 153, 154, 170, 171, 214, 215). The long relationship between Mark Twain and England is analyzed in Howard G. Baetzhold, *Mark Twain and John Bull* (Bloomington, Ind., 1970).

[28] Budd, *Mark Twain: Social Philosopher*, pp. 31, 83; Smith, *Mark Twain*, pp. 14–15. Some of the keenest descriptions of Hawaii are those of Twain, who published twenty-five of them as travel letters in the *Sacramento Union*. This "love affair" with Hawaii foreshadowed his reportorial talents, as can be seen in *The Innocents Abroad*. See A. Grove Day, ed., *Mark Twain's letters from Hawaii* (New York, 1966), pp. v, vii, viii, and passim.

[29] See the following utopian novels, all published during this period: Pruning Knife [Henry F. Allen], *The Key of Industrial Co-operative Government* (St. Louis, 1886), Edward Bellamy, *Looking Backward: 2000–1887* (Boston, 1888), Alfred D. Cridge, *Utopia: The History of an Extinct Planet* (Oakland, 1884), and Frederick V. Worley, *Three Thousand Dollars a Year* (Washington, 1890). See also Allyn B. Forbes, "The Literary Quest for Utopia, 1880–1900," *Social Forces* 1 (1927): 179–189.

they are relevant to the literary movement which looked beyond traditional limits. Instead of directing attention to the established cultures of the world, these novelists enlisted their readers in the imagination's search for the good society.

In *Atlantis* (1882), Ignatius Donnelly (1831–1901) set out to prove Plato's fable of an ancient island kingdom of realized ideals. Donnelly's pseudo-scholarly thesis, that about 10,000 b.c. this great civilization sank into the sea, was the rationale for reconstructing the Platonic ideal of human society. Donnelly's preoccupation with the perfect society, registered in *Atlantis* and such other works as *Caesar's Column* (1890) and *Ragnarok* (1883), grew out of his sympathy for those who had been left behind by America's burgeoning economic development. Although political criticism was his main concern, his utopian quest reflected the expansive view that was typical of his creative, contemporary Americans. Donnelly thought, and hoped, that the United States would eventually "swallow up" Canada. He was unusually bellicose in demanding protection for naturalized American citizens who traveled abroad, and he spoke out in the House of Representatives against the "arrogant pretensions" of monarchical governments in this matter, even asserting that the contest between monarchies and republics would continue until all of the civilized world became one or the other.[30]

Edward Bellamy (1850–1898), in his famous utopian novel *Looking Backward*, drew on his travels to Germany and Hawaii and on his study of Hindu, Judaic, and European thought. Bellamy's political philosophy, manifested in the Nationalist movement, assumed peaceful relations between America and the rest of the world as axiomatic. Bellamy, whose impact upon the European utopian movement was considerable, was perhaps instrumental in creating

---

[30] Ignatius Donnelly, *Atlantis: The Antediluvian World* (New York, 1882), *Caesar's Column: A Story of the Twentieth Century* (Chicago, 1890), *Ragnarok: The Age of Fire and Gravel* (New York, 1883), and Humphrey Doermann, "All my immense labor for nothing," *American Heritage* 12 (June 1961): 60–64, 104–107. See also Martin Ridge, *Ignatius Donnelly: The Portrait of a Politician* (Chicago, 1962), pp. 196–210; *Congressional Globe*, 40th Cong., 2d sess. (Jan. 30, 1868), pt. 1, 865–866; Everett W. Fish, *Donnelliana: an appendix to "Caesar's Column." Excerpts from the Wit, Wisdom, poetry and eloquence of Ignatius Donnelly. Selected and collected, with a biography, . . .* (Chicago, 1892), pp. 67, 71.

theoretical or imaginary societies through his widespread interests in real ones.[31]

Thus the literary cosmopolitanism that developed during the Gilded Age arose, in part, from the transplanted character of American culture, which found the roots of its literature in the Old World. The American *literati* who lived overseas, as well as those who wrote on foreign themes, were—as William Dean Howells described them—"advance agents" of American expansion, not a lost generation of exiles. They were "the vanguard of the great army of adventurers destined to overrun the earth from these shores, and exploit all foreign countries to our advantage." The utopian writers who studied futuristic societies, or who looked backward or outward, were not so much fantastic dreamers as individuals who looked beyond their own country for their themes. These authors possessed a world vision, a haunting American nostalgia for the older European culture and the institutions and forms of that tradition-bound society. From 1865 to 1890, Americans rediscovered the Old World in increasingly large numbers. The flood of travel literature, the descriptions of older cultures, the unique type of international novel, and the utopian epic of the "absurd and fantastic" reflected this new concern.[32]

---

[31] Arthur E. Morgan, *The Philosophy of Edward Bellamy* (New York, 1945), pp. 33–34; John Ransom Bridge, "The Brotherhood of Humanity," *The Nationalist* 1 (May 1889): 13–15; Sylvia Bowman et al., *Edward Bellamy Abroad: An American Prophet's Influence* (New York, 1962), pp. 67, 431 and passim.

[32] Stanley T. Williams, "Cosmopolitanism in American Literature before 1880," in Denny and Gilman, eds., *The American Writer and the European Tradition,* pp. 48, 49, 53; William Dean Howells, "American Literature in Exile," in *Literature and Life-Studies: Writings* (New York and London, 1902), pp. 203, 204; Spiller, *Literary History* 1: 621; 2: 827.

CHAPTER 5

The Eagle's Protective Wing

Some americans who left their native land during the Gilded Age—in ever increasing numbers—searched for economic opportunities abroad, while others (the Christian missionary, the restless intellectual, the Jewish pilgrim, the explorer) were compelled by different reasons to travel around the globe. These roaming citizens, who helped broaden America's international perspective, presented the State Department with the serious problem of protecting them abroad. Although the problem of protection was not resolved during this period, these traveling Americans constitute another important aspect of the deepening foreign involvement of the United States during the years that followed the Civil War.

In the late nineteenth century, the diplomatic protection of nationals played a larger and increasingly important part in the relations between nations. In accord with this worldwide trend, the protection of United States citizens overseas, always a tenet of American democracy, was given legal status on July 27, 1868. By an act of Congress, all citizens, native born or naturalized, were entitled to protection by the President and the Department of State.

Whenever it is made known to the President that any citizen of the United States has been unjustly deprived of his liberty . . . it shall be the duty of the President acting through the State Department and consuls . . . to demand . . . the reason . . . and if it appears to be wrongful and in violation of the rights of American citizenship . . . [the President will demand the restitution of the citizen's liberty, and if this is not forthcoming] the President shall use such means not amounting to acts of war.[1]

As the law made no distinction between native-born and naturalized citizens, and did not discriminate among American citizens on the grounds of religious faith, three groups of Americans—the Irish-American agitator, the Jewish pilgrim, and the Christian missionary—would severely test the terms of this protection.

The political ideals of a number of Irish-Americans presented the State Department with one of its most embarrassing situations. Nearly 4 million people had left Ireland between 1840 and 1880 and settled in American cities, where they became an important political group. The return of some of these citizens to Ireland to agitate for home rule proved a source of tension to the otherwise relatively cordial Anglo-American relations. This problem grew acute in 1881 and 1882, when British authorities imprisoned twelve Irish rebels who claimed United States citizenship and the large Irish-American electorate pressured the Garfield administration to act in their behalf.

Secretary of State Blaine, less anti-British in office than as a candidate, took the position that the United States government could not ask for immunity for its nationals who broke British law, "but prompt and certain justice, under the usual and unstrained operation of the law, would certainly be expected." But prompt and certain justice under the British law was not sufficient for the outraged Irish-Americans, whose loud criticism was voiced by the sons of Erin in Congress and the anglophobe press. The British government, on the other hand, did not see how it could be expected to give the trials of foreigners precedence over those of its own subjects.

---

[1] *U.S. Statutes at Large,* 15: 224; Frederick S. Dunn, *The Protection of Nationals* (Baltimore, 1932), p. 56.

Through private correspondence, former Secretary of State Hamilton Fish and Sir John Rose, a retired British diplomat, found a solution. Rose intervened and the Gladstone ministry released the suspects, deporting them at the expense of the State Department. How much influence American protests had on the release of the prisoners is not clear as the Gladstone ministry was beginning to realize the need for better relations with Ireland. Thus the American protests may only have speeded the acceptance of a policy of conciliation.[2] Whatever the reason behind the solution, the incident demonstrated that the State Department could not ignore the political embroilments of United States citizens abroad.

The radical politics of Irish-American travelers was not the only problem the State Department faced; discrimination against nationals of the Jewish faith also caused the department much concern. Indeed, czarist treatment of the Jews threatened at times to disrupt American-Russian relations. Since many American Jews had returned to Russia for business or sentimental reasons, czarist discrimination against these citizens caused much American protest. The United States objected to Russian discrimination not only from humanitarian considerations but also because the Russian policy violated our national interests. In 1879 the House of Representatives unequivocally denounced discrimination on religious grounds. Secretary of State William M. Evarts, in the following year, instructed our Russian minister, John W. Foster, to petition the Russian government whenever its laws injuriously affected American citizens. Secretary Blaine, who was equally vigorous in his insistence upon the strictest fulfillment of the earlier agreement with Russia (1832), later reminded Foster that the United States did not distinguish between naturalized and native-born citizens, nor did it take note of different creeds.[3]

---

[2] See Pletcher, *The Awkward Years,* pp. 234–245, for a valuable summary. See also Owen D. Edwards, "American Diplomats and Irish Coercion, 1880–1883," *Journal of American Studies* 1 (Oct. 1967): 213–232, and Thomas N. Brown, *Irish-American Nationalism, 1870–1890* (Philadelphia, 1966), passim.

[3] Edward J. Carroll, "The Foreign Relations of the United States with Tsarist Russia," pp. 21–22; George S. Queen, "The United States and the Material Advance in Russia," pp. 85–86; *Congressional Record,* 46th Cong., 1st sess. (June 10, 1879), 9, pt. 2, 1891; John W. Foster, *Diplomatic*

The protection of Jewish nationals in the Middle East also became a salient issue in American-Turkish relations. The Russian pogroms of the 1880s, which hounded thousands of Jews out of that country, forced many of them to migrate southeastward to Asiatic Turkey and Palestine. The American minister to Constantinople was General Lew Wallace, famed as a Civil War hero and author of the best-selling book *Ben Hur*. In 1882, he took to heart the plight of the Jews who were stranded in the Turkish capital en route to the Holy Land. Through his good offices, the Sublime Porte (the Turkish government) allowed these migrants to settle anywhere in Asiatic Turkey except Palestine, provided they accepted Turkish nationality. Wallace's action, typical of the traditional Christian attitude, was unofficial and taken solely on humanitarian grounds.[4] Nevertheless, it was significant.

Turkey's definition of citizenship and its refusal to allow Jews to settle in Palestine frequently brought the United States into conflict with the Porte. In 1884, some thirty-five or forty naturalized American citizens tested Turkish policy by settling in Jerusalem. Elderly and impoverished, these Jews asked the American consul to protect what they claimed was their right to die on holy soil. The Turkish

---

Memoirs, 2 vols. (Boston and New York, 1909), 1:163; Foster to Evarts, Dec. 30, 1880, *Foreign Relations,* 1881, p. 996; Blaine to Foster, July 29, 1881, *Instructions, Russia,* vol. 16; Alice F. Tyler, *The Foreign Policy of James G. Blaine* (Minneapolis, 1927), pp. 272–276.

The commercial treaty with Russia (1832) was eventually terminated because Jewish-American citizens were not recognized by the Russians as the equals of Americans of other faiths.

The persecution of Jews in Austria-Hungary also occasioned American reaction. For example, Secretary Evarts instructed Minister John A. Kasson to transmit this country's sympathy for the oppressed peoples, along with a request for equal treatment, to the Board of Delegates on Civil and Religious Rights of Hebrews (Evarts to Kasson, Nov. 28, 1879, *Instructions, Austria,* vol. 3).

One of the most vigorous American diplomats who assisted Jews abroad was Benjamin F. Peixotto, our consul in Bucharest in the 1870s. See Lloyd P. Gartner, "Roumania, America, and World Jewry: Consul Peixotto in Bucharest, 1870–1876," *American Jewish Historical Quarterly* 58 (Sept. 1968): 25–117.

[4] Wallace to Frelinghuysen, July 11, 1882, *Foreign Relations,* 1882, pp. 516–517. For a discussion of the United States and the protection of Jews in Turkey, see Frank E. Manuel, *The Realities of American-Palestine Relations* (Washington, 1949), pp. 47 ff.

government questioned the validity of their American citizenship because the intruders had originally been Russians, and because they had forsaken that citizenship they were subject to the laws of the Ottoman Empire. According to Turkish understanding of the *jus sanguinis* principle, their naturalization and American citizenship meant nothing.[5]

General Wallace protested this interpretation of citizenship and instructed the consul in Jerusalem to protect those who had taken out citizenship papers in the United States and renounced allegiance to the Czar's government. The Turkish Minister of Foreign Affairs relented in these cases, but pointed to the former Russians in Jerusalem who, not having been in the United States, claimed the privileges of American citizenship. Turkey could only conclude that they were Turkish subjects, but the matter ended in compromise and a clarification of naturalization procedures. Secretary of State Frelinghuysen informed Wallace that, in the future, those who had not applied for citizenship within the United States could not lawfully be naturalized outside American jurisdiction. As for the case at hand, however, those who had taken out citizenship papers in Jerusalem could not be considered Ottoman subjects because their ultimate intention was United States citizenship.[6]

The Turkish policy of limiting Jewish pilgrimages in Palestine

---

[5] Wallace to Frelinghuysen, Jan. 24, 1884 (with enclosures from Aarifi Pasha to Wallace, Jan. 22, 24, 1884), *Foreign Relations,* 1884, pp. 535–537. See also Cyrus Adler and Aaron Margalith, *With Firmness in the Right: American Diplomatic Action Affecting Jews, 1840–1945* (New York, 1946), pp. 44–45.

[6] Wallace to Frelinghuysen, Jan. 26, 1884 (with enclosures from Wallace to Aarifi Pasha, Jan. 25, 1884 and Wallace to Heap, Jan. 4, 1884); Wallace to Frelinghuysen, Mar. 12, 1884 (with enclosure from Aarifi Pasha to Wallace, Mar. 11, 1884); Frelinghuysen to Wallace, Mar. 25, 1884, *Foreign Relations,* 1884, pp. 539–544, 549–552. See also Adler and Margalith, *With Firmness in the Right,* pp. 45–46.

The United States also began to insist that the religion of its nationals should not be the basis for expulsion. Secretary of State Bayard challenged Turkish action in ejecting two American citizens of Jewish origin from Safed, Palestine. Minister Samuel S. Cox informed the secretary that the Turks had asked him " 'Are they not Jews? If so, they must go.' " The American stand was equally forceful: only superior force would bring an American capitulation. Thereupon, the matter was dropped. Bayard to Cox, Aug. 29, 1885; Cox to Bayard, Sept. 24, 1885, Nov. 3, 1885, *Foreign Relations,* 1885, pp. 862, 864, 878.

was another strain on American diplomatic relations. In 1887 the governor of Jerusalem, Raouf Pasha, complained that foreign consuls were not assisting Jerusalem police in forcing foreign Jews to leave Palestine after the expiration of the one-month visitation period. Minister Oscar S. Straus reported this complaint and noted that the Turks justified expulsion on the grounds that Christian fanaticism endangered Jewish travelers. The Turkish minister in Washington explained that his government would allow Jewish travelers free access into Palestine for a more lengthy pilgrimage provided they did not intend to settle or engage in commerce. Straus immediately rejected this offer, which meant the ultimate expulsion of all but the original Jewish community.[7]

In 1888, Turkish policy again tested American principles in religious matters, when three American Jews were ordered expelled from Palestine because their passports had not been approved by the Turkish consul. An American official called the Pasha's attention to the nondiscrimination declaration in Minister Straus's earlier notes and warned that the expulsion of these Americans might lead to "disagreeable complications." This strong language produced results: the Porte ruled that "the measure concerning Israelites going to Palestine shall not be applied, except to those who emigrate in number." [8]

The Turkish government continued to enforce its discriminatory legislation sporadically, but the incidents of the 1880s had clarified the United States' position on such regulations. Acting Secretary of State G. L. Rives summarized this stand in a dispatch to the American consul in Turkey on October 12, 1888.

> The impossibility of making any distinction as to our citizens based upon creed or race precludes any recognition of any curtailment of their treaty rights abroad on such grounds, and in entering into reciprocal stipulations

---

[7] Straus to Bayard, Jan. 28, 1888; Bayard to Straus, Mar. 5, 1888; Mavroyeni Bey to Bayard, Mar. 2, 1888; Straus to the Pasha, May 17, 1888, *Foreign Relations,* 1888, pt. 2, pp. 1559–1560, 1566–1568, 1589–1590, 1627. See also Adler and Margalith, *With Firmness in the Right,* pp. 47, 61.

[8] King to Said Pasha, Sept. 22, 1888, *Foreign Relations,* 1888, pt. 2, pp. 1615–1616.

for the mutual advantage and protection of our citizens abroad and aliens of the United States, no qualifications of the sole condition of citizenship could be implied or imposed by the other contracting party without being expressly consented to by us. No treaty has been entered into between the United States and Turkey to curtail the personal rights or liberty of our citizens.[9]

The United States extended religious freedom to its citizens at home, and would continue to protect this right abroad.

But Jewish pilgrims were not the only American travelers in Palestine who required State Department protection. Shortly after the Civil War an evangelical sect, the Church of the Messiah, boarded the *Nellie Chapin* en route for Palestine. Combining missionary zeal with polygamy and a talent for real estate manipulation, these "restorationists" (led by the Reverend George J. Adams) planned the "speedy restoration of the earthly kingdom of Christian Palestine." Settling near Jaffa, the group almost immediately encountered trouble. The Turks were suspicious, if not hostile, and the Restorationists were literally fenced into a small area and forbidden to purchase land. The country and its inhabitants were strange, the police maintained a constant watch on the group, and the climate was unbearable. Internal strife and bickering added to the external obstacles. The Reverend Adams was later charged with dishonesty in his financial dealings, and the two rival camps that emerged from the quarrel called upon the consular office to mediate the dispute.

It was reported that the Porte approved foreign travel in Palestine but strongly objected to any form of colonization. The American minister, surprised that the American Restorationists wished to settle in a country which objected so vehemently to colonization, contacted the State Department, and Secretary of State Seward replied that there was no law which would authorize the consul to extend financial assistance to the colonists. The American minister therefore recommended that the Adams group sell its effects to defray its traveling expenses back to the United States. Because the colonists had not understood their status under our treaty with a

---

[9] Rives to Gillman, Oct. 12, 1888, ibid., pp. 1617–1619.

non-Christian land, the consular service had been forced to become involved in the unpleasant affair.[10]

While the Irish freedom fighter, the traveling Jew, and even such an evangelical sect as the Restorationists might require occasional governmental protection, it was the Protestant missionary in foreign parts who raised the most serious questions of protection for the State Department. The missionary abroad was an almost constant victim of discrimination, and the United States in the Gilded Age was faced with the problem of protecting their fantastically increasing number.

The growth of the American missionary movement was little short of phenomenal after the Civil War. In 1870, Protestant denominations boasted 18 missions, 95 stations, 537 outstations, and 238 churches abroad, with a membership of 24,142. Almost 16,000 were enrolled in church schools. Similar figures for 1890 reveal a substantial increase: 90 missions, 387 churches, and 36,256 members. Before 1869, there were never more than five Methodist missionaries overseas in any one year, but by 1873 there were twenty-three. In 1882 and 1883, the Presbyterian Board of Foreign Missions appropriated $640,000 for missionary work, a new high for that age. In 1882, the annual meeting of the American Board of Commissioners for Foreign Missions presented another proud listing of overseas accomplishments: the creation of 26 new missions and 23 native churches, the ordination of 80 native pastors, and 1,700 new converts. The board's receipts for 1880 alone amounted to well over $600,000. The works published by missionaries and their societies and the annual reports of the denominational conferences reflected ever increasing activities.[11]

----

[10] J. Augustus Johnson, "The Colonization of Palestine," *Century Magazine* 2 (June 1882): 293–296; *Commercial Relations, 1887–1888,* p. 176. See also James A. Field, Jr., *America and the Mediterranean World, 1776–1882* (Princeton, 1969), pp. 323–327.

[11] *Annual Report of the Board of Foreign Missions of the Presbyterian Church in the United States of America,* 28th–52nd Meetings, 1865–1889 (New York, 1865–1889); *Annual Report of the American Board of Commissioners for Foreign Missions,* 55th–79th Meetings, 1865–1889 (Boston, 1865–1889); Kenneth M. MacKenzie, *The Robe and the Sword: The Methodist Church and the Rise of American Imperialism* (Washington, 1961), pp. 9, 11–12; "Foreign Mission Work," *The Presbyterian* (July 1, 1882), p. 11; "Reports on Missionary Work," *New York Daily Tribune,* Oct. 4, 1882;

Missionary periodicals included letters from overseas clerics, descriptions of foreign lands, statistics, and comments on political issues as they affected missions. Religious weeklies were generally required to devote at least one column to missions and to support fund raising campaigns. The annual reports of the Board of Foreign Missions of the Presbyterian Church in the United States of America was typical of the wealth of such information in church periodicals.[12]

The contributions of the missionaries encompassed a variety of fields—diplomatic, commercial, and humanitarian. Their raison d'être was, of course, religious propagation. But as one missionary put it: "Opportunity is power. What we *ought* to do we *can* do. When God opens a door before a people, that is His command to them to enter." In short, missionary influence, which extended over the entire face of the earth, was a considerable factor in modifying extreme nationalism and promoting a world-oriented outlook. It was in the propagation of commerce with remote areas overseas that the missionaries counted most. Wherever the missionary went, articles of comfort and luxury, imported from the homeland, appealed to natives and opened new avenues of commerce. The missionary journals spoke first of the cross, then of business and good government— a mutual concomitance.[13]

The missions were also vital in the civilizing process—in translating material, in organizing schools and educational systems, and in developing science and art. Many of the American dollars earned in the business expansion of the age were channeled into institutions

---

The News from the American Baptist Mission in Burma, vol. 1 (July 1888); William E. Strong, *The Story of the American Board* (Boston, 1910), p. 312. *Ave Maria* constantly reported similar activities and statistics for Catholic missionaries (see, for example, 19 [Feb. 3, 1883], 95).

[12] The Annual Reports of the Board of Foreign Missions of the Presbyterian Church in the United States of America are an invaluable source for missionary statistics and data. While there is little interpretation, they excel in reporting what was happening in overseas religious efforts.

[13] Bishop Charles Henry Fowler, *Missionary Addresses* (Cincinnati and New York, 1906), p. 92; Dennis, *Christian Missions and Social Progress,* 3:248, 357, 457–463. See also "Do Christian Missions Pay?" *Christian Union* 32 (Dec. 10, 1885): 6–7; Jacob A. Clutz, "The Success of Foreign Missions," *Lutheran Quarterly* 19 (Apr. 1889): 189; MacKenzie, *The Robe and the Sword,* p. 14; Rev. R. S. Storrs, "Commerce and Christianity," *Our Day* 5 (Jan. 1890): 32–40; *Christian Advocate* 60 (Apr. 16, 1885): 245.

sponsored by a missionary board. In the 1880s, Indian primary schools were subsidized, and the well-known Syrian-Protestant College in Beirut and Robert College in Constantinople owed their origin and continued existence to such money. Christopher R. Robert, patron of the Constantinople institution, was a prominent railroad magnate as well as an importer of sugar, tea, and cattle. A Presbyterian missionary, Samuel G. M. McFarland, was appointed superintendent of public instruction and head of the Royal College of the King of Siam. The missionaries also contributed to the development of higher standards in medicine and public health by establishing dispensaries, hospitals, and nurses' training schools. Moreover, curing diseases enhanced the popular image of the missionary, for healing the sick was demonstrable evidence of the compassion of Christianity.[14]

Few areas in both the civilized and the backward parts of the world did not experience the advance of American Protestant missions. Even "Catholic areas," such as Latin America, ranked high among the areas of Protestant missionary endeavor. In the 1880s, for example, the Presbyterians' eleven areas of overseas interest included Brazil, Chile, Colombia, and Mexico. Protestant interest, however, was not enough to produce much success in Latin America. Noting the lack of extensive Protestant missions in Central America, the *Missionary Review* explained that the climate, the volatile political situation, and the religious fanaticism of the people all but precluded a vigorous campaign. In spite of such obstacles, the *Christian Standard* believed that the work of the Baptists in Cuba had brought that "priest-ridden corner of ecclesiastical despotism [closer] to the Lord's domain of liberty." [15]

---

[14] Merle Curti, *American Philanthropy Abroad: A History* (New Brunswick, 1962), pp. 147–149, 151, 163.

Missionaries also increased Western knowledge of other cultures, but their main function was, as always, conversion of the natives. They also interpreted to the Occident their respective areas of assignment, and through reports, articles, addresses, and books popularized the world beyond America. For instance, S. Wells Williams's *The Middle Kingdom* was a classic in the effort to extend the range of American-Chinese cultural interchange. It was first published in London and New York in 1848, and was reprinted several times during the middle 1880s.

[15] "Guatemala," *Missionary Review of the World* 13 (Mar. 1890): 229–231 (hereafter *Missionary Review*); *Christian Standard* 24 (Mar. 9, 1889): 145.

American missionaries found, however, that the Lord's domain could be more easily established in other areas of the world. The Muslim Middle East, though not in the vortex of American thought, nevertheless presented an interesting challenge for the missionary. One correspondent wrote President Harrison that he opposed the appointment of a Jew as minister to Turkey; in view of the great missionary interests throughout the Turkish Empire, he reasoned, a Christian minister was a necessity. Many of the area's institutions of higher education had missionary origins, but medical knowledge proved the best technique for carrying evangelism to otherwise in- accessible Muslims. Through his variegated educational, commercial, and medical roles, the missionary symbolized the growing influence of Western society in the Arab world.[16]

Palestine (or as it was then called, Asiatic Turkey) always occupied a unique place in the dreams and hopes of Americans. The return of the Jews to their traditional home had been a favorite theme of sentimental poetry and schoolboy declamation from time immemorial. But interest in a Hebrew homeland was not confined to the Jew; Christian, even romantic, interest in Palestine was per- sistent in a country long devoted to evangelical, millenarian, and apocalyptic dreams. Many American Protestants have traditionally associated the universal triumph of the Gospel and the Second Ad- vent with the conversion of all the nations and the return of Jesus for the final judgment.

With this belief in mind, it is easy to understand the recurrent publicity given Palestine in the nineteenth-century American secular press. Moreover, Christian missionary papers and journals were intimately concerned with the Jews' return to Palestine, which it was assumed would be accompanied by their wholesale conversion to Christianity. The physical reclamation of the Holy Land was a prime factor for the Gentile in the promulgation of the Gospel throughout the world. Some missionaries felt that the Jews would be converted first and would then return to Zion, while others con- tended that their return to Palestine would result in their conversion.

---

[16] Rev. John P. Newman (Omaha) to Elijah Halford, Apr. 19, 1889, Harrison MSS, vol. 75; Muhyee Al-Din Hatoor Al-Khilidi, "A Century of American Contribution to Arab Nationalism, 1820–1920" (Ph.D. disserta- tion, Vanderbilt University, 1958), pp. 134–139, 150, 165.

But whether converted before or after, in exile or on *terra sancta*, the accent was on "saving" the Jew. Protestants who were so concerned with the conversion of the "chosen people" maintained a missionary corps in the Holy Land, and thus a land with Jews and many Muslims was an inviting territory for the eager missionary.[17]

Because of its novelty and challenge, Africa, and especially the Congo region, was one of the most attractive spots from a proselytizing point of view. The *Missionary Review* asserted that little had been known about the Dark Continent until it had become "girdled" with Christian missions. Although commerce and science had opened Africa to the West, the *Missionary Herald* also contended that purveyors of the Gospel had led the way. The African "episode" was pictured dramatically by the *New York Herald* as one in which missionary and merchant marched side by side in common battle against Islamic influences.[18]

Optimism and naivete abounded in assessing the results of an African mission. In the nineteenth century, it was said, the Anglo-Saxon would make a man of the African savage; in the twentieth century, it was predicted, Christian Europe would seal the continent against the rest of the civilized world. Many believed that the benefits derived from the commercial penetration of the continent depended upon the number of Christian conversions. America's refusal to vie with Europe in colonizing Africa was often lamented, and missionary journals regularly described the various phases of the race for African territory. The *Christian Standard*, which rhetorically asked if the United States, under the banner of nonintervention, should wash its hands of a political role in Africa and care only for the fruits of trade, answered its question with a resounding no.

---

[17] Milton Plesur, "The Relations between the United States and Palestine," *Judaism* 3 (Fall 1954): 469–479; Plesur, "The American Press and Jewish Restoration during the Nineteenth Century," in Isidor S. Meyer, ed., *Early History of Zionism in America* (New York, 1958), pp. 55–58; Selig Adler, "Backgrounds of American Policy toward Zion," in Moshe Davis, ed., *Israel: Its Role in Civilization* (New York, 1956), pp. 255–258; *Catholic World* 25 (1877): 365–378; William Wells, "The Regeneration of Palestine," *Methodist Quarterly Review* 63 (Oct. 1880): 646.

[18] "Africa," *Missionary Review* 11 (Jan. 1888): 52; Johann Heinrich Kurtz, *Church History*, 3 vols. (New York, 1889–1890), 3:214 ff.; "The Opening of Africa," *Missionary Herald* 74 (Mar. 1878): 88; "Mission Work in Africa," *New York Herald*, May 14, 1888.

Thus the missionary contribution to the renewal of interest in Africa was significant.[19]

Although missionaries were often foremost in the commercial penetration of Africa, some missionaries constantly fought against certain forms of business activity. One dissenting voice asserted that some West African tribes, despite three centuries of commercial contact, were more hopelessly backward (and of less value as customers) than many of the tribes in the heartland, implying that the former's condition was the baneful result of commercial traffic. The missionary was the prime lobbyist against the liquor traffic in Africa. J. N. Murdock, the corresponding secretary of the American Baptist Missionary Union, told the State Department that American commerce with Africa would benefit only through "peaceful and moral development" of that continent, which necessitated a ban on intoxicating liquors. The *Missionary Review* called for the cooperation of the churches and other organizations to end the "rum traffic" on the Congo River. The editor entreated for a better way of establishing Christian rule in Africa than by manuring the soil with the bodies of natives ruined and rotted by rum.[20]

Another prominent missionary area was Hawaii, or the Sandwich Islands as they were then called, where in 1863 the Hawaiian Evangelical Association had twenty-four stations. Indeed, some of the most optimistic reports of the American Board of Commissioners for Foreign Missions pertained to these islands. Missions helped lay the foundation for their westernization and eventual American annexation in that the first white men in that part of the world were missionaries, and their descendants very often became businessmen. The story of the famous entrepreneur, Sanford B. Dole, follows such a pattern. The fruits of trade and possible territorial expan-

---

[19] John O. Means, "The Proposed Mission in Central Africa," in *69th Annual Report of the American Board of Commissioners for Foreign Missions* (1879), pp. xxxvi–lx; "Africa," *Missionary Review* 13 (Jan. 1890): 43; *Christian Standard* 24 (Aug. 31, 1889): 567.

[20] Robert E. Speer, *Missions and Modern History,* 2 vols. (New York, 1904), 2: 675–676; Murdock to Secretary Thomas F. Bayard, Mar. 17, 1886, *Miscellaneous Letters, Department of State;* "The United States and the Congo Free State," *Missionary Review* 13 (Mar. 1890): 217–218. For a discussion of missionary concerns in both the Middle East and Mediterranean Africa, see Field, *America and the Mediterranean World,* pp. 345–359.

sion were the two elements that most concerned the Hawaiian missionary.[21]

The mysteries of the Far East proved as alluring to the missionaries as to most Americans. While the vast majority of Americans knew little about Asia, the efforts of the missionaries worked to dispel some of this ignorance. The first missionary was allowed into Japan in 1859 under the terms of the Townsend-Harris treaty (1858), which became the basis for Japanese-American commercial relations. Few successes were apparent until the 1870s, but thereafter missionary prospects improved.

Soon it was widely believed that the time was ripe for Christian success, since the passing of the old order with the Meiji restoration and the resultant Japanese attempt at modernism created a favorable milieu for missionary activity. The Gospel was spread chiefly in the urban areas and achieved its greatest support among the educated middle classes. This meant that Christianity achieved an influence disproportionate to its size, and it was sufficient to help shape Japan's emerging culture. The establishment of Christian schools, a flood of Christian literature in the vernacular, and the equating of Protestantism with social welfare activities were specific contributions of the missionaries. The immediate vogue for things Western caused the missionary to be regarded as a symbol of progress; but after 1889 the situation changed because of the revival of Japanese nationalism, anti-foreign feeling, the derision of Western ways, divisions among the Christian nations, and a worldwide financial crisis. Nevertheless, Christianity had helped introduce Western culture into Japan, and American Protestantism continued to feel a particular obligation toward that country. With the growth of anti-foreignism, missionaries appealed to the President to urge Tokyo to rescind various anti-Christian edicts and allow the missions to continue to participate in what they called the "remarkable revolution." [22]

---

[21] *Minutes of the Meeting of the Hawaiian Evangelical Association* (Honolulu, 1863); Dennis, *Christian Missions and Social Progress,* 3: 386.

[22] "Remarkable Growth of Christianity in the East," *Spirit of Missions* 48 (Oct. 1883): 445–446; John Liggins, "A Supreme Opportunity in Japan," ibid. 49 (Apr. 1884): 185–187; C. M. Williams, "Report of Bishop Williams on Japan," ibid. 25 (Jan. 1870): 51–53; R. S. Maclay, "New

Missionaries were also among the most prominent Sinologues and interpreters of China to the West. On leave from their Oriental stations, these men and women wrote and popularized their views throughout this country. Perhaps their most controversial activity was the role they played as defenders of the Chinese in the debates over the various exclusion acts. Missionaries optimistically predicted that even the remotest provinces of China would soon see the light of Christianity, and that this happy day would be followed by active commercial relations with the Western nations. By 1889 the missionary movement in China had expanded so greatly that there were 1,296 Protestant agents, compared to only 81 in 1858.[23]

Missionaries always spoke of the conquest and challenge of China, but seldom promised an easy victory. Not surprisingly, they were concerned about political affairs. For example, when Anson D. Burlingame, a former American diplomat who was then in the service of the Chinese government, visited the United States in 1868, missionaries hailed this trip as an official link between China and the most Christian nation on earth. And when the American minister to Peking, J. Ross Browne, became interested in introducing opium to the treaty ports, he incurred missionary wrath. But despite its measurable growth, the spread of Christianity in China was not as fast as in Japan, and hence there was a persistent cry for more and more missionaries in the Far East. The underlying religious differences, which were an important aspect of Sino-American cultural conflicts, were especially evident in the antagonism with which Chinese intellectuals viewed the missionary, who was regarded as

---

Japan," *Methodist Quarterly Review* 64 (July 1882): 405–427; Winburn T. Thomas, *Protestant Beginnings in Japan: The First Three Decades, 1859–1899* (Tokyo and Rutland, Vt., 1959), pp. 13–14, 69–128, 163–176, 183–199, 207–210.

[23] LaTourette, *A History of Christian Missions in China,* pp. 842–843; Paul A. Varg, *Missionaries, Chinese, and Diplomats: The American Protestant Missionary Movement in China, 1890–1952* (Princeton, 1958), pp. 6–15; Rev. Judson Smith, "Our Missionary Opportunity in China," *78th Annual Report of the American Board of Commissioners for Foreign Missions* (1888), pp. xxxvi–xli; *Baptist Missionary Magazine (51st Annual Report of the American Baptist Missionary Union)* 45 (July 1865): 193–270; "Missionary Growth in China," *Methodist Review* 80 (May 1888): 467; James M. McCutcheon, "The Missionary and Diplomat in China," *Journal of Presbyterian History* 41 (Dec. 1963): 224–236.

another Western intruder. Thus anti-foreignism was intimately related to missionary activity.[24]

While missionary progress was slower in Korea, it received ever increasing attention. This was especially true because diplomatic relations with the United States were facilitated by Dr. Horace N. Allen, the first American missionary to the Hermit Kingdom. Although Allen seemed to be more attracted to diplomatic work than to missionary activity, he never abandoned his religious labors. At one time he was even accused of trying to convert his diplomatic colleagues.[25]

Thus it is apparent that the increased tempo of overseas proselytizing activities was important as a reflection of America's coming of age. Long before Rudyard Kipling described "the white man's burden," the implications of the challenge had become clear to Americans. Foreign missions helped shape the American attitude toward remote peoples during an era when few other contacts with them existed. Missionaries were among the first to realize that, as a result of rapid communication and the diffusion of knowledge, the "heathen" world was no longer isolated. And, as we have seen, missionaries often preceded merchants in opening new territories for business and commerce and in the promotion of science. In short, missionaries broadened American contacts with the wider world.[26]

A growing affinity between missionaries and the imperialist impulse was also developing. Some men of the cloth gave heed to the clarion call of empire, rationalizing Christianity as an expansive doctrine which looked to the evangelization of the entire world. The religious press was replete with ideas of destiny, racial superiority, and religious zeal. Josiah Strong's *Our Country*, written in 1885,

---

[24] MacKenzie, *The Robe and the Sword*, p. 19; Paul A. Cohen, *China and Christianity: The Missionary Movement and the Growth of Chinese Anti-Foreignism, 1860–1870* (Cambridge, Mass., 1963), pp. 264–270.

[25] Fred H. Harrington, *God, Mammon and the Japanese: Dr. Horace N. Allen and Korean-American Relations, 1884–1905* (Madison, 1944), p. 85; John Liggins, "The New Foreign Mission Field," *Spirit of Missions* 49 (June 1884): 289–292; Dennis, *Christian Missions and Social Progress,* 3: 397.

[26] Rev. N. G. Clark, "The Changed Relations of Foreign Missions," in *70th Annual Report of the American Board of Commissioners for Foreign Missions* (1880), pp. xxi–xxxix; Rev. J. A. Singmaster, "The Reflex Influence of Foreign Missions," *Lutheran Quarterly* 20 (Apr. 1890): 211–220.

was essentially a formula for the creation of missions around the world. Moreover, American missionaries in backward lands often anticipated the annexation to the United States of their areas of endeavor. In another sense, missionary work was related to expansion because it was conceived in terms of the subjugation of "enemy" territory—territory that was either pagan or otherwise deserving of conquest by "true believers." Meanwhile the foreign mission would supply the blessings of American liberty, institutions, and civilization.[27]

The notion of conquest, then, was not alien to the missionary methodology. As the *Christian Standard* put it, despite the possession of more land than it could cultivate, the United States was about to succumb to the annexing, colonizing, and aggrandizing fever. Thus the ideology of American expansion was reinforced by religious bonds. In a sense, missions were a form of foreign service, and few parts of the earth's surface were exempt from their influence. Consciously or unconsciously, missionary zealots were advance agents of Western penetration.[28]

Obviously, the contributions of the missionary were wider than simple labor in the vineyard of God. Professor Merle Curti has asserted that the major impulse in nineteenth-century overseas philanthropy flowed from the evangelical missionary movement, which was becoming global. Such activities, by their very nature, operated against the prevalent isolationist sentiment. The "world outreach" of Christianity was the missionary dream, and these enterprises were important agencies in breaking down American parochialism. Although the missionary never regarded himself primarily as an agent of commercial or national policy, he was nevertheless involved in these policies because he contributed to the impact of Western civilization on Asian and African cultures. In so doing, he also broadened American horizons and helped prepare the stage

---

[27] Phillips Clifton Jackson, "Protestant America and the Pagan World: the First Half Century of the American Board of Commissioners for Foreign Missions, 1810–1860" (Ph.D. dissertation, New York University, 1957); Thomas Dawson to Walter [*sic*] Blaine, Aug. 22, 1881, *Consular Despatches, Apia; Church at Home and Abroad,* 4 (July 1888), 4; Edward Ransford, "The Pan Anglican Conference," *The Churchman* 58 (July 14, 1888): 37.

[28] *Christian Standard,* 24 (Mar. 9, 1889), 145; Thompson, *Future Probation and Foreign Missions,* p. 5.

for a positive American role in the larger world. The obligation of America to evangelize the world, originally conceived by such colonial divines as Cotton Mather and Jonathan Edwards, was being implemented. As one writer put it: "Missionary expansion has . . . given a certain impetus . . . to that interchange of intellectual, spiritual, and material commodities which has become the unique glory of our age." [29]

Because of his increasing number and the widening scope of his activities, the American clergyman in remote outposts around the world could not be forgotten or ignored by the Department of State. Indeed, it may have seemed to the various Secretaries of State that missionaries in the late nineteenth century were perpetually involved in difficulties with the governments of the lands in which they toiled. Problems also arose because missionary efforts were often hindered by conflicts with the political and commercial projects of European governments. For example, two sore points that arose between the missionaries and some of the European chancelleries involved the morality of the opium trade in China and the sale of liquor in Africa. Originally, it was not certain whether the United States would protect missionaries from discrimination, but it soon became apparent that Washington would afford them the same protection as other Americans who were legally abroad.[30]

The cases involving protection in these years are legion. In China, missionaries were frequently persecuted because they established stations in the interior, in violation of existing treaties. In these cases the State Department attempted to restrain missionary influence in the interior, but at the same time it held the Chinese government accountable for the welfare of American citizens. The story of missionary treatment in Japan was also marked by persecutions, petitions, and pleas for protection. In Korea, the missionaries were not overly aggressive, and moreover the Koreans were anxious to retain American friendship and counteract hostile foreign intrigues.

---

[29] LaTourette, *Missions and the American Mind* (Indianapolis, 1949), pp. 29, 35–36; Curti, *American Philanthropy Abroad*, pp. 138–139; Dennis, *Christian Missions and Social Progress*, 3: 402.

[30] James S. Dennis, *Foreign Missions after a Century* (New York, Chicago, Toronto, 1893), pp. 168–169; Foster, *The Relation of Diplomacy to Foreign Missions* (Sewanee, Tenn., 1909), p. 7.

Hence the missionary experience in Korea was perhaps the happiest in all Asia during this period.[31]

The work of American missionaries in the Ottoman Empire posed vexatious problems for the State Department. As early as 1866, the American minister in Turkey, E. Joy Morris, wrote Secretary of State Seward that

> it is a fact . . . that the feeling of disaffection to the Porte is constantly spreading among the Christian subjects. . . . Indeed . . . unless a change for the better soon takes place . . . the Great Powers who have an interest in the preservation of Turkey must eventually interfere to save the empire from the ruin with which it is menaced.

It is therefore hardly surprising that the Christian missionary was not a welcome guest in the Middle East.[32]

In 1885, when the Board of Commissioners for Foreign Missions lodged a formal complaint with the State Department about Turkish annoyances and treatment of missionaries, Secretary Bayard instructed the minister in Constantinople, Samuel B. Cox, to secure protection for them and redress of their grievances. While Washington had previously attempted to remain behind the scenes in cases involving the treatment of American missionaries, this case brought the situation into the open. Representative Rufus R. Dawes of Ohio echoed the sentiments of many Americans when he suggested that it was high time for the State Department to assume a more active role in protecting American missionaries.[33]

Despite the pressure for their protection, the United States government refused to single out missionaries for preferential treatment.

---

[31] Harold J. Bass, "The Policy of the American State Department Toward Missionaries in the Far East" (Ph.D. dissertation, State University of Washington, 1937), passim; McCutcheon; "The Missionary and Diplomat in China," loc. cit.

[32] E. Joy Morris to William H. Seward, Sept. 29, 1866, *Foreign Relations*, 1866, p. 254; *Senate Executive Document* 10, 39th Cong., 2d sess. (1867), pp. 5–11.

[33] Bayard to Cox, Aug. 17, 1885, *Foreign Relations*, 1885, pp. 885–859; *Congressional Record*, 47th Cong., 1st sess. (Aug. 7, 1882), 13, pt. 7, A522; Manuel, *Realities of American-Palestine Relations*, p. 38.

Minister James Russell Young, in China, made this clear to one missionary.

> I do not see that the treaties can be amended to make your rights more secure. An American missionary, in the eyes of the law, is a citizen, no more. He is engaged in an honorable calling, just as if he were a banker, or a teacher of chemistry, or a tiller of the soil. So long as he observes the law, he must have the protection of the law.

Recognizing their need for protection, the State Department afforded American missionaries the same privileges extended to all American citizens, but no special considerations.[34]

By 1890 the political ideals of Irish-Americans and the religious zeal and determination of Jewish pilgrims and Christian missionaries had involved the State Department in innumerable diplomatic entanglements. Although only a few of the cases were satisfactorily resolved, the department was slowly clarifying the terms of protection for traveling Americans. The government's attitude toward citizens discriminated against by Turkish rules, its protests against the treatment of our missionaries in far-off regions, and its treatment of American citizens involved in the Irish revolts exhibit a consistent resolve to uphold a basic principle of American diplomacy: the United States would protect its citizenry overseas— regardless of race, religion, or their purposes overseas. This principle would draw America ever deeper into international affairs.

---

[34] *Foreign Relations,* 1885, p. 157; Harold J. Bass, "The Policy of the American State Department toward Missionaries in the Far East," *Research Studies of the State College of Washington* 5, no. 3 (Sept. 1937): 179–190.

CHAPTER 6

The Nation's
Right
Arm

THE UNITED STATES Navy and its merchant marine, neglected and forgotten after Appomattox, were "rediscovered" during the 1880s. In that decade a new breed of naval thinkers hailed the potential commercial and strategic contributions of a revitalized fleet. A refurbished merchant marine became the prerequisite for overseas carriage while a strong navy was needed to support a spirited and aggressive foreign policy.[1] Naval officers frequently served as roving diplomatic and commercial agents. Commodore Robert W. Shufeldt's exploits in Africa and Asia not only helped to promote American trade in these regions but also enhanced America's diplomatic interests and national prestige.[2]

More often than not it was a naval officer, rather than a civilian

---

[1] "The Navy," *New York Daily Tribune*, Dec. 7, 1875. For concise accounts of the navy's problems and revitalization, consult Robert Seager II, "Ten Years before Mahan: The Unofficial Case for the New Navy, 1880–1890," *MVHR* 40 (Dec. 1953): 491–512; Walter R. Herrick, Jr., *The American Naval Revolution* (Baton Rouge, 1966), esp. pp. 3–85; and Daniel J. Carrison, *The Navy from Wood to Steel: 1860–1890* (New York, 1965).

[2] See chapter 9.

official, who cared for our interests in far-flung outposts. Moral power was considered well and good, but naval strength was also a concomitant of the effective conduct of nineteenth-century diplomacy. The possession of a navy, or even the capacity to stage an effective naval demonstration, was apt to enhance the attention paid to the government's representatives in underdeveloped areas. Indeed, some prescient thinkers had early perceived the relationship between enhanced naval power and a more effective diplomacy. Representative George B. Wise of Virginia thought that the maintenance of a naval establishment was the first step toward the preservation of friendly relations with other powers and the best guarantor against aggression.[3]

Industrialism also speeded the process of naval renewal. Because industrial expansion in the 1880s resulted in surpluses and created international rivalry over foreign markets, sea power was deemed essential in settling the problems which arose from this rivalry. In 1881, President Arthur noted the forces which would drive a decade of naval reform when he told Congress that "every consideration of national safety, economy and honor imperatively demands a thorough rehabilitation of the Navy." [4]

Although some strategists recognized naval force as an offensive arm of overseas political policies, the condition of the navy and merchant marine in the years immediately following the close of the Civil War was deplorable. Uncle Sam possessed only enough ships to cruise leisurely from port to port, looking after the welfare of her citizens abroad, exchanging salutes, and providing officers an opportunity to see the world. In a classic understatement, one admiral warned that the "condition of the Navy of the United States [was] not such as any citizen of the country would desire." [5]

During the Civil War, developments had been made in the use of steam and in the production of iron and steel hulls, but such

---

[3] "The Right Arm of Diplomacy," *Public Opinion* 7 (July 8, 1889): 271; "Our Foreign Relations and the Need of a Navy," *New York Herald,* Dec. 12, 1881; *Congressional Record,* 49th Cong., 1st sess. (June 18, 1886) 17, pt. 8, and spec. sess., A244.

[4] Richardson, *Messages and Papers,* 10: 4638.

[5] Rear Admiral Edward Simpson, "The United States Navy in Transition," *Harper's New Monthly Magazine* 73 (June 1886): 3–26; "The Navy," *New York Daily Tribune,* Dec. 7, 1875.

progress withered with the restoration of peace. At a time when other nations were constructing metal-armored steamships, the United States Navy was composed of obsolescent wooden vessels that relied primarily upon sail power. By 1870 the navy consisted of 200 ships, but when Lee surrendered it had boasted 700 vessels. Deterioration continued, and by the 1880s the navy had less than fifty vessels afloat which could safely fire a gun. Even the ships declared seaworthy were in dire need of repairs and lacked modern artillery. The navy's ships, noted one quipster, presented a greater danger to their crews than to a possible enemy.[6]

Although the navy could have been a source of international prestige, its weakness detracted from our international status. The *San Francisco Evening Bulletin* remarked in 1884 that the United States was in no position to resent even a direct snub by a foreign power. To point up its weakness, our navy was often compared to those of minor powers. In quantity, the United States ranked twelfth among the world's fleets; in quality, all the navies of the European powers reputedly were more modern than that of the United States. Henry Cabot Lodge thought it a disgrace that the United States did not have one warship worthy of the name. Our rich sea coast cities lay at the mercy of any "piratical descent from a hostile power," even a "tenth-rate" state such as Chile. Indeed, inspired by the War of the Pacific (1879–1883), the pro-navy senator, Eugene P. Hale of Maine, confessed "with a sense of shame . . . there is nothing whatever to prevent Chile . . . from laying our towns under contribution, and burning and destroying . . . [the cities] of the Pacific Coast." [7]

Haiti's navy, with its new ironclads, was also considered a potential rival, and, according to the *New York Herald*, Turkey's fleet was not so "sick" that it could not "mortify" us. A report that a member of the Canadian Parliament had inquired into British navi-

---

[6] Pletcher, *The Awkward Years*, pp. 116–118; Foster R. Dulles, *Prelude to World Power* (New York, 1965), pp. 124–125.

[7] "Our Defenseless Condition," *San Francisco Evening Bulletin*, Jan. 10, 1884; H. C. Lodge, ed., *Selections from the Correspondence of Theodore Roosevelt and Henry Cabot Lodge, 1884–1918*, 2 vols. (New York, 1925), 1 : 63; *Congressional Record*, 48th Cong., 1st sess. (July 5, 1884), 15, pt. 6, 6082. See also Martin Meadows, "Eugene Hale and the American Navy," *American Neptune* 22 (July 1962): 187–193.

gation rights in Alaskan waters led the *Herald* to suggest sardonically that Congress concede free navigation to the British; then, if the Indians rebelled, an English gunboat could come to our rescue. The *Boston Commercial Bulletin* pointed out that a strong navy was an economical proposition. The devastation that could be inflicted during the first three months of a war would cost the United States ten times the amount necessary to protect its coastline.[8]

The condition of the navy was much worse than even the naval officers cared to admit. It had not kept pace with the times, and by 1884 the $75 million that had been expended over almost two decades had produced nothing of real value. The *Buffalo Daily Courier* declared that we had a Navy Department, a naval academy, and an annual expenditure of millions "for what is by courtesy called a navy." The navy was, in reality, a myth and, pending its rehabilitation, could serve only as a "butt for the press and football for political parties." The United States, a first-class power in population, wealth, and political importance, possessed a navy "not even third-class." It was obsolete, inefficient—a farcical defense mechanism for our coastlines.[9]

What accounted for this deplorable decline in Admiral David C. Farragut's stalwart navy? First and foremost, the nation was concerned with domestic expansion, and this concern was paralleled by the anti-military tradition that revived after the Civil War. Reaction against the militarism of the Civil War years affected all branches of the American defense system. In 1874 the army was reduced to 25,000 men, and remained at this level until the Spanish-American War. The chief function of our land forces was to police the Indians, and its size made it suitable for little else. Both army and navy alike were either ignored or shamelessly exploited as political footballs.[10]

---

[8] "Hayti's Navy—Where Is It to Fight?," *New York Herald,* June 12, 1883; "An American Navy," ibid., Aug. 12, 1881; "Hope for Alaska," ibid., Mar. 12, 1879; "Congress and Coast Defenses," *Boston Commercial Bulletin,* June 8, 1889.

[9] "The Navy Problem," *The Nation* 41 (Dec. 17, 1885): 502–503; *Buffalo Daily Courier,* Nov. 14, 1881; James R. Soley, "Our Naval Policy—A Lesson from 1861," *Scribner's Magazine* 1 (Feb. 1887): 223–235; Wing (U.S. delegate in Ecuador) to Fish, Feb. 5, 1872, *Foreign Relations,* 1872, pp. 176–177; "The American Navy," *Chicago Tribune,* Feb. 4, 1880.

[10] "The Reduction of the Army," *The Nation* 21 (Dec. 30, 1875): 413–414. See also Richard C. Brown, "General Emory Upton—The Army's

The prevailing notion that the United States was immune from attack by its geographic isolation and the absence of foreign entanglements fostered a sense of security and an unimaginative military and naval policy. Americans felt that they could count on internal strife in the Old World to maintain the balance of power. To many, the navy seemed to be perpetually preparing for eventualities which never would or could occur. Even at the time of the *Virginius* crisis in 1873, the danger to the United States from "superannuated" and "crippled" Spanish ships was pointed out. The Midwest often interpreted the desire for a naval renaissance as a sectional whim of the Eastern seaboard press. The mere suggestion that assistant Secretaries of War and the Navy be appointed was denounced by the Midwestern press as a "martial demonstration" not to be tolerated by a peace-loving nation.[11]

The navy was also weakened by lack of finances. Congressional misers, elected by tax-conscious rural constituents, thought modernization of the military and expenditures for the navy were a foolish waste of money. Representative William S. Holman of Indiana, typical of the small-minded pinch-penny agrarians who then dominated Congress, contended that if we imitated monarchies and impoverished our people by the costly luxury of a great navy, it would not add to the honor and respect accorded us by foreign nations. The Jeffersonian belief still lingered that the chief tasks of the navy were to protect our merchant vessels and provide immediate coastal defense in the unlikely event of an invasion. For such purposes, only cruisers and gunboats were deemed necessary; battleships were a costly extravagance. Because no serious war threat had arisen to stimulate rearmament since 1865, this approach seemed reasonable. One annual report of the Secretary of the Navy was challenged when it included the expenses for rigging ships and stowing shot and powder—all deemed nonessential to a nation blessed by peace. Indeed, the only cause for optimism among strong-navy advocates was the national recovery from the depression of the 1870s. A Treasury

---

Mahan," *Military Affairs* 17 (Fall 1953): 125–131. This article catalogs the recommendations of Upton, which, if adopted, would have revolutionized military policy.

[11] *Buffalo Express*, Dec. 9, 1873; "Our Military Strength," *St. Paul Daily Gazette*, Feb. 10, 1887.

surplus, they hoped, would weaken the economic argument against naval expansion.[12]

Curiously, the Navy Department seemed incapable of reform from within because of reactionary departmental administration. Although its personnel were somewhat better than its ships, the bureau system was inefficient and subject to abuse. Eight naval bureaus divided the overall responsibility and prevented genuine coordination within the department. Feuds between line and staff officers over reorganization were common. As is typical of bureaucracies, there were more chiefs than Indians. Ensigns were in oversupply, and admirals often fought retirement with more zeal than they would have displayed in combat. Discipline was lax and morale was low. Congressional interference and politicking in naval circles did not help the situation. Elements in both major parties regarded the department's offices as legitimate plunder, which made the navy a repository for shopworn political hacks. As a result, Secretaries of the Navy tended to be second-rate officials who were brought to power through the workings of the spoils system. Many sources recommended the removal of the navy from all contact with political influence. The custom of congressmen and other political magnates —stirring heaven and earth to secure a coveted bureau appointment after almost a decade of naval reform—one editor complained, "was still an intolerable abuse." [13]

The uncertainty of domestic politics was another factor deterring naval reform. During the postwar decades, neither major political party was able to retain control of Congress and the White House for any appreciable length of time. In these years of seesaw control (1877 to 1897), the Republicans held the presidency and both houses of Congress for only four years, and the Democrats for only two. The consequent struggle between the opposite ends of Pennsylvania Avenue hindered legislative accomplishment. When Republicans gained control of both houses of Congress in 1881, they took

---

[12] *Congressional Record, 49th Cong.,* 2d sess. (Feb. 26, 1887), 18, pt. 3, A98; "The Navy," *New York Daily Tribune,* Dec. 7, 1875.

[13] "The Naval Controversy," *The Nation* 10 (Mar. 12, 1870): 169–170; "Naval Reorganization," *New York Daily Tribune,* Jan. 11, 1887; *Annual Report of the Secretary of the Navy, 1882,* 3 vols. (Washington, 1882), 1: 7–9; Pletcher, *The Awkward Years,* p. 118; "Reforms in the Navy," *Public Opinion* 7 (July 6, 1889): 270.

steps in the direction of naval reform, but this movement was stifled when the Democrats, who clung to their Jeffersonian small-navy tradition, regained control of the House two years later.[14]

The merchant marine, like the navy, fell into a state of dilapidation in the postwar years. Before the Civil War, American shipping was second only to that of Great Britain in tonnage and carriage. Five years after the South capitulated, only a third of our import-export trade was carried in American bottoms. It was a "monstrous anomaly" that foreign vessels had to transport our goods to and from markets; and legal obstacles account heavily for this deterioration. American tariff laws placed heavy duties on the imported iron and steel that were necessary for the merchant marine's replacement of its now obsolete wooden hulls. The high protective tariff policy also hampered investment in shipping enterprises by making it more profitable to place surplus capital in such domestic enterprises as manufacturing. Congress further obstructed the development of the merchant marine by refusing to grant mail subventions to encourage shipbuilding, and until 1914 it prevented American shippers from buying foreign-made ships for American registry. The postwar government failed to realize that new naval construction would, in turn, stimulate private shipbuilding, and it refused to follow the generous subsidy policy of foreign powers toward their own merchant marines. Despite little private or governmental backing, a few American companies were brave enough to hazard the risks. In the early 1870s, the Pennsylvania Railroad launched the American Steamship Company, and after 1877 the Red-D Line ran three steamers between New York and Venezuela and the Ward Line provided service to Cuba and Mexico.[15]

In desperation, many shippers turned to the government for aid. John Roach, an Irish immigrant, was so vocal in his demands for government subsidy that he has been called the father of American

---

[14] See Vincent DeSantis, "American Politics in the Gilded Age," *Review of Politics* 25 (Oct. 1963): 551–561; Harold and Margaret Sprout, *The Rise of American Naval Power: 1776–1918* (Princeton, 1939), p. 191.

[15] Pletcher, *The Awkward Years,* p. 148. See also "The American Merchant Marine," *New Orleans Daily Picayune,* Oct. 5, 1887; John Totyl, "Shall American Carriers Transport the Products of American Industry?," *Overland Monthly* 14 (Sept. 1889): 305–310; Willard C. McClellan, "A History of American Military Sea Transportation" (Ph.D. dissertation, American University, 1953), p. 57.

iron shipbuilding. A builder of vessels for the government, and a participant in what was to become known as the "new navy," Roach argued that, with its geographic position, labor supply, and economic resources, the United States should be the prime shipowning nation of the world.[16]

Roach found a powerful ally in Secretary of State Blaine, who also saw the necessity of a large merchant fleet for increased freightage and protection of our lengthy coastlines. The secretary and the shipbuilder also set out to challenge British maritime supremacy. Blaine favored steamship subsidies, and gave financial support to the United States and Brazil Mail Steamship Company (established by Roach in 1865), which operated a line between New York and Rio de Janeiro. Blaine justified his actions by pointing to American trade statistics. Between 1870 and 1877, he reported, the United States absorbed 50 percent of Brazil's exports, all of which was carried in foreign bottoms. In the same period, due to the size of the American merchant fleet, the United States furnished only 8 percent of Brazil's imports. The moral was clear: subsidized shipping would mean an increase in American export trade.[17]

State governments and individual business groups added their ideas to Blaine's plan. Legislatures, for example, favored federal contracts to encourage American ships to transport overseas mail. Congressmen offered innumerable resolutions on Capitol Hill to allow their constituents to purchase foreign-made ships and engage

---

[16] Roach wrote many tracts and articles; see, for example, *The Successful Maritime Policy: An Investigation into the Cause of the Decline of Our Shipping Interest* (New York, 1881) and *The American Carrying Trade* (New York, 1880). See also Leonard A. Swann, Jr., *John Roach: Maritime Entrepreneur* (Annapolis, 1966).

[17] Pletcher, *The Awkward Years,* pp. 123–125, 149; David S. Muzzey, *James G. Blaine, A Political Idol of Other Days* (New York, 1931), p. 146.

An excellent example of American overseas shipping entrepreneurial activity was the Anglo-American steamship rivalry in Chinese waters in the 1860s and 1870s. Little known to the Americans of the day, the Shanghai Steam Navigation Company, utilizing the joint stock principle, was typical of individual business enterprise. Eventually, Chinese competition ended the British-American rivalry and monopoly, but the story fills an important page in the American record overseas, especially since this same period witnessed the decline of the merchant marine. See Kwang-Chang Liu, *Anglo-American Steamship Rivalry in China, 1862–1874* (Cambridge, Mass., 1963), pp. 2–4, 152–156.

in the carrying trade. At the same time, they wished to compensate American shipbuilders by reducing the tariffs on the necessary raw materials. Representative William Ward of Pennsylvania felt that, if we would but act with dispatch in this matter, a "new world" was within our reach.[18]

Between 1880 and 1900, the New York State Chamber of Commerce gave special attention to the expansion of merchant shipping. In 1880, a national convention of shipbuilders and shipowners met in New York City and petitioned for the establishment of ocean routes and a national policy toward commerce. *Bradstreet's* constantly voiced the demands of businessmen in this period for steamship subsidies, which it claimed would improve overseas mail facilities and restore the carrying trade to American bottoms. William G. Gibbons, president of the Pusey and Jones Company (shipbuilders), and typical of those who requested subsidized steam travel, also wanted to know how far the United States would go in protecting the rights of its citizens engaged in the carrying trade.[19]

Gibbons's interest in subsidies and federal protection for shipping concerns illustrates how closely the plight of our outdated navy was related to the development of a commercial fleet. Shippers needed naval protection on the high seas, and real improvement in the condition of the navy came only when it was successfully linked with commercial expansion. In the 1880s, the reports of the Secretary of the Navy began to stress the commercial possibilities inherent in a strong fleet. In 1882, for example, Secretary Richard W. Thompson stated that the interests of the navy were "inseparably involved" with those of the merchant marine and that the protection of our commerce was the paramount object of increased naval strength. The exploits of Commodore Shufeldt provided a classic example of the service the navy could perform for commerce. Instrumental in ex-

---

[18] *Report on Shipping and Shipbuilding to the Manufacturers' Association, Board of Trade and Chamber of Commerce of San Francisco* (San Francisco, 1885); *Congressional Record,* 45th Cong., 3d sess. (Feb. 28, 1879), 8, pt. 3, A175.

[19] Joseph Bucklin Bishop, *A Chronicle of One Hundred and Fifty Years: The Chamber of Commerce of the State of New York, 1768–1918* (New York, 1918), p. 222; *New York Daily Tribune,* Oct. 7, 1880; "The American Carrying Trade," *Bradstreet's* 13 (May 15, 1886): 308; William G. Gibbons (Wilmington, Del.) to Blaine, Apr. 7, 1881, *Miscellaneous Letters, Department of State.*

tending American influence in Africa and Asia, Shufeldt argued that no nation could really be great without water-borne commerce and that the man-of-war had to precede the merchant marine. Moreover, the United States needed this commerce to dispose of its industrial and agricultural surplus. Thus the navy became the means to greatness and increased prosperity; it was both the trailblazer and protector of commerce.[20]

Business journals and congressmen lent support to the navy's position. The *Northwest Miller*, which felt strongly about the relationship between the navy and overseas trade, argued that if the government failed to build a strong naval force, business should develop one with its own power and resources. Representative James Wheeler of Alabama believed that effective sea power would act as "midwife" and "handmaid" to foreign commerce. With a strong navy, he predicted, "it will not be long ere we can once more rejoice in the knowledge that the sails of our birds of commerce are whitening every sea, that the smoke of our merchant steamers is ascending to the heavens which bend above all portions of the globe." "Give us such a navy," he asked, "and we shall . . . return [to] those halcyon days." [21]

As the weakness of the navy was advertised by public debate, its crucial importance to both national security and commercial development became slowly but surely apparent. The demands of our diplomats for men-of-war to back up their representations and the concomitant need for bases for American sea power became perennial pleas. The United States, alone among the great powers, lacked coaling stations, and this deficiency aroused apprehension over its ability to withstand the thrusts of European imperialism. New York

---

[20] *Annual Report of the Secretary of the Navy, 1882,* I: 31; R. W. Shufeldt, *The Relation of the Navy to the Commerce of the United States* (Washington, 1878).

In *Domestic Letters, Department of State* (125 [Oct. 23, 1878], p. 23), there is a letter from Secretary Evarts to Secretary of the Navy Thompson declaring that the State Department had "certain unsettled questions" with the inhabitants of the African coast and the Far East and was "deeply interested" in considering measures for the increase of our commercial and friendly relations with "these productive regions."

[21] *Weekly Northwest Miller* 19 (Mar. 20, 1885): 268; *Congressional Record,* 49th Cong., 1st sess. (June 18, 1886), 17, pt. 8, and spec. sess., A311.

City merchants regularly deplored what they called our defenseless coasts. Even the Midwest's *Chicago Tribune* demanded an increase in naval appropriations so as to halt foreign insolence. Fuming over Moroccan piracy on the high seas, the *New York Herald* decried the condition of the American fleet. We had plenty of "young Decaturs," naval men bred in the tradition of the American who had humbled the Barbary pirates in 1815, but we lacked the necessary ships. One senator explained how the weak navy hampered the Committee on Foreign Relations:

> Whoever had been upon the Committee . . . must have felt . . . at almost every meeting . . . that there were questions presented which we did not feel it was best to take hold of and to assert ourselves in the manner that is required of a government with power that this one possesses, merely because . . . we were not provided with the facilities for doing so.[22]

The fear that none of our ships could stand up to a first-class ironclad played a large part in the naval renaissance. Foreign rivalry in territories the United States considered part of its private domain excited fierce nationalism, and a show of naval force was usually prescribed as the antidote to this form of aggression. For example, even in an age of tight naval economy, two American warships were sent to Samana Bay (in 1881 and 1882) in response to a rumored German coup in the Caribbean; and it was Commodore Shufeldt who arbitrated a boundary dispute between Liberia and Great Britain. The *Chicago Tribune* warned that the most effective way to maintain the Monroe Doctrine was not by executive messages or congressional resolutions but by outfitting a navy that could command respect.[23]

Isthmian defense and the need for bases also called attention to the naval situation. Captain Alfred Thayer Mahan, eager to pro-

[22] *Chicago Tribune,* Jan. 31, 1887; "Morocco," *New York Herald,* June 26, 1880; *Congressional Record,* 50th Cong., 1st sess. (July 24, 1888), 19, pt. 7, 6718.

[23] Pletcher, *The Awkward Years,* pp. 132–133; *Instructions, Liberia,* vol. 2, no. 13 (Nov. 12, 1878); "How to Maintain the Monroe Doctrine," *Chicago Tribune,* Mar. 12, 1880; "The Panama Canal and the Navy," *New York Herald,* Dec. 9, 1881; "The Isthmian Canal and the Monroe Doctrine," ibid., Dec. 17, 1881.

mote his expansionist views, capitalized upon the isthmian question in arguing for a bigger navy. There was no sense in piercing the isthmus, he argued, without a navy adequate to defend the "big ditch." The completion of the canal, Mahan predicted, would mark the end of isolation and the indifference of foreign nations toward American opinion. While most Americans in the Gilded Age were content to remain aloof from European involvements, they realized that the American eagle could easily get its feathers badly ruffled in response to foreign interference in the domain of our vital interests.[24]

Labor and religious circles eventually came to favor naval reform. Labor, of course, knew that an expanded navy would create new outlets for American manpower. And a segment of the religious press supported a large navy but emphasized that a naval buildup could not be automatically interpreted as a warlike gesture. Religious groups who found a big navy compatible with their theological views cited their faith in the moral uses of such a fleet. If, perchance, preparation for war did not keep the peace, they made room in their beliefs for waging a righteous war.[25]

Encouraged by the press, business groups, lobbyists, the naval reform program made substantial progress, and by the 1880s had gained the support of important public officials. Secretaries of the Navy William M. Hunt and William E. Chandler, while run-of-the-mill political appointees rather than farsighted statesmen, performed yeoman service in this crusade. Secretary Hunt warned that "the condition of the Navy imperatively demands the prompt and earnest attention of Congress." Unless some action was taken in its behalf, he predicted, our fleet would soon lapse into total insignificance. American mercantile interests, global in scope, depended upon our fighting ships for adequate protection. In March 1881, Hunt created the Naval Advisory Board and requested larger appropriations to build a "new navy."[26] In his report for 1883, Sec-

---

[24] Mahan, *The Influence of Sea Power upon History, 1660–1783* (Boston, 1890), p. 88; Mahan, "The United States Looking Outward," *Atlantic Monthly* 66 (Dec. 1890): 816–824.

[25] *Pittsburgh National Labor Tribune,* Dec. 29, 1888; "Our Navy," *Boston Congregationalist* 34 (Feb. 22, 1882): 64.

[26] *Foreign Relations,* 1881, preface; *Annual Report of the Secretary of the Navy, 1881,* 2 vols. (Washington, 1881), 1: 3.

retary Chandler proposed the establishment of naval bases in the
Caribbean, Brazil, Chile, Central America, Liberia, East Africa,
and Korea. Commodore Shufeldt, as a result of his expeditions to
Africa and the Far East, recommended additional stations. Also,
British actions in the Fiji Islands and German encroachments in
Samoa caused Shufeldt to consider various desirable acquisitions.
Efforts at increasing the size of the navy did not always meet ex-
pectations, but by 1883 the construction of at least four steel ships
had begun. Continuing the work of Hunt and Chandler, Cleveland's
able Secretary of the Navy, William C. Whitney, campaigned vigor-
ously to obtain expenditures for additional ships.[27]

Comments on the pitiful state of the navy and pleas for its reform
were also voiced in the presidential office. President Arthur argued
that the navy would not have declined if "navigation interests [had
been given] a portion of the aid and protection which had been so
wisely bestowed upon our manufacturers." Although peaceful conditions had existed for many years, Arthur argued that the lessons
of history taught that "resort to arms" might alone save the nation
from dishonor in the future. President Cleveland was also a strong
proponent of naval preparedness, despite the fact that, like Arthur,
he viewed the navy largely in terms of coastal defense.[28]

Congress eventually took cognizance of the situation, although in
the 1880s Capitol Hill was restrained by public inertia, depression
conditions, and a political paralysis induced by the seesaw of party
control. For instance, Representative William Henry Calkins of Indiana remarked that he desired to see our navy again put upon a
footing in keeping with the prestige of the "greatest civilized and
Christian nation in the world." [29] Through debate and tortuous
wrangling, new naval legislation was enacted. In 1886, Congress
authorized the building of two armored ships, and in 1888 approved
a large armored cruiser, stipulating in each case that the vessels
be constructed of domestic iron and steel. A Naval War College was

---

[27] See also Annual Reports for 1882 and 1883.

[28] George F. Howe, *Chester A. Arthur: A Quarter-Century of Machine
Politics* (New York, 1934), p. 240; Richardson, *Messages and Papers,*
10: 4638–4639; "The President on 'The Decline of Our Merchant Marine,'"
The Nation 32 (Dec. 15, 1881): 466–467.

[29] *Congressional Record,* 47th Cong., 2d sess. (Jan. 20, 1883), 14, pt. 2,
1401.

opened in Newport, Rhode Island, in 1884, and the entire Navy Department underwent much needed refurbishing.[30]

In less than a decade, the navy was transformed from an "atrophied arm of national power" into an assertive force in American foreign policy. As the *Philadelphia Record* remarked, gradually but surely the United States Navy was rising to a position worthy of our greatness. Although no major international crisis had occurred, money judiciously appropriated for future defense and designed to enhance American honor would not be grudged by the taxpayers, the *Pittsburgh Post* reasoned. The *New Orleans Daily Picayune* observed that, by 1887, the nation was disposed to boast about the number of guns in our new navy. The *New York Herald* expressed its joy in an editorial headline: "At Last a Navy!" [31]

Some sober elements warned, however, that the naval buildup did not include first-class warships but limited its maritime combat force to mere "commercial destroyers." And most Americans still thought in terms of coastal defense and blockade breaking in time of war. In 1887 the *Philadelphia Telegraph* contended that, while improvements had been made, the American fleet was still weak compared to Europe's forces of armored vessels. It argued that a modern fleet required new means of construction and increased numbers of trained workmen. Other critics saw weakness in the large number of foreign seamen manning our commercial ships, and called for provisions to outfit our vessels with native American seamen.[32]

---

[30] See Seager, "Ten Years before Mahan," loc. cit.; John D. Long, *The New American Navy*, 2 vols. (New York, 1903); Pletcher, *The Awkward Years*, chap. 7, passim. For a discussion of the role of Rear Admiral Stephen B. Luce in founding the modern American navy, see John A. S. Grenville and George B. Young, *Politics, Strategy, and American Diplomacy: Studies in Foreign Policy, 1873–1917* (New Haven and London, 1966), chap. 1, passim. The authors point out that Luce deserves to be recognized as the father of the modern American navy because, among other accomplishments, he founded the Naval War College, guided Mahan's first steps as a naval historian, and led in the fight for a battleship fleet.

[31] "A Navy Worthy of the Nation," *Public Opinion* 6 (Nov. 17, 1888): 114; "The Navy Department," ibid. 6 (Feb. 9, 1889): 364; "The New Navy," *New Orleans Daily Picayune*, Mar. 17, 1887; *New York Herald*, June 1, 1887.

[32] "Needs of the Navy," *Boston Commercial Bulletin*, Mar. 2, 1889; "Changes in Naval Conditions," *Public Opinion* 2 (Feb. 26, 1887): 429–430; ibid., 7 (Apr. 13, 1889), 9; Paul S. Holbo, "Economics, Emotion, and Ex-

Despite the need for further improvements, by the time Benjamin Harrison moved into the White House the program for naval reform was more than a partial success, and optimism prevailed. In the 1880s, a former Civil War general predicted that the Atlantic would be crowded with American ships and the United States would ask by what right other nations held naval bases adjacent to the ocean avenues which washed our shores. And the *Philadelphia Telegraph* remarked that, could a cultivated citizen of the early part of the nineteenth century return to life, few things would astonish him more than the "completely revolutionized fleet." [33]

The refurbished fleet was far more important than the actual increase in ships and guns would indicate. The major factor in the naval renaissance was largely psychological and closely related to a growing national maturity. America was in the throes of growth. Industrialization hurried things forward, cities sprang up, and as the country grew more cosmopolitan the foreign scene became more attractive to traders and investors. The navy was bound to benefit as American interest in far-off shores burgeoned. Reciprocally, a newly restored navy helped sweep away parochialism and create new attitudes.

In 1890, Alfred T. Mahan was undoubtedly considering the "new navy" when he wrote: "Indications are not wanting of an approaching change in the thoughts and policy of Americans as to their relations with the world outside their own borders." Indeed, his writings are eloquent testimony to a fading provincialism. "The instinct for commerce, bold enterprise in the pursuit of trade, and a keen scent for the trails that lead to it, all exist." Mahan's mission was to rekindle his country's interest in sea power, an interest which had declined while Americans had been engrossed in developing the continent. Power and national prestige, Mahan stated, resulted from the proper use of ocean highways, ships, and bases. Although Mahan's influence has been exaggerated, and such sentiments had been voiced much earlier, Mahan did the most to popularize these

pansion: An Emerging Foreign Policy," in H. Wayne Morgan, ed., *The Gilded Age,* revised and enlarged, ed. (Syracuse, 1970), p. 213.

[33] George B. McClellan, "The Militia and the Army," *Harper's New Monthly Magazine* 72 (Jan. 1886): 294–303; *Public Opinion* 2 (Feb. 26, 1887): 429–430.

views and exerted the most pressure on governmental agencies for their implementation.[34]

The appropriations for three battleships in 1890 culminated a decade of naval expansion. Yet, as naval enthusiasts predicted, these three ships were only the beginning of what would one day be a mighty battleship navy—a fleet able to trounce the Spanish at Manila, help stem the German tide on the high seas during World War I, and humble the Japanese in their own waters a generation later. In 1890 the world was becoming too small and America too large for the latter to live in seclusion. And the navy was but one of several examples of a new outward focus. Another type of involvement was the official and unofficial travel which took many Americans overseas on private, exploratory, scholarly, and technological missions, which we will investigate in the next chapter.

[34] Mahan, "The United States Looking Outward," loc. cit.; Mahan, *The Influence of Sea Power*, pp. 57–58; William D. Puleston, *Mahan* (London, 1939), p. 118; William E. Livezey, *Mahan on Seapower* (Norman, Okla., 1947), p. 217.

CHAPTER 7

The Overseas Americans: Travelers, Scholars, Technicians, Explorers

PRIOR TO the Civil War, overseas travel was confined to the select few, but among the many changes that followed Appomattox was the desire of a great number of Americans to venture abroad. From archeologists and explorers to the restless *nouveaux riches*, Americans in the Gilded Age seemed especially eager to travel. A young aristocrat, Franklin Delano Roosevelt, went abroad eight times before he entered his adolescence. College presidents Nicholas Murray Butler and Charles W. Eliot, and the lawyer-statesman Henry L. Stimson, were also frequent travelers. For these individuals, travel no doubt influenced their positions on isolationism and world cooperation. If travel did not make internationalists of other Americans who went abroad, it made them at least aware of the world that lay beyond their shores.

No single explanation sufficiently accounts for the increased travel of Americans in the Gilded Age. Some interpreters of the post–Civil War scene cite the restlessness, curiosity, and love of adventure inherent in the Anglo-Saxon heritage. Others see the impulse to cross the seas as one aspect of that mobility which distinguished the whole American development. Indeed, travel was not confined to any one group of Americans, and motivation varied. Immigrants labored to save enough money to revisit their native lands. At the other extreme, the wealthy elite regarded a European trip—the "grand tour" as developed in the eighteenth century—as a necessity for rounding off their education. The grand tour, with its stops at Paris and Rome and side trips to the Low Countries, Germany, and Switzerland, had been established early in the century. In the Gilded Age, it gained new popularity as industrial expansion created a business aristocracy with money and leisure time. Few American tourists could enjoy the luxury of the entire grand tour, but many now had the funds for more modest travel and could satisfy what was called the "vagabond habits" of Americans. By the end of the century, about 30,000 Americans each year received passports for some type of overseas travel.[1]

In addition to the increased wealth of many Americans, technological advances facilitated overseas travel. With marked improvements in steamships, the oceans became highways rather than barriers. New and faster steamers allowed for an Atlantic crossing in less than a week. Constantly improving, these liners were able to reduce costs and at the same time offer greater luxury to first-class passengers, and more comfort for second-class travelers as well. The

---

[1] William Hemstreet, *The Economical European Tourist—A Journalist's Three Months Abroad for $430* (New York, 1875), pp. 3, 4; Foster R. Dulles, *Americans Abroad,* pp. 1, 68; Robert Spiller, *Literary History* 2: 827; "Going to Europe," *The Nation* 10 (Apr. 28, 1870): 269–270; "Americans Abroad," ibid. 27 (Oct. 3, 1878): 208–209.

Most frequently, those who flocked overseas were steel kings, oil lords, railroad magnates, and similar entrepreneurs whose aim was to storm the bastions of Europe's aristocracy. For these social climbers, the "grand tour" had to include stays at elegant resorts, gambling at casinos, betting at famous race tracks, and visiting svelte salons. While atypical of Americans, these *nouveaux riches* were significant because of the wide publicity their activities received. An eager American public soaked up the gossipy items picturing the glamorous activities of the "international set." The ultimate goal of this group was a presentation at court, preferably in London, and possibly the marriage of a daughter to a titled European aristocrat. Such families as the Vanderbilts, Goulds, and Whitneys now included various dukes and counts as in-laws. So prevalent did this custom become that such diverse personalities as Secretary of State James G. Blaine, the scholar-politician Henry Cabot Lodge, and the artist Charles Dana Gibson lamented the sacrifice of the fairest daughters of the republic to fortune-seeking foreign noblemen (Dulles, *Americans Abroad,* pp. 127 ff.).

estimated costs of trips to Europe averaged $400 for three months, $600 for five months, $800 for seven months, and $1,000 for a year. In the late 1860s, steamship passage could be had for between $110 and $160 in gold, and by the 1890s the cost had been reduced. The Cunard Line charged $160 in gold for the Atlantic crossing in the 1860s, and the cost on French and American lines was $160 and $120 respectively.[2]

Tourist companies expanded, making Europe even more attractive to American travelers. In the 1880s, a ten-week first-class tour of the Continent cost between $250 and $300, including $15 for railroad fare and $2.50 per evening for lodging. The famous Thomas Cook's tours, begun in 1841, further minimized expenses by its schedule of attractions. These tours, widely advertised by Cook's *Excursionist*, opened up Europe as never before. In 1874 the company introduced an important convenience for travelers, "circular notes," which today are known as travelers' cheques. In 1868, the Cook and Ravel Company negotiated treaties with local sheiks which enabled travelers to visit holy places in Asiatic Turkey, and in 1889 the company made arrangements with the Arabs which permitted safe trips and pilgrimages to Mecca. Cook's company had branched into so many countries by the turn of the century that it adopted the slogan "When you think of travel, think of Cook's." The invention of the Eastman Kodak camera (1880) also encouraged tourism, and the ever present picture postcards became ineradicably associated with Americans and their trips. European hotels, eager to serve the growing American market, offered more services, elevators, and even installed baths on each floor. English came to dominate the lingua franca of the continent, and such American favorites as ice cream appeared as regular items on European menus.[3]

American tourists in the Gilded Age found an increasing number of guidebooks that covered every conceivable facet of travel—in addition to Cook's *Excursionist*. In the 1860s, Harper began to publish

[2] J. M. Buckley, "The Traveler," *The Chautauquan* 8 (May 1888): 483–486; "Going to Europe," *Indianapolis Journal*, July 1, 1881; Dulles, *Americans Abroad*, pp. 105, 108; "How to Visit Europe," *New York Tribune*, June 14, 1867.

[3] Dulles, *Americans Abroad*, pp. 106–108; *Cook's Excursionist* (London, 1851–1902); "The Story of Travel, 1841–1966" (125th anniversary of Thomas Cook and Son), *New York Times*, Feb. 6, 1966 (special sec.).

an annual *Handbook for Travelers in Europe and the East*, and in
the next decade Baedeker introduced guidebooks for various areas.
Bradshaw's Continental Railway Guide, another popular handbook,
claimed that its 87-cent, 700-page guidebook provided all the information needed for comfortable travel overseas. Tourists were re-
peatedly cautioned to acquaint themselves with the history, customs,
and languages of foreign lands. Guidebooks advised subscribing to
foreign newspapers and discouraged attempts to cover large amounts
of territory in a short period. Travelers were told to establish themselves in various key cities and then to radiate out into the hinterland.
Necessary health precautions, such as boiling water and avoiding
certain foods, and warnings against European swindlers, regularly
appeared in these books. It seemed that the fleecing of American
tourists was to be expected, but they were warned lest they be
swindled twice in one day! Asking the proper questions, keeping a
diary, and writing letters home were also suggested in order to
provide notes for future visits. Travel guides generally included
remedies for seasickness and special advice for ladies traveling alone.
In addition, they suggested types of dress and the amount of fees
and tips to be paid, outlined the legal rights of travelers, listed the
best hotels, and discussed the process of obtaining passports and
visas.[4]

---

[4] J. M. Buckley, "The Traveler," loc. cit.; "Going to Europe," *Indianapolis Journal*, July 1, 1881; "How to Visit Europe," *New York Tribune*,
June 14, 1867; Dulles, *Americans Abroad*, pp. 103–104.

See W. Pembroke Fetridge, *Harper's Handbook for Travelers in Europe
and the East*, 3 vols. (New York, 1884). *Harper's Handbook* was first published in 1861. See also Karl Baedeker Publishers, Handbooks For Various
Areas (i.e., *Egypt, Handbook* [London, 1878–1892]; *Belgium and Holland,
Handbook for Travelers* [Boston, 1874]).

Some of the other guidebooks published in this era are: *A Sketch of the
Route to California, China and Japan via the Isthmus of Panama* (San Fran-
cisco and New York, 1867), James Brooks, *A Seven Months' Run, Up and
Down, and Around the World* (New York, 1872), Samuel S. Cox, *Arctic
Sunbeams, or from Broadway to the Bosphorus by Way of the North Cape*
(New York, 1882), John H. Gould, *Outward and Homeward Bound: A
Journal and Note-Book for Ocean Voyagers* (New York, 1893), William
Hemstreet, *The Economical European Tourist* (New York, 1875), W. J.
Rolfe, *A Satchel Guide for the Vacation Tourist in Europe* (New York,
1872), Thomas W. Knox, *How to Travel: Hints, Advice, and Suggestions to
Travelers by Land and Sea All Over the Globe* (New York, Boston, London,
Geneva, 1881), Lillian Leland, *Traveling Alone: A Woman's Journey around*

Periodicals also popularized travel. Such journals as *A Pointer for the Tourist*, the *Traveler and the Ticket Agent*, and *Travel* were typical of those devoted to the interests of travelers in all lands. They included advertisements, descriptions of routes, tours, sailing times, fares, lists of guidebooks, and maps. One of these periodicals was a monthly which promoted bicycle tours, and sometimes in poetic form:

> Come with me out into the road, my wheel, —
> Out into the road, ere the sun goes down! . . .
> O bicycle! free as the swallows that fly,
> We'll hover, we'll hasten, as joyful as them.

Outing, like other magazines of its type, not only stressed the romance of travel but offered practical advice. A trip through czarist Russia, one writer for *Outing* maintained, could be had for "next to nothing." His 86-day, 11,293-mile journey had cost only $152.90, or an average of 1½ cents per mile.[5]

A spate of travel books, a relatively new literary genre—and sometimes written by such notables as Mark Twain, William Dean Howells, John Hay, Henry James, and Henry Adams—also began to roll off the presses regularly. Because of the speed of transatlantic travel and the innovation of machine-set type, the publication of travel books was greatly facilitated. While many contained little more than listings of bills of fare or railroad time tables, others were literary gems which mirrored the spirit of a country and the life of its people.[6]

---

the *World* (New York, 1890), Lee Meriwether, *A Tramp Trip: How to See Europe on Fifty Cents a Day* (New York, 1887).

[5] See, for example, the following travel periodicals: *Outing* . . . (Albany, May 1882–Apr. 1923), *Travel* (New York, 1883, 1884), *A Pointer for the Tourist, Traveler and the Ticket Agent* (New York, 1889–1894), *Travel*, vol. 1 (June–July, 1883). Charles E. Pratt, "A Song of the Wheel," *Outing* 3 (Oct. 1883): 3; Joseph Ricalton, "My Travels on Next to Nothing," ibid. 11 (Oct. 1887): 50–63.

[6] Some of the travel books produced during this period are: Thomas B. Aldrich, *From Ponkapog to Pesth* (Boston and New York, 1883), Eugene Benson, *Art and Nature in Italy* (Boston, 1882), Francis Marion Crawford, *A Roman Singer* (Boston, 1884), Crawford, *Greifenstein* (London and New York, 1889), Edmondo DeAmicis, *Spain and the Spaniards* (New York, 1881), Henry M. Field, *Old Spain and New Spain* (New York, 1883),

With the romantic appetite for the strange and the mysterious came an appreciation of other peoples, their cultural contributions, and their inspirations. One writer found "our English cousins" to be the "nicest" people outside the United States. Another author confessed that he was inspired by Rome because the idle, easy-going life of that ancient city was congenial to the artistic soul. Exotic Paris, long before the days of Gertrude Stein's Lost Generation, was a favorite haunt of the expatriate and the home of thousands of "parisianized" Americans. Here was a phase of international relations over which the State Department had no control. The reciprocal influence of contrasting civilizations upon each other through social contact and literary exchanges grew into an appreciable force. In part, travel literature helped substitute an air of cosmopolitanism for the traditional American parochialism.[7]

Prominent Americans also increased the popularity of overseas travel. Andrew Carnegie wrote that Americans should not allow their own advances to obscure a recognition of the rich traditions of European culture. Travel was necessary for the truly educated

Phebe H. Gibbons, *French and Belgians* (Philadelphia, 1879), Edward E. Hale, *Seven Spanish Cities, and the Way to Them* (Boston, 1883), James Albert Harrison, *Spain in Profile: A Summer among the Olives and Alves* (Boston, 1879), Helen Hunt Jackson, *Glimpses of Three Coasts* (Boston, 1886), Thomas Allibone Janvier, *The Mexican Guide* (New York, 1886), George P. Lathrop, *Spanish Vistas* (New York, 1883), Percival Lowell, *Chöson, the Land of the Morning Calm: A Sketch of Korea* (Boston, 1886), Herman Melville, *Clarel: A Poem and Pilgrimage in the Holy Land* (New York, 1876), Selah Merrill, *East of the Jordan: A Record of Travel and Observation in the Countries of Moab, Gilead, and Boshan, during the years 1875–1877* (New York, 1881), Major Serpa Pinto, *How I Crossed Africa from the Atlantic to the Indian Ocean* (Philadelphia, 1881), Raphael Pompelly, *Across America and Asia: Notes of a Five Years' Journey around the World* . . . , 5th rev. ed. (New York, 1870), Francis Hopkinson Smith, *A White Umbrella in Mexico* (Boston and New York, 1889), William Wetmore Story, *Vallombrosa* (Edinburgh and London, 1881), Charles Dudley Warner, *My Winter on the Nile, among the Mummies and Moslems* (Hartford, 1876), Warner, *Saunterings* (Boston, 1882), Richard G. White, *England Without and Within* (Boston, 1881).

[7] Marshall P. Wilder, "Our English Cousins," *Lippincott's Magazine* 45 (Mar. 1890): 406–411; Eugene L. Didier, "American Authors and Artists in Rome," ibid. 24 (Nov. 1884): 481–495; "The American Colony in Paris," ibid. 24 (Sept. 1879): 384–386; "A New View of Our International Relations," *New Orleans Daily Picayune*, Mar. 22, 1889; Spiller, *Literary History*, 2: 827.

man because "no nation [has] all that [is] best." While the senior Oliver Wendell Holmes ranked Boston higher than London, he still recommended travel; he felt a "longing to cross the water, to get back to that old home of his fathers." William H. Seward was pleased that the Americans overseas included thoughtful inquirers and observers as well as pure hedonists. The American tourist in Great Britain could not help but notice the similarity between the two societies, and this recognition would enhance Anglo-American friendship. Ulysses S. Grant's triumphant march of peace, as it was called, was pictured as the most remarkable trip in recorded history, as scattering "love and harmony" everywhere (though he naively remarked that Venice would be a fine city if it were only drained!). On another level, one of America's most popular personalities, William "Buffalo Bill" Cody, made another famous pilgrimage. His Wild West Exhibition, composed of Indians, cowboys, buffalo, stage-coaches, and the like, played before queens and commoners alike.[8]

Despite the increasing numbers who traveled and the advantages of an overseas journey, the belief lingered that contact with Europe would somehow taint the American character. Europe's indifference to social reform, its evil land system, the power of the Roman Catholic Church, and the lax moral standards of the Continent were all potential dangers. The *Indianapolis Journal* feared that American youths who studied abroad might return with alien tastes, habits, and ideas. "America firsters" of the Gilded Age felt that their fellow

---

[8] Andrew Carnegie, *Round the World* (Garden City, 1884), pp. 306, 307, 309; M. Elizabeth M. Hillman, "Reluctant Pilgrims: A Study of the Reports on England by American Writers Who Visited Great Britain between 1806 and 1886, Considered in Relation to General American Attitudes towards England" (Ph.D. dissertation, University of Toronto, 1949), p. 106; Oliver Wendell Holmes, Sr., *Our Hundred Days in Europe* (Boston, 1886); William H. Seward, *Travels around the World*, ed. Olive Risley Seward (New York, 1873), pp. 774–776; J. F. Packard, *Grant's Tour around the World* . . . (Philadelphia, 1880), pp. 892–893; *New York Herald*, Sept. 21, 1879; Allan Nevins, *Hamilton Fish*, p. 130; William F. Cody, *Story of the Wild West* . . . *Including a Description of Buffalo Bill's Conquests in England* (Chicago, 1888); Dulles, *Americans Abroad*, p. 96.

The press coverage of celebrities' trips was generally full, but that of Grant's tour was unusually complete; in fact, a *New York Herald* correspondent accompanied the former President. The journey evidently had a salutary effect on foreign relations, and Grant's role as mediator for Chinese-Japanese troubles was noted as a possibility.

countrymen ought to patronize native attractions and spend their travel money at home.[9]

Some critics also lamented the spectacle that American travelers presented to foreigners. Henry James, Henry Adams, and E. L. Godkin were vocal in their concern over the invasion of Europe by *nouveau riche* dilettantes and the unfortunate impression that they created. Uncouth barbarity, wasteful extravagance, ignorance, miserliness, and rude and conceitful behavior too often characterized these "ugly Americans." *The Nation* described this segment of American travelers as ill made, ill mannered, and ill dressed. They took with them not only their "numerous, noisy, and uncontrolled" children but also their "wonderful ignorance" of the habits, behavior, and feelings of Europeans. Despite the eagerness of hotels to make Americans feel at home, many travelers complained when they could not obtain their usual pork and beans or fried ham. These Americans wasted so much time on trivial concerns that one writer asked "How could they see so much and learn so little?" [10]

Despite the wide publicity which marked their visits, the steel kings, oil lords, railroad magnates, and other entrepreneurs were not the only Americans to travel overseas. The largest group of Americans came as students to the superior European centers of fine arts. According to one estimate, Americans in Paris accounted for 1,500 of the 7,000 American students on the Continent in the 1880s. James M. Whistler began his overseas stay in that city in the 1850s; Winslow Homer traveled there in 1867; and John Singer Sargent made his home in Paris from 1874 to 1885. These travelers often congregated on the Left Bank, populated the art schools, and frequented the sidewalk cafés of the Latin Quarter. The American students in Paris blended so easily with the French population that Henry James said they took to Paris like ducks to water. The American colony's celebration of the Fourth of July and its formation of

---

[9] "Educating American Youth Abroad," *Indianapolis Journal*, June 23, 1881; Spiller, *Literary History*, 2: 828.

[10] "Some Americans Who Travel," *Overland Monthly* 2 (May, 1869): 418–424; Dulles, *Americans Abroad*, pp. 5, 111, 112; "American Ministers Abroad," *The Nation*, loc. cit.; "The American Colony in France," ibid. 27 (Apr. 18, 1878): 257–259; "Americans Abroad," ibid. (Oct. 3, 1878), pp. 208–209; "Americans Abroad," *New York Herald*, May 2, 1880; "Home Again," ibid., Sept. 4, 1882.

the Students' Association in Paris are evidence, however, that these young artists had not forgotten their native land.[11]

Italy also attracted American visitors. In the 1760s, Benjamin West (1738–1820) visited the Eternal City, becoming the first American artist to study in Italy. John Singleton Copley (1738?–1815) followed West's example when he fled Boston in 1774. By 1858, an estimated 30,000 Americans visited Italy each year, and in 1890 Rome had a permanent colony of about 200 Americans. Perhaps the leading American in Rome during this period was the sculptor William Wetmore Story (1819–1895), son of Supreme Court Justice Joseph Story. For Story, who made Italy his permanent home after his third visit in 1856, and for other artists, Italy provided vast and varied resources for study. It had the attractions of ancient sites, artistic achievements, and the Holy See.[12]

Germany was another magnet that drew Americans to European culture. The large German population in the United States, the German language newspapers, and German athletic, musical, and communal contributions all contributed to interest in the *Vaterland*. While the enthusiasm for Germany was not as intense as that generated for Paris or Rome, American travelers liked Germany and its people. They admired such German traits as seriousness of purpose, gregariousness, close family ties, steadfastness, and politeness. They envied Germany's libraries and its musical superiority, although it was hard to reconcile German militarism, anti-Semitism, and governmental paternalism with the more pleasant aspects of German culture.[13]

---

[11] Dulles, *Americans Abroad,* p. 128; Speech, Article, and Book File (1888–1890), Whitelaw L. Reid MSS, Library of Congress; "Paris Revisited" (letter from Henry James), *New York Daily Tribune,* Dec. 11, 1875; "The American Student Colony in Paris," *Christian Union* 24 (Aug. 3, 1881): 101–102; "The Fourth in Foreign Lands," *Pittsburgh Press,* July 6, 1890; "Americans Abroad," *Springfield Daily Republican,* Nov. 28, 1878.

[12] Paul R. Baker, *The Fortunate Pilgrims: Americans in Italy, 1880–1860* (Cambridge, Mass., 1964), pp. 3, 21–24, 66, chap. 6 passim, 201 ff., 223; Otto Wittmann, Jr., "The Italian Experience (American Artists in Italy, 1830–1875)," *American Quarterly* 4 (Spring 1952): 3–15; Dulles, *Americans Abroad,* pp. 19–21.

[13] Ruth Ann Musselman, "Attitudes of American Travelers in Germany, 1815–1890: A Study in the Development of Some American Ideas" (Ph.D. dissertation, Michigan State College of Agriculture and Applied Science, 1952), pp. 65, 74, 81, 113, 124, 146, 150, 156, 163, 178, 202, 204.

The high quality of German universities attracted American students. As early as 1766, when Benjamin Franklin visited the University of Göttingen, German universities were registering great numbers of Americans. In the 1880s, over 2,000 Americans studied in these centers. German universities offered excellent professional training and magnificent library resources. They successfully combined scholarship, research, and teaching, and emphasized the professional training of historians, lawyers, physicians, ministers, and teachers. Inadequate graduate instruction in the United States caused many eager young scholars to spend their *Wanderjahre* in Germany.[14] During the period 1870–1914, German medical schools attracted some 15,000 Americans, and American historians, educated in German institutions, introduced "scientific history" into American universities.[15]

Americans schooled in Germany brought back learning and experiences that were to re-create the American university. While this relationship began in the second decade of the nineteenth century, when George Ticknor and Edward Everett studied at Göttingen, and included George Bancroft and Joseph G. Cogswell in the "middle period," the numbers greatly increased in the latter part of the century. The University of Michigan, under its forceful and energetic president, Henry P. Tappan (1852–1863), pioneered in the elevation of American scholarship along German lines. Tappan believed that the university should be the capstone of the entire state system, but his "Prussian" ideas were too advanced for the reactionary Michigan regents, and in 1864 this crusading president was voted into retirement. President Tappan did succeed, however, in building a faculty renowned for its accomplishments. Among his appointments was Andrew D. White as professor of history. White had studied at the University of Berlin under such eminent men as Lesius, Boeckh, von Raumer, Hirsch, and Ritte, and he brought his enthusiasm for German historical methods to Michigan. Reacting against the concept employed by his undergraduate instructors at

---

[14] See "German Universities," *Atlantic Monthly* 7 (Mar. 1861): 257–272, for a description of the organization of German universities.

[15] Thomas N. Bonner, *American Doctors and German Universities: A Chapter in International Intellectual Relations, 1870–1914* (Lincoln, Neb., 1963), pp. 6, 14, 23, 55, 61, 159; Jurgen F. H. Herbst, *The German Historical School in American Scholarship* (Ithaca, N.Y., 1965), pp. 99–106.

Yale, that learning history meant memorizing dates and facts, White aimed "to get at the students" by teaching them history in unconventional ways.[16]

In the 1860s, White left Michigan to become the first president of the newly created university at Ithaca, leaving Charles Kendall Adams, a former student, to continue his work at Michigan. In 1869 Adams introduced the historical seminar, and later campaigned for funds to create better library facilities. As president of Cornell, White continued to develop his ideas on American university education. He maintained that the natural sciences, technical arts, and liberal arts should occupy equal places in the curriculum. Believing that students should be treated as mature individuals, not children, White followed the German theory of *Lernfreiheit* and introduced the elective system into Cornell. To improve the quality and variety of instruction within the confines of a limited budget, White became the first university president to invite eminent scholars to his institution as visiting professors.[17]

Daniel Coit Gilman was another American who used his experiences in German institutions to change the American university system. In 1875 he was appointed president of the recently created Johns Hopkins University, and his pioneering work in Baltimore is probably the most important episode in the development of the modern American university. Unlike many other presidents, Gilman concentrated upon men, not buildings, and gathered a small but eminent faculty that was equipped to give genuine graduate instruction. Most of the first group of postdoctoral fellows Gilman brought to Johns Hopkins were German-trained scholars. Among them was Herbert Baxter Adams, a Heidelberg Ph.D. who began his career at Hopkins in 1876 and remained there until his death in 1907. In 1881, Adams turned the historical seminar at the university into an investigation of American local institutional history. The results

---

[16] Henry P. Tappan, *University Education* (New York, 1851); John A. Walz, *German Influences in American Education and Culture* (Philadelphia, 1936), p. 45; Andrew D. White, *Autobiography of Andrew Dickson White,* 2 vols. (New York, 1905), 1:39; Kent Sagendorph, *Michigan, the Story of a University* (New York, 1948), p. 95; Charles M. Perry, *Henry Philip Tappan* (Ann Arbor, 1933), pp. 212 ff.

[17] See Walter P. Rogers, *Andrew D. White and the Modern University* (Ithaca, 1942), pp. 136 and passim.

were published in Johns Hopkins University's *Studies in History and Political Science*, the first such series in America. Impressed by the German organization of scholarship, Adams suggested the establishment of a society of American historians, and in 1884 played a major role in founding the American Historical Association.[18]

The group of pioneer scholars who studied abroad included John W. Burgess. After studying at various German universities, Burgess returned to Amherst College in 1873 to assume a professorship in the newly established department of history, political science, and political economy. His greatest contributions were made, however, during his association with Columbia University. In 1876 Burgess accepted a position as lecturer on constitutional law at the Columbia College Law School, and four years later he organized that university's first graduate school of political science. The admiration Burgess felt for the German university system was evidenced in the system of exchange professorships between Columbia and the University of Berlin, which he was instrumental in establishing, and in the teaching methods he used in the classroom. Burgess's methods of instruction followed those of the typical German university. He insisted upon the elective system, prepared original lectures based upon primary research, and selected superior students to fill his seminars.[19]

The famous social scientists, Henry Adams and Richard T. Ely, also supplemented their education in Germany. Though, as with so many things, Adams was critical of his German education, his

---

[18] Abraham Flexner, *Daniel Coit Gilman, Creator of the American Type of University* (New York, 1946), p. 71; Fabian Franklin, *The Life of Daniel Coit Gilman* (New York, 1910), 195–196; Gilman, *The Launching of a University* (New York, 1906), pp. 1–56 and passim; John Martin Vincent, "Herbert Baxter Adams," in Howard W. Odum, ed., *American Masters of Social Science* (New York, 1927), pp. 99–127; W. Stull Holt, *Historical Scholarship in the United States, 1876–1901, as Revealed in the Correspondence of Herbert Baxter Adams,* Johns Hopkins University Studies in History and Political Science, 56 (1938), 399–692; Herbert B. Adams, *The Study of History at American Colleges and Universities,* Bureau of Education Circular of Information, No. 2 (Washington, 1887).

[19] William R. Shepherd, "John W. Burgess," in Odum, *American Masters of Social Science,* pp. 23–57; John W. Burgess, *Reminiscences of an American Scholar* (New York, 1934), pp. 84–137, 147; Burgess, "The American University: When Shall It Be? Where Shall It Be? What Shall It Be?" in *Reminiscences,* pp. 349–368.

application of German techniques helped elevate Harvard's department of history to the forefront of advanced scholarship. Critical of Harvard's educational system, he vowed that he would teach "lively history" in his own way. In 1871, Adams introduced the seminar method at Harvard. By 1902 his contributions to the technique of history instruction and his work in improving the collections in Harvard's library had slowed the stream of students to Germany. At the same time that Adams was revamping Harvard's history department, the economist Richard Ely was explaining the role of the trained expert in civil service and welfare activities. Trained at Heidelberg, Ely popularized the German idea of welfare economics and the concept of the state as an agency for obtaining the "good life." During the course of his career, Ely occupied chairs in economics and political economy at Johns Hopkins, Northwestern, and the University of Wisconsin.[20]

Although most American tourists and students traveled to western Europe, distant Russia was attracting increased attention. In an obvious exaggeration, the *New York Herald* reported that "swarms" of Americans had visited Russia in 1886. It was felt that cordiality and understanding between the United States and Russia was enhanced by the kinship that grew out of the purchase of Alaska, the abolition of slavery and serfdom, and the reciprocal visits of Russia's fleets to the United States in 1863 and 1864 and our fleet to Russia three years later. The palaces and churches of the czardom were the chief sightseeing attractions. Economically, American companies were concerned with trade depots, grain harvests, and railroads, and Russia's economic development was often linked with our own. At the same time, the possibility that Russia would become an economic rival of the United States was noted, and Samuel Cox predicted that Russia would eventually rival the United States in grain output. The experiences in Siberia of America's Russian expert, George

---

[20] Samuel E. Morison, ed., *The Development of Harvard University since the Inauguration of President Eliot, 1869–1929* (Cambridge, Mass., 1930), pp. 152 ff., 163; Henry Adams to Charles M. Gaskell, Oct. 25, 1870, in W. C. Ford, ed., *Letters of Henry Adams,* 2 vols. (Boston and New York, 1930–1938), 1: 195–196; Richard T. Ely, "The American Economic Association, 1885–1909," *American Economic Association Quarterly* 11 (Apr. 1910): 68–69.

Kennan (1845–1925), uncle of a future Ambassador to the Soviet Union, attracted much attention, and beginning in 1888 *Century Magazine* carried an important series by Kennan on Siberia and the exile system. Naturally, the remnants of czarist despotism were deplored by liberty-loving Yankees. Americans were also concerned with Russian literature, Siberian expansion, the condition of peasants and women, the Russian educational structure, and the status of religion.[21]

While American institutions profited and perspectives broadened because of citizens' experiences abroad, overseas travel also exerted a clear and lasting effect upon other nations. Although the dissemination of American technical knowledge is often thought of as part of such recent foreign policies as the 1949 Point Four aid program, this policy can be traced to a much earlier origin. As Professors Merle Curti and Kendall Birr have pointed out, the first officially organized efforts to export American know-how were made during the Gilded Age.[22]

There were many American technical missions overseas, but those in Japan approached present-day ventures in scope and complexity. In the 1860s, two American geologists and mining engineers, William P. Blake and Raphael Pumpelly, were employed to explore the Japanese island of Yezo. A Japanese railroad line linking Otaru harbor to the Poronai coal mines was completed in 1882 with American aid, and equipped with American rolling stock. American technical services to Japan also included assistance in establishing a postal system, conducting geological surveys, organizing a customs and internal revenue service, and initiating reforms in the finance ministry (banker George B. Williams served as financial adviser in the 1870s). Direction was provided in the fields of prison administration and naval modernization and expansion. In addition, Ameri-

---

[21] "Americans Abroad," *New York Herald*, Sept. 27, 1886; Anna M. Babey, *Americans in Russia, 1776–1917* (New York, 1938), pp. 9, 13, 17, 19, 23, 105, 107, 125; Samuel S. Cox, *Arctic Sunbeams*, p. 376. Some examples of Kennan's reports are: "Camping Out in Siberia," *Putnam's Magazine* 2 (1868): 257–267; "Siberia and the Exile System," *Century Magazine* 36 (May 1888): 3–4; "My Meeting with Political Exiles," ibid. (Aug. 1888): 508–527.

[22] See Merle Curti and Kendall Birr, *Prelude to Point Four: American Technical Missions Overseas, 1838–1938* (Madison, 1954), p. 11.

can expertise in international law and diplomacy greatly influenced the Japanese foreign office.[23]

Early educational influences in the "New Japan" were almost exclusively American. In 1859 the Meiji government engaged an American missionary, the Reverend Guido F. Verbeck, to modernize the Japanese educational system. Ten years later Verbeck established a school which eventually evolved into the Imperial University of Tokyo. Verbeck also directed a program enabling Japanese to study in the United States at Rutgers University. The vice minister of education, Tamaka Fujimaro, impressed by America's public school movement, sought more American advisers in the 1870s. A Rutgers professor compiled the statement of Japanese educational aims in 1872, and the Japanese educational code of 1879 was drafted with American assistance. Science, music, and physical education were also promoted with American aid. In 1878 Dr. George A. Leland introduced the Amherst College system of class calisthenics and marching. Professor Thomas C. Mendenhall, of Ohio State University, utilized modern experimental methods in his course in physics at the Imperial University of Tokyo. Beginning in 1872, Dr. John C. Berry taught medicine at Doshisha University, managed a hospital, and established a school for nurses. Japanese students were also apprenticed to American physicians and dentists.[24]

Japan also benefited from American agricultural technology. The

---

[23] Curti and Birr, *Prelude to Point Four,* pp. 38–39; Inago O. Nitobe, *The Intercourse between the United States and Japan* (Baltimore, 1891), pp. 123, 137–138; Robert S. Schwantes, *Japanese and Americans: A Century of Cultural Relations* (New York, 1955), pp. 53–54, 86–90.

Japan, a forward-looking nation, increasingly made herself felt in the Western world, but despite the great interest in her, Americans, seemingly, never felt an urgent need to learn from Japan. But Japan refused to fit the stereotype of the Asiatic nation, complacently decaying, and her culture—especially her art—contributed to the expansion of the "American mind." See James R. Bowditch, "The Impact of Japanese Culture on the United States, 1853–1904" (Ph.D. dissertation, Harvard University, 1963), pp. 3–4, 431–433.

For a popular and sprightly account of American merchants, teachers, technologists, and missionaries in Japan, see Pat Barr, *The Deer Cry Pavilion: A Story of Westerners in Japan, 1868–1905* (New York, 1968), pt. 1 and 2.

[24] Curti and Birr, *Prelude to Point Four,* pp. 40–41, 57–65, 168–169; Schwantes, *Japanese and Americans,* pp. 129–133, 153–180, 194–201; William L. Neumann, *America Encounters Japan: From Perry to MacArthur*

United States' insulation from international controversies and competitive land acquisition no doubt influenced the Japanese decision to request American assistance in settling its northern frontier. In 1870, negotiations were instituted with the United States Commissioner of Agriculture, Horace Capron, and President Grant, and the following year Capron left for Japan. His main challenge was to establish agricultural units in the northern islands of Hokkaido, Sakhalin, and the Kurile chain north of Honshu. In drawing up his plans, Capron borrowed heavily from the American experience of settling the trans-Mississippi West. Basing his ideas on the Homestead and Preemption acts, Capron advocated granting land on liberal terms to encourage voluntary settlement. He introduced new crops and American breeds of livestock, and instituted experimental model farms near Tokyo where imported trees and livestock could be developed before being sent to the northern islands. Capron's mission also began engineering projects; developed harbors, water power, canals, and roads; and conducted geological, mining, and hydrographic surveys. Capron even proposed that thirty American families settle in the area to provide an example for the Japanese pioneers. Although there were interruptions, setbacks, and tension in dealing with foreign realities, there were also real gains. When Capron left Japan in 1875, he had laid the foundation for prosperous additions to the Japanese Empire. Replacement of the hoe by the plow was symbolic of the development of the new Japan.[25]

(Baltimore, 1963), pp. 84–85; Nitobe, *Intercourse between the United States and Japan,* pp. 119–120.

From 1868 to 1880, twelve Japanese were allowed to study at Annapolis, but West Point was closed to them (Schwantes, *Japanese and Americans,* pp. 200–201), which may indicate that the United States hoped Japan would remain a naval power but never become a land power in Asia.

See also Guido F. Verbeck, *A Synopsis of All the Conjugations of the Japanese Verbs* . . . (Yokohama, 1887); Herbert Welch, *Men of the Outposts: The Romance of the Modern Christian Movement* (New York, Cincinnati, Chicago, 1937); William E. Griffis, *Verbeck of Japan: A Citizen of No Country* (New York, 1902).

Baseball was introduced into Japan by Americans as early as 1875, and the first team was formed three years later (Schwantes, *Japanese and Americans,* p. 184).

[25] Curti and Birr, *Prelude to Point Four,* pp. 41–53 and passim; John A. Harrison, "The Capron Mission and the Colonization of Hokkaido, 1868–

The Capron mission was supplemented by another American-Japanese agricultural interchange. In 1871, the Japanese ministry of education employed an American, George A. H. Hall, to conduct tests on fruit and vegetables developed in the new experimental gardens. The president of the Massachusetts Agricultural College, William Smith Clark, helped launch the agricultural school at the University of Tokyo in 1872. In the next decade and a half, eight other Americans taught at the school. Many Japanese professors at Tokyo and other agricultural colleges received part of their training at Michigan State and other American universities.[26]

In 1882 the Agriculture Department sent a foreign-aid representative to Brazil to collect data on cotton culture, with the object of improving Brazil's production of this crop. At the same time, Congress continually faced proposals (albeit abortive) to finance corn exhibits at various international expositions. A New York brewer (whom Merle Curti calls a "corn evangelist") felt that popularization of corn in other nations was essential for the prosperity of farmers. But Americans also traveled overseas on various coastal, geodetic, and topographical surveys. During the Civil War, the *Wyoming* was dispatched to China to survey certain ports, and in the 1880s the U.S. Coast and Geodetic Survey participated in an expedition to West Africa to determine the gravity and magnetic elements of that region. America also responded to a Costa Rican request for aid to survey a proposed road or railroad route (1868), conducted an exploratory expedition up the Amazon in the 1870s, helped chart Mexico's west coast and that of the Gulf of California (1873), conducted the first geological work in Brazil (1874), participated with Mexico in deep-sea dredging (1877), made an astronomical survey in Guatemala (1883), and introduced American mining methods to China (1886).[27]

Polar exploration was a form of travel which brought the United States into contact with little-explored parts of the earth. By 1869

1878," *Agricultural History* 25 (1951): 135–142; Nitobe, *Intercourse between the United States and Japan,* p. 134; Foster Rhea Dulles, *Yankees and Samurai* (New York, 1965), pp. 176–185; Schwantes, *Japanese and Americans,* pp. 52–53.

[26] Dulles, *Yankees and Samurai,* pp. 185–189; Schwantes, *Japanese and Americans,* pp. 48–50, 54–55.

[27] Curti and Birr, *Prelude to Point Four,* pp. 16–19, 21, 24–27.

ethnologist and geologist Major John Wesley Powell had explored the last uncharted American terrain in Colorado, and in the new decade Americans began to look to new lands. Alaska provided a natural starting point for new exploration, for little was known of Alaska's resources when the United States acquired it in 1867, and the real work of discovery began in the last two decades of the century. Charting and mapping was done by the Army Signal Corps, the navy and merchant marine, and the Coast and Geodetic Survey. Tourism in Alaska also became an important spur to exploration. As the Western frontier vanished, Alaska became a kind of resort for rugged individuals. Its scenery was breathtaking and the Indian problem negligible. Hardy souls could fish or hunt, climb mountains, or traverse glaciers. Transportation facilities were developed to accommodate tourists and (beginning in the 1880s) luxury steamers meandered through the coastal fjords. Tourists' letters, pamphlets, and books became a major source of information about this region.[28]

Although Alaska attracted many American tourists, the Arctic presented the major challenge to the restless late nineteenth-century pioneer. Business expansionists saw a relation between a charted Arctic and increased trade. Scientists were interested in investigating the origin of the Eskimos and exploring the Arctic terrain. The government also demonstrated interest in the Arctic when a State Department report in 1868, compiled by the United States Coast Survey, attested to the economic and strategic importance of Iceland and Greenland.[29]

In 1870, Congress appropriated $50,000 for an expedition to the North Pole, and in 1871 Captain Charles Francis Hall, commanding the ill-fated *Polaris*, set out to investigate the area north of 80 degrees latitude. Accompanying Hall was Professor Louis Agassiz of Harvard University, who had been asked to advise the expedition on glaciers. Unfortunately, Hall died before the expedition returned, and most of the observations and specimens were lost on an ice floe. Eight years later, Lieutenant George Washington DeLong, USN,

---

[28] Morgan B. Sherwood, *Exploration of Alaska* (New Haven, 1965), pp. 1–10, 70–84, 187–192. See also Farley Mowat, ed., *The Polar Passion: The Quest for the North Pole, with Selections from Arctic Journals* (Boston, 1967), passim.

[29] Curti and Birr, *Prelude to Point Four*, p. 15.

traveled along the Siberian Arctic coast in an expedition financed by James Gordon Bennett of the *New York Herald*. Three relief cruisers were sent to rescue his drifting ship, the *Jeannette*, and although DeLong perished, his reports were brought home intact.[30]

Captain Henry W. Howgate of the Army Signal Corps and Lieutenant Frederick Schwatka were more successful in their explorations. Having obtained a congressional grant of $50,000 in 1877 for the establishment of an Arctic base, Howgate moved rapidly to give the United States the first expedition in the field when the International Polar Year's activities commenced. His effort to establish a camp on Ellesmere Island in the Lady Franklin Bay area of northeastern Canada was an important part in the story of America's scientific explorations. Howgate compared the importance of his efforts to that of the Hudson's Bay Company. Unfortunately, he did not achieve his full purpose, and further aid was withheld. (Howgate was later convicted of embezzlement and forgery.) Schwatka, who undertook a search for the remains of Sir John Franklin's expedition, also made valuable observations on Eskimo life, which were widely disseminated and were among the most fruitful results of his exploration.[31]

In 1881 Congress appropriated $25,000 for another expedition to establish a polar station in the Lady Franklin Bay area for the scientific explorations undertaken as part of the International Polar Year activities. The expeditions of Lieutenants Adolphus Washington Greely to Lady Franklin Bay and Patrick Henry Ray to Point

---

[30] John Edwards Caswell, *Arctic Frontiers: United States Explorations in the Far North* (Norman, Okla., 1956), pp. 42–82 and passim; Curti and Birr, *Prelude to Point Four*, p. 15.

See Charles F. Hall, *Arctic Researches and Life among the Esquimaux* . . . (New York, 1865); U.S. Navy Department, *Narrative of the Second Arctic Expedition Made by Charles F. Hall* . . . (Washington, 1879); Edward Ellsberg, *Hell on Ice: The Saga of the "Jeannette"* (New York, 1938); Emma DeLong, ed., *The Voyage of the "Jeannette": The Ship and Ice Journals of George W. DeLong*, 2 vols. (New York, 1883).

It has recently been suggested that it is "circumstantially possible" that Hall was murdered during the 1871 expedition. See *Time* (Jan. 13, 1969), p. 87; Donald Jackson, " 'Tell Me, Sidney, How Do You Spell Murder?' " *Life* (Apr. 25, 1969), pp. 663–678.

[31] Caswell, *Arctic Frontiers*, pp. 83–95. See also H. W. Howgate, *Polar Colonization: The Preliminary Arctic Expedition of 1877* (Washington, 1877?).

Barrow, Alaska, resulted in our finest scientific achievements of the age. Not only was much learned about fauna and geology, but first-hand contact with the Eskimos was established. Noteworthy, too, was America's cooperative effort in international scientific research. Congress cooperated with eleven nations in establishing plans for a global scientific research system for gathering data on polar weather conditions, flora and fauna, and various features of Arctic geography. (Greely became a founder of the National Geographic Society.) In April 1886, perhaps due to Greely's pioneering efforts, Robert Edwin Peary was planning the first of his expeditions to the North Pole, which—twenty-three years later—he would "discover." [32]

The pecuniary gains that might result from increased commerce, as noted, influenced our early Arctic dreams. One New York paper even predicted that far-northern explorations would yield new trade routes and reopen competition with Britain for Asiatic commerce. But it was chiefly glory and science that motivated the Arctic explorers who carried the American flag into the northernmost reaches of the earth. The Arctic polar cap was no longer a barrier which helped assure our invulnerability; it was slowly becoming a link between the nations of the world, and in time would open a new avenue of destruction. Lieutenant Greely expressed the hope that posterity would ever cherish the proud American spirit, which in his generation had fought a Civil War, penetrated deepest Africa, and attained the ultimate goal in the ice-packed north. [33]

The Holy Land was another area which attracted American explorers. The Palestine Exploration Fund, a private organization formed in 1864, began as an attempt to improve the sanitary conditions in Jerusalem by improving its water supply. By 1870, the fund's activities had expanded to compiling maps of Jerusalem and

---

[32] Caswell, *Arctic Frontiers,* pp. 96–122 and passim; Curti and Birr, *Prelude to Point Four,* pp. 15–16. See Adolphus W. Greely, *Three Years of Arctic Service . . . 1881–1884* (New York, 1885); A. L. Todd, *Abandoned: The Story of the Greely Arctic Expedition, 1881–1884* (New York, 1961); Theodore Powell, *The Long Rescue* (New York, 1960); Patrick H. Ray, *Report of the International Polar Expedition to Point Barrow, Alaska* (Washington, 1885). A popular account of the Greely mission is Major Charles B. van Pelt's "The Greely Arctic Expedition," *American History Illustrated* 2 (Jan. 1968): 36–48.

[33] "Arctic Exploration," *New York Daily Tribune,* Dec. 29, 1877; Caswell, *Arctic Frontiers,* p. 215; Greely, *Three Years of Arctic Service,* p. 720.

the immediate area, as well as conducting excavations. The society further extended itself in 1872 with a proposal for an extensive geographical survey of eastern and western Palestine. The United States government was invited to help survey Moab and the area of Palestine east of the Jordan River; the British would investigate Palestine proper.[34]

The American role in the survey, unfortunately, was stymied by congressional opposition. In 1874, Representative Lewis B. Gunckel of Ohio introduced a joint resolution (H.R. 63) calling for the Secretary of War to detail an army officer to proceed east of the Jordan to assist in the work already begun by the society. Although the work was not to involve the United States in any expense beyond the usual pay and allowances for the officer, the opposition in the House, led by that "watchdog of the Treasury," William S. Holman of Indiana, argued that this was not the proper task of an army officer. Representative Samuel S. Cox of New York opposed the project on other grounds. He believed that while this endeavor was in the interest of science and the discovery of materials related to biblical history, Palestine had already been explored "by everybody." More was known about the Holy Land than about any other country. Citing the voluminous published collections, Cox asserted that he would "never vote to make the United States government a publishing house at the expense of private publishers and citizens." [35]

Gunckel defended his resolution by emphasizing that the officer would only command the survey; the actual work and expense would be carried by the society. Supporters of the resolution pointed out that this action would merely follow established precedents. President Polk and Secretary of the Navy John Young Mason had earlier dispatched Lieutenant William F. Lynch on a similar journey, and it had entailed twenty times the number of men and sup-

---

[34] Joseph P. Thompson, "The Exploration of Palestine," *North American Review* 113 (July 1871): 154–173; Committee of the Palestine Exploration Fund, *Our Work in Palestine* (New York, 1873), pp. 15–19. See also C. R. Conder, *Tent Work in Palestine* (London, 1878); Trelawney Saunders, *An Introduction to the Survey of Western Palestine* (London, 1881); Palestine Exploration Fund, *Quarterly Statements* (London, 1869–   ).

[35] *Congressional Record*, 43d Cong., 1st sess. (Feb. 26, 1874), 2, pt. 2, 1818; ibid. (May 23, 1874), 2, pt. 5, 4203–4204.

plies. Others argued that the society had worked for several years, and it would be a loss to scientific knowledge if the United States refused to cooperate. In spite of a memorial sent by the citizens of New York and New Haven urging the adoption of H.R. 63, and the House vote of 118 to 38 in its favor, the resolution was pigeon-holed in the Senate Committee on Military Affairs.[36]

"Plant explorers" in South America generally fared better than the Palestinian archeologists. Intellectual horizons were broadened by their travels in South America, which resulted in the introduction of new seeds and plants and scholarly interest in the Southern Hemisphere. Programs for cooperative botanical explorations were formulated for the first time. While the effect of these explorations on diplomatic relations was negligible, wider concerns led to better relationships, called the attention of American farmers to our Latin neighbors, and quickened the cause of interamericanism by facilitating a greater exchange of ideas.[37]

The many Americans traveling, studying, and exploring abroad led, perhaps inevitably, to an awakened concern in the areas of foreign aid and humanitarianism. The strained discussions that currently arise over congressional foreign-aid programs are the culmination of a long tradition of American philanthropy and consideration for foreign people in need. In the Gilded Age, this need seemed especially great. Consular and diplomatic officials regularly reported disasters which occurred in their districts and solicited relief contributions. One of the best-organized efforts was led by the veteran reformer Samuel Gridley Howe, who in 1866 campaigned for the independence movement in Crete. France received aid from the American government, as well as from the New York Chamber of Commerce, during her war with Prussia in 1870 and 1871. German-Americans and Irish-Americans spearheaded drives for ameliorating conditions in their homelands. Congressional resolutions of sympathy for the Irish during the nineteenth century were

---

[36] *House Miscellaneous Document* 158, 43d Cong., 1st sess. (1874), pp. 1–2; *Congressional Record,* 43d Cong., 1st sess. (May 23, 1874), 2, pt. 5, 4204–4236.

[37] Wayne D. Rasmussen, "The United States Plant Explorers in South America during the Nineteenth Century" (Ph.D. dissertation, George Washington University, 1950), pp. 321, 365, 366, 374, 375.

sometimes matched by relief donations, but federal aid was small compared to the impressive voluntary assistance.[38]

The increased travel of Americans in the Gilded Age was a natural accompaniment to our growing overseas interests, manifested in economic and naval expansion, the spread of foreign missions, and our deepening diplomatic involvements. American tourists, students, technicians, explorers, and humanitarians probably contributed more to the foreigner's image of the United States than did our diplomats. Contact with the outer world, in turn, changed American attitudes. The newer concerns with Europe had results as culturally significant as the original discovery of the Western Hemisphere. The rediscovery of the rest of the world was equally significant. The experiences of Americans abroad proved to countless citizens that the United States was not all of the world that was worth serious consideration.[39]

---

[38] Merle Curti, *American Philanthropy Abroad,* pp. 65–98 and passim. Such relief, together with the establishment of schools, hospitals, art galleries, orphan asylums, and the like, reflected America's increased wealth in this new age of business consolidation—as well as growing commercial and social ties with foreign lands. This country was thrust further into the international cultural stream by the establishment of the American School of Classical Studies in Athens (1881) and the American Academy in Rome (1894). Further, the philanthropy of financier George Peabody was extended beyond the United States to provide low-cost housing in the London slums, and Andrew Carnegie's beneficence also transcended national borders.

[39] Spiller, *Literary History,* 2: 827.

CHAPTER 8

American
Ambivalence:
Attitudes
toward Europe

Fʀᴏᴍ ɪᴛs ᴠᴇʀʏ ɪɴᴄᴇᴘᴛɪᴏɴ, America viewed the Old
World with mixed emotions. Europe had spawned this country, but
America, as the young often do, labored to break the parental ties.
Yet these links—cultural and traditional—could not be easily sev-
ered; hence the ambivalence in the relationship between the Old and
New Worlds. In the Gilded Age the attitudes of scorn and distrust,
a legacy of the Revolutionary generation, clashed with a new deference, evidenced in part by marriage alliances with European royalty
and by American imitation and praise of various aspects of European culture. The Old World was at one and the same time alluring
and repulsive to Americans.

Similarly, the countries of Europe were no more consistent in
their attitudes toward the United States. Many Europeans continued to regard the United States as an uncouth upstart. One
American newspaper felt that England regarded the United States
as an adolescent boy who was growing up too fast. The reports
brought back by travelers in the United States often ridiculed
Americans and intensified bitter relations. Europeans noted such
features as frontier mannerisms, rowdyism, and expectoration in

the halls of Congress, theaters, and libraries, overlooking the positive aspects of American culture. They described us as materialists, prosaic money makers, and marriage brokers interested in making titled alliances among European society. However, a few English visitors pointed out real flaws in the American experience. Herbert Spencer, for example, contested Andrew Carnegie's belief that American democracy was the cause of world prosperity. Spencer contended that American materialism was not conducive to the finer pursuits of human life and referred to the United States as the land of "unrestrained ambitions." The poet Matthew Arnold also found materialism a dark side of American life. Accustomed to less constructive criticism, Americans generally received these comments as another form of European abuse.[1]

Undoubtedly, negative American views of Europe account for much of the anxiety with which Americans ventured abroad. While hyphenated Americans still loved their mother country, most Americans viewed the United States and Europe as antithetical camps. The United States was free and young; Europe was often dictatorial, despotic, and decrepit. Reacting against English privilege and aristocracy, Americans emphasized a democratic explanation of their own past, sometimes to the point where it seemed the United States evolved in a vacuum. The "frontier thesis" of the historian, Frederick Jackson Turner, who grew up in the Gilded Age, may well be the product of this era. In Italy, American travelers shuddered at what they perceived as rigid class structures, economic indolence, and low standards of morals. The United States, proud of its divorce from such European troubles, must not risk contaminating the American garden with Old World decay. At least in the diplomatic sphere, it seemed better to stay at home and remain uninvolved than to expose our tranquillity to the European "circle of camps and barracks."[2]

---

[1] "America in England," *Hartford Daily Courant,* Dec. 26, 1882; Herbert Spencer to Andrew Carnegie, May 18, 1886, Carnegie MSS, Library of Congress. See also Matthew Arnold, *Civilization in the United States: First and Last Impressions of America* (Boston, 1888), and James Eckman, "The British Traveler in America, 1875–1920" (Ph.D. dissertation, Georgetown University, 1946), passim.

[2] "The Year," *New York Daily Tribune,* Dec. 31, 1887.

During the late nineteenth century, Europe seemed determined to prove the truth of the American point of view as the great powers undertook a worldwide career of conquest, marked by secret alliances, rival armament programs, and military conscription. In the 1870s and 1880s, the European powder keg seemed about to explode at any moment. As nation after nation in continental Europe adopted some form of military conscription, Americans compared their picayune expenditures for military needs with the crippling budgets of European powers. While European nations often spent over half of their revenues on the army, the United States earmarked only one-sixth of its revenues for defense needs. Americans seemed to lose sight of the fact that their oceanic moats and the absence of aggressive neighbors permitted minimum military expenditures, a minimum which shrank even further after the Plains Indians surrendered. Scornful of European deficits, they boasted a Treasury "brimming full"—unaware that this was the last time in their history they would enjoy a clear surplus of revenue. American commercial journals disdainfully pointed out the connection between Europe's financial depression and its destructive wars. American nationalism flowered wildly in the Gilded Age.[3]

The press nurtured the feeling of superiority by noting in detail the problems of the European powers. European nations had spent millions for defense systems but, as the *New York Herald* lamented, almost every nation on the Continent had made war during the past half-century. Europe was unstable. Russia had more nihilists than Siberia could hold; Germany was jealous of Russia on one side and concerned about France on the other; Austria and Russia coveted slices of Turkey; and Spain was on the verge of revolution. Russian persecutions filled humanitarians all over the world with despair. Nihilism, czardom, and despotism were generally depicted in negative terms, and it was noted that Russia was the last of the European nations to respond to modern ideas. At first the press hailed the Dual Alliance of 1879 (and the later alliance of 1887) as a "political event of the first importance," assuming that it would lead to European peace. When the alliance proved disappointing, providing

---

[3] *Buffalo Express,* Aug. 30, 1883, June 9, 1885; "The Year," *New York Daily Tribune,* Dec. 31, 1887; "European Disarmament," *Commercial and Financial Chronicle* 28 (Mar. 15, 1879): 265.

no relief to the persistent political tensions, the American press reverted to its normal position of distrust.[4]

European militarism furnished ready copy for American newspapers. American editors, whenever at a loss for a subject, found speculation on the imminence of a general war in Europe an attractive subject. The Russian, Egyptian, and Irish crises, together with the perennial Franco-German rivalry, always sold newspapers. The American reader may have thanked "his lucky stars that three thousand miles of blue water rolled between him and the oppression and discontent, and intrigue of the Old World," but he also took a kind of sadistic pleasure in watching Europe suffer. He observed the politics of Europe as spectators in the Coliseum once watched gladiatorial combats.[5] He seemed to have little appreciation of the grim fact, so apparent to later Americans, that his vital interests could be jeopardized by a major conflict among the European powers.

Subscribing to a kind of perversion, which has been termed a major factor in American diplomatic history—European distress ensures American advantage—some Americans reasoned that a general European war would be beneficial to this country. For example, when Russia and Turkey entered on one of their periodic wars in 1877, many organs of opinion hoped that other countries in Europe would join the conflict; the United States would then profit by feeding and clothing a larger number of the antagonists. The *Commercial and Financial Chronicle* held that European hostilities would mark a revival of American commerce. The sale of food, clothing, and munitions—at good prices—and the appropriation of European stocks and bonds in payment seemed an attractive proposition to a debtor country just pulling out of a sharp depression.[6]

---

[4] "Mr. Gladstone and the Monroe Doctrine," *New York Herald,* June 1, 1884; "Armed Europe," *Atlanta Constitution,* Feb. 8, 1880; "The Revolution in Russia," *North American Review* 129 (July 1879): 23–36; "The Nihilists in Russia," *Christian Herald and Signs of Our Times* 1 (Apr. 24, 1879): 423; "The Russian Problem," *Cleveland World,* Apr. 25, 1890; "The German-Austrian Alliance," *The Nation* 29 (Oct. 23, 1879): 269–270.

[5] "The Prospect of a General War in Europe," *The Nation* 22 (May 4, 1876): 288; *Buffalo Express,* June 15, 1882; "The State of Europe," *New York Herald,* Apr. 1, 1883. For a description of American concern vis-à-vis the Franco-Prussian War, see Field, *America and the Mediterranean World,* pp. 329–332.

[6] "American Opinion on the War in the East," *The Nation* 24 (May 3, 1877): 260–261; "Preparing for War in Europe—Our Position," *New York*

European conflicts also promised relief to a nation suffering from chronic agricultural overproduction. Farmers were urged to plant their crops with the international situation in mind, and protests by the London press that the United States was "cashing in" on European war talk had some validity. Chicago wheat dealers, for example, reported that the 17-million-bushel surplus, produced in the war-scare year of 1877, had been easily absorbed by the European market. In 1885, in Wyoming, a Cheyenne paper stated that if the recent Sudanese-Russian-French alliance against Egypt, Italy, and Britain turned into a general conflagration, American beef and wheat growers would profit greatly from the "circus." [7]

For the most part, Americans looked on European crises with an insulated sense of self-content. Few exhibited the fear, expressed in a *Chicago Tribune* editorial, that war makes all nations poorer by thinning the ranks of those who produced commodities as well as those who consumed them. Even the State Department seemed immune to this fear. Secretary Bayard stated in 1885: "So long as I am head of this Department, I shall not give myself the slightest trouble to thwart the small politics or staircase intrigues in Europe, in which we have not the slightest share or interest, and upon which I look with impatience and contempt." [8]

Despite Bayard's complacency, the State Department showed concern when Europe's aggressiveness seemed to threaten this hemisphere. Although no real danger existed, Gilded America was highly susceptible to rumors, and the press and official diplomatic dispatches continually warned of new European invasions and acquisitions. Latin America seemed perpetually threatened. When the American minister at Bogota reported a Colombian overture to France, Great Britain, Germany, Spain and Italy, inviting these powers to join in a treaty guaranteeing Colombia's sovereignty over the Isthmus of Panama, Secretary of State Blaine reacted immediately. He sug-

---

Herald, Feb. 3, 1880; *Minneapolis Tribune,* July 21, 1886; "The European War and the United States," *Commercial and Financial Chronicle* 24 (Apr. 21, 1877): 357–358.

[7] *New York Times,* May 12, Aug. 17, 1877; *Cheyenne Democratic Leader,* Apr. 30, 1885.

[8] "Business Effects of a Russo-British War," *Chicago Tribune,* Mar. 31, 1881; quotation from Charles C. Tansill, *The Foreign Policy of Thomas F. Bayard, 1885–1897* (New York, 1940), p. xxviii.

gested that the powers acquaint themselves with the "necessary relation" of the United States toward Colombia. Pointing to the treaty of 1846 between this nation and Colombia, which guaranteed American interest in the isthmus, Blaine declared that the United States alone protected the interests of Latin America. European interference would be considered aggression.[9]

Suspicions of German colonial ambitions particularly aroused American anxiety in the 1880s. In 1883, Minister Aaron A. Sargent in Berlin told Secretary of State Frederick Frelinghuysen that Germany was intent on colonial acquisitions. Pressure by such nationalists as Professor Heinrich von Treitschke, Germany's flag-waving historian, as well as Germany's commercial and industrial expansion, its decreasing supply of agricultural land, and its desire for land on which to settle criminals, pushed Germany into the competition for a colonial empire. Sargent predicted, however, that Germany would have trouble holding overseas colonies because of their distance from the fatherland, as well as general apathy toward naval expansion. Despite the frightening reports about Bismarck's involved structure of European alliances, our minister concluded that German colonial expansion could be held in check.[10]

Sargent's optimism was not shared by the State Department as a whole, and Germany disturbed the pax Americana more than once in the late nineteenth century. In 1880, for example, Secretary William Evarts called Minister Andrew D. White's attention to a report of German activity in San Salvador. The German chargé d'affaires, Werner Von Bergen, had allegedly proposed a German alliance to ensure San Salvador's autonomy in the face of annexation threats by the United States. In effect, Evarts suggested that White inform the chargé of Mr. Monroe's Doctrine and the United States' ability to enforce it. The San Salvador treaty never materialized, but the State Department's problems in this region were hardly over. In February 1881, a Dominican minister arrived at the Wilhelmstrasse to negotiate a commercial treaty. To the department's fear of further German commercial penetration of Latin

---

[9] *Instructions, Germany,* June 25, 1881, vol. 17, no. 229.

[10] A. A. Sargent to F. T. Frelinghuysen, Mar. 12, 1883, *Foreign Relations,* 1883, pp. 349–355; "Russo-German Alliance," *San Francisco Chronicle,* Jan. 6, 1887.

America, Minister White in Berlin added another. He reported that Chancellor Bismarck was encouraging German emigrants in Latin America to retain their unity as *Deutsche-Ausländer*. White reasoned that the Iron Chancellor could not fail "to look with longing" toward Hispaniola, and he feared that if the United States became preoccupied in a serious war, Germany would try to seize New World territory. White concluded that the only course to follow in the face of potential German aggression was firm adherence to the Monroe Doctrine.[11]

The United States was concerned, too, about rumors of German activity in the Pacific. In 1880, Washington became fearful that Celso Caesar Moreno, an Italian who for a few days was the Hawaiian foreign minister, was about to negotiate a treaty with Germany that would be hostile to American interests. The next year, King Kalakaua's projected world tour caused Secretary Blaine to worry that cession of part of the islands to Germany might be concluded during the King's absence. To forestall such a treaty, Blaine made a clear and definite restatement of the 1842 Tyler-Webster doctrine. He declared that Hawaii's position in the Pacific and its intimate commercial and political relations with the United States would lead this country to watch with grave concern any movement, negotiation, or discussion regarding the transfer of those islands to another power. Clearly, the United States was unalterably opposed to any attempt of a foreign power to make Hawaii its political satellite.[12]

---

[11] Evarts to White, Aug. 6, 1880, *Instructions, Germany,* vol. 16, no. 128; White to Blaine, Apr. 4, 1881, *Despatches, Germany,* vol. 28, no. 196. In a report on German trade for 1884 and 1885, Consul General Frederick Raine reported that German colonial policy was to be advanced through commercial intercourse, colonial companies, and the establishment of steamship lines (*Consular Despatches, Germany,* no. 57, Nov. 7, 1885). Secretary Bayard, to forestall German action in Cuba, wrote to Minister George H. Pendleton in 1885: "The geographical proximity of Cuba to the United States makes the condition of that Island an especially American question" (Bayard MSS, Sept. 9, 1885, quoted in Tansill's *Bayard,* pp. 29–30). Earlier, Frelinghuysen had warned Spain not to transfer Cuba to another power (Frelinghuysen to Foster, Aug. 29, 1884, *Instructions, Spain,* 19: 642–643, quoted in ibid., p. 30).

[12] Evarts to White, Oct. 16, 1880, *Instructions, Germany,* vol. 17, no. 145; Blaine to White, Apr. 22, 1881, ibid., no. 212.

German operations in Samoa, a country with which the United States had enjoyed treaty relations since the early 1870s, and persistent rumors that Germany and Great Britain had secretly divided the Pacific among themselves gave American diplomats little rest. Secretary of State Bayard was overwhelmed that two powers could boldly assert the right to control and divide insular possessions which had hitherto been open to the commerce of all. Bayard contended that if the United States chose to pursue a policy of colonial acquisition, it would certainly have an equal claim to the Pacific islands. Asserting that Germany had no "good rights" over the Spanish Carolines, the *New York Herald* suggested that the South Pacific islands be placed under the care of an "international state" and developed for the good of all. The German Reichstag, however, put an end to the "Samoan crisis" by defeating a bill for the extension of trade between the two countries. In spite of pressure from certain elements, German officialdom, happily, was still opposed to both a vigorous colonial policy and a naval increase.[13]

After 1871, we were watchful of victorious Germany, and almost equally so of defeated France. The State Department and the press greeted the Third Republic's aggressiveness in Asia and Africa with open skepticism. Most home newspapers doubted the advantages the French would incur in their imperialistic adventures. The *New York Times* felt that France's overseas policies were intended to appeal to its national passion for glory, denied an outlet in the humiliation of 1871. Imperialism compensated for the demoralizing loss of Alsace-Lorraine. Most journals, however, were at a loss to see any glory in exercising sovereignty over African tribes. Although this attitude no doubt indicates a cynical isolationism rather than a wholesome concern for the French nation, Americans had an interest in the course of its imperialism. For example, when France and

---

[13] Bayard to Pendleton, Feb. 27, 1886, *Instructions, Germany,* vol. 17, no. 102; "Germany and Her Annexations," *New York Herald,* Aug. 25, 1885; White to Evarts, May 3, 1880, *Despatches, Germany,* vol. 26, no. 118. The bill that was defeated in the Reichstag would have guaranteed the bonds of a company which would have assumed the liabilities and continued the business of Godeffrey and Company of Hamburg, thus thwarting English and American trade in Samoa. See also White to Evarts, May 10, 1880, ibid., no. 121. For a discussion of German colonialism in Africa, see "Germans in Africa," *New York Herald,* Aug. 15, 1889.

Liberia became involved in a boundary dispute in 1887, Secretary Bayard warned the Paris government through our minister that the United States might intervene in behalf of Liberia. In reply to a report of French interference in Haiti in 1888, Bayard asserted that Paris should be aware of our "well settled" policy. The United States would insist that the independent lands to our south be free to develop their resources in their own way.[14]

Looking from France across the Channel, Victorian Britain provided the American press with more examples of how not to manage foreign affairs. English bumptiousness in diplomacy was humorously reported, and British imperialistic schemes were publicized as warnings for Americans to keep out of such "grab games." The *New York Herald*, for example, did not doubt that Mexico, Santo Domingo, and Cuba would be more prosperous as part of the United States, but this was no reason to wage war to accomplish such acquisition. Nor were similar rationalizations reason enough for England to wage war upon the Boers. John Bull was in a "peck of trouble" as a result of the Egyptian venture of 1882, and it was remarkable, as one newspaper source put it, how unanimously everyone stood arrayed against him.[15]

Referring to England's Afghanistan and South African policies, the *New York Daily Tribune* noted with irony that the way of annexation was always hard when it was, as usual, the way of the transgressor. In answer to an English journal's remark that Uncle Sam, although rich and powerful, did not carry his share of the "white man's burden," the *Chicago Tribune* predicted that if we mended our ways we could solve many colonial problems: British opium sales in China would be prohibited, Canada would be liberated, and the Union Jack would be expelled from the West Indies. England might do well to mind its *own* business. The *New York Herald* jested that the only real cure for British difficulties was annexation by the United States. But since the American people had

[14] "France and Her Foreign Policy," *Commercial and Financial Chronicle* 37 (Aug. 25, 1883): 190–191; "France on the Offensive," *New York Times*, June 17, 1883; Bayard to McLane, Mar. 22, 1887, *Instructions, France*, vol. 21, no. 209; ibid., Dec. 21, 1888, no. 214.

[15] *New York World*, quoted in "The United States and Africa," *Public Opinion* 7 (July 6, 1889): 271; "Foolish Wars," *New York Herald*, Mar. 3, 1881; "England in Egypt," ibid., Aug. 1, 1882.

rejected Cuba and Mexico, there was no certainty they would accept the mother country.[16]

England's dealings with its Irish ward further prejudiced American attitudes toward Great Britain. Economically and politically suppressed by the British government, the Irish began to pour into the United States in the 1840s. Once established in American cities, many of these immigrants began to work for Irish independence. In the post–Civil War decades, Fenian groups raided Canada, and returned to Ireland with American funds to agitate for home rule. These activities raised problems in enforcing American neutrality laws against a popular cause and upholding the rights of Irish-Americans against the British notion of "indelible" citizenship. Operating in a period of strong anglophobia, the Fenians often mistook the sympathy native Americans showed toward their cause for approval of the means they employed. Indeed, a large segment of the American press, as well as a great number of politicians, declared open season on Great Britain. Pleas for Irish freedom were commonplace and the press speculated continuously on possible solutions to the Irish question. For the most part, however, the mass media and the vote-seeking politicians sought Irish support with promises which never materialized. Terrorists and bomb throwers, so often associated in America with Irish radicalism, were persona non grata. While British policy in Ireland had no doubt produced these individuals, many Americans were becoming unwilling to accept the products of English mismanagement.[17]

The floodtide of immigrants from Europe was bound to give new shape to our foreign conceptions. The impact made by the newly

---

[16] "England's Annexation Schemes," *New York Daily Tribune*, Feb. 3, 1880; *Chicago Tribune*, Dec. 28, 1880; "Shall We Annex England?" *New York Herald*, Oct. 26, 1878.

[17] "England and the Irish-Americans," *The Nation* 27 (Mar. 29, 1883): 268; Goldwin Smith, "Great Britain, America, and Ireland," *Princeton Review* 58 (Nov. 1882): 283–305; "Gladstone and the Irish," *Salt Lake City Deseret Evening News*, Jan. 28, 1886. See also Charles C. Tansill, *America and the Fight for Irish Freedom, 1866–1922* (New York, 1957); Florence E. Gibson, *The Attitudes of the New York Irish toward State and National Affairs, 1848–1892* (New York, 1951), pp. 327 ff.; James M. Mahoney, "The Influence of the Irish Americans upon the Foreign Policy of the United States, 1865–1872" (Ph.D. dissertation, Clark University, 1947), pp. 415–419; Brown, *Irish-American Nationalism*, passim.

arrived helped shape the American image of the Old World, and in large part confirmed ancient prejudices, and even reinforced feelings of American superiority. Certainly some of the most volatile and negative immigration publicity stemmed from Irish activities in this country. Some immigration, such as that from Scandinavia, was believed to be composed of sound elements and was generally well received; but most Americans began to look with suspicion and concern at the masses who flooded our ports and points of entry. Fear of "corrupting" influences and the inability of most of the newly arrived to become assimilated caused many journals and politicians to denounce the immigrants as undesirables. Business, reputed to be pro-immigration, was in fact rather hostile to unskilled foreigners who came during slack times, thus aggravating the relief problems. Our representatives abroad were constantly admonished to prevent, as best they could, the immigration of paupers and other undesirables. The evils of tenement existence, the callousness of steamship companies and immigration agents, and the difficulties of assimilation into the mainstream of American life received constant attention in the press.[18]

The cry against immigration became louder as the foreign-born came to be closely linked with increasing radicalism and labor unrest. German socialists were denounced as the "pests of civilization," and the *New York Daily Tribune* called upon the President to stop the immigration of such people. The emerging socialist movement gave a fillip to a new form of Know-Nothingism, culminating in the formation of the American Protective Association. "Patricians," as Professor Cushing Strout has pointed out, were especially unhappy. European manners were fine, and even quaint, as long as tourists could observe them while visiting abroad. In the New World, however, they became offensive, and nostrils twitched in disgust. The "foreign peril" stemmed from a deep-rooted nostalgia for an older

---

[18] "The Scandinavian Emigrants," *Salt Lake City Deseret Evening News,* July 13, 1886; "Evils of Immigration," *Boston Commercial Bulletin,* July 21, 1888; "Immigration Evils," *Burlington (Vt.) Free Press,* July 13, 1888; "The Emigration Question," *New Haven Evening Register,* Jan. 4, 1889; *Pittsburgh Post,* Aug. 11, 1888; Charlotte Erickson, *American Industry and the European Immigrant, 1860–1885* (Cambridge, Mass., 1957), pp. vii, 86; Morrell Heald, "Business Attitudes toward European Immigration, 1880–1900," *Journal of Economic History* 13 (Summer 1953): 291–304.

world untouched by the European evils symbolized by the immigrants to our shores.[19]

Despite the anti-foreign prejudice and such other drawbacks as share cropping and labor violence, the persistent needs of our open West and the requirements of a burgeoning economy attracted immigrants in staggering numbers. The United States was pictured as a nation with a high standard of living, thriving agriculture, available land, no military service requirements, and high wages. Immigrants, simply by coming to America, awakened interest in the nations of their birth. Nevertheless, and although this country needed the labor of the immigrants, their ways were alien, and much of the interest they awakened was uncomplimentary, mirroring American feelings of superiority.

The condition of Ireland and the so-called immigration question only confirmed the popular conception of an unbreachable gap between America and Europe. The European story was a chronicle of rapacious endeavors to compensate for empty policies at home by equally empty adventures and acquisitions abroad. Diplomatically, the United States would react to European policies only when they seemed to threaten us close to home. Having absorbed the choicest section of the North American continent through expansion and the mass murder of its native inhabitants, the United States nevertheless felt free to criticize imperialistic nations. Until 1898, when America went on the prowl for new territory, she all too often exhibited the self-righteousness of the retired-bank-robber-turned-honest.

At the same time that the United States condemned many European institutions, it was awakening to the possibilities of its influence overseas. Hating Europe's tyranny, craftiness, and indolence, Americans of the Gilded Age prepared to act out their role as a chosen people, destined to be a guide to others—an almost religious inspiration for the rest of the world. Europe had only to reproduce American governmental forms and follow American economic policies and the Old World would be saved.

With the advent of Germany and Italy to the roster of great

---

[19] "Immigration of German Socialists," *New York Daily Tribune,* Dec. 4, 1878; "Our Foreign Element," *Minneapolis Tribune,* July 29, 1886; Cushing Strout, *The American Image of the Old World* (New York, 1963), pp. 132–133, 137.

powers, the consolidation of the Austrian Empire, and the weakened condition of France, many Americans hoped that Europe would follow the American example and form a United States of Europe. Andrew Carnegie told William Gladstone that the union of Britain and the United States was the truest hope for the progress of the world. At another time, the industrialist informed the Prime Minister that a British republic would serve the cause of world progress. In his *Triumphant Democracy*, Carnegie asserted that the older nations of the world crept at a snail's pace while this country thundered forward with the rush of an express train. He effusively described our superiority in population, agriculture, manufacturing, and indeed all areas of accomplishment. The *New York Herald* even urged that the Irish party in the British Parliament consider the American experience. The best solution to the vexing problem of home rule was to reconstruct the empire upon the basis of the American republic. One American writer was bold enough to contend that the United States had the right to be heard on European questions and to have a voice in final decisions.[20]

Although Europeans did not seem to be in a rush to change their political institutions, some Americans seemed pleased with European adoption of economic nationalism. Convinced that our own prosperity was based on a high tariff policy, they celebrated increased tariff rates in Europe as a Yankee exportation. The arguments of the American protectionists were no longer "whistled down the wind in the British Parliament." Ironically, the United States seemed unaware that economic nationalism was a one-way street that was crowded with fellow travelers.[21]

It was not only smug superiority or a desire to change European institutions which led the United States to consider its role vis-à-vis Europe. Our ideas about Europe were parochial, antipathetic, patronizing, but at the same time envious and respectful. Our culture was recognized as derivative, and though we could condemn Euro-

---

[20] *Old and New* 5 (Jan. 1872): 3; Andrew Carnegie to Gladstone, July 14, 1885, Feb. 7, 1890, Carnegie MSS, Library of Congress; Carnegie, *Triumphant Democracy* (New York, 1886), pp. 508–509; "American Ideas in Europe," *New York Herald*, June 21, 1881; *Buffalo Daily Dispatch*, Jan. 3, 1878. See also Nathan Appleton, *Europe and America in 1870* (New York, 1870), esp. pp. 21–25.

[21] "American Ideas Abroad," *New York Daily Tribune*, May 12, 1879.

pean militarism, at the same time we acknowledged European supremacy in matters of the mind. Sensitive Americans still felt a magnetic pull toward the matrix of culture. European homes, fashions, polite society, sports, reform movements, labor, religion, and culinary habits all were of some interest to Americans. The social contributions of William Morris (as well as his famous Morris chair), the vogue of Sarah Bernhardt, Gilbert and Sullivan, and Leopold Damrosch, and even the borrowed French taste for frog legs, or for Napoleon III mustaches on American faces, took on deep significance and represented a heightened degree of deference to Old World habits and institutions.[22]

English and French writers often surpassed Americans, and the highest aim of our literary journals was to emulate the English or continental periodicals. Such magazines featured discussions on the less romantic foreign developments, as well as descriptions of the economic and political life of other countries. *Scribner's* noted a tendency to "frenchify" American fiction, and interest in Russian literature, especially Turgenev, Tolstoi, Dostoevski, and Gogol, seemed more than a passing interest or novelty. Though foreign events counted for so much, it is significant that, when *The Nation* began to devote increased attention to such themes and literature, it was criticized for not being thoroughly American in spirit.[23] Thus the dichotomy in America's attitude toward the Old World.

A reciprocal cultural influence could also be discerned in a renewed European interest in America. While European publications were popular in this country, there was much interest in American periodicals in England. More issues of *Harper's* and *Century Magazine* were sold in Great Britain than any British monthly of similar price. The popularity of these and other American periodicals called the attention of English readers to American authors, thus heightening the cultural affinity between the two English speaking nations. American literature had come into its own in Great Britain. Moreover, popular novels were translated into French and German, and soon European girls, like their American counterparts, were en-

---

[22] Van Wyck Brooks, *New England: Indian Summer, 1865–1915,* p. 286.
[23] Mott, *History of American Magazines,* 3: 248–250, 278–279; 4: 134–135, 223; Gustav Pollak, *Fifty Years of American Idealism: The New York Nation, 1865–1915* (Boston and New York, 1915), p. 35.

tranced by the trials and tribulations of Louisa May Alcott's *Little Women*. British audiences heard the American revivalists Dwight Moody and Ira Sankey, and enjoyed such American songs as *Camp Town Races*. American historians who stressed the Teutonic origins of American democracy aroused enthusiasm for American scholarship. British universities began to be endowed with chairs in American history and literature, and Europe's radicals studied the works of the economist Henry George and utopian writer Edward Bellamy.[24]

American inventions, such as Thomas A. Edison's incandescent lamp and phonograph, Alexander G. Bell's telephone, and Philo Remington's typewriter, also found ready adoption in the Old World. The American press gave new ideas to European papers, which in the 1880s imitated such American features as oversize headlines, pictures, cartoons, stunts, and terse language. Perhaps the only feature of the American press that was not copied was the comic strips.[25]

More attention was also paid American civilization by the Germans, who learned much from American scholars studying in Germany. American characters even found their way into German fiction. Early American history, colonial and national, was not an uncommon subject matter. James Fenimore Cooper and Bret Harte were favorite writers. Frankness as a trait of American girls and the American sense of superiority figured conspicuously in German literature which dealt with the United States.[26]

American civilization and culture, which had branched off from that of Europe, were rediscovered as a part of Europe's heritage.

---

[24] *Cosmopolitan* 2 (Sept. 1886): 41; Clarence Gohdes, *American Literature in Nineteenth Century England* (New York, 1944), pp. 6, 70; "American Periodicals in England," *Detroit Free Press*, Jan. 21, 1883; Mott, *History of American Magazines*, 4: 229; Sigmund Skard, *The American Myth and the European Mind: American Studies in Europe, 1776–1960* (Philadelphia, 1961), pp. 39, 40; George S. Gordon, *Anglo-American Literary Relations* (London, New York, etc., 1942), p. 113; Halvdan Koht, *The American Spirit in Europe: A Survey of Transatlantic Influences* (Philadelphia, 1949), pp. 189, 202, 204, 228.

[25] Koht, *The American Spirit in Europe*, pp. 173, 175, 232, 233.

[26] Lida von Krockow, "American Characters in German Novels," *Atlantic Monthly* 68 (Dec. 1891): 824–838; John H. Nelson, "Some Germanic Surveys of American Literature," *American Literature* 1 (1929–1930): 148–160.

The continuing vogue in America for things European, and the reciprocal influence of American ideas and products, proved that the United States was coming into its own as an active participant in Western civilization. Even before the cocktail party, football games, jazz, and tourists who demanded daily towel changes, America left its mark on the Old World.

James Russell Lowell, who knew England as few other outsiders did, predicted that it would take the English a great deal of time to rid themselves of their patronizing attitude, since in their eyes we were but "lusty juveniles." James Bryce, however, was more sentimental and optimistic; he was convinced of the efficacy of travel improvements in fostering Anglo-American amity. And while Herbert Spencer was pessimistic about American materialism, he observed that the United States would soon be the most powerful nation in the world. While the majority of foreign comments on America were hardly flattering, Europeans manifested grudging respect for the United States.[27]

An excellent example of increased cultural interchange involved the copyright problem. As early as 1790, Congress had passed the first domestic copyright bill for the protection of American citizens, with the proviso that nothing in the act should prevent Americans from publishing works by foreign authors. In the absence of an international agreement, publishing prospered, though American piracy or unauthorized printings reduced the victims' royalties. Thus American authors were forced to compete in their own country with foreign authors whose reprinted books sold for less than their own copyrighted works. From 1866 to 1891, American copyright laws permitted the reprinting of books by foreign authors, and, since the best of Europe's authors could be published cheaply, it is no wonder that this country depended on English models and thereby fostered the imitative spirit of American letters.[28]

---

[27] James Russell Lowell, "On a Certain Condescension in Foreigners," *Atlantic Monthly* 23 (Jan. 1869): 82–94; James Bryce, *American Commonwealth*, 2 vols. (New York, 1893), 2:785; Herbert Spencer, "The Americans," *Essays Scientific, Political, and Speculative*, 3 vols. (New York, 1891), 3:474.

[28] Aubert J. Clark, *The Movement for International Copyright in Nineteenth-Century America* (Washington, 1960), pp. vii–viii; Warren B. Bezanson, "The American Struggle for International Copyright, 1866–1891" (Ph.D. dissertation, University of Maryland, 1953), pp. 72, 214; I. Joel

Charles Dickens's second visit to the United States, in 1867, focused particular attention on the copyright problem, for he had lost much money by American pirating of his books. Meanwhile, advances in the printing industry and technical improvements made possible the spectacular growth of an inexpensive book and magazine trade, whose promoters relied heavily on the fact that they did not have to pay royalties. Established publishers, badly hurt by the competition, complained that piracy reduced the incentive for building an American literature. Great controversy ensued among authors, publishers, and printers. Periodicals referred to America's insensitive conscience and its crude and barbarous attitude toward authors. The United States persistently refused to protect nonresident alien authors from literary piracy, and the public ignored the fact that the American practice was not in accord with that of most civilized states. Americans were satisfied with cheap reprints; so why should they pay more? [29]

But the ultimate success in achieving a copyright bill showed the power of pressure groups: manufacturers, unions, and professional associations such as the International Copyright Association and the American Copyright League. Finally, in 1891, a lame-duck GOP Congress, faced with a Democratic majority in the House of Representatives, passed the Platt-Symonds bill and the United States was no longer regarded as the "literary Ishmael of the civilized world." The settlement of this issue assisted considerably in creating a milieu of more positive reciprocal understanding between America and England.[30]

Larus, "The Origin and Development of the 1891 International Copyright Law of the United States" (Ph.D. dissertation, Columbia University, 1960), pp. 34, 125–126.

[29] Clark, *The Movement for International Copyright,* pp. 87–88, 92–100; Bezanson, "The American Struggle for International Copyright," p. 286; Larus, "The Origin and Development of the 1891 International Copyright Law," pp. 219–224; "Copyright," *New York Daily Tribune,* July 24, 1875; "The Copyright Bill," *Christian Union,* 24 (Feb. 14, 1884), p. 147; "International Copyright," *Book News,* 2 (Mar. 1884), p. 118.

[30] Clark, *The Movement for International Copyright,* pp. 118–148, 182–186; Bezanson, "The American Struggle for International Copyright," pp. 335, 349, 354; Larus, "The Origin and Development of the 1891 International Copyright Law," pp. 180, 218; *Hartford Daily Courant,* Jan. 9, 1885; "The Copyright Bill," *Washington Post,* Jan. 14, 1889; Richardson,

Increased American travel and European appreciation of our culture would, by 1890, break down some of the barriers between the two continents. Americans still viewed Europe with suspicion, and many continue to do so even today. In many respects, Europe remained the symbol of monarchical despotism, belligerent militarism, rapacious imperialism, economic indolence, and widespread corruption. But Gilded America was increasingly intrigued by European markets, society, culture, and institutions, and more certain of its own position in the world. With certainty as a nation came revived missionary zeal. Schooled in a revivalist tradition, the "chosen people" were becoming anxious to spread their doctrines, and Europe was in need of American assistance. Americans, then, were not ready to send the Old World to eternal damnation. As the *New York Herald* reminded its readers, the United States was only part of the world worth thinking about, and it spoke glowingly about the deeper implications of European-American interchanges and cooperation.[31] Whether this spirit of exchange would lessen America's smug isolationism and engender genuine international interests remained to be seen.

Messages and Papers, 12: 5478; *Congressional Record,* 51st Cong., 2d sess., 22, pt. 7, pp. 4221, 4284.

[31] "America's Influence on Europe," *New York Herald,* June 19, 1882.

CHAPTER 9

Spotlight
on Darkest
Africa

$\mathbf{A}$FRICA had traditionally been a realm of mystery and romance and, as such, had fascinated scholars, explorers, philanthropists, businessmen, and laymen alike. Although the origins of American activity in sub-Sahara Africa date back to the lucrative slave trade and to the American Colonization Society's establishment of a colony of freed Negroes in Liberia in 1822, the Dark Continent drew only momentary attention from Americans in the next fifty years. In the Grant Era, however, Americans renewed their interest in Africa, particularly in the region surrounding the Congo River.[1]

Men came to believe that the Congo territory was possibly the germ of another New World. Discoveries of lakes, mountains, and other geographical features in Africa became items of newspaper reporting in this country. The Dark Continent, ripe for exploration, was described as teeming with treasures for the adventurous traveler. In the name of Christian civilization, trade, and humani-

---

[1] Gilbert Haven, "America in Africa," *North American Review* 125 (July 1877): 147–158; "Discoveries on the Congo," *Louisville Commercial*, Sept. 19, 1885.

tarianism, Americans were exhorted to disregard Washington's advice on aloofness from foreign complications and to join the scramble for territory already begun by the post-1871 European imperialists. Commercial potentialities and missionary pursuits combined to produce the ever brightening spotlight that was being played upon the darkness of Africa. The time was at hand, many sources indicated, for Africa to undergo vast change, and for Americans to participate. The press, scientific societies, business and missionary groups, and the imperialistic activities of foreign nations pushed the United States into a new relationship with the Dark Continent.[2]

In the press, the *New York Herald* played a leading role in developing American interest in Africa. Demanding that the Congo be opened to the trade of the world, its editor urged the New York Chamber of Commerce to call the government's attention to the resources and potentialities of the Congo, likening the opening of that region to the discovery of gold in California. The paper also gave financial support to private exploratory missions. In 1869, James Gordon Bennett commissioned the journalist Henry M. Stanley to find the English missionary, David Livingstone. Stanley's search for Livingstone, and later his unsuccessful attempt to rescue the Emin Pasha from a revolt in equatorial Egypt, brought the African continent to the attention of an excited public.[3]

Traversing the continent for two decades, Stanley was perhaps the greatest voice for Africa in the United States. Stanley discovered the vast commercial possibilities of the Congo, and it was perhaps because the initial impetus was American that the economic lure of that region attracted special interest in the United States. American journals portrayed Stanley as one of the great pioneers of the day and the best prototype of the man of action since Garibaldi. On his return from his celebrated search for Livingstone, Stanley received a huge ovation, complete with a banquet at Delmonico's in New York.[4]

---

[2] "American Opportunities in Africa," *Our Day* 5 (June 1890): 490–499; "The Development of Africa," *New York Daily Commercial Bulletin*, Feb. 12, 1881; "Prying into Africa," *New York Times*, Mar. 19, 1879. For general American-Mediterranean-African relations, see Field, *America and the Mediterranean World*, pp. 378 ff.

[3] "The Congo," *New York Herald*, Sept. 7, 1884; "The New Africa," ibid., Dec. 30, 1883; ibid., Oct. 30, 1882.

[4] "Henry M. Stanley," *Eclectic Magazine of Foreign Literature, Science,*

The American Geographical Society was another agency which purveyed the progress of African exploration to the public. Founded in New York City in 1852, it soon became a headquarters for scientists, diplomats, explorers, various kinds of sponsors, and geographers. Here they could meet, exchange views, and read or listen to reports and recollections. Judge Charles P. Daly, the association's longtime president (1864–1899), was especially noted for his addresses on Africa.[5]

Recognition that Africa was a fertile territory for missionary enterprise also contributed to American interest and activity, and the *Christian Advocate* maintained that never in all history had there been more intense evangelical work. The challenge of redeeming millions of heathens became not only a Christian act of love but a necessary step in the development of commerce and other concomitants of civilization. Business interests were linked with the spiritual concerns of Christianity—at least in the thinking of many of the missionaries. These evangelists held that the Almighty had revealed to them the future he held in store for the Congo, and that it was America's manifest duty to develop Africa. The growing numbers of American clergymen and missionaries in Africa not only publicized the continent in this country but caused anxiety for their safety. Negotiations for the protection of these overseas nationals brought the State Department into closer contact with Africa.[6]

---

and *Art* (hereafter *Eclectic Magazine*) 52 (July 1890): 78–85; "The Congo Commission," *Bradstreet's* 10 (Sept. 6, 1884): 146; "Africa for the Americans," *Review of Reviews* 2 (Dec. 1890): 541; "A Policy of Action," *New York Daily Tribune,* Apr. 12, 1890. See also Stanley's *Through the Dark Continent,* 2 vols. (New York, 1878), *The Congo and the Founding of Its Free State,* 2 vols. (New York, 1885), *In Darkest Africa,* 2 vols. (New York, 1890), *My Kalulu Prince, King, and Slave: A Story of Central Africa* (New York, 1889) (an adventure book for boys, based upon the search for Livingstone); *The Autobiography of Sir Henry Morton Stanley,* ed. Dorothy Stanley (Boston and New York, 1909); Olivia Manning, *The Reluctant Rescue* [of Emin Pasha] (New York, 1947); and Byron Farwell, *The Man Who Presumed* [a biography of Stanley] (New York, 1957).

[5] Harold E. Hammond, "American Interest in the Exploration of the Dark Continent," *The Historian* 18 (Spring 1956): 202–229.

Judge Daly (1816–1899) led a romantic career which included such activities as cabin boy on a trading vessel, a carpenter's apprentice, and judge and chief judge of New York City's Court of Common Pleas.

[6] "The Race for the Heart of Africa," *Christian Advocate* 56 (Oct. 6, 1881): 625; George Mooar, "Some Problems of the Congo," *Overland*

Perhaps the most important force pushing the United States into involvement in Africa was the fear among commercial and missionary circles that the continent would soon fall under foreign domination. That Europe was "absorbing Africa" with "wonderful rapidity" was the cry of the *San Francisco Evening Bulletin.* The *Hartford Daily Courant* felt that the generation of the 1880s might well witness Africa's "coming out." Asserting that the continent was not just the final recipient of Sunday school pennies, it predicted a contest comparable to the epic struggle of England and France for control of North America in the eighteenth century. As Russia was gradually absorbing Asia, Germany and France seemed to be concentrating on Africa, and the *Courant* believed war was inevitable.[7]

While some Americans were content to see the United States merely look on, ready—as usual—to profit from the trade that would be thrust upon us in the event of a European power struggle over Africa, others wanted bolder action. Repeating the stand taken on Samoa, Hawaii, and parts of Latin America, the *New York Herald* demanded commercial freedom for all the nations in the Congo. And there was congressional concern as well. As early as 1877, Senator Roscoe Conkling presented a petition by a group of his New York constituents urging the appointment of a commission to discuss the possibility of a trans-Africa railroad with other nations. One year later, the American Colonization Society submitted a petition calling for an American survey of the West African coast.[8]

The growing American concern with the sub-Sahara was shown in the 1878 mission of Commodore Robert W. Shufeldt to West Africa, the first leg of a voyage that carried him eventually to Korea and the Far East. The *New York Herald* praised Shufeldt for his reports on the possibility of trade with the natives and hoped, with the commodore, that this region would soon become the "great com-

---

Monthly 5 (Apr. 1885): 366–372; "The Opening of the Congo," *The Friend* 56 (1883): 372; Joseph Cook, "American Opportunities in Africa," *Our Day* 5 (June 1890): 490–499; *Missionary Review* 8 (May 1885): 219–220.

[7] "Europe Absorbing Africa," *San Francisco Evening Bulletin,* June 8, 1888; "The Day of Africa," *Hartford Daily Courant,* Jan. 24, 1885.

[8] "American Interest in the Congo," *New York Herald,* Apr. 13, 1884; *Senate Journal,* 45th Cong., 2d sess. (Dec. 7, 1877), p. 33; ibid., 3d sess. (Feb. 12, 1879), p. 259.

mercial prize of the world." He was congratulated for having sent the Secretary of the Navy some specimens of the colored cotton goods that were most in demand by the natives. Shufeldt warned, however, that a consular service on the West African coast was essential if the United States wished to share in the economic opportunities of Africa. The American merchant could not compete with European capital unless he was sustained by consular service and reinforced by the presence of American gunboats. Shufeldt's report found support in the State Department.[9]

Taking note of Commodore Shufeldt's recommendations and the efforts of France to gain commercial supremacy in the rich African interior, Alvey A. Adee of the department's permanent staff suggested a government investigation of commercial opportunities on the continent. Only a government commission could make American influence authoritative. Although no immediate action was taken on Adee's proposal, these were strong words to come from the State Department in supposedly quiet years.[10]

The first steps toward a more positive African policy were taken during the Arthur administration. In his annual message of 1883, President Arthur pointed out that the United States could not afford to remain indifferent to the development of African commerce. In marked contrast to his predecessors, who had generally ignored the region, Arthur suggested cooperation with other commercial powers in maintaining freedom of trade and residence in the Congo.[11]

A year later, Senator John Tyler Morgan of Alabama put the President's suggestion into stronger form in a congressional resolution (on February 26, 1884). An aggressively expansionist member of the Foreign Relations Committee since 1878, Senator Morgan

---

[9] See chapter 6. The prime source for Shufeldt is "Letters from Commodore R. W. Shufeldt, October 1878–November 1880," Department of Navy Archives. These volumes also contain notes from Shufeldt's journal, and instructions to and reports from the expedition.

Shufeldt to Thompson, Aug. 2, 1879, "Letters from Commodore Shufeldt"; "A New Feature of Naval Operations," *New York Herald*, Sept. 6, 1879. See also George L. Allen, *The Pilgrimage of the "Ticonderoga"* (San Francisco, 1880); Shufeldt, *The Relation of the Navy to the Commerce of the United States* (Washington, 1878).

[10] *Reports of the Diplomatic Bureau*, Aug. 14, 1879, vol. 3, no. 32 (memorandum by Adee); F. W. Seward to Edward F. Noyes, Aug. 29, *Foreign Relations*, 1879, pp. 342–344.

[11] *Foreign Relations*, 1883, preface.

viewed the furtherance of American interests in the Congo as part of a larger policy, including a Nicaraguan canal and the annexation of Cuba and the Philippines. Morgan's initial resolution called upon the President to take positive measures to protect American traders and missionaries in the Congo basin. He was especially concerned lest any one nation receive rights of exclusive sovereignty. Morgan also proposed that a scientific commission be set up "to lay down a foundation of facts upon which commerce [could] be established between this country and [Africa]." Specifically, Morgan believed in the necessity for a steamship line connecting Charleston, New Orleans, and the mouth of the Congo River. The African Trade Society, an organization formed to promote intercourse with the Dark Continent, also pressed for the establishment of steam and mail service between New Orleans and Liberia.[12]

The racist assumptions behind Morgan's resolutions were apparent. In an article for *North American Review* in 1884, Morgan noted that while the black race had advanced numerically in the United States, competition with the white majority continued to halt its material progress. Integration of the races, he maintained, was desired neither by whites or blacks, and thus the return of black Americans to Africa might well afford a solution to this vexing problem. The Congo would provide a "natural theater" for Negro development. Later, in "The Race Question in the United States," Morgan took a more positive stand. It was the "very peculiar duty" of this country to return the descendants of the slaves to the land from which they had been brought. Africa must be opened up so that these Negroes could return and promote commerce among "their own people."[13]

---

[12] *Senate Miscellaneous Document* 59, 48th Cong., 1st sess. (Feb. 26, 1884); *Congressional Record,* 48th Cong., 1st sess. (Feb. 26, 1884), 15, pt. 2, 1378; *House Journal,* 48th Cong., 2d sess. (Feb. 18, 1884); ibid., p. 594. As a matter of fact, many resolutions called upon various agencies to inquire into trade possibilities with Africa and asked them to report upon possible action to further American commerce (see for example, *Senate Journal,* 48th Cong., 1st sess. [Jan. 21, 1884], p. 195).

[13] John T. Morgan, "The Future of the Negro," *North American Review* 139 (July 1884): 81–84; Morgan, "The Race Question in the United States," *Arena* 2 (Sept. 1890): 384–398; *Congressional Record,* 50th Cong., 1st sess. (June 28, 1888), 19, pt. 6, 5671–5672.

For appraisals of Morgan's work, see Joseph O. Baylen, "Senator John Tyler Morgan, E. D. Morel, and the Congo Reform Association," *Alabama*

While Morgan saw Africa as a potential means of redemption from national guilt, other Americans worried about America's responsibilities in Africa. Rumors of a French takeover in Liberia, a republic which owed its existence to the benevolence of the American Colonization Society, caused the State Department much concern. Secretary Evarts's dispatches referred to the "peculiar relations" between the United States and Liberia and predicted that these relations would increase as Liberia's economic importance was realized. Commodore Shufeldt called for closer economic ties with Liberia, which he described as "the *objective* point of American trade on [the African] Coast, and . . . really the garden of Africa." Shufeldt even favored keeping a gunboat off Liberia's coast to ensure governmental stability.[14]

The rumors of an intended French protectorate over Liberia were not the only cause for American concern. In 1882, for example, the American Colonization Society, which represented the Liberian government in Washington, had appealed for American aid in a Liberian dispute with Great Britain and the British colony of Sierra Leone. During the 1880s, the weakness of Liberia and the difficulty of maintaining effective sovereignty over its outlying districts continued to expose that republic to foreign encroachment and to arouse American sympathy. In his annual message for 1886, Grover Cleveland maintained that although a formal protectorate over Liberia was contrary to United States policy, it was the moral right and duty of this country to assist Liberia in maintaining its territorial integrity. The President recommended that a small naval vessel, no longer adequate for American needs, be presented to Liberia for the protection of its coastal revenues. Even skeptical Americans, such as Henry Adams, were becoming aware that "on the whole [Africa] is worth some trouble." [15]

Review 15 (Apr. 1962): 117–132 and August C. Radke, Jr., "John Tyler Morgan, An Expansionist Senator, 1877–1907" (Ph.D. dissertation, University of Washington, 1953), passim.

[14] *North American Review* 125, pt. 2 (Nov. 1877): 517–528; Elizabeth Brett White, *American Opinion of France* (New York, 1927), p. 215; Roy Olton, "Problems of American Foreign Relations in the African Area During the Nineteenth Century" (Ph.D. dissertation, Fletcher School of Law and Diplomacy, 1954), pp. 200 ff.; Pletcher, *The Awkward Years*, p. 225.

[15] Pletcher, *The Awkward Years*, pp. 225–227; Olton, "Problems of American Foreign Relations in the African Area," pp. 195 ff.; Richardson,

American response to the International African Association and the Berlin conference on the Congo is probably the best illustration of American sentiment toward involvement in Africa. Organized in 1876 under the leadership of King Leopold II of Belgium, the association sought American recognition in the 1880s. At first, President Arthur and Secretary Frelinghuysen opposed recognition. But in April 1884—after pressure from General Henry S. Sanford, a former minister to Belgium and experienced diplomat, as well as from business organizations such as the New York Chamber of Commerce—the President extended recognition to the association. Many believed that recognition was necessary to end the slave trade, and some hoped that American contact with the association would block any European monopoly of the African trade. Secretary Frelinghuysen testified before the Senate that the recognition of the International African Association by the United States was in harmony with the traditional policy of the government toward the financial interests of its citizens. He declared, however, that the United States would avoid all political entanglements.[16]

Messages and Papers, 11: 5086; Adams to Charles Milnes Gaskell, Feb. 8, 1885, in Ford, ed., *Letters of Henry Adams,* 1: 362.

In answer to a suggestion that the United States mediate a dispute between France and Madagascar, Adee advised Frelinghuysen to pursue a "hands off" policy, despite the threat to our growing trade with the latter country (*Reports of the Diplomatic Bureau,* Oct. 1, 1884, vol. 6, no. 149).

We were even more suspicious of Germany in Africa than of France or Britain. For example, Washington was warned of the German occupation of the east coast of Africa north of Zanzibar. Again, in Polynesia, Berlin's interest in far-off regions seemed to excite American jealousy more than that of other capitals. In 1886, when the *Methodist Review* reported that Germany was making a serious inquiry into East African products, American suspicions seemed justified. See Tisdel to Bayard, Aug. 25, 1885, *Special Agents, Department of State,* vol. 32, and *Methodist Review* 68 (Nov. 1886): 917–918.

[16] Leon Felde, "An American General and the Congo," *Belgium* 5 (Apr. 1944): 110–112; Hammond, "American Interest in the Exploration of the Dark Continent," loc. cit.; Olton, "Problems of American Foreign Relations in the African Area," pp. 218, 232–239; *Senate Executive Document 196,* 49th Cong., 1st sess. (Apr. 22, 1884), p. 260; Edward Younger, *John A. Kasson* (Iowa City, 1955), pp. 322–329.

The issue that aroused humanitarians the world over was the encouragement of the slave trade in Africa, especially to extend the influence of foreign powers. Many American papers and journals found it hard to believe that Britain, France, Germany, and Belgium were moved to intervene in

Despite the guarantees of the International African Association, Bismarck feared that one power could easily gain control of the Congo territory and exclude German trade. This fear prompted the Chancellor (in October 1884) to invite the great powers to a conference in Berlin to discuss the African situation. After much debate over the extent of America's involvement, Secretary Frelinghuysen instructed Minister John A. Kasson in Berlin to accept the German invitation with the stipulation that he would confine his participation to matters of commerce and navigation and avoid all political discussion. Graham H. Stuart, a historian of the State Department, has termed Frelinghuysen's "courageous acceptance" of Bismarck's invitation his greatest accomplishment because he departed from the tradition of noninterference in his belief that only neutralization would hold the Congo in trust for the benefit of all. Professor Samuel F. Bemis suggests, further, that Frelinghuysen anticipated the concept of an international mandate for backward areas. If this is so, the deliberations of the conference take on heightened meaning.[17]

The Berlin conference adopted a resolution establishing freedom of commerce and navigation in the Congo basin. The conferees also outlawed the slave trade, agreed upon the principle of freedom of religion in the area, drew up rules for the occupation of the African interior, and recognized the International African Association as a sovereign state. Kasson followed his instructions, and American participation in the congress was limited to discussions of an economic and social nature. Although it was obvious that American commercial and humanitarian commitments depended upon the political stability of the Congo, Kasson avoided matters dealing with international politics.[18]

African affairs for the humanitarian reason of suppressing that evil trade. Missionaries were especially critical of such a convenient precept.

[17] Frelinghuysen to Kasson, Oct. 15, 1884, *Instructions, Germany,* vol. 17, no. 345; Graham H. Stuart, *The Department of State,* p. 162; Samuel F. Bemis, *Diplomatic History* (5th ed.), p. 576.

[18] See U.S. Congress, Senate Committee on Foreign Relations, *Report* 393, 48th Cong., 1st sess. (Mar. 26, 1884) on the occupation of the Congo; *House Executive Document* 247, 48th Cong., 2d sess. (Feb. 28, 1885); *Senate Executive Document* 196, 49th Cong., 1st sess.; *Missionary Review* 8 (Jan. 1885): 81.

For background on the slave trade, see James C. Duram, "A Study of Frustration: Britain, the U.S.A., and the African Slave Trade, 1815–1870," *Social Science* 40 (Oct. 1965): 220–225.

Ratification of the Berlin agreement occasioned considerable debate in the American press and on Capitol Hill. Anxious to enhance the prestige of the United States, Kasson staunchly defended American participation at Berlin. He contended that ratification was essential for the protection of American commercial interests. The agreement, he further noted, was "the very substance of the American constitution extended to Africa." It should be added, too, that no political alliance had been authorized or concluded, as some quarters feared. The *Commercial and Financial Chronicle*, while skeptical at first, saw American attendance at the Berlin conference as a sign of new and more realistic diplomatic endeavors. Thus as early as 1885 the commercially powerful Eastern seaboard may have been preparing to scrap isolation in favor of a more sophisticated outlook. The missionary press also endorsed American adherence to the conference's resolutions. The *Boston Congregationalist*, for example, hailed the International Association as a wise device for settling the problems of the Congo with words rather than arms.[19]

The Berlin conference did not limit itself to commercial policy, and because political interests and territorial jurisdiction were discussed in Berlin, traditionalists in this country resurrected the ghosts of Washington, Jefferson, and Monroe. Opponents of ratification argued that Americans were being deceived, beguiled into forgetting that a neutral course was the only wise policy to follow. After all, they asked, and inasmuch as the talks did advance farther than the deliberative stage, why throw overboard all the sanctified and time-tested traditions of our foreign policy? Beyond a remote and questionable commercial interest, the United States had no concern with the Congo. Others feared that the conference might lead to a new departure and "engraft upon the peaceful precedents of our diplomacy . . . a precedent liable to become pregnant with foreign discord and domestic unrest." *The Nation* felt that American participation in the proceedings was odd and inconsistent since the

---

[19] John A. Kasson, "The Congo Conference and the President's Message," loc. cit.; Younger, *Kasson*, pp. 329–339; *House Executive Document 156*, 48th Cong., 2d sess. (Jan. 30, 1885), pp. 9–10; "The Congo Conference and the Nicaragua Canal," *Commercial and Financial Chronicle* 40 (Jan. 3, 1885): 5–6; "The Congo Conference," *Boston Congregationalist* 36 (Nov. 20, 1884): 394.

United States so zealously guarded the Americas from any foreign interference. What, they asked, were Americans doing in carving up Africa? [20]

Congressmen were also skeptical. Representative Perry Belmont, one of the most vigorous critics of American participation at Berlin, asserted that our action was unjustified. Any interests the United States wished to maintain in Africa could be secured by special treaty arrangements. Moreover, "no prospect of commercial advantage warrants a departure from the traditional policy of this Government." The participation of the United States in "the so-called Congo Conference" was an unfortunate departure from that "policy which forbids the [United States] to participate in any political combination . . . outside of the American continent." [21]

In the end, despite American participation in the Berlin conference, ratification of its proposals never came to congressional vote. President Cleveland, foreshadowing his later action vis-à-vis Hawaii's annexation, stuck to a Jeffersonian position and refused to submit the treaty for Senate approval. Despite our steadily increasing commercial interests, the Congo issue fell victim to tradition and isolation.

America's African hopes were also reduced by damaging reports made by Willard P. Tisdel on commercial possibilities in the Congo valley. Tisdel, a businessman, a onetime South American explorer, and an agent of John Roach's Brazilian steamship line (who was also a friend of Senator Morgan), had been sent by the State Department in 1884 to explore the political, geographic, and commercial situation in the Congo. His special instructions were to investigate the commercial possibilities of the Congo, with special emphasis on determining promising markets for American products, but his directives included a denial of political interests. Tisdel's reports, though optimistic and encouraging at first, eventually dashed cold water on the hopes of the ardent enthusiasts.[22]

---

[20] "The Congo Conference," *New York Herald,* Jan. 30, 1885; "Our Diplomacy," ibid., Dec. 10, 1884; *House Report* 2655, 48th Cong., 2d sess. (Feb. 28, 1885), p. 1; "A Strange Proceeding," *The Nation* 40 (Jan. 1, 1885): 8–9.

[21] Perry Belmont, *An American Democrat: The Recollections of Perry Belmont,* 2d ed. (New York, 1941), p. 313.

[22] Frelinghuysen to Tisdel, Sept. 8, 1884, *Special Missions, Department*

In 1884, Tisdel had reported that America needed the Congo's products and that the natives were eager to use our manufactured goods. He even suggested that Americans establish themselves in the Congo to compete with foreign mercantile houses. By 1885, however, he struck a different note; in a series of reports to Secretary Bayard and others during 1885 and 1886, he painted a more gloomy picture. The land was unsuitable for many types of agriculture, inland travel was difficult, and white men were unable to bear the torrid climate. Although the territory had development possibilities, Tisdel could not envision a paying business in the upcountry. Besides, the natives were "a lazy, treacherous, wild and cruel sort of people"; they had few wants and were therefore a poor market for American exports. Furthermore, Dutch, English, and German merchants already controlled most of the trade of the west coast, and large quantities of capital would be necessary to establish effective competition. Although men like Stanley continued to promote interest in African trade, Tisdel flatly reported: "I do not deem it advisable or desirable that the United States should become the possessor of lands here under existing circumstances." Predicting meager results from the activity of enthusiasts, Tisdel said "I do not believe that Americans want or should want anything to do with Central Africa." [23]

Despite Tisdel's findings and advice, his mission is evidence that the United States entered into a new relationship with Africa in the Gilded Age. Senator Edmunds of Vermont was typical of many who

---

of State, vol. 3, no. 1; Frelinghuysen to Tisdel, Sept. 8, 1884, *Foreign Relations,* 1885, pp. 282–284. See also Pletcher, *The Awkward Years,* p. 317.

[23] Tisdel to Frelinghuysen, Nov. 23, 1884, *Special Agents, Department of State,* vol. 32; Tisdel to Bayard, Apr. 25, 1885, Tisdel to Frelinghuysen, Nov. 23, 1884, Frelinghuysen to Tisdel, Dec. 12, 1884, Tisdel to Bayard, Apr. 25, 1885, June 29, 1885, *Foreign Relations,* 1885, pp. 285–289, 293, 294–300, 300–311. See also a report by Tisdel in *Consular Reports,* 16, no. 54 (July 1885), pp. 331–337 and Pletcher, *The Awkward Years,* pp. 344–345.

Lieutenant Emory H. Taunt, commissioned by the Navy to conduct explorations in the Congo area, was a bit more optimistic than Tisdel. He insisted that the immense wealth of Africa had not been exaggerated, but his comments were more cautious than expansive. See "Up the Congo," *New York Herald,* Dec. 31, 1885; letter from Secretary of the Navy W. C. Whitney, with Taunt's report, *Senate Executive Document 77,* 49th Cong., 2d sess. (Feb. 5, 1887), pp. 39–41.

felt that the United States had too long stood "silently and idly by in seeing our rivals . . . and competitors in the world cover the globe." "I think," he added, "we ought to adopt a different and a better policy." Senator John Sherman of Ohio categorically asserted that the Congo was the most "interesting" of any region still open for exploration and occupation by civilized nations. It was apparent that the United States, or at least a segment of it, was anxious that the door to economic riches in Africa be left open for the profit of all nations. This popular aspect of American thinking, later called the "open door" principle, was manifest even in Africa.[24]

Although American policy vis-à-vis the Dark Continent was not wholly consistent and (as our participation at Berlin attests) was limited to commercial and humanitarian considerations, the United States *had* become involved. The country refused to cooperate officially in the partitioning of Africa, but it had anxious moments over the possibility that it might be excluded from Africa's trade. Commodore Shufeldt followed the trail blazed by Stanley, but the fruits of his enterprise and the realization of Africa's potentialities would not be fully obtained until after the passage of many years. Although our trade with Africa remained relatively small until well into the twentieth century, the *New York Herald*, in 1889, said that the Dark Continent would become the next fertile field for American enterprise. Another newspaper predicted that "in the end the indomitable energy of the white man will conquer and hold this mysterious land and all its treasures." As the interests of Americans in this "last unconquered spot on the earth" expanded, political responsibility would be harder to avoid.[25]

---

[24] *Congressional Record,* 50th Cong., 1st sess. (June 28, 1888), 19, pt. 6, 5671–5672.

[25] Olton, "Problems of American Foreign Relations in the African Area," p. 340; "Africa Five Hundred Years From Now," *New York Herald,* Aug. 30, 1889; *Atlanta Constitution,* Aug. 24, 1888.

For a brief analysis of American interest in Africa, see Clarence Clendenen, Robert Collins, and Peter Duignan, *Americans in Africa, 1865–1900* (Stanford, 1966), passim.

CHAPTER 10

The Persistent
Monroe Doctrine:
Increasing Involvement
in Latin America

Between the time of Appomattox and Manila Bay, activity south of the Rio Grande warranted the constant interest and concern of the United States. While America's attitude toward Europe remained ambivalent, our Latin America policy was firmly encased in the framework of the Monroe Doctrine. John A. Kasson, for instance, felt that the Monroe Doctrine represented the supreme, indisputable, irreversible judgment of the United States. That doctrine had been expanded, however, since the days of Monroe. Some Americans now believed that the United States should not intervene only in instances of direct European aggression but also in cases of indirect European pressure.[1]

Secretary Blaine's constant interest in America's role "as the natural protector of Central American integrity," as well as her growing commercial involvement in that area, no doubt added to the importance of the Monroe Doctrine. Yet one impressive success was

---

[1] "The Monroe Doctrine in South America," *New York Herald,* Sept. 19, 1887; John A. Kasson, "The Monroe Doctrine," *North American Review* 133 (Sept. 1881): 241–254; *Buffalo Express,* Dec. 5, 1881; H. C. Bunts, "The Scope of the Monroe Doctrine," *Forum* 7 (Apr. 1889): 192–200.

probably most responsible for its wider popularity—when, during the Civil War, the government of Napoleon III established a French protectorate in Mexico. On the pretext of imposing a stable government, Napoleon installed the Austrian Archduke, Maximilian, as puppet emperor. After the collapse of the Confederacy, the State Department made it clear to the French government that the Maximilian regime was in violation of American policy and would not be tolerated, and the subsequent French troop removal was viewed by Gilded Age America as an important victory for the Monroe Doctrine. This success of the doctrine, and its support by both major political parties, helped make the Monroe Doctrine a cardinal tenet of American foreign policy.[2]

The importance of the areas to the south was again highlighted by the War of the Pacific (1879–1883) and the role this country played in trying to terminate that conflict. At war against Bolivia and Peru over rival claims to guano and nitrate deposits, Chile easily emerged the victor. When Peru rejected the latter's peace proposals, the United States began mediation efforts, which would culminate in a pitiful story of blundering diplomacy. Secretary Blaine's attempts to play the role of impartial mediator only increased the distrust which the squabbling nations had for the northern colossus. The American ministers accredited to the several countries involved seemed more committed to the nations to which they were assigned and their territorial aspirations than to arranging an impartial peace. They merely complicated the situation, like the proverbial bull in the china shop.[3]

Fear of European intervention, and the subsequent loss of markets in South America, pushed the United States into the conflict. According to our representative in Peru, the Monroe Doctrine would become a myth in South America unless the United States intervened.

---

[2] *Foreign Relations,* 1881, p. 599; John B. Sherman, *Recollections of Forty Years in the House, Senate, and Cabinet* (Chicago, London, New York, Berlin, 1895), pp. 1057–1058.

[3] Herbert Millington, *American Diplomacy and the War of the Pacific* (New York, 1948), pp. 9, 30; see also *Senate Executive Document* 181, 47th Cong., 1st sess., for the Trescot mission, as well as *Senate Executive Document* 79, 47th Cong., 1st sess.; *House Report* 1790, 47th Cong., 1st sess. See also Pletcher, *The Awkward Years,* chap. 3, 5; Dulles, *Prelude to World Power,* p. 40.

Perry Belmont, chairman of the House Foreign Affairs Committee, summed up the situation:

> The treatment of the questions arising out of the . . . war between Chili and Peru and Bolivia . . . contrived . . . to gamble away the moral influence of the United States in South America, and to discredit American diplomacy throughout the world, but [also has opened] the way to a direct European interference in South American affairs.[4]

The State Department also feared European intervention, with some justification. In response to Bismarck's suggestion that the United States, England, and Germany make a joint attempt to enforce a peace, Andrew D. White, our minister at Berlin, promptly cited Washington's Farewell Address. Traditional American policy implied unilateral action. Blaine parried a similar peace proposal from the President of the French republic, stating that this kind of intervention was common only in European diplomacy. The American republics were "the younger sisters" of the United States, politically, commercially and geographically, and the United States' interest in the region necessarily transcended that of other nations. Yet the United States was in a quandary. As the *New York Herald* pointed out, the country could neither wash its hands of the South American imbroglio nor intervene in a forceful manner. Nonetheless, American mediation efforts were quickened because of the danger of foreign intervention. The American minister to Peru, Isaac D. Christiancy, wrote Blaine that the United States had only two alternatives if it wished to continue "to control the commerce of Peru and to preserve a commanding or even material influence" in that region. Either the United States must intervene and establish a peace (without the danger of European aggression) or it must convert Peru into an American protectorate.[5]

---

[4] *Senate Executive Document* 79, 47th Cong., 1st sess.; Dyer, *Public Career of William M. Evarts,* pp. 229–230; Millington, *American Diplomacy and the War of the Pacific,* pp. 34, 53; Isaac D. Christiancy to Blaine, May 4, 1881, *Foreign Relations,* 1881, pp. 899–904; Belmont, *An American Democrat: The Recollections of Perry Belmont,* p. 221.

[5] Andrew Dickson White, *Autobiography,* 1: 596; Blaine to L. P. Morton, Sept. 5, 1881, quoted in Blaine, *Political Discussions: Legislative, Diplo-*

Several months later, in the fall of 1881, General Stephen J. Hurlbut was dispatched as minister to Peru, and he too urged Blaine to intervene in order to save the Lima government. Hurlbut also suggested that an American coaling station be established in Chimbote Bay, a plan which Blaine disavowed. Indeed, by December 1881 Secretary Blaine found it necessary to send William H. Trescot and his son, Walker Blaine, on a special mission to repair the damage done by the impetuous Hurlbut. These envoys were directed to make it clear that the President did not wish to dictate to South America. On the contrary, the White House was merely following the nonintervention policy laid down by George Washington! However, these efforts at mediation ended in complete failure. The mission was recalled in disgust, and in October 1883 Chile imposed a harsh peace upon Peru and Bolivia. Despite the fact that American diplomacy failed to bring about the desired results, our concern with this conflict reflected more than our growing commercial and strategic maturity and jealous insistence that all facets of the Monroe Doctrine be observed. The chance that Peru might appeal to Europe for assistance made a distinct impression on the United States.[6]

Although Blaine was unwilling to go so far as to demand a base in Latin America, considerable support for such a project existed well before the keels of the Great White Fleet had been laid. Even the Hayes administration, which certainly was not dominated by expansionism, showed ambitions in this direction. In 1880, a House resolution authorized the Secretary of the Navy to secure coaling stations and harbors at "proper points" on the Atlantic and Pacific coasts of Central America and on the Isthmus of Panama. Secretary

matic, and Popular, 1856–1886 (Norwich, Conn., 1887), pp. 401–402; Christiancy to Blaine, May 4, 1881, *Foreign Relations,* 1881, pp. 889–904; "Another Chapter of Our South American Diplomacy," *New York Herald,* Oct. 6, 1883.

[6] See Seward W. Livermore, "American Strategy Diplomacy in the South Pacific, 1890–1914," *Pacific Historical Review* 12 (1943): 33–41. See *Foreign Relations,* 1881, p. 938, for Hurlbut's message to Blaine (Oct. 5, 1881) on the Chimbote station. Tyler, *Foreign Policy of James G. Blaine,* pp. 118–120; Millington, *American Diplomacy and the War of the Pacific,* pp. 87, 89, 95; Frelinghuysen to Trescot, Jan. 9, 1882, *Instructions, Chile,* vol. 16, no. 6; Trescot to Frelinghuysen, June 5, 1882, *Despatches, Chile,* vol. 31, no. 26. For Hurlbut's apologia, see his *Meddling and Muddling—Mr. Blaine's Foreign Policy* (New York, 1884), p. 68.

of the Navy Richard W. Thompson contended that, since our material wealth was in large degree a product of ocean commerce, Congress should extend protection to shipbuilding and commercial interests. Therefore one facet of this protection should be the establishment of naval bases in Latin America, where our trade was increasing at a rapid rate.[7]

The question of bases soon became linked with our general policy in Central America, and refueling stations were potential items in international bartering. For example, President Justo Rufino Barrios of Guatemala expected to win American support for the modernization of his country and for the settlement of border disputes with Mexico by assisting America in the acquisition of naval bases. In this case, however, our minister informed Blaine that Barrios' proposition for bases in the provinces of Chiapas and Soconusco was impractical because of their doubtful utility to the United States.[8]

The desire for naval bases was also coupled with the demand for an American-owned interocean canal and with resentment at the restrictions of the Clayton-Bulwer treaty. In the fall of 1882, President Arthur directed Captain Seth L. Phelps, USN, to secure from Nicaragua—as part of the overall Nicaraguan canal project—islands in Lake Nicaragua to serve as coaling and refitting stations for our navy. *La Tribuna*, the chief anti-American organ in Nicaragua, sardonically charged that "the great republic" to the north was rearing its proud crest over the Atlantic and Pacific shores and casting its "protecting" arms about countries that otherwise would be quickly "swallowed up" by other governments. Although the Phelps mission proved abortive, Secretary Frelinghuysen two years later requested our minister in Nicaragua to reopen negotiations for coaling stations. These plans also proved premature, but the idea lingered; and in 1889 the superintendent of the Nicaraguan Railroad Company suggested that a Costa Rican island (Cocos), 100

---

[7] *House Journal*, 46th Cong., 2d sess. (Apr. 12, 1880), p. 1006; *Annual Report of the Secretary of the Navy*, 1880, pp. 24–26, 34.

[8] J. Fred Rippy, "Relations of the United States and Guatemala during the Epoch of Justo Rufino Barrios," *Hispanic American Historical Review* 22 (1942): 595–605; Cornelius P. Logan to Blaine, May 2, 1881, *Despatches, Central America*, vol. 17, no. 177.

miles west of Nicaragua in the Pacific, would make a "first class" American naval coaling station.[9]

While naval bases would provide security for American interests in Latin America, some Americans saw a union of the Central American states as a necessity for stability in that region. The ceaseless quarrels between Guatemala, Nicaragua, San Salvador, Honduras, and Costa Rica aroused fear that some European power would use the situation as an excuse for intervention. Moreover, such a union would not be permanent or solid unless the United States took a directing part. "Jingo Jim" Blaine, always on the lookout for more power in that area, argued that Central American union was needed to facilitate commerce, further the cause of republicanism and, of course, forestall European intervention.[10]

In a discussion of a quarrel between England and the Guatemalan Central Railroad, our representative in Guatemala complained of a British effort to discriminate against American trade in Central America. When Britain later made overtures toward the Mosquito Coast territory, Secretary Bayard informed our minister that the United States could not assent to any interference, indirect or direct, by Great Britain. Meanwhile, Blaine had denied that the United States had expansionist interests in this region. Rather, it was the chronic fear of foreign intervention that led the Department of State to request that it be promptly informed of rumors of such intervention. Though Blaine did not expect it to happen, he contended that such a danger was always present in view of Europe's financial investment in Central America. Thus general distrust of the overseas powers was a persistent theme in the diplomatic notes that passed between Washington and Central America.[11]

The press generally blessed pan-American schemes as consistent

---

[9] *Special Missions, Department of State,* 3 (Sept. 23, 1882), 347–349; Phelps to F. J. Medina, Minister of Foreign Affairs, Nov. 10, 1882, *Special Missions, Department of State,* vol. 3; Frelinghuysen to Hall, Apr. 7, 1884, *Instructions, Central America,* vol. 18, no. 136; P. W. Chamberlain to Blaine, June 20, 1889, *Miscellaneous Letters, Department of State.*

[10] Blaine to Logan, May 7, 1881, *Instructions, Central America,* vol. 18, no. 145.

[11] Logan to Evarts, Jan. 9, 1881, *Despatches, Central America,* vol. 17, no. 134; Logan to Blaine, June 2, 1881, ibid. For a discussion of miscellaneous Latin American-Central American relationships, see Pletcher, *The Awkward Years,* chap. 4 passim, 6, 10 passim, 16.

with our traditional hegemony over the area. The *New York Herald* thought such a union was worthy of the best efforts of all the statesmen in the American republics. It also reproved the United States, as an "elder republic," for being remiss in its duty toward South and Central America. Minister Cornelius A. Logan, who was even more enthusiastic than Blaine for Central American union, wrote in answer to the secretary's early declaration of our policy: "Your dispatch so clearly foreshadows a more vigorous policy, as to give one renewed hope that something substantial may be accomplished for these miserable people." The Secretary of State's final instruction to an American diplomat prior to the latter's departure was "I have but one instruction to give you . . . do what you can to unite those Central American States." Some felt so strongly about Central American unity that it was suggested the navy might well stand by to assist in such efforts.[12]

Still further testimony of America's interest to the south was the plan urged by Blaine for closer cooperation among all states of the Western Hemisphere. Whatever positive place in history James G. Blaine occupies rests not upon his florid oratory but, rather, on his part in the early foundation of the Good Neighbor Policy. Following Henry Clay's suggestion of sixty-two years earlier, Blaine summoned the first inter-American conference, in Washington in March 1882, to promote permanent and lasting peace, as well as friendship and commerce. One congressman dramatically insisted that such a policy was essential "in the name of American commerce, American manufacturers, American progress, American statesmanship, American honor, and all American interests." But Blaine maintained that America's sole motive was humane: to help save the Latin countries from internecine struggles. He assured a skeptical world that the United States did not assume the role of counselor, nor did it desire to become the protector of its neighbors. A recent student of Blaine's diplomacy has asserted, however, that there is a strong likelihood that Blaine was partly motivated to call such a conference to paper over his earlier South American blunders.[13]

---

[12] "A New Effort for a South American Union," *New York Herald,* Oct. 19, 1878; Logan to Blaine, July 7, 1881, *Despatches, Central America,* vol. 17, no. 188; Mizener to Blaine, Oct. 28, 1889, ibid., vol. 31, no. 39; "Central American Disturbances," *Cleveland Plain Dealer,* Apr. 1, 1885.

[13] See U.S. Department of State, *The International American Conference*

Some congressmen, too, grasped the importance of closer inter-American relations. As early as 1879 the New Jersey legislature sent Congress a resolution advocating that measures be taken to develop further commercial intercourse between the two American continents. Similar resolutions were soon forthcoming on Capitol Hill. In 1882, for example, one measure called for the Secretary of State to negotiate a reciprocity treaty between the United States and Central or South America. In April of that year, a bill was introduced authorizing the creation of a special commission to promote commercial intercourse and railroad ties between the two continents. Unfortunately, these and numerous other resolutions and bills were referred to committees, and apparently perished there. The *New York Herald* observed that, while it was unwise to enter into the sort of political relationships that would lead to protectorates, it would be even more foolhardy to allow potential trade to escape from our hands.[14]

In addition to such support, there was constant criticism. One editorial referred to Blaine's plan as a sentimental notion based upon a private pecuniary interest. Another critic thought it was anomalous that the United States, pledged to an unreasonably high tariff, should talk so much about closer commercial relations. Imperialistic ambitions were also attributed to Blaine. Some critics suggested that, if the secretary were a Frenchman, he could well have been a political opportunist like the Third French Republic's "Man on Horseback," Georges Boulanger. The inter-American congress was described by this source as a piece of "political claptrap, a pyrotechnic exhibition" on Blaine's part. Godkin's *Nation* was so anti-

(Washington, 1890); Tyler, *Foreign Policy of James G. Blaine*, pp. 165 ff.; Theodore Clarke Smith, *The Life and Letters of James Abram Garfield*, 2 vols. (New Haven, 1925), 2: 1166–1168; *Congressional Record*, 47th Cong., 2d sess. (Feb. 15, 1883), 14, pt. 4, A46–51 (remarks of Rep. James B. Belford of Colorado); M. M. De Meza, M.D., New York City, to Blaine, Apr. 12, 1881, *Miscellaneous Letters, Department of State;* Russell H. Bastert, "A New Approach to the Origins of Blaine's Pan-American Policy," *Hispanic American Historical Review* 39 (Aug. 1959): 375–412.

[14] *Senate Journal*, 46th Cong., 1st sess. (Mar. 24, 1879), p. 25; *Congressional Record*, 47th Cong., 1st sess. (Feb. 8, 1882), 13, pt. 1, p. 978; ibid. (Apr. 24, 1882), pt. 4, p. 3209; "A Congress of the Three Americas," *New York Herald*, Oct. 4, 1889.

Blaine that it predicted only "empty talk" would come from the meeting. The British, as a matter of course, regarded the conference as the biggest farce of the season.[15]

The subsequent history of the pan-American Conference is familiar. Secretary Frelinghuysen canceled the invitations, and the intervening years, from 1882 to 1889, saw commissions proposed and bills introduced dealing with such subjects as railroads, customs unions, and commercial and arbitration congresses. By an unforeseen turn of events, Blaine was back at the State Department in time to preside at the long-awaited congress in October 1889. On the whole, the conference was disappointing, arousing much European antagonism, becoming enmeshed with domestic problems, and rejecting many far-reaching proposals. It did, however, accept an arbitration plan, and established what in time came to be called the Pan American Union.[16]

Much of the press praised the conference. A proposed international railroad to connect the Americas was looked upon with much favor. The rise of cities along its route would spell the end of isolationism, which was pictured as the handmaiden of ignorance. While the annexation of people who did not speak English was undesirable, there was no reason for not trading with nations who shared similar interests. One journal commented that the conference was the "only solid chunk of statesmanship heaved at the people from Washington in many a long year." Andrew Carnegie, a delegate to the earlier conference, asserted that no act of the Harrison administration was likely to exert so great an influence for the welfare of the American continent as the conference, which in his view anticipated the coming brotherhood of man. Carnegie felt that arbitration provisions and a customs union were important accomplishments. He was, however, practical enough to pressure for a steamship

---

[15] "The Conference Vagary," *New York Times,* Apr. 12, 1886; "The American People Will Enter into No Entangling Alliances," *New York Herald,* Oct. 10, 1889; *The Nation* 41 (May 9, 1889): 376; "The Pan-American Congress," *New Haven Evening Register,* Nov. 26, 1889.

[16] Russell H. Bastert, "Diplomatic Reversal: Frelinghuysen's Opposition to Blaine's Pan-American Policy in 1882," *MVHR* 42 (Mar. 1956): 653–671; Pan-American Act, May 24, 1888, *U.S. Statutes at Large,* 25: 155–156. See also J. Lloyd Mecham, *The United States and Inter-American Security, 1889–1960* (Austin, Tex., 1961), pp. 48–57.

line between North and Central and South America in order to capture the intercontinental trade.[17]

Unhappily, E. L. Godkin was typical of a sizable segment of the press that could find no good in Blaine's efforts. Despite the conference's announced aim to secure commerce and stabilize the peace among our southern neighbors, Godkin dubbed the congress a piece of diplomatic meddling. To be sure, Blaine's political opportunism and big-business orientation rendered him in some ways unfit for the exercise of the impartial deliberation so essential in diplomacy.[18] Yet it is in the matter of the inter-American congress and the resultant reciprocity movement that Blaine's positive plans for Latin America can be best discerned. His was an era of transition, combining a vestigial belief in manifest destiny with the newer mercantilistic spirit of post–1870 Europe. While Blaine was eager to further the domination of the United States in the Western Hemisphere, he seems also to have been a genuine advocate of international peace.

American attempts to unite various states in the Southern Hemisphere coincided with increased relations with each nation. While relations with Argentina were not intimate or cordial, the United States expressed neighborly interest in its welfare. An eagerness to offer mediation and arbitration during various hostilities involving Argentina was the principal manifestation of this good will. Although commerce between the two nations remained at a low level until the 1890s, American agents made repeated efforts to increase trade, and the annual messages of Presidents Arthur, Cleveland, and Harrison appealed for more congressional aid for American shipping lines to Argentina. Domingo F. Sarmiento, President of Argentina in the early 1870s and a firm protagonist of "northamericanization," helped inspire greater cordiality in American-Argentinian relations.[19]

---

[17] "An International Railroad," *Memphis Advocate,* Mar. 3, 1890; *Pittsburgh National Labor Tribune,* July 13, 1889; Andrew Carnegie to Blaine, Apr. 20, July 22, 1889, Blaine MSS.

[18] "More of Blaine's International Law," *The Nation* 34 (Mar. 30, 1882): 264; Tyler, *Foreign Policy of Blaine,* p. 189.

[19] Thomas F. McGann, *Argentina, The United States, and the Inter-American System, 1880–1914* (Cambridge, Mass., 1957), pp. 85 ff.; Harold F. Peterson, *Argentina and the United States, 1810–1960* (Albany, 1964), pp. 205, 207, 216, 222, 230.

With the pro-American feeling that accompanied the politically and economically stable Porfirio Díaz regime, which began in Mexico in 1876, our official attitude toward that country combined respect for her territorial sovereignty and a disclaimer of our need for additional land. The central problem threatening relations between the United States and Mexico during the Gilded Age was the raids of bandits and cattle thieves along the Rio Grande border. Indeed, Secretary of State Evarts felt "the first duty of a government is to protect life and property. . . . Protection . . . of American lives and property is the sole point upon which the United States is tenacious." Thus "hot pursuit" of Mexican marauders in safeguarding life and property became standard practice, and occasional war cries rose on both sides of the border. To some Mexicans, the United States was the "rapacious northern giant," and the American press often confirmed this impression. After a punitive border raid in 1875, for example, the *Cleveland Leader* threatened that if Mexico refused to do its duty and let our federal troops punish the guilty, we would have to "give the greaser government another lesson." During a similar crisis in August 1886, the *Minneapolis Tribune* commented that a second Mexican war would be popular in the United States, if only to serve the interests of railroad and mining magnates. Acting in character, young Theodore Roosevelt offered to raise some cavalry companies of riflemen.[20]

---

[20] For a full treatment of the United States-Mexican border dispute, see Robert D. Gregg, *The Influence of Border Trouble on Relations between the United States and Mexico, 1875–1910,* Johns Hopkins University Studies in History and Political Science, 55, no. 3 (Baltimore, 1937), 375–564. See also Barrows, *William M. Evarts; Lawyer, Diplomat, Statesman,* pp. 350–362; Dyer, *Public Career of William M. Evarts,* pp. 194–202; John W. Foster, *Diplomatic Memoirs,* 2 vols. (New York, 1909), 1 : 92–93; Chester C. Kesier, "John Watson Foster, United States Minister to Mexico, 1873–1880" (Ph.D. dissertation, American University, 1953).

Evarts to Foster, Aug. 13, 1878, quoted in Francis B. Wharton, *Digest of International Law,* 8 vols. (Washington, 1906), 1 : 232; Foster to Evarts, June 22, 30, 1877, *Despatches, Mexico,* vol. 59 in Dyer, *Evarts,* p. 196; *Cleveland Leader,* Dec. 27, 1875; "As to a War with Mexico," *Minneapolis Tribune,* Aug. 13, 1886; "The South and a Mexican War," ibid., Aug. 20, 1886; Theodore Roosevelt to Henry Cabot Lodge, Aug. 10, 1886, in Lodge, ed., *Selections from the Correspondence of Theodore Roosevelt and Henry Cabot Lodge, 1884–1918,* 1 : 44–45.

For an excellent analysis of American-Mexican relations during the Díaz regime, see Daniel Cosío Villegas, *The United States versus Porfirio Díaz*

Generally speaking, certain groups, smarting under Mexican treatment, wished to force hostilities. This was usually true of certain holders of Mexican mining and railroad franchises, militaristically minded Americans, idle Confederate veterans, some Catholic clerics, and certain bellicose politicians. One element of the population undoubtedly felt that a "just war" with Mexico would be vastly popular because it could consolidate the Union and wipe out the last lingering bitterness arising from the Civil War. But conquest or annexation a la Roosevelt did not materialize. The stability of the Díaz regime brought increased respect for Mexico and further American economic investments in that nation. Other elements contributed to the desire for peace. The United States, one group pointed out, had adequate territory, and experience with unassimilable Chinese coolies and the flood of newer immigrants made many Americans loath to add further disparate elements to our variegated population. Even the *Catholic World* predicted that the annexation of Mexico would be disastrous. The *Buffalo Express* thought a war with Mexico would be barren of results unless territory was desired— which, it emphatically added, was not the case.[21]

The Mexican market aroused more interest in the United States than the annexation of Mexican territory. Even those who desired an intimate political relationship with Mexico saw commercial liaison as a prerequisite. A nation that was about to become the leading manufacturing country of the world was anxious for a *Zollverein* with a neighbor who could buy much and sell little. Between 1883 and 1884, for example, American exports to Mexico increased by $3.25 million dollars. Recognizing the importance of the Mexican market, the State Department continually expressed concern about European interference. Secretary Blaine warned Minister Philip H. Morgan that the great surge of foreign interest in Mexico could

(Lincoln, Neb., 1963). Cosío Villegas's work is based on Mexican and American sources and emphasizes the struggle between American diplomats and the Mexican Foreign Ministry over the questions of special concessions for Americans, border raids, and the claims of both countries.

[21] "The Mexican Border Grievances," *The Nation* 27 (Aug. 29, 1878): 125–126; Edwards Pierrepont to Bayard, Aug. 21, 1886, Bayard MSS; Evarts to Foster, Aug. 13, 1878, *Instructions, Mexico,* vol. 19, no. 495; "The Reciprocal Needs of Mexico and the United States," *New York Herald,* Feb. 27, 1883; "The United States and Mexico," *Catholic World* 34 (Mar. 1882): 721–731; *Buffalo Express,* Nov. 29, 1877.

well get out of hand. Morgan responded that he constantly spoke to Mexican businessmen about the benefits to be gained by closer American relations, but he believed that, because the United States was not predominantly Roman Catholic, it was discriminated against by the Mexicans.[22]

Whatever the reasons for discrimination, commercial reciprocity seemed to many to be the answer to the difficulties in trade relations. Indeed, reciprocity talk became a staple of almost every congressional session during the Gilded Age. For example, in 1877 Senator Roscoe Conkling offered a resolution for the appointment of a committee which would report on measures to promote commercial intercourse with Mexico. Manufacturers' associations constantly pressured for the appointment of a congressional committee or subcommittee to look into more direct commercial relations between the countries. In 1878, a resolution was passed calling for the Secretary of State and the Postmaster General to inform the House of Representatives about commercial and postal relations with South America, particularly with Mexico.[23]

The threat to American trade by European merchants was usually sufficient to shock American producers and legislators alike into action. *Bradstreet's,* a commercial journal, wondered why Europe should monopolize trade between two countries that were separated by no more than an easily forded stream. The *New York Herald* proposed an "invasion" of Mexico by American merchants armed with sample cases. Mexico was generally pictured as an almost virgin outlet for the products of America's industrial might. Secretary Frelinghuysen even favored discussing the possibilities of transporting Mexican produce on American rail lines. Northern interests had consolidated our Southern railroads, and could do the same across the Rio Grande. A veritable "railway invasion" of Mexico was at

---

[22] "Relations with Mexico," *New Orleans Daily Picayune,* Mar. 23, 1889; *Boston Economist,* 9 (Feb. 17, 1883), 99; Blaine to Morgan, June 16, 1881, *Instructions, Mexico,* vol. 20, no. 137; Philip H. Morgan to Blaine, Aug. 13, 1881, *Despatches, Mexico,* vol. 73, no. 254. See also Joseph Nimmo, *Commerce between the United States and Mexico* (Washington, 1884).

[23] *Congressional Record,* 45th Cong., 2d sess. (Dec. 11, 1877), 7, pt. 1, 120. In 1884, reciprocity arrangements were finally ratified (*Senate Executive Journal,* 29 [Mar. 11, 1884], 209–212); *Senate Journal,* 45th Cong., 3d sess. (Dec. 16, 1878), p. 56; *Congressional Record,* 45th Cong., 3d sess. (Dec. 4, 1878), 8, pt. 1, 32.

hand, and the *Chicago Tribune*, always concerned with the special interest Chicago had in the Mexican trade, predicted that the United States would find a tremendous market to the south with immense potentialities. The *San Francisco Evening Bulletin* reminded its readers that "capital does not stop at State boundaries" and that a new era of railroad and mining development in Mexico, under American auspices, would soon become a reality. *Dixie*, a Southern commercial journal, even went so far as to dispatch a special agent to Mexico to assist in the distribution of that magazine.[24]

While Congress discussed commercial reciprocity with Mexico, the Caribbean islands were attracting the attention of American expansionists and businessmen. Officially, the United States declined to play an active role in this area, preferring to maintain its role of backdoor guardian of Caribbean territorial integrity. Congressional opposition to Grant's attempt to annex Santo Domingo no doubt strengthened this stand. When President Salomon of Haiti offered to cede to the United States the island of La Fortue, the Arthur administration declined the offer. Haiti was referred to as our good neighbor and sister republic, and because she was peopled by Negroes her experiment in popular government was all the more interesting. However, some were not anxious to forgo a new source of wealth, and Haiti became a goal for expansionists. As a protectorate, Haiti could absorb discontented American Negroes, and would certainly prove no more embarrassing than the protectorate the United States had, in practice, over Liberia.[25]

---

[24] "The Proposed Mexican Reciprocity Treaty," *Bradstreet's* 8 (Oct. 27, 1883): 258; "Proposed Invasion of Mexico," *New York Herald*, Dec. 30, 1878; "Chicago and Mexico," *Chicago Tribune*, Apr. 20, 1883; "Letter-Books of Frederick T. Frelinghuysen," vol. 4, Jan. 13, 1883, Frelinghuysen MSS, Library of Congress; "American Railroads into Mexico," *Chicago Tribune*, Jan. 8, 1881; "Closer Relations with Mexico," *San Francisco Evening Bulletin*, Jan. 26, 1881; *Dixie* 5 (June 1889): 420. See also Jules Davids, "American Political and Economic Penetration of Mexico, 1877–1920," (Ph.D. dissertation, Georgetown University, 1947), passim.

The leading American interests in Mexico were summarized by Consul David H. Strother (Strother to Hunter, Oct. 24, 1884, *Consular Despatches, Mexico City*, no. 247): two international railroad companies; mercantile houses dealing in arms, agricultural implements, machinery, hardware, furniture, and sundries; several houses dealing in sewing machines and fancy goods; branches of the American Life Insurance Company and Equitable Life; two American newspapers; and American mining interests in Hidalgo.

[25] *Senate Executive Document 64*, 49th Cong., 2d sess., p. 15; "The Revo-

Although Haiti attracted some interest, Cuba, the Pearl of the Antilles, received more persistent interest from American expansionists. President Grant gave several reasons for this concern in his discussion of the island's Ten Years' War (1868–1878) against Spain:

> The protracted continuance of this strife seriously affects the interests of all commercial nations, but those of the United States more than others, by reason of close proximity, its larger trade . . . with Cuba, and the frequent and intimate personal and social relations which have grown up between its citizens and those of the island.

In addition, many feared that a strong foreign power in control of Cuba could convert the Gulf of Mexico into a *mare clausum*. Because Cuba lay broadside to our commerce with Latin America, this fear was not overlooked by various ambitious merchants. The *Atlanta Constitution* remarked that "when this ripe plum gets ready to drop into Columbia's [the United States'] lap, it is not likely that there will be any protest on the part of our Republic." [26]

Not all Americans, however, wished to exert American domination over Cuba. The *Springfield* (Mass.) *Daily Republican*, tired of hearing of the "need" for Cuba, protested that we should be concerned only with peace in Cuba, abolition of its slavery, and freedom of commerce with the island. The *New York Times* declared that Madrid was wrong in thinking that the United States hungered for Cuba, while its sister daily, the *Herald*, maintained that it would be a great misfortune to annex Cuba, even if it came as a gift. The problem of defense, the differences in governmental institutions,

---

lution in Hayti," *New York Herald,* Dec. 13, 1888; George Prothwell to Blaine, June 18, 1899, *Miscellaneous Letters, Department of State;* Blaine to Harrison, Aug. 10, 1891, quoted in Volwiler, *The Correspondence between Benjamin Harrison and James G. Blaine, 1882–1893* (Philadelphia, 1940), pp. 173–174; "Our Commercial Relations with Hayti," *Chicago Tribune,* Mar. 29, 1889; *House Journal,* 46th Cong., 3d sess. (Jan. 10, 1881), p. 151. For a fuller treatment of American-Haitian relations, see Ludwell Lee Montague, *Haiti and the United States, 1714–1938* (Durham, N.C., 1940).

[26] *Foreign Relations,* 1875, annual message, vol. 1; General Thomas Jordan, "Why We Need Cuba," *Literary Digest* 3 (July 11, 1891): 281–282; "Annexation of Cuba," *Public Opinion* 3 (Oct. 8, 1887): 551.

and Cuba's heterogeneous population became arguments against annexation.[27]

Yet most Americans were not averse to establishing American commercial supremacy in the island, for such an arrangement would give the United States the advantages of annexation without its responsibilities. Tradewise, Cuba seemed to gravitate toward the United States by virtue of proximity, but Spain required her to buy most of her goods from the motherland. But the situation was somewhat improved by the signing of a reciprocity treaty between the United States and Spain on January 2, 1884, which American commercial circles viewed as a triumph of diplomacy, as a foretaste of a long-held dream of commercial union which would eventually embrace the whole North American continent.[28]

The increasing attention which the United States directed southward during the Gilded Age was a portent of a more aggressive policy that was to characterize the early twentieth century. Curiously, neither Central American union nor any of the other projects discussed above were strong enough to produce this change. Rather, it was the isthmian canal issue which finally stimulated a bolder Latin American policy. One periodical was not far from the truth when it predicted, in 1884, that canal diplomacy would require an overhaul of our entire foreign policy.[29]

The idea of uniting the two great oceans, at the isthmus or elsewhere in Central America, was a hardy perennial. In 1846, New Granada (later Colombia) offered the United States transit rights across the isthmus in return for an American guarantee of Colombian sovereignty over the area. The Senate approved this arrangement, but intense rivalry between Great Britain and the United States over a Nicaraguan route helped prevent construction of a canal on the Colombian site. The Nicaraguan route, with its natural, sea-level waterways, appeared to have more potential than the Colombian route. Construction of a canal was also stalled by the

[27] *Springfield* (Mass.) *Daily Republican*, Nov. 23, 1875; *New York Times,* Dec. 4, 1879; "Who Wants Cuba?" *New York Herald,* May 9, 1885.

[28] V. Perry Atwill, "Our Hold on Cuba," *North American Review* 146 (May 1888): 581–582; Ramon O. Williams, vice-consul general, to F. W. Seward, Aug. 8, 1878, *Consular Despatches, Havana,* no. 968; *Bradstreet's* 10 (Dec. 6, 1884): 356–357; *Buffalo Express,* Nov. 21, 1884.

[29] "The Nicaragua Treaty," *Watchman* 44 (Dec. 25, 1884).

Clayton-Bulwer treaty, by which the United States and Great Britain agreed never to obtain or maintain exclusive control over such a route. This is how matters stood at mid-century.

After the interruption of the Civil War and with the opening of the Suez Canal in 1871, canal advocates in the New World renewed their pressure. In the next year, President Grant obtained senatorial approval for an Interoceanic Canal Commission to evaluate earlier canal surveys, and in 1876 the commission concluded its study with a recommendation of the Nicaraguan route.

External events also intensified American discussion of the canal route. In the late 1870s the aging but still dashing hero of the Suez Canal, Ferdinand De Lesseps, began organizing a private company, with Colombia's approval, to build a canal in Panama. American alarm mounted at this European invasion of what was considered a private preserve of the United States under the Monroe Doctrine. De Lesseps attempted to allay American fears during a tour of this country in 1880, but President Hayes was not reassured. In a special message to Congress, he advocated strict American control over any projected canal.

One of the main priorities in American foreign policy now became the abrogation of the restrictive Clayton-Bulwer treaty. In December 1884, Secretary Frelinghuysen ignored the agreement with Britain in negotiating a treaty with Nicaragua granting exclusive rights for a jointly owned canal. The Senate rejected the treaty, however, and it was ultimately withdrawn by Grover Cleveland. American promoters then proceeded privately, through the Maritime Canal Company of Nicaragua. Despite the bankruptcy of De Lesseps's company, which ended serious competition, the American company eventually experienced financial difficulty. Governmental assistance was not forthcoming, and by 1893 all plans for American canal projects in the isthmus had foundered. The tortuous details of intricate canal diplomacy, involving politicians and intriguers in Paris, Panama, Managua, and Washington, continued into the twentieth century, but the arguments presented by partisans of particular routes remained the same. Like other forms of expansionism, "canal fever" had its beginnings in the Gilded Age.[30]

---

[30] For full details on the diplomacy of the canal, see *The Interoceanic Canal Correspondence, Senate Document* 237, 46th Cong., 1st sess. (contains

The growing American concern with isthmian affairs was reflected in the various readings given the Monroe Doctrine. Some maintained that the hallowed words of our forefathers prohibited United States involvement in any foreign complications, including canal construction. At the opposite extreme, others felt that the Monroe Doctrine encouraged the construction of a canal for the protection of American rights in Latin America. In between these two positions, a third group maintained that the doctrine allowed America to play a limited role in Latin American affairs. Those who subscribed to the "small policy" of America's role were rudely awakened by the attitude taken by both the government and the press regarding foreign interests in an American canal. The dichotomy which developed between the wish to steer clear of foreign troubles and the desire to own (or at least control) an interoceanic canal ushered in, as the *New York World* put it, a vexed and disagreeable chapter in our diplomacy.[31]

In an America so absorbed with domestic matters, it is not surprising that many found no room in their thinking for an adventurous canal policy. The *New York Times* thought the canal issue was purely commercial and denied that an American-owned canal was in keeping with the Monroe Doctrine concept against political controls by non-American states. In other words, the doctrine gave us no more right to exclusive sovereignty over the isthmus than to exclusive control of the Caribbean. One writer asserted that Monroe's principles had as much bearing on the canal issue as they had on construction of a viaduct to the moon. The *Times* could find no real

---

all documents to 1900); *Diplomatic History of the Panama Canal (1914)*, Senate Document 474, 63rd Cong., 2d sess.; *Correspondence in Relation to the Proposed Interoceanic Canal between the Atlantic and Pacific Oceans* (Washington, 1885); *Reports of the Diplomatic Bureau*, vol. 2 (Dec. 1878) (report by A. A. Adee).

The following secondary accounts are useful: Dexter Perkins, *The Monroe Doctrine, 1867–1907* (Baltimore, 1937), pp. 64 ff.; Perkins, *Hands Off: A History of the Monroe Doctrine* (Boston, 1946), pp. 162 ff.; Dwight A. Miner, *The Fight for the Panama Route* (New York, 1940); Gerstle Mack, *The Land Divided: A History of the Panama Canal and Other Isthmian Projects* (New York, 1944); Pletcher, *The Awkward Years*, chap. 2, 4 passim, 15.

[31] *Buffalo Express*, Jan. 12, 1885; "Concerning an Interoceanic Canal," *New York Herald*, Jan. 4, 1884; "The Panama Canal," *Public Opinion* 6 (Dec. 22, 1888): 214.

evidence that a European state proposed to interfere in the New World and it warned Americans that, if they expected Europe to mind its own business, the United States should set the example. The *Chicago Tribune* contended that it would be premature and ill advised to assert the Monroe Doctrine in arguments against a foreign-built canal, for such action would necessarily involve broader authority than the United States was ready to assume. The *Catholic World* even declared that, as far as a canal was concerned, there was no warrant in the doctrine for declaring that an independent nation in this hemisphere could not make concessions to European capitalists. The United States, it added, exercised no suzerainty over sovereign states in the Western Hemisphere, any more than it did over the nations of Europe. Hence some quarters were decidedly opposed to disturbing the status quo in this "piping time of peace." [32]

Despite disclaimers of interest, the imagination of many Americans evidently was fired by the prospect of an isthmian canal. Such limitations as the Clayton-Bulwer treaty posed only temporary problems, because the laws of progress required America's extension into Central America. The *New York Herald* predicted that the canal would be the "entering wedge" that would pry America loose from its traditional aloofness in foreign policy, and the *Buffalo Express* suggested that a canal would offset our ingrained parochialism. National pride was also a factor in canal discussions. De Lesseps's completion of the Suez Canal in 1869 sparked American competitiveness. What had been fashioned in the Old World could easily be duplicated in the New, and advocates of an American canal often referred to their project as the "brother" and "complement" of the Suez Canal. [33]

---

[32] "The Panama Canal Humbug," *Chicago Tribune,* Apr. 24, 1883; "A False Step Threatened," *New York Times,* Mar. 9, 1880; "The Interoceanic Canal and the Monroe Doctrine," *Atlanta Constitution,* Mar. 24, 1880; "The U.S. and Other Nations," *New York Times,* Feb. 9, 1881; "The Monroe Doctrine," *Chicago Tribune,* Feb. 11, 1880; "The Monroe Doctrine," *Catholic World* 31 (Apr. 1880): 116–133; *House Report* 4167, 50th Cong., 2d sess. (Mar. 2, 1889), p. 24.

[33] George W. Hobbs, "Clayton-Bulwer Treaty vs. the Monroe Doctrine," *Bay State Monthly,* 3 (Apr. 1885), 17–26; "A Foothold on the Isthmus," *New York Herald,* Feb. 14, 1880; *Buffalo Express,* Jan. 18, 1887; "The Interoceanic Canal," *Commercial and Financial Chronicle,* 28 (June 14, 1879), 588; "DeLesseps and the Interoceanic Canal," *Friends' Intelligencer,* 37 (Mar. 13, 1880), 57.

Even so cautious an observer as Godkin of *The Nation* came out in favor of an American-controlled canal. The *New York Times* publicized an interesting "pan-anglican idea," calling for English recognition of an American canal in exchange for American concessions to British commercial interests. The *Buffalo Daily Courier* contended that only England might dispute America's position, but, since England held Gibraltar, Aden, and the Suez, it could not justly interfere. The *New York Herald* advised Britain to "take another turn" at the Zulus or Boers or Afghans if it had to maintain its imperialistic policies in the "outer world." "She need not bother about this side of the sea. We are a good enough England for this hemisphere." [34]

The advantages of an American canal were clear. Farmers and merchants would benefit by the opening of an interocean canal since their products would be many days nearer the European and Atlantic coast markets. Indeed, the construction of a canal was linked to the new importance the West was assuming in American politics. A canal would assure the domination of the Pacific and its commerce by our West Coast ports, and optimists believed the Pacific coast alone would furnish enough business to render the enterprise profitable. The *Commercial and Financial Chronicle* felt that America ought to wish the canal project godspeed no matter by whom it was built, and whoever managed or protected it, because the profits from the venture would be American. If the United States was not going to build it, this should not hinder others from going ahead with the project. "With a territory washed by both oceans," our minister to Colombia wrote, "a waterway by means of . . . a canal . . . is to be desired, both on account of commercial as well as political reasons." [35]

With the exception of Grover Cleveland, the Presidents during

---

[34] "The United States Government and the Panama Canal," *The Nation* 30 (Feb. 5, 1880): 90–91; "The Pan-Anglican Idea," *New York Times,* Sept. 17, 1888; *Buffalo Daily Courier,* Dec. 18, 1880; "England and the Panama Canal," *New York Herald,* Jan. 16, 1882.

[35] *Congressional Record,* 47th Cong., 2d sess. (Feb. 5, 1883), 14, pt. 4, A33; H. C. Taylor, "The Control of the Pacific," *Forum* 3 (June 1887): 407–416; "The Isthmus Canal as a Commercial Enterprise," *New York Herald,* May 20, 1879; "Secretary Blaine and the Panama Canal," *Commercial and Financial Chronicle,* 33 (Oct. 29, 1881), 456–467; Ernest Dichman to Evarts, July 13, 1879, *Foreign Relations,* 1879, pp. 290–295.

the Gilded Age worked for an American-built canal. Out of office, Ulysses S. Grant spoke out in favor of the project. His analysis, in an article written for the *North American Review*, listed the advantages of a Nicaragua canal—commercial and political. The difficulties in Panama, he maintained, included floods, swamps, the need for tunnels and viaducts, and great distance from the United States.[36]

The interest evinced by President Rutherford B. Hayes was striking, for he was a conservative who was not given to supporting expansionist projects. Hayes believed that an isthmian canal, constructed and controlled by the United States, was necessary as a protective measure against European aggression. An isthmian canal was "virtually a part of the coastline of the United States," where a European power could not intervene without adopting measures running athwart the Monroe Doctrine. In his diary, President Hayes confided that the United States regarded all types of commercial communication across the isthmus as essential to its prosperity and safety. "It must be held and controlled by America," he wrote. Because of the peculiar commercial and strategic value to this country of a canal, Hayes asserted that our motto should be "either an American canal or no canal." [37]

In his inaugural address, President James A. Garfield took a less rigid position. He assured the world that the United States sought no exclusive privilege in any canal route, but he reaffirmed the "right and duty" of the United States to exercise full authority over such an isthmian project. His successor, Arthur, reaffirmed Hayes's position. Strongly in favor of a canal, Arthur termed it a matter of "grave national importance" and proposed immediate abrogation of the Clayton-Bulwer treaty.[38]

Characteristically cautious, Grover Cleveland was opposed to exercising American authority outside our own territory. He could

[36] U. S. Grant, "The Nicaragua Canal," *North American Review* 122 (Feb. 1881): 107–116.

[37] *Senate Executive Document* 112, 46th Cong., 2d sess. (1885); Richardson, *Messages and Papers,* 10: 4537–4538; Charles R. Williams, ed., *Diary and Letters of Rutherford Birchard Hayes,* 5 vols. (Columbus, O., 1922–1926), 3: 586, 587, 589.

[38] Richardson, *Messages and Papers,* 10: 4601 (Garfield), 4628 (Arthur); George F. Howe, *Chester A. Arthur,* p. 374.

not "recommend propositions involving paramount privileges of ownership or right outside of our own territory, when coupled with absolute . . . engagements to defend the territorial integrity of the state where such interests lie." Although Cleveland personally favored a canal, he believed that one constructed, owned, and operated by the United States would be inconsistent with its "dedication to universal and neutral use." His mild endorsement of the Clayton-Bulwer treaty gave logic to the charge made against him in the 1888 Murchison episode that he was an anglophile.[39]

The Secretaries of State (again with one exception) were equally zealous in safeguarding American rights and destiny vis-à-vis a canal. Always the prudent lawyer, William M. Evarts, while more temperate than President Hayes, maintained that the United States had a paramount interest in the region, and as the "great commercial and political power of America" must exert its control. Evarts regarded concessions to Great Britain in this region as incompatible with proper Colombian-American relations, and he instructed our minister to work constantly for modification of the 1846 treaty.[40]

James G. Blaine—as in other areas of diplomacy—unequivocally asserted America's right to construct and control an isthmian canal. He even prepared a circular, addressed to all American representatives in Europe, directing them, if necessary, to acquaint the governments to which they were accredited with the terms of the New Granada treaty of 1846. As for revision of the Clayton-Bulwer treaty, Blaine wrote Minister James Russell Lowell in London that the "remarkable development of the United States on the Pacific coast . . . has created new duties for this Government, [and] for self protection to her own interests . . . the United States asserts her right to control the Isthmus transit." Blaine also instructed Lowell to inform Britain that any foreign attempt to supplement

---

[39] Richardson, *Messages and Papers,* 10: 4912–4913. In 1888 a letter, signed by one Charles F. Murchison, was sent to Lord Sackville-West, the British minister in Washington, saying that the signer was a naturalized citizen and asking how he should vote in the coming presidential election. Sackville-West answered that Cleveland was more friendly to Great Britain than Harrison. The Republicans published this reply, hoping to lure the Irish vote from Cleveland.

[40] *Senate Executive Document* 112, 46th Cong., 3d sess., quoted in Barrows, *Evarts,* pp. 364, 368; Dyer, *Evarts,* p. 226; Evarts to Trescot, Feb. 15, 1881, *Special Missions, Department of State,* 3: 329.

American guarantees would be regarded as an unwarranted intrusion into a field where, save for Colombia, the United States regarded itself as paramount. He further stated that foreign commercial interest was of no concern to us; foreign *political* control alone aroused our fear. For Blaine, such a canal was purely an American waterway, and part of our coastline.[41]

If the United States followed Blaine's policy, *The Nation* predicted, our interest would prove so great that we would have to assume a protectorate over the isthmus and, possibly, wage war with any power that challenged our jurisdiction. However, even the pacifist and anglophile Andrew Carnegie agreed with Blaine that the treaty of 1850 needed to be modified: "America is going to control anything and everything on this continent. . . . America will take this Continent in hand alone." In seeking to modify the Clayton-Bulwer treaty, Blaine went even further than his predecessors. His overriding goal was an American continental system. Viewed in this light, Blaine's canal policy—together with his interest in Central America union, his fostering of inter-American commerce, and his defense of the Monroe Doctrine—are all interrelated.[42]

When Blaine left office to make room for Arthur's choice, the shift in personnel produced little change in American policy. Secretary Frelinghuysen attempted to negotiate a canal treaty with Nicaragua in 1884 despite British claims under the Clayton-Bulwer treaty. In instructing our minister he wrote: "I think the . . . United States has determined that the canal shall be built and that its control shall not pass to foreign interests." Secretary of State Thomas Bayard also argued the need for American control: "Our power may be questioned, but it will be maintained." [43]

---

[41] Blaine to Dichman, June 24, 1881, *Foreign Relations,* 1881, pp. 356–357; Blaine to Lowell, Nov. 19, 1881, *Senate Executive Document* 161, 56th Cong., 1st sess., pp. 178–184; Blaine to Lowell, June 24, 1881, Blaine MSS; Blaine to James M. Comly, Dec. 1, 1881, *Foreign Relations,* 1881, pp. 635–639.

[42] "American Policy towards the Isthmus Canal," *The Nation* 33 (Nov. 3, 1881): 348–349; Carnegie to Blaine, Jan. 14, 1882, Blaine MSS; Tyler, *Foreign Policy of Blaine,* p. 17; Blaine, *Political Discussions,* pp. 311–313.

[43] Frelinghuysen to Hall, Feb. 8, 1884, *Instructions, Central America,* vol. 18, no. 128; C. C. Tansill, *The Congressional Career of Thomas Francis Bayard, 1869–1885* (Washington, 1946), p. 290.

Congress also seemed to be aware of the advantages of an American canal as long as it did not mean financial appropriations. On May 29, 1879, a resolution called upon the President to report what measures should be adopted to promote American interests in the building of an isthmian canal. Chairman Samuel S. Cox, of the House Committee on Foreign Affairs, even introduced a joint resolution requesting the President to call a convention of the United States and Latin American republics to consider an interoceanic canal. In 1880, Representative William J. Crapo of Massachusetts introduced a bill which held that the construction of a canal by foreign capital and under the auspices of a European government would be hostile to America's established policy. The next year, a joint resolution of Congress stated that it was in the interest of America that no foreign government build a canal, but—if one were constructed—no foreign power other than the state through which the canal passed should exercise control. A resolution was also introduced which asserted that American interests were so involved in the canal question that the United States must consent to it as a necessary condition of its construction.[44]

Senator John Tyler Morgan of Alabama, more than any of his colleagues, fostered American interest in a canal. Though a former Confederate officer and a major Southern voice during Reconstruction, places like Hawaii, Nicaragua, Cuba, and the Congo were as much part of his life as Mobile, Montgomery, and Birmingham. In contrast to his posture as a defender of states' rights, Morgan was always an ardent and embarrassingly outspoken expansionist in foreign affairs. He endorsed the isthmian canal project (preferring the Nicaragua route to that of Panama), and in 1884 bluntly asked his colleagues in the Senate "Are we blind?" implying that the United States would be foolish not to become involved. His resolution, introduced in April 1881, stated that America's consent was necessary for the construction of a canal. Congressmen such as Morgan were as displeased with the proposed European projects as they were with congressional reluctance to encourage private American canal ventures. Senator Edmunds of Vermont, a canal enthusi-

---

[44] *Congressional Record*, 46th Cong., 1st sess. (May 29, 1878), 9, pt. 2, 1709; ibid., 2d sess. (Apr. 16, 1880), pp. 2480, 2489; ibid., 3d sess. (Dec. 13, 1880), 11, pt. 1, 107; *House Report* 224, 46th Cong., 3d sess. (Feb. 14, 1881); *Senate Journal*, 46th Cong., 3d sess. (Feb. 16, 1881), p. 263.

ast of the first order, urged that the least the United States could do was incorporate a company composed of reputable citizens to construct the waterway. And one Missouri representative felt that the first step to take in this direction was the annulment of the Clayton-Bulwer treaty.[45]

The "do-it-ourself" isthmian canal faction found other supporters. Representative Thomas R. Stockdale of Massachusetts announced he would not cast a vote to exempt any part of the isthmus from the Monroe Doctrine. Attacking the Clayton-Bulwer treaty, the *Hartford Courant* asserted that it was not what John Bull wanted but what Uncle Sam wanted that counted. The threat to the United States in event of war made it totally incomprehensible that a foreign power should control such a canal. Senator Ambrose Burnside of Rhode Island predicted that the United States, of necessity, would be required to take a new look into the management of noncontiguous territory. Such action was a requirement for peace, he reasoned, and a European-constructed canal would endanger peace.[46]

Despite the pressure on the government to act, the champions of a United States-built canal had to await another day and more propitious circumstances to consummate their plans. But, even during the Gilded Age, America's attention was increasingly drawn to events within the hemisphere. The range and span of this attention varied considerably, but it appears to have been constant.

---

[45] Radke, "John Tyler Morgan, An Expansionist Senator," esp. pp. 5, 144, 313–316, 391–393; Radke, "Senator Morgan and the Nicaragua Canal," *Alabama History* 12 (Jan. 1959): 5–34; George F. Edmunds, "The Nicaragua Canal Treaty," *Harper's Weekly* 45 (Jan. 19, 1901): 53; *Congressional Record*, 48th Cong., 1st sess. (July 5, 1884), 11, pt. 6, A502.

[46] *Congressional Record*, 50th Cong., 2d sess. (Feb. 6, 1889), 20, pt. 3, 1565–1574; "England and the Canal," *Hartford Courant*, Jan. 3, 1885; Benjamin Perley Poore, *The Life and Public Services of Ambrose E. Burnside* (Providence, 1882), pp. 350–353.

CHAPTER 11

The Quest for
a Canadian-American
Consensus

As AMERICAN interests extended south of the Rio Grande, our neighbor to the north could hardly escape the covetous glances of our expansionists. During the Revolution, Americans had attempted to lure Canada from Britain, and annexation became a central project of the war hawks of 1812. Strained relations with Great Britain in the Civil War decade again stimulated American thoughts of wooing away the crown's brightest jewel. In the Gilded Age, the leaders of what one historian called "little expansionism" regarded Canada as the most likely candidate for inclusion in the American system.[1] As with Samoa, Hawaii, and Latin America, interest in Canada was strong among those concerned primarily with commercial possibilities, as well as among expansionists who regarded commercial union as a step toward eventual political annexation.

The most outspoken and easily recognizable expansionists in Congress were those who entertained grandiose ideas of an americanized Canada. Massachusetts Senator Charles Sumner maintained that

---

[1] Albert K. Weinberg, *Manifest Destiny* (Baltimore, 1935), p. 354.

annexation of Canada would only be just payment for Great Britain's failure to observe neutrality in the Civil War. Another Radical Republican, the demagogic Benjamin F. Butler, urged American expansion "so far north that wandering Esquimau will mistake the flashings of the midnight sun reflected from our glorious flag for the scintillations of an *aurora borealis.*" All territory north of the St. Lawrence River and thence to the North Pole, he predicted, would some day be American. He held that the great diversity of interests between Americans and Canadians, often regarded as disadvantages by those opposed to eventual union, would in fact weld the two nations more closely together.[2]

Then there was Representative Randall L. Gibson of Louisiana, who declared that the idea of a "Grand Republic" must look to the stars and stripes flying over Canada. The United States was pictured as a modern Rome whose motto would be *urbis et orbis.* John Sherman, in a fiery oration, asserted unequivocally: "I want Canada to be part of the United States." He also told the Senate, in 1888, that Canada and the United States could not be at peace with one another without political as well as commercial union. He looked forward to "the good time coming when the American flag [would] be the signal and sign of the Union of all the English speaking people of the continent from the Rio Grande to the Arctic Ocean." [3]

Many annexation advocates in both the United States and Canada believed that political union was the inevitable result of natural law. Young Henry Cabot Lodge demonstrated his disdain for England when he declared that union with Canada was our "manifest destiny" and the "inevitable result" of the law of politics, finances, and society. Even English-born Goldwin Smith of Toronto, formerly a professor of history at Cornell University, believed Canada's annexation to the United States to be inevitable. Writing in the *North*

---

[2] Benjamin F. Butler, "Defenseless Canada," loc. cit.; Butler, *Should There Be a Union of the English-speaking Peoples of the Earth? A Dissertation Delivered . . . July 2, 1889* (Boston, 1889); *Home Market Bulletin* 2 (March, 1891): 9.

[3] *Congressional Record,* 47th Cong., 1st sess. (Mar. 10, 1882), 13, pt. 7, A33; Sherman, *Recollections of Forty Years in the House, Senate, and Cabinet;* 2: 1019; *Congressional Record,* 50th Cong., 1st sess. (Sept. 18, 1888), 19: 7286, 8666–8667; "Senator Sherman on Canadian Relations," *New York Times,* Sept. 20, 1888.

American Review in 1883, one Canadian predicted that annexation would become a fait accompli within his generation. Several years later, a New York congressman observed that the 46,000 "brave men of the north" who had served in the Union army during the Civil War would soon be enrolled as permanent citizens. "God speed the day!" he added; "her people are ready. . . . 'Commercial union' we will not favor except as a means to a speedy end [political control]." [4]

The attitude of the press, while enthusiastic, was generally less nationalistic and extreme than that of the more expansion-conscious legislators. The journalists of the day were naturally interested in a good story, and while most of the papers frowned upon an annexationist movement per se, stories on that topic made prime copy and the journals and newspapers were replete with them. The *New York Herald*, in voicing pessimism over the possibilities of Canadian annexation, called such stories sentimental discussions. The *Chicago Tribune*, alarmed at what it called the "flight" of Canadians southward to the United States, suggested that the exodus could be stopped by simply extending our northern boundary. In its predictions for the year 1889, the *Tribune* observed that although it was hardly probable that "Miss Canada" would be at the "Yankee round table" in the near future, there would always be a chair reserved for her. [5]

The *Louisville Courier* urged speedy annexation, perhaps because the Canadians were progressing so fast that they would soon demand independence. The *Pittsburgh Commercial Gazette* could find no good reason why we should not take Canada under "our protecting wing." The *Washington Post* announced bluntly that the spirit of manifest destiny was still vibrant and it urged the Canadians to "walk in" to the American union. There was the possibility, the paper proclaimed editorially, that Canada, Cuba, Mexico, and Central America would soon join the United States. Probably with

⁴ Lodge, "The Fisheries Question," loc. cit.; Goldwin Smith, "Canada and the United States," *North American Review* 131 (July 1880): 14–25; P. Bender, "A Canadian View of Annexation," ibid. 136 (Apr. 1883): 326–336; *Congressional Record*, 50th Cong., 2d sess. (Mar. 1, 1889), 20, pt. 3, A181.

⁵ "Canadian Annexation," *New York Herald*, Oct. 1, 1888; "The Trouble with Canada," *Chicago Tribune*, Aug. 5, 1880; "The Old Year Abroad," ibid., Jan. 1, 1889.

tongue in cheek, the *New Haven Evening Register* urged annexation if only to lower the high American divorce rate by combining it with the low Canadian rate.[6]

Economic considerations also played a role in the argument for political annexation. Canadian wheat fields, it was contended, would act as a welcome guarantee against American crop failures, and Canadian bituminous coal, conveniently deposited near our Eastern states, would enhance the economic position of both nations. Indeed, most of the annexationists in the United States promised that Canada would receive the greater rewards for union due to the resulting increase in commercial intercourse.[7]

Unionist advocates, anxious to "cement" all the different peoples of North America into one great nation, were also motivated by the desire to achieve "continental solidarity." Canadian-born Jacob G. Schurman, professor of philosophy and later president of Cornell University, felt that union was the secret wish of all Americans and that manifest destiny decreed a single continental empire. Union with Canada would usher in the beginning of a new era in world history. The unity of the Anglo-Saxons of North America was important, not for material considerations but because it would result in a more enlightened civilization. One writer felt that the annexation of Canada would be the first step in a movement reuniting the entire Anglo-Saxon race. "Canada may be content to pass away," said this would-be prophet, "having more than justified her short existence, for . . . that movement will bring peace upon earth, justice among nations, and the growth of that true wealth whose virtue is most excellent—true and wise men." Those who favored union were so imbued with missionary zest that they referred to union as "irresistible" and predicted that it "must come to pass." Annexation and the resultant "grand domain" would bring a "great day." [8]

---

[6] "To Be Done Quickly," *Louisville Courier,* Feb. 7, 1889; "Canadian Agitation," *Pittsburgh Commercial Gazette,* Nov. 22, 1881; "Manifest Destiny," *Washington Post,* Feb. 26, 1889; *New Haven Evening Register,* Feb. 22, 1889.

[7] Justin S. Morrill, "Is Union with Canada Desirable?" *Forum* 6 (Jan. 1889): 451–464; "Canadian Annexation," *New York Daily Tribune,* June 5, 1887.

[8] W. Blackburn Harte, "The Drift toward Annexation," *Forum* 7 (June

Despite all the talk and fiery speeches extolling annexation and the predictions of marvelous things to come if only the United States and Canada would merge, annexationist sentiment was not really that widespread on either side of the border; in the United States, it was primarily the issue of the Young America movement. Although annexationist talk was heard even in the Canadian Parliament, discussions of joining New England to Canada were probably uttered in levity.[9]

Most journals in the United States were against the annexation of Canada. The *New York Times*, which could discover no genuine expansionist sentiment in the country, claimed that we had territory enough. Like so many others who were to be proved wrong, it asserted that many years would pass before the frontier was eliminated. The *Buffalo Courier* informed her neighbor across the Niagara River that she need not fear "American bluster," and the *San Francisco Evening Bulletin* stated that expansionism was not a "taking idea" in the United States. The *Buffalo Express*, as early as 1877, felt that if Canada did not want union with the United States, the United States certainly would not absorb it. The majority of Americans probably agreed with Representative Oscar L. Jackson of Pennsylvania: it was a sufficiently Herculean task to harmonize interests in a country the size of the United States without adding Canadian problems to our task. Opponents of annexation especially looked askance at the inclusion of the French-Canadian regions and their alien Catholic majority. Swallowing a country was hard enough to begin with, but digesting such a large and disparate segment of the population was even more difficult.[10] The publication of Josiah Strong's *Our Country* in 1885 no doubt publicized

---

1889): 361–372; Jacob G. Schurman, "Is Union with Canada Desirable?" ibid. 6 (Jan. 1889): 451–464; Schurman, "The Manifest Destiny of Canada," ibid. 7 (Mar. 1889): 1–17; "Is the Annexation of Canada Desirable?" *Cosmopolitan* 6 (Jan. 1889): 303–304; *Age of Steel* 64 (Sept. 1, 1888): 10; David A. Poe, "The Position of Canada," *Forum* 3 (July 1887): 443–457; *Sitka Alaskan*, July 31, 1886.

[9] "Another Annexation Scheme," *Washington Post*, Mar. 9, 1889.

[10] "Commercial and Political Union," *New York Times*, May 29, 1887; *Buffalo Courier*, Sept. 23, 1888; "Not Seeking Territory," *San Francisco Evening Bulletin*, Sept. 5, 1888; *Buffalo Express*, June 14, 1887; *Congressional Record*, 50th Cong., 2d sess. (Mar. 1, 1889), 20, pt. 3, 216–217; "Obstacles to Annexation," *Forum* 6 (Feb. 1889): 634–643.

this racist notion of the necessity of a completely homogeneous population.

Although political union with Canada was hardly feasible, closer economic ties were favored on both sides of the border. By the 1880s, Canada's economy had become heavily dependent on its export trade, and Canadian liberals desired a closer American association in order to pull out of an economic slump. With the lapse in 1864 of the Elgin-Marcy reciprocity arrangements with the United States and the general decline in world prices for Canadian goods, the national debt and trade deficits soared. As a result, the 1880s witnessed increased Canadian discussion of "annexation," which for the most part meant commercial union and reciprocity. In 1890, for example, the Manitoba legislature voted unanimously to urge Ottawa to negotiate an agreement with the United States looking toward unrestricted reciprocity.[11]

Many Americans also favored a renewal of reciprocity arrangements as a more attractive alternative than political affiliation. According to George S. Boutwell, a former congressman and Secretary of the Treasury under Grant, Canada needed the American market; indeed, if commercial ties were not reestablished, the Canadian farmer would soon be unable even to sell his land in Canada and purchase a home in the United States. Therefore, to better his economic position, he would demand annexation. The future president of the Anti-Imperialist League saw free commercial intercourse as at least postponing political union.[12]

American consuls and commercial agents consistently reported the hard times in Canada and observed that, while Canada was friendly to the United States and desired closer commercial contact, annexation was not the answer. Canadian-American commercial union was often put in the same category with Blaine's projected

---

[11] Donald F. Warner, *Idea of Continental Union,* pp. 155–156 and chap. 6; Pletcher, *The Awkward Years,* pp. 170 ff.; "Annexation of Canada," *American Economist* 5 (Jan. 10, 1890): 17–18; "Hard Times in Canada," *Chicago Tribune,* Aug. 22, 1885; Consul James W. Taylor, Winnipeg, Mar. 24, 1890, in *Commercial Relations,* 1888–1889 (Washington, 1891), pp. 292–293.

For an excellent discussion of reciprocity, see Warner, *Idea of Continental Union,* chap. 3–8 and Charles C. Tansill, *Canadian-American Relations, 1875–1911* (New Haven, 1943), chap. 13.

[12] George S. Boutwell, *Reminiscences of Sixty Years in Public Affairs,* 2 vols. (New York, 1902), 2: 278–279.

Zollverein with Latin America. In fact the *Chicago Tribune* felt that closer Canadian ties were more important than Blaine's trade projects south of the border. After all, it asserted, the Canadian trade amounted to twice as much as our Latin American trade. The *New York Herald* boldly stated that America's commercial interests rested with the countries closest to us. Trade with Korea, Europe, and Latin America was important, but to neglect the obvious was foolhardy. In refusing to renew reciprocity, the United States was "stupid" and "pig headed." Why, asked one newspaper, should we have a reciprocity treaty with the "half-naked and half-civilized greasers of Mexico" while trade in the "most natural direction"—to the north—was forgotten? [13]

The *Buffalo Commercial Advertiser* pointed out that the advantages of free trade between the United States and Canada were as obvious as the benefits of unrestricted interstate commerce between the states. Eventually, it predicted, Canada would have to become part of the "North American Union." The *Commercial and Financial Chronicle* felt that Canada's high tariff operated unfavorably against the United States and that Americans should face this fact and take the initiative for reciprocity. And the *Christian Advocate* invoked divine support for the "blessing" of reciprocity.[14]

Booster organizations and businessmen naturally discussed the question of reciprocity. American businessmen displayed great interest in the northern trade, but their action was largely limited to resolutions, petitions, and memorials. Almost every chamber of commerce, agricultural association, and manufacturers' and producers' societies expressed themselves in favor of reciprocity. For example, in 1881 over 500 New York mercantile houses petitioned Congress for the creation of a commission to investigate the possibility of reciprocity and five years later, a group of Minnesota citizens voiced their approval of such legislation. The Detroit Board of Trade con-

---

[13] Theodore J. Barnett, "Canada and the United States," *Consular Reports*, 2 (Feb. 1881), 193–196; "Commercial and Political Union," *New York Times*, May 29, 1887; "Commercial Union with Canada," *Chicago Tribune*, Sept. 2, 1887; "Trade with Canada," *New York Herald*, Jan. 14, 1884; *Buffalo Express*, Mar. 22, 1883.

[14] *Buffalo Commercial Advertiser*, Sept. 4, 1885; "Canadian Commerce," *Commercial and Financial Chronicle* 33 (July 30, 1881): 114–115; *Christian Advocate*, Feb. 5, 1873.

tinually pressed for new reciprocity agreements. The Businessmen's Association of Buffalo held regular meetings to discuss the issue, and the New York City Chamber of Commerce passed a resolution calling for the appointment of a national commission to study the entire problem.[15]

S. J. Ritchie, as we have already seen, was one of those entrepreneurs who constantly and eloquently urged unrestricted reciprocity. Ritchie, perhaps the unofficial leader of the commercial union movement, was a persistent petitioner of such Ohio politicians as Senator John Sherman and Representative Benjamin B. Butterworth, who voiced Ritchie's views on the subject. Another reciprocity leader was Erastus Wiman, a native Canadian who was president of an American firm, the Great Northwestern Telegraph Company, who argued that both countries would obviously profit if the tariff barriers were removed. A Philadelphia banker, Wharton Barker, felt that commercial union would furnish the best solution of the fisheries problem, which complicated our economic and political relationships with Canada. Reciprocity would bring closer cooperation in the administration of what Barker referred to as a common heritage of resources and capacities.[16]

Congress generally reflected this interest in Canadian commerce. Democrat Richard W. Townshend of Illinois advocated the establishment of a commercial union among American nations and explained his reasons to Secretary of State Bayard. Representative Butterworth introduced resolutions for commercial union (which never came to a vote). In 1888 he introduced a resolution that would mandate the United States, "in the interest of peace and amity be-

---

[15] *Senate Journal*, 49th Cong., 1st sess. (Feb. 17, 1886), p. 300; *House Journal*, 46th Cong., 3d sess. (Jan. 20, 1881), p. 214; "Reciprocity with Canada," *New York Times*, Jan. 1, 1883; ibid., July 29, 1887; *New York Herald*, Nov. 4, 1887.

[16] Tansill, *Canadian-American Relations*, pp. 382–383, 385, 388–392, 394; Warner, *Idea of Continental Union*, pp. 180–182. See also S. J. Ritchie, *Commercial Union between the United States and Canada* (Toronto, 1887) and Goldwin Smith, ed., *Handbook of Commercial Union* (Toronto, 1888).

Erastus Wiman was a prolific pamphleteer for the cause of closer Canadian-American relations. Some of his works are *The Advantages of Commercial Union to Canada and the United States* (New York, 1887), *Commercial Union between the United States and Canada* (New York, 1887), and *Does Annexation Follow? Commercial Union and British Connection* (New York, 1887?).

tween nations, and in response to the demands of our manufacturers, [to] remove all obstacles to trade and commerce with Canada." Butterworth even went so far as to urge every chamber of commerce, agricultural association, and manufacturers' society to support his views.[17]

Representative Robert R. Hitt of Illinois, chairman of the House Committee on Foreign Affairs, also spoke for the pro-reciprocity legislators when he asserted that such legislation was practical, timely, and in the "liberal spirit." Speaking of the natural law of gravitation which pulled Canada to our markets, Hitt proposed a joint resolution to promote commercial union with Canada, citing numerous "practical business reasons" for it. Representative Cox of New York stated that Canada's large and ever increasing trade was too valuable to be lost to the United States. In the late 1880s and early 1890s there were at least three motions that would have incorporated Canada into the United States' economic system, but they were buried in committee.[18]

Commercial union without political ties was obviously attended by grave difficulties. As *The Nation* put it, commercial union was regarded in some quarters as merely a stepping-stone to political unity. Certainly Canada's hard times could be cured by annexation, some felt, but there were as many advocates of closer economic ties who had no ulterior political motives as there were those who saw economic union as inevitably leading to political union.[19]

In any event, reciprocity encountered opposition from the staunch protectionists and from some extreme advocates of political union. The latter group maintained that our commercial ties with Canada would be weakened unless we made political *Anschluss* a prerequisite for reciprocity. Canada's ties with Great Britain presented another

---

[17] Richard W. Townshend to Bayard, Oct. 17, 1885, Bayard MSS; Benjamin Butterworth, *Commercial Union between Canada and the United States* (New York, 1887); *Congressional Record,* 49th Cong., 2d sess. (Feb. 14, 1887), 18, pt. 2, 1735; ibid., 50th Cong., 1st sess. (Jan. 23, 1888), 19, pt. 1, 635; Warner, *Idea of Continental Union,* p. 185; Tansill, *Canadian-American Relations,* pp. 386, 391, 396.

[18] *Congressional Record,* 50th Cong., 2d sess. (Mar. 1, 1889), 20, pt. 3, A125; "Union with Canada," *Washington Post,* Mar. 3, 1889; Warner, *Idea of Continental Union,* pp. 185–186; Tansill, *Canadian-American Relations,* pp. 395–396; *House Report* 1127, 46th Cong., 2d sess. (Apr. 23, 1880).

[19] "The Wooing of Canada," *The Nation* 47 (Dec. 20, 1888): 491–492.

obstacle. Reciprocity negotiations with Canada, some contended, were worthless in a day when Britain still called the tune. Canada desired advantages from the United States that it could not acquire elsewhere, but the trade advantages we desired were controlled by England. Thus there could be no commercial union unless Canada was separated from Britain. And it was most unlikely that John Bull could be induced to negotiate a treaty which discriminated against his own people in favor of a rival—especially in the absence of a cordial spirit between the two great English speaking nations.[20]

Even more pessimistic notes were sounded. Some quarters felt that reciprocity would require the United States to take all of the commercial risk; Canada would be dependent upon us and would not really reciprocate. In a note to President Harrison, Secretary Blaine explained this position.

> They [the Canadians] will aim at natural products, to get all the products of the farm on us in exchange for Heaven knows what. They certainly will not give us manufactured articles, as that will interfere with their own and break down their tariff. . . . We do not want any intercourse with Canada except through the medium of a tariff, and she will find that she has had a hard row to hoe and will ultimately, I believe, seek admission to the Union.[21]

Perhaps the dreary agrarian outlook in the 1880s and the Republicans' desire to satisfy their Western wing provided the force that ultimately doomed all discussions of reciprocity legislation.

Thus reciprocity, as well as talk of political union, was far from wholly popular in both Canada and the United States. Canadians in general, and French-Canadians in particular, were reputed not to possess the educational, religious, political, or business acumen of Yankees, and fear was voiced that reciprocity would harm the farmers of Maine, Vermont, and New York and the lumbermen of Michigan and Ohio. No advantage could be seen for American

---

[20] *House Report* 1127, 46th Cong., 2d sess. (Apr. 23, 1880); *Toronto World*, quoted in *Buffalo Daily Courier*, May 17, 1887.

[21] *Buffalo Express*, Jan. 27, 1877; Gail Hamilton, *Biography of James G. Blaine* (Norwich, Conn., 1896), pp. 693–694; Tyler, *Foreign Policy of Blaine*, p. 20.

manufacturers in closer Canadian ties until Great Britain abrogated her exclusive right to furnish Canada with British goods. Zealous advocates of reciprocity could not dispel the impression in Canada and the United States that their plans were but veiled and diabolical attempts to seduce our northern neighbors into a political union. Thus the reciprocity issue proved abortive.[22]

In addition to debates on annexation and reciprocity, another issue continued to play a significant role in Canadian-American relations. The problems surrounding American fishing rights off the Canadian and Newfoundland coasts began early in the history of the Republic, continued during the Gilded Age, and were not finally resolved until the presidency of William H. Taft. At the conclusion of the Revolution, Americans received the privilege of fishing off the coast of British North America within the three-mile limit. In 1818, these inshore fishing rights were eliminated except at specified locations. Difficulties arose in determining the three-mile limit at these locations, and for the next thirty-six years American fishing vessels were sporadically seized. The 1854 reciprocity treaty restored the inshore privileges in return for granting Canadian trade reciprocity, but in the 1860s, with the lapse of the Elgin-Marcy agreement, the United States and especially New England was again deprived of inshore fishing rights.

The Treaty of Washington, in 1871, brought the fisheries issue to a head. Under the terms of this agreement, which resolved many other Anglo-American problems, Great Britain agreed to restore inshore fishing rights in return for limited free-trade grants for Canada in the United States and the payment of certain monies to Great Britain. The United States, dissatisfied with these provisions, terminated this arrangement on July 1, 1885. The Canadians retaliated the next year by narrowly interpreting the convention of 1818 and resuming the seizure of American fishing vessels for alleged infractions. Twisting the lion's tail—which had been ultimately responsible for congressional action in 1885—was renewed by the Canadian reaction. The fishery situation, which attracted much

---

[22] See "Proposed Reciprocity with Canada," *Bradstreet's* 9 (Feb. 2, 1884): 66–67, for a list of objections to reciprocity. See also Gary Pennanen, "American Interest in Commercial Union with Canada, 1854–1898," *Mid-America* 47 (Jan. 1965): 24–39.

attention in the United States in an age of strong anglophobia, led
to violent anti-Canadian and anti-English utterances. Although the
business community was usually divided on foreign-policy matters,
its attitude on this issue reflected not only a high point in its concern
but also a remarkable consensus.[23]

The fisheries issue also created editorial agreement in the nation's
press. The *Boston Transcript* cried for " 'a single hour' of Andrew
Jackson" to save our fishermen. The *Rochester Herald* demanded
that our government abandon none of its rights and that it protect
the fishing fleet. By what title, asked the *New York Herald,* did
Canada, a mere British dependency, raise and maintain a navy
hostile to the United States? The *St. Paul Daily Gazette* asked
Canada to remember that staying on good terms with the United
States was more valuable than the fisheries; if American ports were
closed to Canadian goods, the dominion's commerce would be crippled. The *New York Daily Tribune,* urging American fishermen to
demand congressional protection, said they should not place much
confidence in a State Department filled with free-trade advocates.
Finally, an American commercial magazine suggested that annexation was the most direct means of solving the fisheries dispute.[24]

Congressional expansionists quickly championed the fishermen's
cause. Congressman Henry Cabot Lodge, speaking for the fishing
interests of Massachusetts, asserted that his constituents were not
the only victims of Canadian policy: when Canada sought, through
blackmail, to extort commercial concessions from the United States,
all Americans were involved. He exclaimed that whenever the American flag on an American fishing vessel was insulted by a foreigner,
the great American heart was touched. Senator George F. Edmunds
of Vermont, who had a passion for baiting John Bull, demanded
naval protection for the fishermen. He suggested that the United
States send its "best vessel" into "the northern seas at a due and
respectful distance from the dominions of her majesty . . . to give

---

[23] For the background of the fisheries issue, see Warner, *Idea of Continental Union,* pp. 151–152, 159–160, 185 and Tansill, *Canadian-American
Relations,* chap. 1–3.

[24] "The Fisheries Question," *Public Opinion* 1 (May 22, 1886): 106;
"Canada's Stake," *St. Paul Daily Gazette,* Jan. 26, 1887; "The Fisheries
Question," *New York Daily Tribune,* May 12, 1886; *American Manufactur-
ing and Iron World* 39 (Dec. 17, 1886): 11.

a little . . . encouragement to men who are engaged in clearly lawful occupation in clearly lawful places." [25]

Protests and excitement reached fever pitch in 1887 when Congress authorized the President to retaliate against Canadians by barring their ships from American ports. Although President Cleveland signed the bill, he had no wish to execute it; he intended to use it as a means for extorting concessions. The press generally favored the measure, but feared that war might result. In the spring of that year *The Nation* warned that a prolonged conflict between England and the United States was "peculiarly liable" to lead to war.[26] However, peaceful solutions to the fisheries crises were also explored. The *New Orleans Times-Picayune* reported one such plan, made by Edward Atkinson, a Boston statistician who proposed that the United States purchase New Brunswick, Nova Scotia, and Cape Breton Island for $58 million dollars. Eventually the United States had to own these territories, he maintained, and the sooner they were acquired the less excuse there would be for withholding government resources from the "paramount business" of expansion and development. According to a Sacramento newspaper, retaliatory legislation was indefensible. Earlier, historian Worthington Chauncy Ford also had pleaded for a sane policy. Canada had acted unwisely, but that was no reason for the United States to do the same. Ford felt that Secretary Bayard's policy showed dignified restraint, and he hoped Bayard would continue to control the hotheads.[27]

In November 1887, the Anglo-American joint commission met in Washington and began to search for a peaceful solution. On February 15, 1888, Secretary Bayard and Britain's representative, Joseph Chamberlain, signed a compromise agreement. In addition to lifting the limitations on waters in which Yankee fishermen could operate, the settlement removed restrictions in other areas: American purchases of bait, supplies, and outfits in Canada; the trans-

---

[25] Lodge, "The Fisheries Question," loc. cit.; *The Nation* 46 (May 19, 1887): 417; *Congressional Record,* 49th Cong., 1st sess. (June 3, 1886), 17, pt. 5, 5182.

[26] "Fisheries Fallacies," *The Nation* 46 (May 26, 1887): 443–444.

[27] "A Project to Buy the Canadian Fisheries," *New Orleans Times-Picayune,* Nov. 20, 1887; *Sacramento Daily Record-Union,* Jan. 26, 1887; Worthington C. Ford, "The Fisheries Dispute," *Forum* 2 (Oct. 1886): 174–181.

shipment of catches; and the shipping of crews. In return for these concessions, the United States would remove its duties on the fish products of Canada and Newfoundland. Republican pressures on the Cleveland administration to assert American interests in this dispute were obviously intended to court the usually Democratic Irish vote.

The *New York Times* urged ratification of this pact, for its rejection would mean the reopening of a complicated and senseless quarrel. The *Christian Standard* urged Canada and the United States to rise above party differences for the sake of mankind, since the progress of Christian civilization was at stake. But despite all pleas for moderation, the argument was still heard that the matter involved the national interest and honor of the whole country. A New York representative even called for the exclusion of Canadian rolling stock from American railroads. Despite the sensible provisions of the Bayard-Chamberlain treaty, the issue was bound up in patriotic assertions of America's supremacy.[28]

Because the treaty contained reciprocal tariff provisions, its opponents in the Senate labeled it a sellout to Great Britain. Gaining support by this tactic, they rejected the treaty on August 21, 1888, by a vote of 27 to 30. President Cleveland thereupon reacted with a measure which seemed more a retaliation against the Senate than against Canada. In a strongly worded message to Congress (August 23, 1888), he asked that he be granted extreme retaliatory power so as to halt all trade across the border. The Republicans, to avoid being held responsible for business losses, refused to heed the President's request.

A good portion of the press was critical of this turn in the Cleveland-Bayard policy. The State Department, it asserted, had done nothing to protect American fishermen, and indeed had surrendered our historic rights. In commenting upon a plea by the president of the National Fishery Association for the protection of the industry, the *New York Times* criticized his "laborious and anxious reasoning" that the United States subordinate questions of national and

---

[28] "The Fisheries Treaty," *New York Times,* Feb. 22, 1888; *Christian Standard,* 23 (Apr. 14, 1888), 225; *Congressional Record,* 50th Cong., 1st sess. (June 13, 1888), 19, pt. 6, 5197; ibid., 50th Cong., 1st sess. (Sept. 7, 1888), 19, pt. 10, A480. For a summary of press reaction, see *Public Opinion* 5 (Aug. 25, 1888): 428.

international policy to the protection of a petty special interest. *The Nation* felt that the people at large would not manifest great interest in the dispute. The very idea of coercing the world's greatest naval power brought smiles to many critics of our extreme nationalistic proposals. On the other hand, the President's retaliation plan, as revealed in his message to Congress, was praised by some as reflecting Mr. Cleveland's faculty of doing the right thing in the right way without sacrificing American pride. The *Pittsburgh Post* lauded the President as a cautious executive who was not given to jingo-like tendencies.[29]

The fisheries dispute had tremendous ramifications; for example, it dampened all hopes for serious talks on reciprocity. As a whole, Congress was not ready to entertain the idea of even limited reciprocity, and although a few of its members advocated annexation, the sentiment for political union was largely spotty and localized in the East and Midwest. Yet the minority of politicians who spoke for reciprocity and/or championed annexation was strongly motivated. If one can speak of destiny in the historical process, both groups moved in that direction. Both groups sensed the limitation that is placed on a country which has no new areas to occupy—which in the next decade Frederick Jackson Turner would term the "closing of the frontier." The expansion of its industrial complex attracted the United States to the undeveloped opportunities in the Canadian economy. In Canada, the situation was reversed because the provinces sold their raw products and bought their manufactured goods in the United States. Because neither nation could operate efficiently with a tariff wall between them, some Americans continued to pressure for reciprocity while others argued for annexation, and with a certain degree of common sense. Yet both groups believed that

---

[29] The treaty and Cleveland's message is contained in *Senate Executive Document* 176, 50th Cong., 1st sess. See also Allan Nevins, *Grover Cleveland, A Study in Courage* (New York, 1933), pp. 406 ff. "Nobody Will Thank Bayard," *New York Daily Tribune*, Nov. 2, 1888; "The President's Plan of Retaliation," *New York Times*, Aug. 24, 1888; "The Reasoning of Babson," *New York Times*, Nov. 29, 1887; "The Senate and the Treaty," *The Nation* 46 (May 24, 1888): 420–421; "Canada and Retaliation," *Pittsburgh Post*, Aug. 7, 1888. See also Charles S. Campbell, Jr., "American Tariff Interests and the Northeastern Fisheries, 1883–1888," *Canadian Historical Review* 45 (Sept. 1964): 212–228.

Canada should take the first step, and that step was not taken during the Gilded Age.[30] Indeed, better trade relations would not come until the administration of Franklin D. Roosevelt. By some irony of fate—or perhaps merely the belief that Canada should take the first step—the manifest destiny of the "quiet years," which would lead to the absorption of Hawaii but not Canada, carried us westward into the Pacific.

---

[30] "Canada's Vain Hopes," *New York Times,* Feb. 8, 1879; Warner, *Idea of Continental Union,* pp. 251, 254; Erastus Wiman, "The Greater Half of the Continent," *North American Review* 148 (Jan. 1889): 54–72; "Canadian Annexation," *New York Daily Tribune,* June 5, 1887; "Canadian Annexation," *Public Opinion* 1 (Sept. 18, 1886): 445.

In a chapter dealing with the period 1874–1896, Gerald M. Graig summarizes American-Canadian relationships in terms of little American interest in commercial relations and disinterest in closer ties in general (*The United States and Canada* [Cambridge, Mass., 1968], chap. 11). See also Robert C. Brown, *Canada's National Policy, 1883–1900* (Princeton, 1964), chap. 1–3.

CHAPTER 12

Across
the Pacific

THE VAST PACIFIC stirred the imagination of Americans from the days of Confederation ginseng traders, whalers, and missionaries. In the Gilded Age, the Samoan and Hawaiian archipelagoes and the Far East were special areas of increasing American political and economic interest. While the mikado image of Gilbert and Sullivan still dominated American conceptions of the Far East, some Americans were beginning to want a share of what one newspaper called the "Harvest which ripens on Asiatic fields." America's growing commercial interests in the East, as well as Europe's disturbing presence in the Pacific islands, made these important trade links to Asia a cause for concern. In the Pacific, as in the Orient itself, the United States seemed to be taking a second place to Britain, France, and Germany. America began to realize that its international role extended well beyond its three-mile limit.[1]

Excellent harbors first attracted Americans to the Samoan Islands. Early American whalers found that the island harbors

---

[1] See William E. F. Krause, *The Influence of the United States Abroad* (San Francisco, 1868).

afforded convenient haven, and the government, pressured by the whaling interest, sent Lieutenant Charles Wilkes, USN, to explore the region in 1838. It was not until after Appomattox, however, that other commercial interests began to give the islands serious attention. In the postwar decade, the Union Pacific Central Railroad facilitated the shipment of American goods bound for Australia and New Zealand, and this expanded trade in turn stimulated a desire for coaling stations and protective naval bases in the South Pacific islands.

Early attempts to secure bases in Samoa failed. In the 1860s, William H. Webb, a New York shipbuilder, seeking a coaling station in Samoa for a projected steamship line between San Francisco and Australia, requested government support. Webb submitted his agent's encouraging report to the Secretary of the Navy and the admiral of the Pacific squadron, but the desired support did not materialize. Several years later, in 1872, the Navy Department itself met a similar failure when it commissioned Commodore Richard W. Meade to secure a coaling station at Pago Pago. Meade accomplished his mission by means of an unauthorized treaty (which President Grant nevertheless submitted to the Senate) that granted the United States exclusive control of the bay and harbor of Pago Pago, but this came at a time of political turmoil and the treaty was easily defeated by anti-expansionists in the Senate.

In January 1878, however, Meade's work came to fruition with the signing of a treaty to establish a naval station at Pago Pago. Negotiating with a native aristocrat, La Mamea, who had come to Washington seeking American support for his government, Secretary Evarts promised that in return for rights to a coaling station the United States would use its good offices to adjust future differences between Samoa and foreign powers. Because the arrangement did not involve the establishment of a formal protectorate, the Senate gave the treaty its speedy approval. But this 1878 treaty would soon prove more consequential. Events in this remote paradise during the next decade would require the United States to change its traditional policy of noninterference in external affairs.[2]

---

[2] For early American interest in Samoa, see Sylvia Masterman, *The Origins of International Rivalry in Samoa, 1845–1884* (Stanford, 1934), passim; G. H. Ryden, *The Foreign Policy of the United States in Relation*

In the 1880s, foreign intervention in Polynesia grew as Great Britain and Germany, capitalizing on intertribal warfare in the islands, obtained valuable commercial privileges. While, officially, the United States wished only to help the Samoan authorities in maintaining a stable government and denied any desire to annex the islands, individuals within the State Department did not always agree with this position. Thomas M. Dawson, our energetic consul in Apia from 1879 to 1882, saw an American protectorate as the only means of maintaining political stability in the islands, and reports of English and German plots filled his dispatches from Samoa. In March 1880 he suggested that British designs on Samoa could be forestalled only if we cooperated in a joint protectorate. If the United States did not cooperate in the establishment of a municipal council in Apia, Dawson reported, Britain would act unilaterally. Later American representatives in Samoa offered similar predictions about the dangers of European interference. One consul invited American merchants and manufacturers on the Pacific coast to supply him with samples, circulars, catalogs, and business cards in the hope that the introduction of American products in Samoa would prevent foreign monopolization of the island's trade.[3]

Alvey A. Adee, chief of the State Department's diplomatic bureau, also questioned the United States' passive role in Samoa. Doubtful that a native government could exist in Samoa or anywhere else in the South Pacific without the implied or actual protection of some "civilized" power, Adee hinted that the United States should assume this role. This nation alone had the right to take the initiative in Samoa because it was the first country to

---

to *Samoa* (New Haven, 1933), passim; Clara E. Schieber, *The Transformation of American Sentiment toward Germany, 1870–1914* (Boston and New York, 1923), pp. 40 ff., 66 ff.; Robert Louis Stevenson, *A Footnote to History: Eight Years of Trouble in Samoa* (New York, 1892); Dulles, *Prelude to World Power,* pp. 99–101.

[3] Ryden, *Foreign Policy of the United States in Relation to Samoa,* pp. 173–174; Thomas M. Dawson to Walker Blaine, *Consular Despatches, Apia,* Aug. 22, 1881, vol. 8, no. 261; Dawson to Charles Payson, Sept. 10, 1880, ibid., no. 188; Dawson to Payson, Mar. 13, 1880, ibid., 7, no. 142; Dawson to Payson, Dec. 1, 1879, ibid., no. 125; Dawson to Payson, Sept. 13, 1879, ibid., no. 102; Berthold Greenebaum to James D. Porter, Aug. 8, 1885, ibid., no. 12; "Consul Greenebaum and Samoa," *Public Opinion* 1 (Aug. 28, 1886): 389; Pletcher, *The Awkward Years,* pp. 127–128.

conclude a treaty with the Samoan kingdom and the only power to pledge its good offices in case of need. In anticipation of such action, Adee wanted the salary of our representative increased to equal that of his German and British colleagues and his rank raised to "political agent and consul general." Only a strong agent, backed by an occasional visit from an American man-of-war, and the establishment of a coaling station would give the United States the necessary foothold in the South Pacific.[4]

In July 1886, the State Department sent George H. Bates to investigate the rumors of power rivalry which filled the dispatches sent home by our Apian consuls. Bates found the situation intolerable and suggested that the United States either renounce all interests in the islands or adopt a more vigorous policy. However, a strict interpretation of the Monroe Doctrine imposed impossible restrictions upon the Republic's growth and its new and wider interests throughout the world. The extension of commerce and the settlement of our Pacific coast made it apparent, Bates contended, that European possession of the Samoan islands would be a danger to the peace. Having acquired the right in the 1878 treaty to assist Samoa in its problems with foreign powers, we should not hesitate to do so, promptly and at any reasonable hazard. Material considerations aside, national self-respect dictated that the United States preserve Samoan neutrality and maintain a "commanding position" in the Pacific.[5]

While Adee and Bates pressured the State Department for more active involvement in Samoa, Pacific coast merchants, Western farmers, and Eastern shipbuilders, whose profits were affected by the existence of an American market in the South Pacific, became increasingly vocal about the future of the islands. Gustavus Goward,

---

[4] *Reports of the Diplomatic Bureau, Department of State,* vol. 4, no. 10 (Mar. 30, 1880); ibid., vol. 5, no. 66 (Dec. 22, 1881).

Most consuls in Samoa believed that a man-of-war in Apia harbor would not only protect American citizens but perhaps forestall a foreign protectorate (see Dawson to Hunter, Jan. 1, 1879, *Consular Despatches, Apia,* vol. 7, no. 35). The *San Francisco Chronicle* (Nov. 10, 1877) believed that if a commercial footing was established, or even if annexation was projected, a naval vessel was needed.

[5] *Special Missions, Department of State,* 3, no. 1, 451–464 (July 22, 1886); Bates to Bayard, Dec. 10, 1886, ibid. See also George H. Bates, "Some Aspects of the Samoan Question," *Century* 15 (Apr. 1889): 945–949.

an American commercial agent in Pago Pago during the late 1870s, advocated the establishment of a naval station and the inclusion of Pago Pago as a port of call for Pacific mail steamers. He believed the need for this "controlling" commercial point in the Pacific was so important to the Pacific coast merchants that it required their immediate attention and support. Consular and diplomatic reports in the early 1880s invariably listed the economic advantages which would fall into American hands (and particularly the enhancement of San Francisco's market) from an improved position in the islands.[6]

In the 1880s, a new series of events began to unfold in Samoa. The numerous intrigues of commercial agents, consuls, land speculators, and naval officers of several countries had created so much tension that, in the summer of 1887, Secretary of State Bayard called the British and German ministers in Washington into conference. The German representative urged that his country—the dominant commercial power—be allowed supreme control in the islands. And because Britain had recently benefited from German concessions elsewhere, she supported the German request. However, the United States persisted in its support of Samoan autonomy, and the conference proved abortive. Conditions in Samoa became even more confused after the failure of the Washington conference.

The next year German forces succeeded in deposing and deporting the native Samoan ruler. Threats and insults to American citizens and damage to their property provided fuel for those who had long considered annexation the proper American course of action. Finally, in January 1889, President Cleveland sent Congress all the correspondence relative to the situation, with a warning that German aims threatened the independence of the islands and the equal positions of the foreign powers. Congress, in reply, appropriated $500,000 to be used for the protection of American citizens and property in Samoa and $100,000 for further development of the

---

[6] Bates to Bayard, Dec. 10, 1886, *Special Agents, Department of State,* vol. 33; Goward to Seward, Dec. 28, 1878, ibid., vol. 13. For statements on Samoa's commercial value to the United States, see *Consular Reports* (*House Miscellaneous Documents*): 47th Cong., 1st sess. (Sept. 18, 1880), vol. 2, no. 3; (Dec. 31, 1882), vol. 10, no. 31; (Sept. 3, 1883), vol. 11, no. 36; 48th Cong., 2d sess. (June 30, 1884), no. 45; 49th Cong., 1st sess. (Dec. 31, 1884), vol. 16, no. 54; 50th Cong., 1st sess. (Aug. 15, 1888), no. 97.

Pago Pago harbor. Faced with a crisis that threatened war, Germany's Chancellor, Bismarck, agreed to a renewal of the earlier discussions and called for a three-power conference in Berlin in April. The Berlin conference set up a tripartite protectorate in which Germany, Great Britain, and the United States shared Samoan responsibilities.[7] President Harrison's approval of the protectorate and the Senate's confirmation constituted an unprecedented involvement in the Pacific. Although most officials considered the arrangement temporary, America had taken the initial step toward a more complete involvement in the affairs of the Pacific islands.

The press, meanwhile, had taken a strong stand on the German threat to Samoa. While many papers did not approve the final tripartite arrangement, most had been willing to risk war to protect the "open door" in Samoa. The *Boston Globe* wanted American property rights protected even if war resulted. The *New Orleans Daily Picayune* even sought to unite the blue and the gray with the motto "Peace and friendship with all the world if possible, but where honor and rights are concerned any nation can get a fight for the asking." The *American Exporter* feared that, if we did not take a strong stand, Britain or Germany would gobble up Samoa and end American trade. The events of 1888 had left the country with only two alternatives: action that involved risks or inaction that would bring discredit. The *Louisville Commercial* suggested that Secretary Bayard could redeem the Cleveland administration from the general public disdain felt for its foreign policy in other spheres by a more assertive stand on the Samoan issue. The *Washington Post* said that the State Department would not panic even if the German fleet sailed up the Potomac to bombard the capital; indeed, a 10-inch shell exploding in the Secretary of State's office would be required to awaken the administration to the country's interests.[8]

---

[7] Bayard to Greenebaum, Oct. 8, 1887, *Consular Instructions, Apia,* vol. 114, no. 35; Tyler, *Foreign Policy of James G. Blaine,* p. 225.

[8] "The Samoan Difficulty," *Public Opinion* 4 (Oct. 15, 1887): 7; "Possible Naval Fight at Samoa," *New Orleans Daily Picayune,* Mar. 9, 1889; *American Exporter* 20 (June 1887): 18; "The Samoan Problem," *Louisville Commercial,* Jan. 22, 1889; "Wake Up, Mr. Bayard," *Washington Post,* Jan. 21, 1889.

Public opinion, however, was not as unified on the settlement made in Berlin as it had been on the defense of American honor. The *New York Times*, which opposed the establishment of an American penal colony in the islands, felt that the country ought not to continue collecting "out-of-the-way islands." The *Times* further maintained that our interests in the South Pacific were more superficial than real. The Berlin agreement over Samoa, this so-called "triumph" of diplomacy, the *Times* feared, would jeopardize America's policy of isolation. The *New York Herald* also believed that the 1889 agreement with the European governments was contrary to the fixed policy of the United States. Its editors hoped that the Senate would at least add a proviso so that the treaty would not become a legal precedent. *The Nation* felt our participation in great power negotiations was a wild goose chase—a policy of sheer jingoism and meddlesomeness.[9]

Thus the three-power protectorate proved unpopular in this country and, eventually, unmanageable in Samoa. Jealousy and intrigue persisted. With the end of the Spanish-American War and the reshaping of American attitudes toward the permanent acquisition of Pacific territory, Samoa became a logical addition to our new empire. Late in 1899, the islands were divided between Germany and the United States, with Britain receiving compensation elsewhere in the Pacific. Yet the determination with which the United States faced the threat of war with Germany ten years earlier—rather than lose what were only potential commercial and strategic advantages in a faraway island—was a preview of American imperialism.

The early morning raid by the Japanese on Pearl Harbor on December 7, 1941, substantiates the importance of Hawaii in terms of twentieth-century military logistics. Yet the geographical position that made the islands so vital was also apparent early in the Republic's history. Uncle Sam had evinced strong concern for the land occupied by the Kanakas ever since the days when American whalers and shippers began to make the Sandwich (Hawaiian)

---

[9] *New York Times,* Nov. 11, 1888; "Samoa in Politics," ibid., Jan. 27, 1889; *New York Times,* June 24, 1889; "The Samoan Treaty," *New York Herald,* Jan. 25, 1890; *New York Daily Tribune,* Jan. 18, 1889; *The Nation* 48 (Jan. 31, 1889): 84.

Islands a port of call on their Pacific voyages. By the 1840s, five of every six ships in Hawaii's harbors flew the stars and stripes.

In Hawaii, as in Samoa, the threat of foreign intervention prompted a strong American stand. As early as 1842, Secretary of State Daniel Webster explained that although the United States had no desire to annex Hawaii, it would oppose such action by other powers. In effect, therefore, the principles of the Monroe Doctrine were applied against British encroachment into what was now regarded as within the American sphere of influence. A decade later, after further British and French penetration, President Millard Fillmore reiterated Webster's interpretation of the Monroe Doctrine: "Our true mission is not to propagate our opinions or impose upon other countries our form of government, by artifice or force, but to teach by example and show by our success, moderation, and justice the blessings of self-government." The United States, therefore, was "influenced by a desire that [Hawaii] should not pass under the control of any other great maritime State, but should remain in an independent condition and so be accessible and useful to the commerce of all nations." [10]

However, various attempts were made in the ante-bellum period to secure a commercial monopoly for American citizens. In 1854 William Marcy, Secretary of State in the Franklin Pierce administration, drafted a treaty of annexation, but the plan proved abortive when Hawaiian interests opposed to annexation managed to include a provision for granting it immediate statehood. A reciprocity treaty, concluded a year later, also failed to gain senatorial approval, primarily because of the opposition of Louisiana's sugar lobby. Reciprocity arrangements were again defeated in 1867.

But the fear of foreign interference and the commercial possibilities the Hawaiian Islands offered American businessmen continued to pull the United States deeper into diplomatic involvement in the Pacific in the postwar decades. In the 1870s, the Hawaiian Commercial Company, whose chief promoter was Claus Spreckels, a California businessman of German extraction, was the only large enterprise on the islands to receive foreign financial support. In 1874, eighty prominent Americans in Hawaii asked the support of the United States legation in Honolulu for their economic interests.

---

[10] Richardson, *Messages and Papers* (Dec. 2, 1851), 6: 2652–2653, 2656.

"Since the expansion of our own territory on the Pacific Coast has made us commercially and politically the near neighbor of the Hawaiian kingdom," they said, "it is on all accounts desirable that our interests here should be increasingly and abundantly protected." [11]

Despite the unhappiness of some businessmen, this protection came in January of the following year in the form of a reciprocity treaty. Debated and attacked by the strong protectionists in Congress, the treaty provided that Hawaiian sugar could enter the United States duty free on the stipulation that the kingdom would never grant territorial concessions to any other country. Hawaii's sugar production boomed as a result of the treaty, and the country's economy in effect became mortgaged to the United States. [12]

During the next decade, American representatives continually complained that the islands were violating the terms of the reciprocity agreement. However, labor problems on the islands were most often the cause of this American anxiety. Chinese labor, which many thought to be unsatisfactory, and the general labor shortage for harvesting the sugar crop, prompted State Department concern that the Hawaiian monarchy would contract with England to secure coolie immigration from British colonies in the Far East. Secretary Blaine informed our London minister, James Russell Lowell, of the suspected British plan to acquire a controlling influence in Hawaiian commerce by encouraging such immigration. Our minister in the islands, James M. Comly, warned his superiors that the Hawaiian King, Kalakaua, was planning to ally himself with China in creating a Polynesian confederacy. The labor shortage presented a very real danger that Hawaii would become an Asiatic possession, or at least a British protectorate. [13]

---

[11] John M. Morton to William Hunter, Nov. 25, 1879, *Consular Despatches, Honolulu,* no. 18; Merze Tate, *The United States and the Hawaiian Kingdom* (New Haven and London, 1965), pp. 38–43 and passim; Pletcher, *The Awkward Years,* pp. 173–177.

[12] Donald M. Dozer, "The Opposition to Hawaiian Reciprocity, 1876–1888," *Pacific Historical Review,* 14 (1945), 157–183; Pletcher, *The Awkward Years,* pp. 175–177; Tate, *Hawaii: Reciprocity or Annexation* (East Lansing, Mich., 1968), chap. 1–7. See also Sylvester K. Stevens, *American Expansion in Hawaii, 1842–1898* (New York, 1968), passim.

[13] Blaine to Lowell, Dec. 10, 1881, *Foreign Relations,* 1881, pp. 569–570,

The world tour of King Kalakaua in 1881 seemed to confirm these American fears. Although the King admired both European and American institutions, and was known for his naive attempts to reconcile the two types, Americans in Hawaii were so concerned that their interests might be betrayed that they chose some of their fellow citizens to accompany the royal entourage. Secretary Blaine expressed similar alarm. He alerted Minister James B. Angell in China to the projected visit of Kalakaua and sent notes stating the United States' position against the alienation of Hawaiian territory to the American ministers in London, Paris, and Berlin.[14]

The events of 1881 illustrate the more stringent tone the United States was adopting toward Hawaii; and Blaine's large vision of America's new role in world affairs is nowhere better illustrated than in his notes regarding Hawaii, which clearly reveal his plan to reactivate the Monroe Doctrine to meet the new situation. Following tradition, the United States would respect Hawaiian independence, but would under no circumstances allow the transfer of its territory to any other power. The Hawaiian Islands, according to Blaine, were in the zone or belt of American commercial dominance and should be considered a part of the American system. As the key to the Pacific, Hawaii's "benevolent neutrality" was essential. If such a policy was impractical, the United States would have to meet the situation with an "avowedly American solution." What that solution was, Blaine did not say. Although he denied any desire for political acquisition, his statements in response to the fears of coolie immigration and the King's world tour in effect made the Hawaiian Islands a protectorate of the United States.[15]

Later Secretaries of State accepted Blaine's position. In 1882, Secretary Frelinghuysen told the chairman of the House Committee on Foreign Affairs that although the United States did not desire supremacy in Hawaii's domestic councils, it was equally clear that

---

635–639; Comly to Frelinghuysen, Apr. 10, 1882, *Despatches, Hawaii,* vol. 20, no. 213.

[14] Blaine to Angell, Apr. 22, 1881, *Instructions, China,* vol. 3, no. 90. See also William N. Armstrong, *Around the World with a King* (New York, 1904) and Ralph S. Kuykendall, *The Hawaiiañ Kingdom: The Kalakaua Dynasty, 1874–1893* (Honolulu, 1967), passim.

[15] Blaine to Comly, Nov. 19, 1881, *Instructions, Hawaii,* no. 111; Blaine to Comly, Dec. 1, 1881, ibid., vol. 2, no. 113–114.

any other established foreign influence would conflict with our national interests. He added that if the United States had favored the establishment of protectorates, Hawaii would have been the foremost candidate. Frelinghuysen, like Blaine, felt that Hawaii belonged in the American commonwealth rather than in a grouping of Asian nations.[16]

Surprisingly, Secretary Bayard took a more aggressive stand on Hawaii than he did with regard to the isthmian canal. "We desire no domination in the Pacific for ourselves," he wrote, "nor can we be expected to sanction a doctrine whereby any one [nation] might roam at will over the Pacific Seas and absorb the jurisdiction of Islands." He informed our minister of a proposed $2 million British loan to Hawaii that would call for pledging the islands' revenues as collateral. He also noted that such action would violate Hawaiian-American treaty arrangements (the reciprocity treaty of 1875). Regarding Hawaii's annexation as inevitable by the 1890s, Bayard urged the establishment of closer ties with the islands by—for example—laying a cable between San Francisco and Honolulu. Such a cable, as the *New York Herald* had already pointed out, would have greater political than commercial implications, and could be legitimately considered a necessary measure for coastal defense. While less convinced of the inevitability of annexation, Bayard's chief, President Cleveland, also saw the value of our Hawaiian contacts. In his annual message for 1886, the chief executive emphasized the intimacy of those relations and summarized Hawaii's role as an outpost of American commerce. Both the President and the Secretary of State viewed the islands as way stations on the road to Asia. By maintaining a close relationship with Hawaii, we would make the markets of Asia more easily accessible.[17]

The Eastern press generally regarded our Hawaiian interests as vital to our political and economic stability. Displaying an interest

---

[16] Frelinghuysen to C. G. Williams, Dec. 20, 1882, "Frelinghuysen Letter Books," vol. 4, Frelinghuysen MSS, Library of Congress.

[17] Bayard to H. A. P. Carter, Nov. 11, 1885, *Instructions, Hawaii,* vol. 1, quoted in Tansill, *Bayard,* p. 373; Bayard to George W. Merrill, Jan. 8, 1887, *Instructions, Hawaii,* vol. 3, no. 36; Bayard to Gresham, Aug. 5, 1893, quoted in Tansill, *Bayard,* p. 409; *New York Herald,* Dec. 12, 1887; *Foreign Relations,* 1886, p. vi (Cleveland's Message of Dec. 6, 1886); LaFeber, *The New Empire,* pp. 53–56.

unusual in those "contented years," the *New York Herald* thought Hawaii was as important to the United States as Malta was to Great Britain. "If the Sandwich Islands are to remain independent, well and good," this editorial observed; "we are in no hurry. [But if they] seek protection from a foreign Power, the United States will know when to put in its claim and how to urge it." The islands would never belong to another country as long as the United States "does its duty to itself." The *New York Daily Tribune* regarded Hawaii as a natural "commercial appendage" of the United States and felt that annexation was thwarted only by our own indifference. It forecast the replacement of apathy by aggressive, intelligent enterprise that would safeguard our mercantile penetration of the islands. A San Francisco business paper, by remarking that America was holding Hawaii by trade relations and not by the use of fleets or armies, made the comparison with European methods obvious. The *Sacramento Daily Record-Union* bluntly asserted that the Hawaiian trade could not be allowed to go to foreign nations.[18]

The reciprocity treaty with Hawaii was renewed in 1884, with a Senate proviso that Pearl Harbor be secured as a naval station. While the extension of the treaty primarily concerned Hawaiian sugar planters and refiners and San Francisco consumers, the grant of Pearl Harbor concerned all nations, and Great Britain suggested that the islands be neutralized and that equal accessibility be proclaimed for all powers. America's reply was an assurance that there would be no prejudice against British shipping. Both nations were becoming more aware that Hawaii was the base for exploiting the Asian market, and reciprocity was rapidly becoming an economic substitute for American political annexation.[19]

The press was aware of this substitution, and some segments bitterly criticized the reciprocity arrangements and the wider economic role being played by the United States. The *San Francisco Chron-*

---

[18] "Honolulu, the American Malta: *Civis Americanus Sum*," *New York Herald*, July 25, 1887; "England Must Not Interfere with Our Rights in the Sandwich Islands," ibid., Sept. 12, 1887; "American Influence Abroad," *New York Daily Tribune*, June 24, 1879; "American Influence in the Hawaiian Islands," *San Francisco Merchant*, Feb. 10, 1882; "The Hawaiian Treaty," *Sacramento Daily Record-Union*, Jan. 24, 1887.

[19] Merze Tate, "British Opposition to the Cession of Pearl Harbor," *Pacific Historical Review* 29 (Nov. 1960): 381–394.

icle, which felt that reciprocal trade would have a pernicious effect on manufacturing, contended that it would be cheaper for the government to pay San Francisco merchants for their goods than to admit duty-free Hawaiian products. Those opposed to reciprocity always claimed that it was improper for Americans to be taxed for the benefit of sugar planters and speculators. The *New York Times*, denying that great advantages would come to the United States, maintained that the benefits which were supposed to compensate for a loss of revenue were, instead, unnecessary political advantages for a nation which did not involve itself in foreign turmoil.[20] Yet international involvement was the direction in which the United States was moving, and Hawaiian reciprocity marked the beginnings of this shift in the attitude of the American people toward foreign problems.

The situation in the Far East, as in the Samoan and Hawaiian islands, contributed to further American involvement in the outside world. During the Gilded Age, the Department of State and the executive branch feared the threat to international stability arising out of rapid Japanese westernization, the Russian *Drang nach Osten*, and the impending collapse of China. Disavowing political ambitions abroad, the United States was quick to denounce all foreign schemes of territorial aggrandizement. Some Americans even advocated the enunciation of an "Asiatic Monroe Doctrine," by which the United States would safeguard the Far East and keep it open to commercial penetration by all nations.[21]

Threats to the status quo in the Orient came so frequently that it is possible to list only a few of the most important. In the 1880s there were widespread rumors of a colonizing movement by Germany, especially in the islands south of Korea, and of future German annexation of that peninsula. Korea's relationships not only to Germany but also to France, China, and Russia were critically analyzed by the American press. Especially serious were French threats

---

[20] "The Hawaiian Treaty," *San Francisco Chronicle,* Jan. 13, 1887; "The Hawaiian Treaty," *New York Herald,* Jan. 13, 1883; "The Hawaiian Treaty," *New York Times,* Dec. 11, 1884.

[21] *Reports of the Diplomatic Bureau,* vol. 6, no. 61½ (May 1, 1881); "American Influence in the East," *New York Herald,* Nov. 21, 1887.

against Indo China and the Manchu Empire, and Russian intrigues in China and Korea were a chronic source of anxiety.[22]

America's attitude toward European penetration of Asia is difficult to evaluate. The press often took a rigorous tone, but official State Department and executive policy wavered between concern and apathy. When China requested Washington's intervention in 1879 in a dispute with Japan over the Liukiu Islands, Secretary Evarts stated that the United States would use its good offices to mediate if Japan would agree and cooperate. He added that, because the United States was the most "prominent advocate of arbitration," it was natural that "the wise counselors" in each nation would turn to this country for assistance. Yet two years later, when the British requested that the United States join in revising treaties between Siam and the West, the State Department seemed almost unconcerned about the possibility of European penetration. Secretary Blaine felt that the United States should act independently in all negotiations dealing with our Far Eastern interests. In a similar mood, the United States refused a Korean request for diplomatic assistance against the British occupation of Port Arthur.[23]

However, our relations with Japan followed a more consistent pattern than our relations with other Far Eastern powers. Because the United States had been instrumental in opening Japan to the world, to abandon our "protégé" to other powers would have been tantamount to renouncing all interest in trans-Pacific affairs. This the United States would not do. Thus one of the problems in the Gilded Age was maintaining, rather than increasing, our interests in Japan.[24]

---

[22] *Boston Economist* 7 (May 6, 1882): 275; Rev. Luther H. Gulick, "China and Korea," *New York Observer,* 61 (June 21, 1883), 197; "France in China and Bismarck in Europe," *New York Herald,* June 19, 1883; Bayard to Richard D. Hubbard, Aug. 19, 1884, *Instructions, Japan,* vol. 3, no. 11.

[23] Evarts to Bingham, Oct. 25, 1879, *Instructions, Japan,* 2: 543–544, quoted in Bemis, *American Secretaries of State and their Diplomacy,* 7: 232 (Bowers and Reid, "William M. Evarts," pp. 217–259); Barrows, *Evarts,* pp. 384–385; Blaine to Consul General John A. Halderman, *Consular Despatches,* vol. 100, no. 4 (June 24, 1881); Lester B. Shippee, "Thomas Francis Bayard," in Bemis, *American Secretaries of State,* 8: 85.

[24] "Japan," *Missionary Herald* 66 (Mar. 1870): 74–77; "English Chin-Chinning with Japan," *New York Herald,* Oct. 9, 1887.

The tradition of empathy between these two nations manifested itself in several ways. The first American consul to Japan, Townsend Harris, who arrived in 1856, opened the way for a close relationship between the two countries through his considerate dealings with the Japanese and his far-reaching treaty, which opened the Japanese ports and allowed Americans considerable latitude of action. The westernization of the nation really went forward, however, with the Meiji restoration in the 1860s. When the Meiji Emperor established his authority over the military ruler, the Shogun, he directed his country toward the ways of the West. Japan adopted American products: condensed milk, clocks, frock coats, silk tophats, chairs and tables in government offices, gas lamps, lightning conductors, baseball, postal service, the diatonic scale in music, crayons, and railroads. Part of this almost slavish imitation was later modified or abandoned, but many of the conveniences of American life became central to Japanese culture.[25]

We have already seen the importance of American education and technology to Japan, and how Japanese agriculture was updated by American methods.[26] American science, medicine, and music were all adapted to Japanese life. In the field of government, the constitution of 1868 drew in large measure upon the American experience. The *Federalist* essays explaining the American Constitution were consulted by the fathers of a similar document for Japan, drawn up in the 1880s, even though the parliament devised at that time followed the English model. In 1872 and 1873, as part of a world trip, a Japanese mission studied American government in operation, and six years later, when ex-President Grant visited Japan, he advised the Japanese on political matters. The visit of so famous a person no doubt flattered the Japanese. His interest in their material progress encouraged the Japanese and represented a type of international concern on the part of Americans. Although Christianity was forbidden until 1873, missionary activity expanded so rapidly after that date that it may well have been the most ambitious American cultural activity in Japan.[27]

---

[25] "Trade Prospects in Japan," *Washington Post,* Mar. 5, 1889; Dulles, *Yankees and Samurai,* pp. 143–153; Neumann, *America Encounters Japan,* pp. 52 ff., 61.

[26] See chapter 7 above. See also Dulles, *Yankees and Samurai,* pp. 153–162.

[27] Dulles, *Yankees and Samurai,* pp. 162–173; Schwantes, *Japanese and*

America's pride swelled when she was chosen to assist in Japanese military planning. The United States Navy was studied very closely, and though Great Britain was the chief source of foreign-built ships, many American ships and munitions were purchased. Japanese students studied at the United States Naval Academy, and the first of the six who survived the training graduated in 1877. An American, Henry W. Grinnell of New York, rose to high rank in the Japanese navy and directed a Japanese naval school. American concern with Japanese navalism was not a departure from our traditional anti-imperialist attitude; instead, it grew in part from a fear that Japan, like China, might be exploited by Europe to the disadvantage of America's commercial interests. But, of course, the growth of Japan's national consciousness led to ventures in imperialism, especially in Formosa and Korea. The American consul in Amoy, Charles LeGendre, an adventurer and Civil War brigadier general, encouraged the Japanese and even guided them in their dealings with China.[28]

Our relationship with Japan, however, was not one sided. In 1860 Japan sent her first mission to tour the United States, and although the Japanese came here to learn, Americans learned to appreciate Japanese art, architecture, and culture. Japanese curios were displayed at the Philadelphia Centennial Exhibition of 1876, and the next year were on sale at Tiffany's in New York City. Indeed, the celebrated artist, James M. Whistler, was reputed to be a collector of Japanese art. Japanese art became more widely appreciated in the United States through the efforts of art critic Ernest Fenollosa. One of the Japanese imperial art commissioners, Fenollosa opened ancient storehouses and rounded up priceless treasures for the Japanese government, thereby spurring enthusiasm in the United States and providing the impetus for such fine Oriental collections as those of the Boston Museum of Fine Arts and the Freer Gallery.[29]

Americans, pp. 86–90; Neumann, *America Encounters Japan,* p. 51; Pletcher, *The Awkward Years,* p. 198.

[28] Dulles, *Yankees and Samurai,* pp. 154–155; Neumann, *America Encounters Japan,* pp. 75–83, 89–97.

[29] Dulles, *Yankees and Samurai,* pp. 214–222; Neumann, *America Encounters Japan,* pp. 61–66; Benjamin Smith Lyman, "The Character of the Japanese: A Study of Human Nature," *Journal of Speculative Philosophy* 5 (Apr. 1885): 133–172.

Commercially, China as well as Japan offered great possibilities for the ever expanding markets of American enterprise. Even before the Civil War and the onslaught of American industrialism, some Americans recognized the commercial potential of the Orient. Hannibal Hamlin—Lincoln's first Vice President, a Radical Republican, and a longtime senator from Maine—was ahead of his time when, in his college valedictory address, he said: "I see . . . a mighty country, an empire upon the Pacific; . . . I look beyond, and I see the mighty commerce that shall come . . . to us if we are wise." [30] In the 1880s, Hamlin's vision was coming true. Our minister in Peking, John Russell Young, thought that America's first duty in foreign affairs was to protect its interests in the Far East, which in 1883 rivaled those of Great Britain. Representative Richard W. Townshend of Illinois thought the commercial possibilities in China so promising that he advocated elevating the legation at Peking to that of a "first class" mission. The United States was the greatest power bordering the Pacific, Townshend boasted, and its destiny was to maintain supremacy throughout that area. While some felt it might be possible to dispense with ministers in Europe so long as consuls were retained, consuls and ministers were needed if only because of European encroachments in the Far East.[31]

Newspapers and periodicals frequently mentioned the need for increased trade with Asia. In 1870, approximately fifty American firms were doing business in China; at the turn of the century the number had increased to over eighty. San Francisco merchants early envisioned their city as the future center of the growing trade with the Orient. In the 1880s, a San Francisco steamer took 27 days to reach Shanghai, compared with 58 to London via the Suez Canal, and much publicity was given to the advantages of the shorter route. In 1880, a third of San Francisco's export and import trade was with China; only a little over 50 percent of the latter was in tea and silk for Eastern cities, and the rest was for San Francisco's Chinatown. Nevertheless, the *San Francisco Journal of Commerce* pre-

---

[30] A. A. Hayes, "China and the United States," *Atlantic Monthly* 59 (May 1887): 586–590; Charles Eugene Hamlin, *The Life and Times of Hannibal Hamlin* (Cambridge, Mass., 1899), p. 543.

[31] Frelinghuysen to Young, Feb. 26, 1883, *Instructions, China*, vol. 3, no. 86; *Congressional Record,* 49th Cong., 2d sess. (Feb. 3, 1887), 18, pt. 3, 81–82.

dicted that very soon China would cease to be a *terra incognita* to Americans and would increase her trade with this country. Another trade journal felt that the best way to solve Chinese problems (including the one that was fast emerging in America over Chinese immigration) was to encourage Chinese railroad ventures. Railroads would provide employment in China as well as facilitate commercial intercourse with Western powers. Indeed, China's "railroad revolution" later prompted Anglo-American competition for contracts.[32]

On the other hand, there was a feeling in some quarters that our trade with China was overvalued, and that the time had come to prick the bubble of speculation. While the United States sent China less goods than any other nation (with the possible exception of Russia), this small volume did not indicate a lack of interest in the sprawling Asian nation. A Southern magazine, for example, admonished Dixie to concentrate on furnishing China and Japan with such products as cotton goods lest other parts of the country provide for these needs. Chinese backwardness and conservatism could be, as the *Engineering News* pointed out, an impenetrable bar to American enterprise.[33]

Also, shipping difficulties and depreciated currency in large part explain America's small volume of trade with China after the Civil War. In contrast to Japan, which recognized the value of foreign trade and Occidental techniques, the Chinese refused to initiate trade. In 1868 the Japanese deliberately set out to imitate the West in trade, industry, and governmental administration, but no such conscious effort was ever evident in the case of China. Trade statistics tell much of the story. In 1865 the percentage of American imports from China was 2.2, and two decades later the figure had risen to only 2.8. In those same years the percentage of American exports to China declined from 2.0 to 0.9. These statistics involve

---

[32] Kwang-Ching Liu, *Americans and Chinese* (Cambridge, Mass., 1963), p. 3; "San Francisco, the Future Centre of Chinese and Japanese Trade," *San Francisco Journal of Commerce,* Aug. 11, 1881; "Chinese Trade with San Francisco," ibid., Sept. 9, 1880; "Trade with China," *Home Market Bulletin* 1 (Sept. 1889): 3; *Pittsburgh National Labor Tribune,* Oct. 26, 1889.

[33] Hayes, "China and the United States," loc. cit.; *San Francisco Merchant,* Jan. 6, 1882; E. E. Overholt, "Applied Mechanics and Civilization," *Dixie* 4 (Aug. 1888): 607–608; *Engineering News* 18 (Sept. 17, 1887): 206.

more than lack of interest on the American side: our exports to China declined because the latter was not receptive to many American goods (especially after beaver pelts declined in importance). European competition was another problem; and Chinese officials were uncooperative toward Americans despite our treaty agreements. Considering the state of the merchant marine, our navy, and foreign service (discussed earlier), these sorry statistics should not be too surprising.[34]

In contrast to the low volume of trade with China, the service performed by Commodore Shufeldt as special adviser to the Manchu government is striking testimony of the larger role China was beginning to play in our foreign policy. China's pressing need in the 1880s was to strengthen her naval forces because of the threat of war with Russia. In 1880, Secretary Evarts informed Minister Angell that the government would allow an American citizen to help improve the material well-being of China, and he instructed the minister to encourage a request for such aid. Reflecting our traditional ambivalence toward the Far East, however, Angell was cautioned to act slowly and not take the initiative by *offering* assistance for China. But James G. Blaine, of course, could be counted on for more vigorous action, and the secretary took note that Shufeldt's presence in China might prove advantageous to our entire Far Eastern position. Traditionally, Paris or London had led in the task of modernization, but China was becoming apprehensive of their voracious territorial appetites and was increasingly turning to Washington. The *New York Herald* remarked that England was becoming anxious about decreases in her Asian trade and asserting—perhaps more enthusiastically than the facts warranted—that the United States had driven her out of that market![35]

President Chester A. Arthur furthered the cause of closer Chinese-American relations, perhaps unwittingly, by his appointment of John Russell Young as minister to China—one of the most competent nineteenth-century American ministers in the Far East. An

---

[34] Mildred A. Preen, "Statistical Analysis of the Trade of the United States with China" (M.A. thesis, Columbia University, 1941), pp. 90–91.

[35] Evarts to Angell, Oct. 29, 1880, *Instructions, China,* vol. 3, no. 50; Blaine to Angell, May 9, 1881, ibid., vol. 3, no. 94; "Commodore Shufeldt and the Chinese Navy," *New York Herald,* Mar. 26, 1881; "England's Trade with China," ibid., Apr. 19, 1879.

example of his efforts to expand American influence in China came during an incident between China and France in 1884, when French demands for control of Indo China caused China to seek America's assistance. Young used the opportunity to lecture the Chinese on the necessity of adapting Western ways for self-defense. The links between an ancient China and a youthful United States were also pointed up with a prediction that, within a century, the two nations would be *the* two great powers on earth. Such a forecast did not reckon with a Communist revolution in China, for it portrayed the oldest nation on earth and Uncle Sam marching "hand in hand along the path of [democratic] progress." [36]

The Far East was also given generous publicity in James Gordon Bennett Jr.'s *New York Herald*. The paper believed that no power save the United States could treat Chinese problems objectively, since it had so little to lose or gain in a material way. Indeed, it lamented this fact and urged Congress to recognize the commercial possibilities inherent in closer political relations with China. The *Herald* also contended that our ties with Asia should be closer than those with Europe, and it described the Orient as the "next door neighbors" of our Pacific states.[37]

The problem of Oriental immigration increased, as well as vexed, Sino-American relations in the late nineteenth century. The Chinese coolie had been welcomed in the 1840s, but his welcome faded as America's technological development abridged the usefulness of the unskilled laborer. By the 1870s the new attitude was noticeable, and the spirit of the 1868 Burlingame treaty ebbed rapidly when the 1880 census revealed that there were 75,000 Chinese in California, or almost 10 percent of the population. While immigration from Asia was predominantly a domestic question, it had broad foreign implications, and economic expansionists feared the effect of America's restrictive policy. Minister George F. Seward told Secretary Evarts that it would be shortsighted for the United States to set the

---

[36] Pletcher, *The Awkward Years,* pp. 198–199, 216–217; *Cleveland Leader,* Dec. 29, 1868.

[37] "France and China—The Possibility of American Arbitration," *New York Herald,* Sept. 9, 1883; "The Treaties with China and Our Policy in Asia," ibid., Jan. 15, 1881; "American Commerce with China," ibid., Mar. 29, 1880.

example of a willful violation of treaty rights. We would be, he predicted, the chief loser in such a course.[38]

Opinions in the United States were sharply divided between the business- and religious-oriented Sinophiles and the men who felt that the influx of more coolies would endanger our institutions. The *International Review* felt sure that the Chinese could never be assimilated in the American "melting pot." The staid *New Englander* feared that a further influx of Chinese might endanger both our economy and our republican institutions. *Bradstreet's* pointed up the threat to native labor and possibly ruinous competition among manufacturers. Sympathetic because of the race issue, the *Atlanta Constitution* feared the consequences if California had to assimilate a swarm of Mongolians for the economic benefit of a few who were eager to exploit a cheap labor supply. On the other hand, Chinese exclusion disappointed business and religious elements that were anxious for closer Chinese relations. President Hayes, in vetoing the first Exclusion Act (1879), noted that the United States had capitalized upon the missionary, commercial, and travel advantages granted in the Burlingame treaty. "Important interests have grown up under the treaty," he insisted, "and rest upon faith and its observance." This action of Hayes, and the subsequent veto by President Arthur of a similar bill in 1882 to suspend immigration from China for twenty years, was praised in some quarters.[39]

Press opinion generally opposed exclusion by law. While some business journals regarded Chinese immigration as a threat, the

---

[38] Tyler Dennett, *Americans in Eastern Asia* (New York, 1922), pp. 535 ff.; Seward to Evarts, Mar. 22, 1878, *Despatches, China,* vol. 47, no. 425 (for a full consideration of the Chinese immigration issue, see Mary R. Coolidge, *Chinese Immigration* [New York, 1909]; Elmer C. Sandmeyer, *The Anti-Chinese Movement in California* [Urbana, Ill., 1939]). For the background of exclusion and general problems of the Chinese in America, see Gunther Barth, *Bitter Strength: A History of the Chinese in the United States, 1850–1870* (Cambridge, Mass., 1964); see also Stuart C. Miller, *The Unwelcome Immigrant: The American Image of the Chinese, 1785–1882* (Berkeley and Los Angeles, 1969).

[39] "The Chinese Question in the United States," *International Review* 3 (1876): 833–841; D. McGregor Means, "Chinese Immigration and Political Economy," *New Englander* 36 (Jan. 1877): 1–10; "Chinese Immigration," *Bradstreet's* 5 (Mar. 18, 1882): 162; "Chinese Immigration," *Atlanta Constitution,* Mar. 14, 1880; "The Chinese Exclusion Act," *Public Opinion* 7 (July 27, 1889): 331; Williams, *Diary and Letters of Hayes,* 3: 523 (Feb. 23, 1879, entry).

majority urged closer relationships with the Orient. The *American Economist*, for example, lauded the resolution of the New York Chamber of Commerce that urged President Harrison to reopen negotiations with China. The *Boston Commercial Bulletin* asserted that the United States could not afford to treat a foreign nation in ways that outraged the spirit of American institutions. The *Hartford Daily Courant* simply labeled the bill un-American. Our former minister to China, George F. Seward, felt that Arthur's veto upheld the honor of the nation. The *New York Times* admitted that, though restricted immigration was necessary, less radical action should have been taken. The *Indianapolis Journal* raised the question of sectional politics, claiming that certain Pacific coast legislators and demagogues fostered such a policy. *The Nation* felt that Californians' aversion to China was a "shocking piece of barbarism" and an "absurd prejudice." Preaching a compromise solution and urging moderation and less emotionalism, *The Nation* derided the idea that a flow of coolies would prove fatal to American government or Western civilization.[40]

Hayes's veto led one writer to observe that the President's action had thwarted "the obloquy that Congressmen tried to fasten on our national reputation." Churchmen also lashed out against exclusion, arguing that to check the movement of people between Asia and America would be to impede the progress of civilization and Christianity. One religious journal pointed out that, since America was a land of refuge, a policy of racial discrimination was inappropriate. The missionary's role in the Far East was obviously complicated by this country's hostility toward Orientals: his opposition to exclusion put him in the awkward position of opposing the policy of the American government, on which he depended for protection in China.[41] Thus the debate over Chinese exclusion revealed the dis-

---

[40] "Our Relations with China," *American Economist* 4 (Dec. 20, 1889): 395; *Boston Commercial Bulletin*, Mar. 11, 1882; *Hartford Daily Courant*, Mar. 10, 1882; G. F. Seward, "Mongolian Immigration," *North American Review* 307 (June 1882): 562–577; "The President's Veto," *New York Times*, Apr. 5, 1882; *Indianapolis Journal*, Jan. 15, 1881; "The California Disturbance," *The Nation* 22 (Apr. 13, 1876): 241–242; *The Nation* 11 (July 14, 1870): 18; "Sand-Lot Ratiocination," ibid. (Feb. 27, 1879): 145.

[41] S. Wells Williams, "Our Treaties with China," *New Englander* 38 (May 1879): 301–324; "The Anti-Chinese Bill," *Christian Union* 25 (Mar. 23,

parity that was already apparent between those who had larger horizons and the older, isolationist view which even at that time was tinged with racism.

While serious American concern with Korea began only with the attack by the North against the South on June 25, 1950, the peninsula had been within the American sphere of interest ever since the United States opened the Hermit Kingdom to world trade. Some authorities contend that perhaps the most significant work the navy undertook between the Civil and Spanish-American Wars was its part in opening Korea to the world. It began in 1878, when Aaron A. Sargent of California, chairman of the Senate Committee on Naval Affairs, introduced a joint resolution to authorize the President to appoint a commission to negotiate a treaty of amity and commerce with Korea by enlisting the good offices of Japan. This resolution was referred to the Senate Committee on Foreign Relations, where it was buried. Sargent described the Koreans as waiting patiently for the United States to extend the same friendly hand we had proffered Japan. He felt that the Koreans were a "new people," contiguous by water to the outside world, receptive to our advanced ways, and eager to buy our manufactured goods.[42]

Almost simultaneously the Navy Department, in cooperation with the Department of State, commissioned Shufeldt on that far-ranging mission which, as we have seen, included not only the extension of American commercial interests in the Congo but the opening of Korea to world commerce. Our minister in Japan, John A. Bingham, was instructed to apply to the Japanese Minister of Foreign Affairs for aid in smoothing Shufeldt's way. Specifically, Shufeldt was to obtain a treaty for the relief of American vessels and crews shipwrecked off the Korean coast and, if possible, negotiate a treaty of

---

1882): 270; "Chinese Emigration," *Friends' Intelligencer* 26 (Aug. 7, 1869): 360; James M. McCutcheon, "The Missionary and Diplomacy in China," loc. cit. See also Gary Pennanen, "Public Opinion and the Chinese Question, 1876–1879," *Ohio History* 77 (1968): 139–148, 201–203.

[42] Paullin, *The Opening of Korea by Commodore Shufeldt,* p. 470; Tyler Dennett, *Americans in Eastern Asia,* p. 450; *Congressional Record,* 45th Cong., 2d sess. (Apr. 8, 17, 1878), 7, pt. 3, 2324, 2599–2601. See also "The Beginnings of Medical Work in Korea," *Korean Repository* 1 (Dec. 1892): 353–358, in Horace N. Allen MSS, New York Public Library.

amity and commerce. With this charge, Shufeldt hopefully set sail in 1878.[43]

Aid for American sailors shipwrecked in Oriental waters had been a long-standing problem. In 1866, when an American ship was wrecked off the Korean coast and its crew and passengers were killed, Secretary Seward considered intervention. The original impetus for such action came from his nephew, George F. Seward, the consul general in Shanghai, but the idea was dropped until 1871, when five ships under the command of Commodore John Rodgers attempted to open negotiations with Korea and secure promises for the protection of American lives. The expedition had been fired upon from the Korean forts, American blood was spilled, and Rodgers destroyed the forts, killing about 200 Koreans. Such American papers as took note of the incident urged extreme measures for the redress of what they called barbarous and injurious insults to our flag. Indeed, Secretary Blaine seemed more interested in remedying this type of situation than in expanding the American dominion. Holding that no political or commercial interest made a Korean treaty a matter of urgent importance, he felt only that an area near China and Japan should be made available for American trade. If Korea was willing to open its ports, the United States would be willing to establish friendly relations. However, in uncharacteristic fashion—considering his stand in Latin America and elsewhere—Blaine proclaimed that his country did not propose to use force to convince the Koreans.[44]

Besides Secretary Blaine's relative disinterest in a Korean treaty,

---

[43] Evarts to Thompson, Nov. 9, 1878; "Cruise of 'Ticonderoga,' " 1: 19–20, in Navy Department, National Archives; Blaine to Shufeldt, Nov. 14, 1881; Frelinghuysen to Shufeldt, Jan. 6, 1882, in Shufeldt MSS, quoted in Paullin, *Diplomatic Negotiations of American Naval Officers*, p. 309.

[44] *Cleveland Leader*, June 19, 1871, in *Annals of Cleveland*, 54 (1871), 281; "Our Little Battle in Corean Waters," *Overland Monthly* 8 (Aug. 1886): 725–728; Dennett, *Americans in Eastern Asia*, p. 453; Dulles, *Prelude to World Power*, pp. 85–88; Tyler, *Foreign Policy of James G. Blaine*, pp. 262 ff.

The 1871 Rodgers Expedition was the largest American military action between the Civil and the Spanish-American wars. For a brief discussion of its genesis and implications, see William M. Leary, Jr., "Our Other War in Korea," *United States Naval Institute Proceedings* 94 (June 1968): 47–53.

our diplomatic staff in the Far East charged that Shufeldt's mission was further handicapped by foreign influences, especially those of England and France. Minister Bingham in Tokyo informed Evarts that the Mikado refused to give the commodore letters of introduction to the Korean officials. In fact, however, Bingham doubted the wisdom of relations with so unpromising a country. Shufeldt himself suspected that certain Chinese officials, anxious that Korea not conclude treaty arrangements with the United States, advised the Hermit Kingdom to enter into relations with other powers. Despite all the obstacles which beset him, Shufeldt remained optimistic and persistent. He never lost his faith in America's future in the Pacific, and he held fast to his belief that the treaty with Korea would form another link in the chain which would eventually unite East and West. While he opposed the use of force in the Far East, he insisted that America be the "pioneer of the Pacific." [45]

Perhaps the zeal with which Shufeldt pursued his mission caused him to commit a monumental blunder, which resulted in his temporary recall to Washington. Frustrated by his failure to gain an interview with the King of Korea, the commodore vented his feelings in 1880 in a personal letter to Senator Sargent, who was being considered by President Arthur for a cabinet appointment. Shufeldt referred to Li Hung-chang, the Chinese viceroy of a coastal province adjacent to Shanghai, with whom he was negotiating, as "the Bismarck of the East," who existed at the whim of the Chinese Empress, "an ignorant, capricious and immoral woman." He also said that American policy toward China ought to be "purely selfish." Because of a misunderstanding, Sargent allowed the letter to be published, thus creating a sensation which aroused emotions on both sides of the Pacific. Li Hung-chang, who had been working for renewed Chinese-Korean bonds, was angered; Frelinghuysen recalled Shufeldt; and the navy assigned him to a desk job. Yet in the spring of 1882, Li Hung-chang and Shufeldt drew up a comprehensive commercial treaty which accomplished the latter's mission. The fol-

---

[45] Bingham to Evarts, May 6, 1880, *Despatches, Japan,* vol. 42, no. 1112; Shufeldt to Bingham, Apr. 27, 1880, enclosure in ibid.; Bingham to Evarts, May 31, 1880, ibid.; ibid., no. 1126; Shufeldt to Secretary of Navy Thompson, Oct. 13, 1880, "Letters from Commodore R. W. Shufeldt, 'Ticonderoga,'" 1.

lowing January, the treaty was ratified, and in February General Lucius H. Foote was appointed minister to Korea.[46]

Curiously, the Shufeldt mission attracted relatively little interest at home. President Arthur paid scant attention to the Far East, and simply told Congress that "the treaty lately concluded with Korea awaits the action of the Senate." The negotiations were lengthy and intimately involved in tortuous Far Eastern relationships, a subject beyond the purposes of this study. Secretary Bayard instructed chargé George C. Foulk to use great discretion in the diplomatic tug-of-war in the Far East, insisting that the United States had no concern in any matters beyond that of a friendly state which had always regarded Korea as an independent nation. He added that we could support Korean independence only by intervention, which, in the absence of an international guarantee, would entail grave risks that our policy would run counter to those of Britain, Russia, China, and Japan.[47]

The press generally supported America's role in ending Korea's isolation. However, the *New York Herald* commented that one could not help but pity the poor Koreans, who were so soon to enjoy railroads, telegraphs, and the other blessings of Christian civilization. Of course the *Times* was jesting, for it was so proud of America's role that it suggested its readers carry a copy of Shufeldt's treaty with them as an almost unique example of the positive features of American foreign policy.[48]

After the final visit of Shufeldt in 1882 and the subsequent treaty of Inch'ŏn, Korea witnessed rapid progress. As might be expected,

---

[46] Pletcher, *The Awkward Years,* pp. 206 ff. The text of the treaty can be found in *Senate Executive Document* 47, 48th Cong., 2d sess., and William N. Malloy, *Treaties, Conventions, International Acts, Protocols and Agreements between the United States of America and Other Powers, 1776–1909,* 4 vols. (Washington, 1920), 1: 334–339.

[47] Paullin, *Opening of Korea,* p. 498; Richardson, *Messages and Papers,* 11: 4715 (Arthur's annual message, Dec. 4, 1882); Tansill, *Bayard,* p. 418; Bayard to Foulk, Aug. 18, 1885, *Instructions, Corea,* vol. 1, quoted in ibid., pp. 427–428; Tyler Dennett, "Early American Policy in Korea, 1883–1887," *Political Science Quarterly* 38 (1923): 83–103. See also H. G. Appenzeller, "The Opening of Korea: Admiral Shufeldt's Account of It," *Korean Repository* 1 (Feb. 1892): 57–62 in Horace N. Allen MSS, New York Public Library.

[48] "Opening of Korea," *New York Herald,* Sept. 2, 1880; "Trade with Korea," ibid., Sept. 10, 1883.

missionary enthusiasm was strong, and many hoped that through diplomatic and/or commercial intercourse Korea would soon permit the teaching of Christianity. American influence was paramount in the Korean government, and an American Judge, Owen N. Denny, served as the King's chief foreign counselor. Korea soon realized that the United States was the only great power that did not want additional territory and that would not tolerate the advance of Russia, England, or any other foreign state in Asia. According to one editorial, the threat to our trade and to the independence of China, Japan, and Korea was as of much concern to the Great Powers as the Monroe Doctrine was to the United States. Despite this American interest and role in Korea, the Diplomatic and Consular Act of July 7, 1884, reduced the rank of the Seoul post to that of minister resident and consul general. Foote thereupon resigned, but the State Department requested him to take a leave so that he would not have to explain to the Koreans that the post had been reduced in importance.[49]

America's relations with Siam were of less significance than those with China, Japan, Korea, and the Pacific islands. However, Siam was the first Oriental country with which the United States entered into formal diplomatic relations (1833), and we were the first nation to relinquish various extraterritorial restrictions in that country without compensation. While the initial contacts between America and Siam were commercial, and the Siamese trade was a valuable adjunct to that of China, the chief American activity in this region came in the missionary field. The traditional Siamese cordiality to the United States manifested itself in extending privileges gratuitously to Americans. The well-known story of the King of Siam's offer of elephants to Abraham Lincoln for use in the Civil War, while perhaps overdramatized, points up the attitude of that kingdom to the United States vis-à-vis the attitude of other Oriental nations. In May 1884 a Siamese legation visited the United States, which resulted in an agreement regulating the liquor traffic in Siam. It is also significant that Siam gave the United States the land upon which

[49] "The Korean Embassy," *New York Times*, Dec. 31, 1887; "Korean Independence," *New York Herald*, Oct. 29, 1888; "Korea and the East," ibid., Nov. 13, 1888; Dennett, *Americans in Eastern Asia*, p. 693.

we built our legation. In happy contrast with other areas in the Orient, America's relations with Siam were generally those of cheerful neighborliness.[50]

The interest evinced by this country in Hawaii and Samoa, when understood in connection with the treaties negotiated with Korea, China, and Japan, demonstrates America's deepening penetration of the regions adjacent to the Pacific. What is more, European nations that had a stake in the area voiced concern over America's growing role in the Pacific long before 1890. For example, the uncertainty with which England observed our intentions in the Pacific was significant in the development of British policy toward the Fiji Islands. Even more significantly, it was British concern over the intensity of our Pacific penetration and the strategic balance of power there that led the British Colonial Office to welcome Germany's entrance in that area after 1870.[51] Hence even before the United States "officially" adopted the role of great power, it was a power to be reckoned with in the Pacific.

America's official policy in the Pacific was basically commercial and philanthropic. To these ends, we insisted that the doors to trade, real or potential, be left open, and we scrutinized every European advance that threatened to close the portals to Eastern riches. We jealously guarded the most-favored-nation clause in our treaties and insisted on the security of the lives and property of our citizens. Because of our close relations with China and Japan and the Pacific islands, American isolation was less pronounced toward Asia than toward Europe. By maintaining the political status quo and by beginning an expansive commercial policy, the United States was setting a foundation for the far-reaching actions of a later day.

---

[50] James V. Martin, Jr., "A History of the Diplomatic Relations between Siam and the United States of America, 1833–1929" (Ph.D. dissertation, Fletcher School of Law and Diplomacy, 1947), pp. iv, 96, 97; Chang Wook Moon, "American Relations with Siam: Diplomatic, Commercial, Religious and Educational" (Ph.D. dissertation, University of Southern California, 1935), pp. 180–182, 237–238.

[51] W. D. McIntyre, "Anglo-American Rivalry in the Pacific: The British Annexation of the Fiji Islands in 1874," *Pacific Historical Review* 29 (Nov. 1960): 361–380.

CHAPTER 13

Epilogue:
Out of the Doldrums

HISTORY IS a continuous drama, and the events of today are but later acts performed on the existing staging. Thus the prolonged debate of the present century over the complexities of our foreign entanglements can easily be related to post–Civil War America and the new role that international relations began to play after Appomattox. Whether one considers American foreign policy in terms of practical responses to immediate needs or as a systematic striving for the fulfillment of basic tenets of our philosophy of government, it reflects our contemporary needs and beliefs. In the early days, the fledgling United States required a policy of noninvolvement. Today our peace and security depends to a great extent on our relationships with other nations. Perhaps the period between our early immaturity and our present sophistication can be considered as an intermediate period. Having fulfilled our manifest destiny of conquering the continent and establishing the stars and stripes from shore to shore, the United States, after 1865, could take greater interest in events beyond those shores.

During these quiet years, however, preoccupation with internal improvements and the westward push obscured our vigorous and conscious overseas programs. Most men of this era were concerned with exploiting the natural resources of the trans-Mississippi West and were often too preoccupied to consider more distant challenges. They were much more concerned about "barbecuing the natural resources of a continent."

Great controversies arose over such internal problems as Reconstruction, the New South, the national debt, currency, and taxation. Such concerns, superimposed upon the time-hallowed concept of isolation, explain the apparent lack of interest in classic expansionism or imperialism. The pax Britannia and American preoccupation with industrialization and the vanishing frontier created a complacent feeling of ocean-locked security. Historians have assumed that at no other time since independence did foreign affairs so little concern this nation. Such treaties as were concluded were basically routine and such international conferences as were held proved for the most part abortive. The issues seemed unimportant and undramatic compared with the more exciting international situations which preceded and followed the period. Politicians reiterated their conviction that the United States was not concerned, except in limited ways, with the rest of the world.

The Department of State was antiquated, inefficient, and poorly suited to meet the needs of a nation which, despite the declarations of its politicians, was assuming greater international responsibilities. The State Department's staff of sixty, with some twenty-five ministers accredited to foreign capitals, and appointed chiefly for their political connections, exhibited scorn or at least disdain for the outside world. In 1880, for example, the European balance of power seemed intact. The Age of Disraeli was waning in London; Berlin was uncommonly placid; and the United States had ended its internecine warfare and was trying to forget the ordeal by concentrating on internal development.

Annual newspaper reports, summarizing the events of each year and prognosticating the future, emphasized American happiness and contentment in contrast to the discontent overseas. Part of this euphoria was inspired, it was held, by our limited foreign contact. President Hayes's second annual message devoted almost as much space to the District of Columbia as to the international situation.[1]

---

[1] Seymour H. Fersh, *The View from the White House, A Study of the Presidential State of the Union Message* (Washington, 1961), pp. 54–55.

America's indifference and preoccupation were due not only to its concentration on internal events and developments but also to the absence of any feeling of imminent peril. Indeed, except for relatively isolated clashes, European guns were silent from 1815 to 1914. There was little reason, therefore, to fear complications from the Old World, and the insulation afforded by the "American garden" or the agrarian myth stimulated men to rationalize their parochial attitude. Facing outward was not necessary since the United States possessed everything then considered desirable. America was, after all, the *summum bonum* of the world. The typical attitude seemed to be an amalgam of swollen national pride, moral superiority, and a strong aversion to foreign affairs.[2]

The well-defined anti-imperialist movement that followed the post-1898 swirl of events had its origins in the Gilded Age, in which one can note the opposition to Seward's Alaskan and Grant's Caribbean ventures. This attitude defeated or postponed such plans as the acquisition of the Danish West Indies, Santo Domingo, and Cuba and commercial reciprocity with Canada and the nations of Latin America. National concern over international relations was manifested by our defensive posture against the vigorous imperialist activities of the European powers, especially Great Britain and Germany. Americans, while denying their own interest in territorial acquisitions, were not willing to stand idly by and watch other countries seize land in the oceanic wilderness of the South Pacific or the lusher parts of Africa and Asia. Despite our assumption of some new obligations, we protested various annexationist projects all over the world, although our protests were often futile. This, then, was the domestic background of the organized resistance to the imperialism of the New America.[3]

It would be futile indeed to ignore this very obvious neglect of foreign affairs. Even the most superficial scanning of the contemporary records buttresses this interpretation of the American *Zeitgeist*. But, despite its supposed diplomatic tranquillity, the post-Reconstruction period was a seedbed of future interests. This

[2] Thomas A. Bailey, *The Man in the Street,* p. 123; Foster R. Dulles, *The Imperial Years* (New York, 1956), p. 15.

[3] Dozer, "Anti-Imperialism in the United States, 1865–1895," pp. 252–256.

was a time of flux, a period of transition, during which the signs of a more vigorous foreign policy began to appear on the American horizon. Interest in the world beyond our shores was quiescent rather than dead; in truth, America was never isolated from the world. From the very beginning of our history we were concerned over the ultimate disposition of Cuba and Hawaii and bothered by the prospect of unfriendly powers exercising control in Latin America, while Canada figured in expansionist thinking from the days of 1782 when our peace commissioners attempted to wrest it from England.

Pre–Civil War expansion aimed at land conquest or purchase, but beginning with Secretary Seward's tenure the nature of that expansion changed. The economic-industrial growth of the United States prompted overseas interests and Americans cast their eyes in all directions for markets. Business expansion and a maturing economy led to the quickening of interest in America's overseas economic destiny. For a nation fast developing a favorable balance of trade, dreams of commercial isolation were no longer possible. After 1914, our expanded business penetration and new status as a creditor nation eventually doomed political isolation. Farmers, too, were market oriented, and they projected their vision for a better life into the wider world. Speaker of the House Thomas B. Reed once described the United States as a billion-dollar country; and such oversize wealth necessarily sought egress beyond our shores. In these confident, optimistic times, all America was "breaking out." A modern nation was becoming highly urbanized and, characterized by accelerated industrialization, it was bound to become involved in the world economy.

Our later political concerns and embroilments grew out of these economic pressures. Professor Walter LaFeber refers to this period as that of the New American Empire, different from classic imperialist interests. Thus the United States was "expansive" but perhaps not "expansionist"—at least in traditional terms. The desire for the acquisition of land, or "real estate," derived from earlier times. The events of 1898 were foreshadowed by Seward's acquisitions, by the work of each Secretary of State, and by many prominent legislators of this period. Americans were not suddenly catapulted to the top of the world hierarchy in 1898; no nation achieves such power in a few years. The itch of destiny was always present, and was ever an American characteristic. The climax may have come in 1898, but the preceding years were years of preparation, for the roots of empire were deeply embedded. The acquisition of territory in the Caribbean and the Pacific, which ushered in America's great power status, was a result of a persistent commercial impulse—the desire and the need to secure markets. Political ties rather easily and neatly followed this commercial pattern.[4]

Concomitant with these national developments was the consensus that we did not have the international standing and respect that a nation of great wealth and resources required. Diplomat John A. Kasson, in assessing the Monroe Doctrine in 1881, stated that there was no longer a question of despotism extending into the Americas; there was, instead, commercial rivalry and conflict between the Old World and the New. He urged that the President and Congress be released from "interior political struggles" in order to assess the future properly. The halcyon days of isolated independence belonged to the past. It was obvious to such advanced thinkers as Kasson that the magnitude of foreign affairs had increased and was ever increasing.[5]

As we have seen, there was an awareness of such broader horizons among various groups. To realize the increasing impact of the world on Americans, one need only contemplate the new concern with steamships (especially those making the transatlantic trek), the growing awareness of the strategic and commercial uses of a merchant and naval fleet, and the quickening of demand for overseas investments and markets. Then, too, the worldwide humanitarian and commercial activities of the missionaries were evident, and the religious journals of the day were replete with ideas of racial superiority and nationalistic expansion as the ordained will of God. More and more foreign correspondents were sent overseas, and our literary people evinced more than the usual interest in the foreign scene as sources of inspiration and themes.

---

[4] See LaFeber, *The New Empire,* pp. 1–2, 407–409.

The expansionism of the 1890s and after was due in large part to the American farmers' "marketplace" image of the world: the necessity for markets and for their expansion—views adopted and transformed by the industrial community. See William A. Williams, *The Roots of the Modern American Empire* (New York, 1969).

[5] John A. Kasson, "The Monroe Doctrine in 1881," *North American Review* 133 (Dec. 1881): 523–533.

Another way of examining the extent of the awakening American interest in foreign events during this period is to concentrate on particular geographic areas. (American attitudes toward different countries cannot be generalized, for those attitudes were shaped by a variety of factors and rooted in diverse traditions.) While American conceptions of foreign areas varied considerably, they were often characterized by chauvinism and an air of superiority, accompanied by genuine interest and curiosity. The children of 1890 have lived to see the United States intimately concerned with maintaining peace in every quarter of the globe. It has been a long and tortuous route to Pearl Harbor, Hiroshima, the Yalu River, and the jungles of Vietnam, but the nation set out on this path before the dawn of the twentieth century.

America's feelings toward the Old World were contradictory. Undoubtedly, many Americans felt that Europe's institutions and history of warfare were illustrations of degeneration and none of our concern. The older feelings of cultural deference and economic dependence upon Europe lingered, but they were mixed with a bumptious nationalism, optimism, power, and even a messianic fervor.

Our conception of Latin America was encased in the Monroe Doctrine. Expansionist sentiment, which evidenced itself in the desire for naval bases, an American-owned canal, the promotion of pan-Americanism, and the movement for trade reciprocity, was cultivated in the name of that hallowed doctrine.

Americans seemed far less alert to the vast potentialities of Africa and the Orient; such concern as existed was wholly economic and humanitarian, revolving around the need for markets and the protection of American nationals. Economic motivations, rather than grandiose political ambitions, also characterized our relationship with Samoa, Hawaii, and Canada. Indeed—despite the fulminations of a few diehards—political control, annexation, or expansion had to await a more propitious day.

Thus the United States, taking a very limited political interest in Europe, tended to concentrate on cultural contacts. Meanwhile, in the Western Hemisphere, the United States regarded herself as the paramount power. As for Africa and Asia, America was willing—under very carefully regulated circumstances—to cooperate with other powers for the maintenance of open door policies.

Captain Alfred Thayer Mahan summed up the new feeling toward foreign problems: "I am frankly an imperialist, in the sense that I believe that no nation . . . should henceforth maintain the policy of isolation which fitted our early history." Yet Mahan was a result rather than the cause of the impulse he did so much to stimulate and enhance. It would be all but impossible to conceive of an American Mahan in the days of Lincoln, or even Grant.[6]

Another interpreter of the new trend was Senator John Tyler Morgan, a conservative Southerner in domestic affairs but an unswerving expansionist. For twenty-nine years (beginning in 1878) a member of the Senate Foreign Relations Committee, he took it as his task to forward the cause of America overseas. Envisaging American control of the Pacific and Caribbean areas, he aligned himself with the "new navy" and was an eloquent spokesman for commercial destiny. As a recent student of Morgan put it, he worked the same side of the street as Theodore Roosevelt and Henry Cabot Lodge.[7]

Less spectacular was a longtime member of the State Department, Alvey A. Adee, chief of the diplomatic bureau and later third assistant Secretary of State. Adee's knowledge of international relations and usages was encyclopedic. He was a mentally sharp and energetic number-two man who influenced secretary after secretary. The memoranda Adee prepared for his superiors were detailed, well researched, and reflected the larger view of America's present and future roles. This "admirable Crichton" of the State Department was considered the only permanent official in that hierarchy, as well as the only one who was indispensable. These men, leaders all, were signs of the times as well as molders of opinion.[8]

As nineteenth-century simplicity gave way to twentieth-century complexity, there was bound to be some overlapping between the shades of the past and the portents of the future. Perhaps this explains the character of the work of each Secretary of State from the administrations of Lincoln and Johnson to those of Cleveland

---

[6] A. T. Mahan, *From Sail to Steam: Recollections of Naval Life* (New York and London, 1906), p. 324.

[7] Radke, "John Tyler Morgan, Expansionist Senator," pp. 197, 198 (see also pp. 203–207, 215, 313–316, 391–393).

[8] O. G. Villard, "The Anchor Man of the State Department," *The Nation* 101 (Aug. 5, 1915): 170–171; Edward G. Lowry, "Adee the Remarkable," *Harper's Weekly* 55 (Nov. 18, 1911): 9.

and Harrison. The path to empire was carefully paved by the statesmen of this period, who were precursors of the later and better-
known expansionists.

William Henry Seward was perhaps the most astute philosopher-
statesman of that day. His vision was based on the "higher law" that
empire was moving westward, across the United States and the
Pacific to the continent of Asia, and that our supremacy as a nation
in these areas was ordained from on high. It was Seward who devised
an integrated plan for the creation of a base of power on the American continent. Of course, Latin America and Canada figured intimately in a new American system. Way stations or bases in the
Pacific would be required so as better to fight the inevitable battle
for power and status in Asia. Seward's Caribbean and Hawaiian
plans proved abortive, but he lived long enough to witness the completion of the first transcontinental railroad and the acquisition of
Alaska, which he did so much to bring about.[9]

The ambitious President Grant and his more restrained Secretary
of State, Hamilton Fish, provided the chains of economic expansion
that linked Seward with the McKinley era. In their relations with
Latin America, the Pacific islands, and Canada, Grant and Fish
left a legacy in foreign affairs that stood in sharp contrast to the
dismal record of "Grantism" in domestic affairs. Under their aegis,
America's first successful reciprocity treaty with Hawaii and first
political contacts with Samoa were obtained. However, it was Latin
America that most fascinated Grant and Fish, and while the results
in this area were inconclusive, the nontransfer idea was a positive
achievement.[10]

William M. Evarts, whose record as Secretary of State has generally been underrated, was acute and witty, and he appreciated the
goals of his friend, Seward. That Evarts understood the need for a
commercial empire is evident in his support of trade expansion and
foreign outlets. The consular reports, which he initiated, reflected
America's desire for this new type of empire. Evarts reasoned that
foreign markets would serve to placate the labor unrest and discontent arising from the panic in 1873. While hopeful of cooperation

---

[9] Excellent descriptions of the secretaries of state in the Gilded Age are
provided by LaFeber in *The New Empire*. For Seward, see pp. 24–32.

[10] See ibid., pp. 32–39.

with England and France in order to maintain the type of world in which commercial activities could function effectively, Evarts viewed foreign encroachment, political and commercial, as a subject for righteous protest. Indeed, he was the real author of President Hayes's firm statement on an American-owned isthmian canal. Evarts especially appreciated the great trade potential of Latin America. It was also under Evarts that the State Department paid increased attention to Asia, and while trade with that great continent was as yet only potential, that potentiality was jealously regarded by American commercial expansionists.[11]

In domestic affairs, James G. Blaine undoubtedly was one of the milder corruptionists of the Gilded Age, but in diplomacy he was far ahead of his generation with his definite plans for commercial expansion. Twice in one decade, he was appointed Secretary of State by two different Presidents, for in many respects he was the embodiment of the national forces lurking beneath a placid surface. Those who sensed the "wave of the future" felt that Blaine spoke with special authority, that he was a harbinger of a union between the new European mercantilism and militant American nationalism. Blaine's ideas all pointed toward a positive foreign policy that befitted a first-rate power. He therefore advocated increased trade, naval expansion, and a wider interpretation of the Monroe Doctrine, implemented by closer ties among all nations of the New World. His constant hope was that his plans for closer cooperation with the republics of the Western Hemisphere would result in a commercially welded "ocean-bound Republic."

When the "plumed knight" returned as Secretary of State in the Harrison administration, the search for markets was accelerated. Both President and secretary correctly maintained that only the export of surplus agricultural products saved the United States from serious economic trouble. Their approach posited American dominance, at least economically, of much of the world. On the other hand, those who still thought in limited, parochial terms described Blaine's diplomacy as vulgar intrigue—dirty, dishonorable, shifty, and uncertain. His critics contended that this country had no need for a Disraeli or a Bismarck. Little did they realize that, within a generation, the United States would have use for such abilities. Thus

---

[11] See ibid., pp. 39–46.

Blaine's policies, which forged the major link between the ideas of Seward and those of the first Roosevelt, excited either violent criticism or warm praise, which accurately reflected the ambivalence toward external problems that was so typical of his age.[12]

Secretaries Frederick Frelinghuysen and Thomas Bayard were cautious but nevertheless zealous watchdogs of America's rights. Frelinghuysen emphasized a vigorous commercial foreign policy, especially in the negotiation of reciprocity treaties. In this way, he reasoned, the United States might exert a beneficial economic influence without burdening herself with the political problems arising from outright imperialism. Frelinghuysen's vigorous canal diplomacy (including his violation of the Clayton-Bulwer treaty) and interest in the Congo placed him in the camp of the commercial imperialists. Although President Cleveland and Secretary Bayard terminated our earlier involvements in Africa and Latin America, they were expansionists in their own way. The renewal of Hawaiian reciprocity, Bayard realized, meant that American primacy in the islands would be ensured, that foreign powers could never acquire the dominant interest. This same thinking resulted in the cooperation of the great powers in the disposition of Samoa, reflecting our increased emphasis on Pacific affairs. Bayard also felt that the islands were needed as stepping-stones to American influence in Asia proper.[13]

Rummaging through the sources for this period, one encounters latent expansionist sentiment at all points. The Gilded Age was not a low point in American diplomacy, unless by low point one means that much greater things were yet to come. Our intellectual contacts with the rest of the world and our growing cosmopolitanism are suggestive of increasing awareness and preparation for the pursuit of a more active foreign policy. The "large policy" had its origins in the very years of our supposed satisfaction with continental expansion and rapid domestic industrialization. Eventually, this new policy was rationalized on the bases of racial and moral superiority, a sense of national mission, strategic considerations, enhancement

---

[12] See ibid., pp. 46–47. See also, Richard C. Winchester, "James G. Blaine and the Ideology of American Expansionism" (Ph.D. dissertation, University of Rochester, 1966), esp. pp. 1–6, 241–253.

[13] See LaFeber, *The New Empire,* pp. 47–58.

of national prestige, and aversion to a worldwide imperialism from which we were excluded economically. Though originally not seeking territory for ourselves, we could not allow other powers to jeopardize what we thought were our legitimate interests. The restless pioneer spirit typified the "expand or bust" philosophy which developed as the depression clouds of 1893 lifted.[14]

Soon the sunshine of the McKinley Era burst through, prosperity quickened, and the United States took its place in the front ranks of the nations of the world. As the new century dawned, America constructed a new ship of state and put it on a course that led through unknown seas. This course would lead to war, one of the concomitants of world leadership, and to a never ending series of frustrating and unprecedented foreign dilemmas.

---

[14] James M. Callahan, *American Relations in the Pacific and the Far East, 1784–1900* (Baltimore, 1901), p. 164.

Bibliography

THIS BIBLIOGRAPHY is designed as a brief guide to America's diplomatic awakening during part of the Gilded Age (1865–1890). It is not meant to be inclusive, but is selective; for additional items or for more detailed information, the reader is directed to the documentation for the individual chapters.

GENERAL

While manuscript collections were helpful, they were not emphasized since this work is conceived as an attitudinal study, stressing rather newspaper and periodical sources. However, the papers of the following, all housed in the Library of Congress, are a selected list of those appearing in the text: Thomas F. Bayard, James G. Blaine, Grover Cleveland, J. C. Bancroft Davis, William M. Evarts, Frederick T. Frelinghuysen, Benjamin Harrison, Rutherford B. Hayes, Robert M. Shufeldt. The Horace N. Allen papers, located in The New York Public Library, were also consulted.

Among the unpublished United States Official Papers in the National Archives are the following: Department of Navy: *Letters from Commodore R. W. Shufeldt—"Ticonderoga." Africa and Asia, 1878–1880.* Department of State: Domestic Letters (from government departments to the State Department), Miscellaneous Letters (from non-diplomatic sources), Records of Foreign Service Posts: Instructions to United States Ministers, Despatches from United States Ministers, Instructions to Consuls, Consular Despatches, Instructions to Special Missions, Reports from Special Agents, Reports of the Diplomatic Bureau. Among the consular outposts studied were: Colon-Aspinwell, Apia, Berlin, Mexico City, Moscow, Odessa, Port-au-Prince, Quebec City, and St. Thomas. Despatches to and from our ministers in Chile, Central America, China, Colombia, Corea, France, Germany, Hawaii, Hayti, Japan, Mexico, Santo-Domingo, and Spain proved especially revealing.

Published United States Public Documents (for the most part by the Government Printing Office) include the pertinent volumes of the *Congressional Record* for the years 1865–1890, various House and Senate documents (i.e., *House Reports, House Miscellaneous Documents, House Executive Documents, Senate Executive Documents, Senate Miscellaneous Documents, Senate Reports, Senate Documents* dealing with such subjects as United States-Mexican border troubles, Chinese immigration, an American-owned canal, trade with various countries, international conferences, overseas diplomatic missions, trade reciprocity, etc.) and the *Journals of the Executive Proceedings of the House of Representatives* and the *Executive Journal of the Senate.* Published Department of State publications include: *Commercial Relations of the United States with Foreign Countries* (Washington: 1856–1914), providing excellent consular reportage; *Papers Relating to the Foreign Relations of the United States* (Washington: 1862–   ), incorporating selected diplomatic correspondence; *Register of the Department of State* (Washington: 1869–   ); *Reports from the Consuls of the United States on the Commerce, Manufactures, etc. of their Consular Districts* (Washington: 1880–   ); and such miscellaneous works as *Commercial Relations between the United States and Central and South America* (Washington: 1884); *Correspondence in Relation to the Proposed Interoceanic Canal between the Atlantic and Pacific Oceans* (Washington: 1885); *The Inter-American Conference* (Washington: 1890); and *Regulations Prescribed for the Use of the Consular Service of the United States* (Washington: 1881, 1888). Bureau of Foreign Commerce publications consulted were: *American Pork* (Washington: 1881); *Commerce of the World, and The Share of the United States Therein* (Washington: 1883); and *Exports Declared for the United States, Returns from Consular Districts,* 9 vols. (Washington: 1883–1903).

The Annual Reports of the Secretary of the Navy and The Department of Commerce, Bureau of the Census, *Historical Statistics of the*

United States, 1789–1945 (Washington: 1949) provided many helpful insights. Among other published official sources are: William M. Malloy, ed., *Treaties, Conventions, International Acts, Protocols and Agreements between the United States and Other Powers, 1776–1909*, 4 vols. (Washington: 1910–1938); James D. Richardson, ed., *A Compilation of the Messages and Papers of the Presidents*, 20 vols. (New York: 1897–1916); and *Statutes at Large of the United States* 15 (Washington: 1869); 25 (Washington: 1889). Party platform pronouncements are contained in Thomas H. McKee, ed., *The National Convention and Platforms of all Political Parties, 1789–1901* (Baltimore: Friedenwald, 1901) and Kirk H. Porter and Donald B. Johnson, eds., *National Party Platforms, 1840–1956* (Urbana: University of Illinois Press, 1956).

Among the newspapers consulted were: *Atlanta Constitution, Buffalo Commercial Advertiser, Buffalo Daily Courier, Buffalo Daily Dispatch, Buffalo Express, Burlington Free Press, Cheyenne Democratic Leader, Chicago Tribune, Cleveland Leader, Cleveland Plain Dealer, Cleveland World, Des Moines Iowa State Register, Detroit Free Press, Hartford Daily Courant, Indianapolis Journal, Louisville Commercial, Memphis Advocate, Minneapolis Tribune, New Haven Evening Register, New Orleans Daily Picayune, New York Daily Tribune, New York Herald, New York Observer, New York Times, Pittsburgh Press, St. Paul Daily Gazette, Salt Lake City Deseret Evening News, Samoan Times, San Francisco Chronicle, San Francisco Evening Bulletin, Sitka Alaskan, Springfield* (Mass.) *Daily Republican*, and the *Washington Post.*

General periodicals of importance included: *Arena, Atlantic Monthly, Bay State Monthly, Century Magazine, The Chautauquan, Cosmopolitan, Eclectic Magazine of Foreign Literature, Science, and Art, The Forum, The Galaxy, Harper's New Monthly Magazine, Harper's Weekly, Historical Outlook, International Review, Lippincott's Monthly Magazine, Literary Digest, The Nation, The Nationalist, New Englander, North American Review, Overland Monthly, Phrenological Journal, Princeton Review, Public Opinion, Putnam's Magazine, Review of Reviews*, and *Scribner's Magazine.*

Selected religious periodicals that were studied were: *American Missionary, Ave Maria, Baptist Missionary Magazine, Boston Congregationalist, Buffalo Christian Advocate, Christian Herald and Signs of Our Times, Christian Standard, Christian Union, The Churchman, The Friend, Friends' Intelligencer, Lutheran Quarterly, Methodist Quarterly Review, Methodist Review, Missionary Herald, Missionary Review of the World, Our Day, The Presbyterian, The Presbyterian Review, Spirit of Missions, Tidings*, and *Watchman.*

Commercial periodicals were abundant in this period. Those researched were: *Age of Steel, American Economist, American Manufacturer and Iron World, American Protectionist, Boston Commercial Bulletin, Boston Economist, Bradstreet's, Commercial and Financial Chronicle, Dixie, Engineering News, Export and Finance, Home Market Bulletin, Iron Age, Manufacturer and Builder, Manufacturer's Gazette, Manufacturer's Record, New York Daily Commercial Bulletin, New York Journal of Commerce, Northwestern Miller, Pittsburgh National Labor Tribune,* and *San Francisco Journal of Commerce.*

Standard textbooks on the history of American diplomacy which can be used profitably are Samuel F. Bemis, *A Diplomatic History of the United States,* 5th ed. (New York: Holt, 1965), perhaps the most scholarly and distinguished of its kind; Thomas A. Bailey, *A Diplomatic History of the American People,* 8th ed. (New York: Appleton, 1969), a popular account and helpful especially for an up-to-date bibliography; Wayne S. Cole, *An Interpretive History of American Foreign Relations* (Homewood, Ill.: Dorsey, 1968), a provocative treatment; Alexander De Conde, *A History of American Foreign Policy* (New York: Scribner, 1963), a succinct statement; L. Ethan Ellis, *A Short History of American Diplomacy* (New York: Harper, 1951); Robert H. Ferrell, *American Diplomacy: A History* (New York: Norton, 1969), quite interpretive; Richard W. Leopold, *The Growth of American Foreign Policy: A History* (New York: Knopf, 1962), useful chiefly for the twentieth century but affording background for the earlier period; and Julius W. Pratt, *A History of the United States Foreign Policy,* 2nd ed. (Englewood Cliffs, N.J.: Prentice-Hall, 1965), a concise and factually correct treatment. Pratt's *America's Colonial Experiment* (Englewood Cliffs, N.J.: Prentice-Hall, 1950) also has some useful background. See also two interesting works by Dexter Perkins, the highly interpretive *The American Approach to Foreign Policy* (Cambridge, Mass.: Harvard University Press, 1952) and *The Evolution of American Foreign Policy* (New York: Oxford University Press, 1948), an excellent summary.

Three fairly recent works dealing with aspects of the Gilded Age must be utilized for a proper understanding of this period. Since they illuminate many topics, they will rarely be cited specifically for each chapter. Foster R. Dulles's *Prelude to World Power; American Diplomatic History, 1860–1900* (New York: Macmillan, 1965) is a very brief account and is useful as an introduction. Walter LaFeber, *The New Empire: An Interpretation of American Expansion, 1860–1898* (Ithaca, N.Y.: Cornell University Press, 1963) is a first-rate account. While emphasizing the 1890s, background chapters are quite helpful.

LaFeber emphasizes economic motivation behind diplomatic happenings. Lastly, David M. Pletcher, *The Awkward Years: American Foreign Relations under Garfield and Arthur* (Columbia: University of Missouri Press, 1962), is an unrivaled treatment of the years 1881–1885. See also the present author's chapter in the first edition of H. Wayne Morgan, ed., *The Gilded Age, a Reappraisal* (Syracuse, N.Y.: Syracuse University Press, 1963) "Rumblings Beneath the Surface: America's Outward Thrust, 1865–1890" and a doctoral dissertation by Ralph D. Bald, Jr., "The Development of Expansionist Sentiment in the United States, 1885–1895, as Reflected in Periodical Literature," University of Pittsburgh, 1953.

The following biographies and treatments of the Presidents and their Secretaries of State, 1865–1890, can be helpful. *Johnson-Seward:* Glyndon G. Van Deusen, *William Henry Seward* (New York: Oxford University Press, 1967); see also Joseph G. Whelan, "William Henry Seward, Expansionist," Ph.D. dissertation, University of Rochester, 1959. *Grant-Fish:* William B. Hesseltine, *Ulysses S. Grant, Politician* (New York: Dodd, Mead & Co., 1935); Allan Nevins, *Hamilton Fish: The Inner History of the Grant Administration* (New York: Dodd, 1936). *Hayes-Evarts:* Hamilton J. Eckenrode, *Rutherford B. Hayes: Statesman of Reunion* (New York: Dodd, 1930); Charles R. Williams, ed., *Diary and Letters of Rutherford B. Hayes*, 5 vols. (Columbus: Ohio State Archeological & Historical Society, 1922–1926); Harry Barnard, *Rutherford B. Hayes and His America* (Indianapolis, Bobbs-Merrill, 1954); Chester L. Barrows, *William M. Evarts, Lawyer, Diplomat, Statesman* (Chapel Hill: University of North Carolina Press, 1941); Brainerd Dyer, *The Public Career of William M. Evarts* (Berkeley: University of California Press, 1933). *Garfield-Blaine:* Robert J. Caldwell, *James A. Garfield, Party Chieftain* (New York: Dodd, 1931); David S. Muzzey, *James G. Blaine, a Political Idol of Other Days* (New York: Dodd, 1934); Alice F. Tyler, *The Foreign Policy of James G. Blaine* (Minneapolis: University of Minnesota Press, 1927); see also Richard C. Winchester, "James G. Blaine and the Ideology of American Expansion," Ph.D. dissertation, University of Rochester, 1966; A. T. Volwiler's collection, *The Correspondence between Benjamin Harrison and James G. Blaine, 1882–1893* (Philadelphia: The American Philosophical Society, 1940) is an important source. *Arthur-Frelinghuysen:* George F. Howe, *Chester A. Arthur, a Quarter-Century of Machine Politics* (New York: Dodd, 1934); (see *The American Secretaries of State* article on Frelinghuysen); *Cleveland-Bayard:* Allan Nevins, *Grover Cleveland: a Study in Courage* (New York: Dodd, 1933); George R. Dulebohn, "Principles of Foreign Policy Under the Cleveland Administration," Ph.D. dissertation, University of Pennsylvania, 1941; Charles C. Tansill, *The Foreign Policy of Thomas F. Bayard, 1885–1897* (New York: Fordham University Press, 1940) and his *The Congressional Career of Thomas Francis Bayard, 1869–1885* (Washington: Georgetown University Press, 1946).

The biographies in Samuel F. Bemis, ed., *American Secretaries of State and their Diplomacy*, 10 vols. (New York: Knopf, 1927–1929) are still useful: vol. 7–Henry W. Temple, *William H. Seward;* Joseph V. Fuller, *Hamilton Fish;* Claude G. Bowers and Helen D. Reid, *William M. Evarts;* James B. Lockey, *James G. Blaine;* vol. 8–Philip M. Brown, *Frederick T. Frelinghuysen;* Lester B. Shippee, *Thomas F. Bayard.*

Note: Works already cited will not be listed by full title again.

CHAPTER 1: SETTING THE STAGE

Post–Civil War expansionist schemes and the eventual "nadir" of expansionism are treated in the older treatments: Joe Patterson Smith, *The Republican Expansionists of the Early Reconstruction Era* (Chicago: University of Chicago Press, 1933); Theodore Clarke Smith, "Expansion After the Civil War, 1865–1871," *Political Science Quarterly* 16 (1901): 412–436; Donald M. Dozer, "Anti-Imperialism in the United States, 1865–1895," Ph.D. dissertation, Harvard University, 1936; and his "Anti-Expansionism during the Johnson Administration," *Pacific Historical Review* 12 (1943): 243–275.

General interpretive statements useful for a comprehension of the period as a whole include Thomas A. Bailey, *The Man in the Street, The Impact of American Public Opinion on Foreign Policy* (New York: Macmillan, 1948), an excellent example of Bailey's concern for the role of public opinion on policy formulation; Selig Adler, *The Isolationist Impulse: Its Twentieth Century Reaction* (New York: Abelard, 1957), good for perspective and background; and two philosophically oriented works: Edward McNall Burns, *The American Idea of Mission: Concepts of National Purpose and Destiny* (New Brunswick, N.J.: Rutgers University Press, 1957) and Frederick Merk, *Manifest Destiny and Mission in American History: A Reinterpretation* (New York: Knopf, 1963).

For discussions of Seward's and Blaine's ideas and ideologies, see in addition to the biographies cited above, Frederic Bancroft, "Seward's Ideas of Territorial Expansion," *North American Review* 167 (July 1898): 79–89 and A. T. Volwiler, "Harrison, Blaine, and American

Foreign Policy, 1889–1893," *American Philosophical Society, Proceedings* 79 (1938): 637–648.

In addition to what the diplomatic history textbooks say, the following address themselves to the question of when the United States became a world power. Bailey ("America's Emergence as a World Power: The Myth and the Verity," *Pacific Historical Review* 30 [1961]: 1–16) feels that such status came as early as independence, while Ernest R. May (*Imperial Democracy: The Emergence of America as a Great Power* [New York: Harcourt, 1961]) dates it from the 1890s. May's *American Imperialism: A Speculative Essay* (New York: Atheneum, 1968) amplifies this thesis. See also the works of Dulles, LaFeber, Pletcher, and Plesur, all of whom feel that the seeds of world status are contained in the Gilded Age.

CHAPTER 2: EARLY ECONOMIC IMPERIALISM

Much of America's destiny abroad was explained or rationalized in terms of economic gain. A blunt statement of this sentiment is that of Brooks Adams (*America's Economic Supremacy* [New York: Macmillan, 1900]). See also John P. Mallon, "Roosevelt, Brooks Adams, and Lea: The Warrior Critique of the Business Civilization," *American Quarterly* 8 (Feb. 1956): 216–230; William A. Williams, "Brooks Adams and American Expansion," *New England Quarterly* 25 (June 1952): 217–232; and Charles Vevier, "Brooks Adams and the Ambivalence of American Foreign Policy," *World Affairs Quarterly* 30 (Apr. 1959): 3–18.

Although concentrating on a later period, Frank A. Vanderlip, *The American "Commercial Invasion" of Europe* (New York, reprinted from *Scribner's*, 1902), sets the theme for increased trade interests during the earlier era as well. The role of America's navy in the promotion of overseas commerce is treated in Charles O. Paullin's *Diplomatic Negotiations of American Naval Officers, 1778–1883* (Baltimore: The Johns Hopkins Press, 1912) and his *The Opening of Korea by Commodore Shufeldt* (Boston: Ginn, 1910) (reprinted from *Political Science Quarterly* 25 [Sept. 1910]: 470–499). Missionary economic interests are adequately treated in Kenneth S. LaTourette, *A History of Christian Missions in China* (New York: Macmillan, 1929); Rev. James Johnston, ed., *Report of the Centenary Conference on the Protestant Missions*, 2 vols. (New York: Revell, 1888); Rev. James S. Dennis, *Christian Missions and Social Progress*, 3 vols. (Chicago, Toronto, New York: Revell, 1899–1906); Augustus C. Thompson, *Future Probation and Foreign Missions* (Boston: Beacon, 1886); and two works by Josiah Strong, the classic *Our Country: Its Possible*

Future and its Present Crisis (New York: Baker & Taylor, 1885) and *Expansion Under New World Conditions* (New York: Baker & Taylor, 1900). See, too, Dorothea R. Muller, "Josiah Strong and American Nationalism: A Reevaluation," *Journal of American History* 53 (Dec. 1966): 487–503.

The publications of various Chambers of Commerce (i.e., *Annual Reports of the Corporation of the Chamber of Commerce of the State of New York*) are prime sources on the pressure activities for a more vigorous overseas economic policy. Two examples of entrepreneurial foreign activity are Robert B. Davies, " 'Peacefully Working to Conquer the World': The Singer Manufacturing Company in Foreign Markets, 1854–1889," *Business History Review* 43 (Autumn 1969): 299–325 and R. A. Church, "The Effect of the American Export Invasion on the British Boot and Shoe Industry, 1885–1914," *Journal of Economic History* 28 (June 1968): 223–254. An intriguing article on the business attitude toward America's export invasion is David E. Novack and Matthew Simon, "Commercial Responses to the American Export Invasion, 1871–1914, An Essay in Attitudinal History," *Explorations in Entrepreneurial History* (Winter 1966), 121–147.

On America's burgeoning agricultural exports, see Morton Rothstein, "America in the International Rivalry for the British Wheat Market, 1860–1914," *Mississippi Valley Historical Review* 47 (Dec. 1960): 401–418; William D. Zimmerman, "Live Cattle Export Trade between the United States and Great Britain, 1868–1885," *Agricultural History* 36 (Jan. 1962): 46–52; and Joseph Nimmo, Jr., *Report in Regard to the Range and Ranch Cattle Business of the United States* (Washington: Government Printing Office, 1885). For the "pork issue" and the business response to overseas discrimination against American pork products, the following should be consulted: Louis L. Snyder, "The American-German Pork Dispute, 1879–1891," *Journal of Modern History* 17 (1945): 16–28; John L. Gignilliat, "Pigs, Politics, and Protection: The European Boycott of American Pork, 1879–1891," *Agricultural History* 25 (Jan. 1961): 3–12; and Robert M. Packard, "The French Pork Prohibition in American Diplomacy, 1881–1891," Ph.D. dissertation, Harvard University, 1954.

America's growing investments overseas are adequately treated in Paul D. Dickens, *American Direct Investments in Foreign Countries* (Washington: Government Printing Office, 1930) and Cleona Lewis, *America's Stake in International Investments* (Washington: The Brookings Institution, 1939). Specific overseas American trade contacts can be gleaned from David M. Pletcher, *Rails, Mines, and Progress: Seven American Promoters in Mexico, 1867–1911* (Ithaca, N.Y.:

Cornell University Press, 1958). Donald F. Warner, *The Idea of Continental Union: Agitation for the Annexation of Canada to the United States, 1849–1893* (Lexington: University of Kentucky Press, 1960), a study of United States-Canadian relations, emphasizing the abortive attempts at economic union; and two doctoral dissertations on Russian interests: Edward J. Carroll, "The Foreign Relations of the United States with Tsarist Russia, 1867–1900," Georgetown University, 1953, and George S. Queen, "The United States and Material Advance in Russia, 1887–1906," University of Illinois, 1941.

The slight labor concern in overseas economic matters is apparent from a study of the *Proceedings of the . . . Knights of Labor* and the *Reports of the . . . Federation of Organized Trade and Labor Unions of the United States and Canada.*

Economic topics receive due attention in Paul S. Holbo, "Economics, Emotion, and Expansion: An Emerging Foreign Policy" in H. Wayne Morgan, ed., *The Gilded Age*, revised and enlarged (Syracuse, N.Y.: Syracuse University Press, 1970). Especially interesting is his treatment of tariffs and his feeling that the search for markets as a force in diplomatic motivation needs qualification. John A. Garraty, *The New Commonwealth, 1877–1890* (New York: Harper, 1968), also feels that there has been an over-emphasis upon economic motivation. However, Howard B. Schonberger's forthcoming study, *Transportation to the Seaboard, A Study in the "Communication Revolution" and American Foreign Policy, 1860–1900* (Westport, Conn.: Greenwood Pub. Corp.) again stresses the market-impulse. Provocative, too, and germane to this discussion, is Thomas C. Cochran, "Did the Civil War Retard Industrialization?" *Mississippi Valley Historical Review* 48 (Sept. 1961): 197–210. For a general survey, see Edward C. Kirkland, *Industry Comes of Age: Business, Labor, and Public Policy, 1860–1897* (New York: Holt, 1961).

CHAPTER 3: STIRRINGS IN THE STATE DEPARTMENT

While the major sources for opinion about the foreign service are periodicals, newspapers, and the *Congressional Record*, the following will be helpful for background: William Barnes and John Heath Morgan, *The Foreign Service of the United States: Origins, Development, and Functions* (Washington: Department of State, 1961) and F. Warren Ilchman, *Professional Diplomacy in the United States, 1779–1939* (Chicago: University of Chicago Press, 1961). More specific statements about our diplomatic establishment can be found in Edward L. Younger, *John A. Kasson: Politics and Diplomacy from Lincoln to McKinley* (Iowa City: State Historical Society of Iowa,

1955), the detailed account of one of the period's fine diplomats; Frederick H. Gillett, *George Frisbie Hoar* (Boston and New York: Houghton, 1934), about a defender of the service; and William N. Armstrong, *E. L. Godkin and American Foreign Policy, 1865–1900* (New York: Bookman Associates, 1957), the standard account of the beliefs, held by the editor of *The Nation*. See also Joseph P. O'Grady "Politics and Diplomacy: The Appointment of Anthony M. Keiley to Rome in 1885," *Virginia Magazine of History and Biography* 76 (Apr. 1968): 191–209, for a "case-study" of the motivation behind one diplomatic appointment. An interesting contemporary criticism of "the system" is contained in James B. Angell, "The Inadequate Recognition of Diplomatists by Historians," *Annual Report of the American Historical Association*, 1893, 15–23. A defense of our consular establishment was naturally part of the thinking of native industrialists. See, for example, Harold F. Williamson and Arnold R. Daum, *The American Petroleum Industry*, 2 vols. (Evanston, Ill.: Northwestern University Press, 1959).

Other international contacts embracing cables, conferences, fairs and exhibitions, and miscellaneous global relationships of perhaps a less dramatic character can be studied in the following works: Clyde E. Persinger, "Internationalism in the '60s," *The Historical Outlook* 20 (Nov. 1929): 324–327; George A. Schreiner, *Cables and Wireless and Their Role in the Foreign Relations of the United States* (Boston: Stratford, 1924); Merle Curti, "America at the World Fairs, 1841–1893," *American Historical Review* 55 (July 1950): 833–856; Foster R. Dulles, *The American Red Cross* (New York: Harper, 1950); Melville Clyde Kelly, *United States Postal Policy* (New York and London: D. Appleton, 1931); Daniel C. Roper, *The United States Post Office, Its Past Record, Present Condition, and Potential Relation to the New World Era* (New York and London: Funk & Wagnalls, 1917); John F. Sly, "The Genesis of the Universal Postal Union," *International Conciliation* (Oct. 1927): 393–443; Norman L. Hill, *The Public International Conferences* (Stanford, Cal.: Stanford University Press, 1929); James B. Childs, *International Exchange of Government Publications* (Washington: Government Printing Office, 1927); Budd Gambee, "The Great Junket . . . ," *Journal of Library History* 2 (Jan. 1967): 9–44, an interesting account of a conference of librarians in London (1877) coinciding with the birth of the library profession in both England and America; two articles by Jeanette P. Nichols, "A Painful Lesson in Silver Diplomacy," *South Atlantic Quarterly* 35 (July 1936): 251–273 and "Silver Diplomacy," *Political Science Quarterly* 48 (Dec. 1933): 565–588; Henry B. Russell, *International Monetary Conferences* . . . (New York and London: Harper, 1898);

George B. Young, "The Influence of Politics in American Diplomacy During Cleveland's Administrations, 1885–1889, 1893–1897," Ph.D. dissertation, Yale University, 1939, used for the material on monetary diplomacy; and Curti, *Peace Or War: The American Struggle, 1636–1936* (New York: Norton, 1936), the standard treatment of the peace movement.

CHAPTER 4: THE "LITERATI" CROSS THE SEA

Citations of works, letters or reminiscences by the authors included in this chapter will not be listed here. See the documentation in footnotes.

General treatments of American *literati*, their contributions, and the milieu in which they functioned, are contained in: Beckles Willson, *America's Ambassadors to England (1785–1929)* (New York: Frederick A. Stokes, 1929); Van Wyck Brooks, *New England: Indian Summer, 1865–1915* (New York: Dutton, 1940), a refreshing and penetrating study; Margaret Denny and William H. Gilman, eds., *The American Writer and the European Tradition* (Minneapolis: University of Minnesota Press, 1950); Foster R. Dulles, *Americans Abroad, Two Centuries of European Travel* (Ann Arbor: University of Michigan Press, 1964), a pioneer-type survey of overseas travel; Matthew Josephson, *Portraits of the Artist as American* (New York: Harcourt, 1930); Frank L. Mott, *A History of American Magazines*, 5 vols. (Cambridge, Mass.: Harvard University Press, 1938–1968), the able and standard treatment of the subject; Robert B. Mowat, *Americans in England* (Cambridge, Mass.: Houghton, 1935); Robert E. Spiller et al., *Literary History of the United States*, 3 vols. (New York: Macmillan, 1948), an indispensable treatment; Walter F. Taylor, *A History of American Letters* (Boston: American Book Co., 1947); Merle Curti's textbook, *The Growth of American Thought*, 3rd ed. (New York: Harper & Row, 1964), and Vernon L. Parrington's seminal *Main Currents of American Thought*, 3 vols. (New York: Harcourt, 1927–1930) are also of great value.

For James Russell Lowell, see Richard Croom Beatty, *James Russell Lowell* (Nashville, Tenn.: Vanderbilt University Press, 1942) and Charles Oran Stewart, *Lowell and France* (Nashville, Tenn.: Vanderbilt University Press, 1951), a perceptive and original work. The finest biography of Lowell is Martin Duberman, *James Russell Lowell* (Boston: Houghton, 1966).

There are many volumes on Henry James. Among the most useful are Osborn Andreas, *Henry James and the Expanding Horizon* (Seattle: University of Washington Press, 1948); Van Wyck Brooks, *The Pil-*

grimage of Henry James (New York: Dutton, 1928); Henry S. Canby, *Turn West, Turn East, Mark Twain and Henry James* (Boston: Houghton, 1951); F. W. Dupee, ed., *The Question of Henry James* (New York: Holt, 1945); Leon Edel, *Henry James,* 4 vols. (Philadelphia and New York: Lippincott, 1953–1969), the definitive study; George A. Finch, *The Development of the Fiction of Henry James from 1879 to 1886* (New York: New York University Press, 1949); Richard Grozier, Jr., "Henry James and American Moral Attitudes," Master's thesis, Georgetown University, 1954; Robert C. LeClair, "Three American Travellers in Europe: James Russell Lowell, Henry Adams, Henry James," Ph.D. thesis, University of Pennsylvania, 1945; Elizabeth Stevenson, *The Crooked Corridor, A Study of Henry James* (New York: Macmillan, 1949); Christof Wegelin, *The Image of Europe in Henry James* (Dallas, Tex.: Southern Methodist University Press, 1958); and Morton D. Zabel, ed., *The Art of Travel, Scenes and Journeys in America, England, France and Italy from the Travel Writings of Henry James* (Garden City, N.Y.: Doubleday, 1958). Several articles should also be studied. See especially, Robert L. Gale, "Henry James and Italy," *Studi Americani* 3 (Rome, 1957): 189–203, and Edna Kenton, "Henry James in the World," *Hound and Horn* 7 (April-May 1934): 506–513.

On William Dean Howells, consult: Van Wyck Brooks, *Howells, His Life and World* (New York: Dutton, 1959); Edwin D. Cady, *The Road to Realism, The Early Years, 1837–1885, of William Dean Howells* (Syracuse, N.Y.: Syracuse University Press, 1956); Cady, *The Realist at War; The Mature Years, 1885–1920, of William D. Howells* (Syracuse, N.Y.: Syracuse University Press, 1958); Everett Carter, *Howells and the Age of Realism* (Philadelphia: Lippincott, 1950); Kenneth E. Eble, ed., *Howells, A Century of Criticism* (Dallas, Tex.: Southern Methodist University Press, 1962); Robert L. Hough, *The Quiet Rebel, William Dean Howells as Social Commentator* (Lincoln: University of Nebraska Press, 1959); Clara M. and Rudolph Kirk, *William Dean Howells* (New York: Twayne, 1962); Albert Mordell, comp. and ed., *Discovery of a Genius: William Dean Howells and Henry James* (New York: Twayne, 1961); and James L. Woodress, Jr., *Howells and Italy* (Durham: University of North Carolina Press, 1952).

Bret Harte is adequately treated in George R. Stewart, Jr., *Bret Harte: Argonaut and Exile* (Boston: Houghton, 1931). For Lafcadio Hearn, see especially Elizabeth Bisland, ed., *The Life and Letters of Lafcadio Hearn,* 2 vols. (Boston and New York: Houghton, 1906) and her *The Japanese Letters of Lafcadio Hearn* (Boston and New York: Houghton, 1910); Vera McWilliams, *Lafcadio Hearn* (Boston: Houghton, 1946) ; and Elizabeth Stevenson, *Lafcadio Hearn* (New York: Macmillan, 1961). See also William W. Clary, "Japan: The Warnings and Prophecies of Lafcadio Hearn," *Claremont Oriental Studies*, no. 5 (April 1963) : 1–17 and Daniel Stempel, "Lafcadio Hearn, Interpreter of Japan," *American Literature* 20 (March 1958) : 1–19. Two works were consulted on Joaquin Miller: M. M. Marberry, *Splendid Poseur: Joaquin Miller American Poet* (New York: Crowell, 1953) and Martin S. Peterson, *Joaquin Miller, Literary Frontiersman* (Stanford, Cal.: Stanford University Press, 1937). Of the volumes on Henry Adams, Elizabeth Stevenson's *Henry Adams, A Biography* (New York: Macmillan, 1955) was the most pertinent.

Selected volumes on Samuel Clemens (Mark Twain) include Howard G. Baetzhold, *Mark Twain and John Bull* (Bloomington: Indiana University Press, 1970), an excellent analysis, as is Justin Kaplan, *Mr. Clemens and Mark Twain* (New York: Simon and Schuster, 1966), especially useful for a study of the author's contradictory views of overseas society. See also Louis J. Budd, *Mark Twain: Social Philosopher* (Bloomington: Indiana University Press, 1962) ; Philip S. Foner, *Mark Twain, Social Critic* (New York: International Publishers, 1958) ; and Henry Nash Smith, *Mark Twain, The Development of a Writer* (Cambridge, Mass.: Harvard University Press, 1962). Mark Twain's views of Europe can also be seen in Baetzhold, "Mark Twain: England's Advocate," *American Literature* 28 (Nov. 1956) : 328–346 and John C. McCloskey, "Mark Twain as Critic in 'The Innocents Abroad,' " ibid. 25 (May 1953) : 139–151. On his views of Hawaii, see Frederick W. Lorch, "Hawaiian Federalism and Mark Twain's 'A Connecticut Yankee in King Arthur's Court,' " ibid. 30 (March 1958) : 55–66 and A. Grove Day, ed., *Mark Twain's letters from Hawaii, 1835–1910* (New York: Appleton, 1966).

Relevant sources for Utopian literature are Allyn B. Forbes, "The Literary Quest for Utopia, 1880–1900," *Social Forces* 1 (1927) : 179–189; Humphrey Doermann, "All my immense labor for nothing . . . ," *American Heritage* 12 (June 1961) : 60–64, 104–107 (on Donnelly); Everett W. Fish, *Donnelliana: an appendix to "Caesar's Column." Excerpts from the wit, wisdom, poetry and eloquence of Ignatius Donnelly. Selected and collated, with a biography, . . .* (Chicago: F. J. Schulte & Co., 1892) ; Martin Ridge, *Ignatius Donnelly: The Portrait of a Politician* (Chicago: University of Chicago Press, 1962) ; Sylvia Bowman et al., *Edward Bellamy Abroad, An American Prophet's Influence* (New York: Twayne, 1962) ; and Arthur E. Morgan, *The Philosophy of Edward Bellamy* (New York: King's Crown Press, 1945).

CHAPTER 5: THE EAGLE'S PROTECTIVE WING

The main sources for the protection of overseas Americans are official documents (i.e., *Foreign Relations of the United States*). For an introduction, see Frederick S. Dunn, *The Protection of Nationals* (Baltimore: Johns Hopkins Press, 1932). On Irish-American protection, Thomas N. Brown, *Irish-American Nationalism, 1870–1890* (Philadelphia: Lippincott, 1966) is invaluable. See, too, Owen D. Edwards, "American Diplomats and Irish Coercion, 1880–1883," *Journal of American Studies* 1 (Oct. 1967): 213–232, who feels that arrests of Americans in Ireland was a "major" diplomatic problem. The problem of protecting Jewish nationals in Russia is treated in Carroll's and Queen's dissertations (see ch. 2), John W. Foster, *Diplomatic Memoirs*, 2 vols. (Boston and New York: Houghton, 1909), and Tyler's *Blaine*. See also Lloyd P. Gartner, "Roumania, America, and World Jewry: Consul Peixotto in Bucharest, 1870–1876," *American Jewish Historical Quarterly* 58 (Sept. 1968): 25–117. The issue of Jewish-Americans in the Holy Land is described in detail in Cyrus Adler and Aaron M. Margalith, *With Firmness in the Right, American Diplomatic Action Affecting Jews, 1840–1945* (New York: The American Jewish Committee, 1946), an excellent treatment, and Frank E. Manuel, *The Realities of American-Palestine Relations* (Washington: Public Affairs Press, 1949), a convenient and lucid survey. James A. Field, Jr.'s *America and the Mediterranean World, 1776–1882* (Princeton, N.J.: Princeton University Press, 1969) is also very helpful. This work blends diplomatic and cultural history and emphasizes the following topics: foreign trade, non-military aspects of the navy, missionaries, and education-cultural contributions.

For research on Protestant missionary activities, the reader is directed to The Missionary Research Library of The Union Theological Seminary (New York). Its strength lies in four areas: history of missions, religion and religions, the environment of missions and churches (especially the holdings in Orientalia, Africana, and Oceania), and international affairs and world trends as they affect the mission (Professor Robert T. Handy to author, June 17, 1970).

In addition to the religious periodicals listed above, and the works previously cited for chapter 2, see the *Annual Reports of the Board of Foreign Missions of the Presbyterian Church in the United States of America*, the *Annual Report of the American Board of Commissioners for Foreign Missions*, excellent for reports of progress and statistical data. See also Kenneth M. MacKenzie, *The Robe and the Sword, The*

Methodist Church and the Rise of American Imperialism (Washington: Public Affairs Press, 1961) ; Merle Curti, *American Philanthropy Abroad: A History* (New Brunswick, N.J.: Rutgers University Press, 1963), a pioneer study of this subject; and Muhyee Al-Din Hatoor Al-Khilidi, "A Century of American Contribution to Arab Nationalism, 1820–1920," Ph.D. dissertation, Vanderbilt University, 1958, for material on Christian efforts in the Moslem world.

For information on the relationship between Christian missions and Jewish interests in Palestine, consult Plesur, "The Relations Between the United States and Palestine," *Judaism* . . . 3 (Fall 1954): 469–479; Plesur, "The American Press and Jewish Restoration During the Nineteenth Century," in Isidore S. Meyer, ed., *Early History of Zionism in America* (New York: American Jewish Historical Society and Theodor Herzl Foundation, 1958) ; and Selig Adler, "Backgrounds of American Policy Toward Zion," in Moshe Davis, ed., *Israel: Its Role in Civilization* (New York: Seminary Israel Institute of the Jewish Theological Seminary of America, 1956).

Many of the works previously cited (ch. 2) treat missionary activity in Asia, Africa, and elsewhere. Dennis's work is especially vital. See also Robert E. Speer, *Missions and Modern History*, 2 vols. (New York: Revell, 1904) ; Field's volume cited immediately above; Winburn T. Thomas, *Protestant Beginnings in Japan: The First Three Decades, 1859–1899* (Tokyo and Rutland, Vt.: Tuttle, 1959) ; Paul A. Varg, *Missionaries, Chinese, and Diplomats: The American Protestant Missionary Movement in China, 1890–1952* (Princeton, N.J.: Princeton University Press, 1958) ; Paul A. Cohen, *China and Christianity: The Missionary Movement and the Growth of Chinese Anti-Foreignism, 1860–1870* (Cambridge, Mass.: Harvard University Press, 1963) ; James M. McCutcheon, "The Missionary and Diplomat in China," *Journal of Presbyterian History* 41 (Dec. 1963): 224–236; and Fred H. Harrington, *God, Mammon and the Japanese: Dr. Horace N. Allen and Korean-American Relations, 1884–1905* (Madison: University of Wisconsin Press, 1944). LaTourette, *Missions and the American Mind* (Indianapolis: National Foundation Press, 1949), a succinct summary of the implications of missionary activity, and Foster, *The Relation of Diplomacy to Foreign Missions* [address and pamphlet] (Sewanee, Tenn.: University Press, 1906) are also pertinent.

Christian missionary protection is explored in Harold J. Bass, "The Policy of the American State Department Toward Missionaries in the Far East," *Research Studies of the State College of Washington* 5 (Sept. 1937): 179–190 and McCutcheon's article cited above.

CHAPTER 6: THE NATION'S RIGHT ARM

The *Annual Reports of the Secretaries of the Navy* are obviously a prime source. There are a number of fine general treatments of the navy, describing its weaknesses and eventual rehabilitation. For example, see Robert Seager II, "Ten Years Before Mahan: The Unofficial Case for the New Navy, 1880–1890," *Mississippi Valley Historical Review* 40 (Dec. 1953): 491–512; Harold and Margaret Sprout, *The Rise of American Naval Power: 1776–1918* (Princeton, N.J.: Princeton University Press, 1939), a standard; Daniel J. Carrison, *The Navy from Wood to Steel: 1860–1890* (New York: Watts, 1965); and Walter R. Herrick, Jr., *The American Naval Revolution* (Baton Rouge: Louisiana State University Press, 1966). According to Herrick, Secretary of Navy Benjamin F. Tracy emerges as the real architect of a new navy.

Henry Cabot Lodge's views on the need for a "new" navy are contained in a letter quoted in *Selections from the Correspondence of Theodore Roosevelt and Henry Cabot Lodge, 1884–1918*, 2 vols. (New York: Scribner, 1925). A study of the views of another bigger navy enthusiast is Martin Meadows, "Eugene Hale and the American Navy," *The American Neptune* 22 (July 1962): 187–193. Richard C. Brown's article, "General Emory Upton—The Army's Mahan," *Military Affairs* 17 (Fall 1953): 125–131, demonstrates the army's problems, not unlike those of the navy. Upton was the precursor of the "preparedness movement." One reason for a weak navy was the political stalemate in Washington. See the excellent article by Vincent DeSantis, "American Politics in the Gilded Age," *Review of Politics* 25 (Oct. 1963): 551–561.

On the merchant marine, its activities, problems, and plans proposed for its revival, consult Willard C. McClellan, "A History of American Military Sea Transportation," Ph.D. dissertation, American University, 1953; Leonard A. Swann, Jr., *John Roach, Maritime Entrepreneur* (Annapolis, Md.: U.S. Naval Institute, 1965) on one of the leading lobbyists; Kwang-Chang Liu, *Anglo-American Steamship Rivalry in China, 1862–1874* (Cambridge, Mass.: Harvard University Press, 1963); Joseph Bucklin Bishop, *A Chronicle of One Hundred and Fifty Years, The Chamber of Commerce of the State of New York, 1768–1918* (New York: Scribner, 1918). See also Roach's own writings, two of which are quoted in the documentation. Pletcher, "Inter-American Shipping in the 1880s: A Loosening Tie," *Inter-American Economic Affairs* 10 (Winter 1956): 14–41 is also illuminating.

For the navy's relation to commerce, see in addition to the works cited for chapter 2, Commodore R. W. Shufeldt's brief but important statement, *The Relation of the Navy to the Commerce of the United States* (Washington: J. L. Ginck, 1878). On the subject of the defense and diplomatic implications of a bigger navy, Alfred T. Mahan's works are essential. See his *The Influence of Seapower Upon History, 1660–1783* (Boston: Little, Brown, 1890) and "The United States Looking Outward," *Atlantic Monthly* 66 (Dec. 1890): 816–824. In addition, for other statements about Mahan and his work, consult William D. Puleston, *Mahan* (New Haven, Conn.: Yale University Press, 1939) and William E. Livezey, *Mahan on Seapower* (Norman: University of Oklahoma Press, 1947).

The "new navy" has been chronicled by Seager, the Sprouts, Carrison, and Herrick, cited above. See also John D. Long, *The New American Navy*, 2 vols. (New York: Outlook, 1903) for an earlier account and Howe's *Arthur*. In the first chapter of John A. S. Grenville and George B. Young, *Politics, Strategy, and American Diplomacy, Studies in Foreign Policy, 1873–1917* (New Haven and London: Yale University Press, 1966), the authors discuss the role of Rear Admiral Stephen R. Luce in creating the new navy. Revisionist in tone, Grenville and Young feel that Luce's role was even greater than that of Mahan. Holbo also has interesting comments on the navy in his chapter in the revised edition of *The Gilded Age.*

CHAPTER 7: THE OVERSEAS AMERICANS: TRAVELERS, SCHOLARS, TECHNICIANS, EXPLORERS

Important for an understanding of the travel impulse in Gilded Age America are the many handbooks, guidebooks, and travel accounts published during this period. Many are listed in the documentation for this chapter. In addition to travel accounts written by relative unknowns, those reports by such traveling notables as Andrew Carnegie, ex-President Grant, Oliver W. Holmes, Sr., William H. Seward, and "Buffalo Bill" Cody, pointed up the allure and romance of overseas visitation. (See documentation.) See also Elizabeth Hillman's doctoral dissertation, University of Toronto, 1949, "Reluctant Pilgrims: A Study of the Reports on England by American Writers Who Visited Great Britain Between 1806 and 1886. . . ." Especially helpful are "How to Visit Europe," *New York Tribune*, June 14, 1867; periodicals such as *Cook's Excursionist* and *Outing*, to name but two. Perhaps the most satisfactory secondary account is Dulles, *Americans Abroad*, an excellent introduction and summation of the motivation for travel and also the main attractions. Spiller's *Literary History* also contains valuable insights.

There is much material on specific American groups who visited and studied abroad. See Dulles, *Americans Abroad;* Paul R. Baker, *The Fortunate Pilgrims, Americans in Italy, 1800–1860* (Cambridge, Mass.: Harvard University Press, 1964), good for background; Otto Wittmann, Jr., "The Italian Experience (American Artists in Italy 1830–1875)," *American Quarterly* 4 (Spring 1952): 3–15; and Ruth Ann Musselman, "Attitudes of American Travelers in Germany, 1815–1890 . . . ," Ph.D. dissertation, Michigan State College of Agriculture and Applied Science, 1952. Thomas N. Bonner, *American Doctors and German Universities, A Chapter in International Relations 1870–1914* (Lincoln: University of Nebraska Press, 1963) and Jurgen F. H. Herbst, *The German Historical School in American Scholarship* (Ithaca, N.Y.: Cornell University Press, 1965) describe the overseas study of American scholars in the medical and historical fields and the application of their new learning in the United States. There are many accounts of the educational contributions of scholars who studied in Germany, written both by the academicians themselves as well as secondary accounts by other scholars. (See documentation for the chapter.) See also John A. Walz, *German Influence in American Education and Culture* (Philadelphia: Carl Schurz Memorial Foundation, 1936). On travel in Russia, there is Anna M. Babey, *Americans in Russia, 1776–1917* (New York: Comet Press, 1938).

Unquestionably, Merle Curti and Kendall Birr, *Prelude to Point Four, American Technical Missions Overseas, 1838–1938* (Madison: University of Wisconsin Press, 1954) is a seminal work in its field. While there were many overseas areas which attracted and invited American technical know-how, there was none more interesting than Japan. The following monographs detail the educational, military, agricultural, and cultural contributions of the United States: Pat Barr, *The Deer Cry Pavilion: A Story of Westerners in Japan 1868–1905* (New York: Harcourt, 1969), a popular account; James R. Bowditch, "The Impact of Japanese Culture on the United States, 1853–1904," Ph.D. dissertation, Harvard University, 1963; Foster R. Dulles, *Yankees and Samurai; America's Role in the Emergence of Modern Japan: 1791–1900* (New York: Harper, 1965); William E. Griffis, *Verbeck of Japan, A Citizen of No Country* (New York: Revell, 1900); John A. Harrison, "The Capron Mission and the Colonization of Hokkaido, 1868–1878," *Agricultural History* 25 (1951): 135–142, a description of an agricultural mission; William L. Neumann, *America Encounters Japan: From Perry to MacArthur* (Baltimore: Johns Hopkins Press, 1963); Inazo O. Nitobé, *The Intercourse Between the United States and Japan* (Baltimore: Johns Hopkins Press, 1891);

and Robert S. Schwantes, *Japanese and Americans: A Century of Cultural Relations* (New York: Published for the Council on Foreign Relations by Harper, 1955).

The most valuable monograph on Arctic exploration is John Edwards Caswell, *Arctic Frontiers, United States Explorations in the Far North* (Norman: University of Oklahoma Press, 1965). See also Morgan B. Sherwood, *Exploration of Alaska* (New Haven, Conn.: Yale University Press, 1965); Farley Mowat, comp., *The Polar Passion: The Quest for the North Pole, with Selections from Arctic Journals* (Boston: Little, Brown, 1967). The reports of such explorers as Hall, Howgate, Greely, and Ray and by the wife of one (DeLong), are also important. (See documentation.) Other secondary accounts are Edward Ellsberg, *Hell on Ice. The Saga of the 'Jeannette'* (New York: Dodd, 1938); A. L. Todd, *Abandoned: The Story of the Greely Arctic Expedition; 1881–1884* (New York: McGraw-Hill, 1961); and Theodore Powell, *The Long Rescue* (Garden City, N.Y.: Doubleday, 1960). Two popular accounts are interesting: Donald Jackson, " 'Tell me, Sidney, how do you spell murder?' " *Life* 66 (Apr. 25, 1969): 663–678 (depicting the Hall death as a possible murder mystery) and Charles B. van Pelt, "The Greely Arctic Expedition," *American History Illustrated* 2 (Jan. 1968): 36–48.

Prime sources for the exploration of Palestine, in which this country was invited to participate, are Joseph P. Thompson, "The Exploration of Palestine," *North American Review* 113 (July 1871): 154–173 and the discussions in the *Congressional Record*, 43 Cong., 1st sess., 2, pts. 2, 5. In the documentation are also listed other original sources for the Palestine project.

That form of exploration done by the "plant explorers" is described by Wayne D. Rasmussen, "The United States Plant Explorers in South America During the Nineteenth Century," Ph.D. dissertation, George Washington University, 1950.

As with technical missions overseas, Merle Curti's analysis of overseas philanthropy is a standard. See his *American Philanthropy Abroad*, cited previously.

Chapter 8: American Ambivalence: Attitudes Toward Europe

The American attitude toward Europe and the Old World's view of this country was a mixture of both criticism and admiration. Two English men of letters who were skeptical of American values were Matthew Arnold and Herbert Spencer. See Arnold, *Civilization in the United States, First and Last Impressions of America* (Boston: Cupples &

Hurd, 1888) and also James Eckman, "The British Traveler in America, 1875–1920," Ph.D. dissertation, Georgetown University, 1946, a convenient survey. A chauvinistic reply to our critics came from Andrew Carnegie. See his *Triumphant Democracy* (New York: Scribner, 1886). Another contemporary account, Nathan Appleton, *Europe and America in 1870* (New York: printed for the author, 1870), is quite interesting and useful. While Spencer voiced negative comments on America's materialism, he was not completely antagonistic. See his *Essays, Scientific, Political, and Speculative*, 3 vols. (New York: D. Appleton, 1891: 3: "The Americans"). Also, James Bryce evinced optimism in the classic *American Commonwealth*, 2 vols. (New York: Macmillan, 1893:2).

America's feeling toward Europe was to a large extent predicated on disdain for her militarism and imperial ventures. Both official sources and the periodicals and newspapers are replete with such sentiments. See, for example, Field, *America and the Mediterranean World* for a discussion of how the Franco-Prussian War affected the United States. Because of prodding from Irish-Americans, Britain's relationship with Ireland aroused special feelings on this side of the Atlantic. Casting light on this subject are Charles C. Tansill, *America and the Fight for Irish Freedom, 1866–1922* (New York: Devin, 1957); Florence E. Gibson, *The Attitudes of the New York Irish Toward State and National Affairs 1848–1892* (New York: Columbia University Press, 1951); James M. Mahoney, "The Influence of the Irish-Americans Upon the Foreign Policy of the United States, 1865–1872," Ph.D. dissertation, Clark University, 1947; and Brown, *Irish-American Nationalism*, previously cited.

Immigration of Europeans to these shores was always a heated subject in the public press. Revisionist views of the business attitude can be seen in Charlotte Erickson, *American Industry and the European Immigrant, 1860–1885* (Cambridge, Mass.: Harvard University Press, 1957) and Morrell Heald, "Business Attitudes Toward European Immigration, 1880–1900," *Journal of Economic History* 13 (Summer 1953): 291–304. Cushing Strout's *The American Image of the Old World* (New York: Harper, 1963) is also helpful in not only this connection, but it is an excellent analysis of the general ambivalence in the United States toward Europe.

The European cultural impact upon the United States receives some attention in Brooks, *New England Indian Summer, 1865–1915* (previously cited); Mott's *History of American Magazines* (cited), describing the concern of some American periodicals for European news and developments; and Gustav Pollak, *Fifty Years of American Idealism, The New York Nation, 1865–1915* (Boston and New York: Houghton, 1915). The following works provide excellent insights into European-American cultural relations: Halvdan Koht, *The American Spirit in Europe, A Survey of Transatlantic Influences* (Philadelphia: University of Pennsylvania Press, 1949) and Sigmund Skard, *The American Myth and the European Mind, American Studies in Europe, 1776–1960* (Philadelphia: University of Pennsylvania Press, 1961). Also of some use are Clarence Gohdes, *American Literature in Nineteenth-Century England* (New York: Columbia University Press, 1944); George S. Gordon, *Anglo-American Literary Relations* (London, New York: Oxford University Press, 1942); Lida von Krockow, "American Characters in German Novels," *Atlantic Monthly* 68 (Dec. 1891): 824–838; and John H. Nelson, "Some Germanic Surveys of American Literature," *American Literature* 1 (1929–1930): 148–160.

The copyright issue proved to be a practical test of Old-New World relationships. Aubert J. Clark, *The Movement for International Copyright in Nineteenth-Century America* (Washington: Catholic University of America Press, 1960) is the standard treatment. Several doctoral dissertations proved quite helpful: Warren B. Bezanson, "The American Struggle for International Copyright, 1866–1891," University of Maryland, 1953; Wallace P. Bishop, "The Struggle for International Copyright in the United States," Boston University, 1959; and I. Joel Larus, "The Origin and Development of the 1891 International Copyright Law of the United States," Columbia University, 1960.

CHAPTER 9: SPOTLIGHT ON DARKEST AFRICA

An excellent contemporary introduction to the subject of American interest in mid-Africa is Gilbert Haven, "America in Africa," *North American Review* 125 (July 1877): 147–158 and (November 1877): 517–528. A recent secondary account, while brief, gives a good summary: Clarence Clendenen, Robert Collins, Peter Duignan, *Americans in Africa, 1865–1900* (Stanford, Cal.: Hoover Institution on War, Revolution, & Peace, Stanford University, 1966). Specifically, the questions of trade, Liberian relations, the story of H. M. Stanley, the opening up of the Congo, and American exploiters of Africa, are treated. Roy Olton's doctoral dissertation, "Problems of American Foreign Relations in the African Area During the Nineteenth Century," Fletcher School of Law and Diplomacy, 1954, is a lengthy and complete study. Field's *America and the Mediterranean World* and Harold E. Hammond, "American Interest in the Exploration of the Dark Continent," *The Historian* 18 (Spring 1956) : 202–229 are also of value.

For interesting and thrilling background, the reader is directed to the writings of Henry M. Stanley (see documentation for chapter). Secondary accounts of the legendary Stanley that will also prove fascinating are Byron Farwell, *The Man Who Presumed* (New York: Holt, 1957), a biography; and Olivia Manning, *The Reluctant Rescue* [of Emin Pasha] (Garden City, N.Y.: Doubleday, 1947). Of course, since the *New York Herald* was a sponsor of the Stanley search for Livingstone, its pages afford an excellent, if somewhat understandably biased account, of the increased attention Africa was beginning to play in America's thinking.

The missionary activity in Africa can be seen in practically every missionary periodical or reminiscence listed elsewhere in this bibliography.

While Africa was a questionable commercial outlet for the United States, it did receive some attention. The works by and about Commodore Shufeldt (previously cited) are pertinent. Senator John T. Morgan was another proponent of Africa as an area to develop commercially as well as a potential haven for American blacks. See his "The Future of the Negro," *North American Review* 139 (July 1884) : 81–84 and "The Race Question in the United States," *Arena* 2 (Sept. 1890) : 384–398. For background on Morgan, consult August C. Radke, Jr., "John Tyler Morgan, An Expansionist Senator, 1877–1907," Ph.D. dissertation, University of Washington, 1953, and Joseph O. Baylen, "Senator John Tyler Morgan, E. D. Morel, and the Congo Reform Association," *Alabama Review* 15 (Apr. 1962) : 117–132.

In addition to the general works on African interests cited above, Elizabeth Brett White, *American Opinion of France* (New York: Knopf, 1927) and Pletcher's *The Awkward Years* have information on American concern over the Great Power role in Africa. For details on The International African Association and The Berlin Conference on the Congo, see in addition to works already mentioned, S. E. Crowe, *The Berlin West African Conference, 1884–1885* (New York: Longmans, Green, 1942); Leon Felde, "An American General and The Congo," *Belgium* 5 (Apr. 1944), 110–112; Edward Younger, *Kasson* (previously cited); and *An American Democrat, The Recollections of Perry Belmont*, 2nd ed. (New York: Columbia University Press, 1941). On an issue that plagued the Great Powers in Africa—the slave trade—see James C. Duram, "A Study of Frustration: Britain, the U.S.A., and the African Slave Trade, 1815–1870," *Social Science* 40 (Oct. 1965) : 220–225.

CHAPTER 10: THE PERSISTENT MONROE DOCTRINE: INCREASING INVOLVEMENT IN LATIN AMERICA

A contemporary judgment of the Monroe Doctrine is John A. Kasson, "The Monroe Doctrine," *North American Review* 133 (Sept. 1881): 241–254. The study of the Doctrine by Dexter Perkins (*The Monroe Doctrine, 1867–1907* [Baltimore: Johns Hopkins Press, 1937]) is still pertinent and is the standard statement.

For America's reaction to the War of the Pacific, see the solid study of Herbert Millington, *American Diplomacy and the War of the Pacific* (New York: Columbia University Press, 1948). Official concern over possible European involvement was voiced by Perry Belmont *An American Democrat* (previously cited) and Andrew D. White, *Autobiography*, 2 vols. (New York: Century Co., 1908). Blaine's apologia is contained in *Political Discussions: Legislative, Diplomatic, and Popular, 1856–1886* (Norwich, Conn.: Henry Bill, 1887). See also Tyler's *Foreign Policy of Blaine;* Seward W. Livermore, "American Strategy Diplomacy in the South Pacific, 1890–1914," *Pacific Historical Review* 12 (1943): 33–41; and V. G. Kiernan, "Foreign Interests in the War of the Pacific," *Hispanic American Historical Review* 35 (Feb. 1955): 14–36.

On other aspects of Blaine's policy, see J. Fred Rippy, "Relations of the United States and Guatemala During the Epoch of Justo Rufino Barrios," *Hispanic American Historical Review* 22 (1942): 595–605; A. Curtis Wilgus, "James G. Blaine and the Pan-American Movement," ibid. 5 (1922), 662–708; Russell H. Bastert, "A New Approach to the Origins of Blaine's Pan-American Policy," ibid. 39 (Aug. 1959), 375–412. Bastert has also studied the reversal of Blaine's program: "Diplomatic Reversal: Frelinghuysen's Opposition to Blaine's Pan-American Policy in 1882," *Mississippi Valley Historical Review* 42 (March 1965): 653–671. The background of the Pan-American Conference is treated in J. Lloyd Mecham, *The United States and Inter-American Security, 1889–1960* (Austin: University of Texas Press, 1961).

Relations with Argentina during the Gilded Age were never intimate but there were efforts on both sides to improve contacts. Both Thomas F. McGann, *Argentina, The United States, and the Inter-American System, 1880–1914* (Cambridge, Mass.: Harvard University Press, 1957) and Harold F. Peterson, *Argentina and the United States, 1810–1960* (Albany: State University of New York Press, 1964) should be consulted. Peterson's book is solid and reliable.

Mexican-United States relations in general are treated in Daniel Cosió Villegas, *The United States Versus Porfirio Díaz* (Lincoln: University of Nebraska Press, 1963). Based on archival research both north and south of the border, this work by an eminent Mexican historian presents a most balanced point of view. Also of value is James M. Callahan, *American Foreign Policy in Mexican Relations* (New York: Macmillan, 1932). See also Jules Davids, "American Political and Economic Penetration of Mexico, 1877–1920," Ph.D. dissertation, Georgetown University, 1947, and Chester C. Kesier, "John Watson Foster, United States Minister to Mexico, 1873–1880," Ph.D. dissertation, American University, 1953. Foster's *Diplomatic Memoirs* are also important. On border troubles, consult Robert D. Gregg, *The Influence of Border Troubles on Relations Between the United States and Mexico, 1875–1910*, Johns Hopkins University Studies in History and Political Science 55, no. 3 (Baltimore: Johns Hopkins University Press, 1937), 375–564. Pletcher's *Rails, Mines and Progress: Seven American Promoters in Mexico* (already cited) is vital to an understanding of America's Mexican relations. Joseph Nimmo's *Commerce Between the United States and Mexico* (Washington: Government Printing Office, 1884) is a contemporary account.

Other Latin-American interests are explored in Ludwell Lee Montague, *Haiti and the United States, 1714–1938* (Durham, N.C.: Duke University Press, 1940) and Rayford W. Logan, *The Diplomatic Relations of the United States with Haiti, 1776–1891* (Chapel Hill: University of North Carolina Press, 1941).

The last major subject explored in this chapter is the inter-oceanic canal issue. Standard monographs include Perkins's *Monroe Doctrine, 1867–1907* and his *Hands Off: A History of the Monroe Doctrine* (Boston: Little, Brown, 1946), a shorter one-volume study of the Monroe Doctrine; Gerstle Mack, *The Land Divided, A History of the Panama Canal and Other Isthmian Projects* (New York: Knopf, 1944); and Dwight C. Miner, *The Fight for the Panama Route* (New York: Columbia University Press, 1940). Senator Morgan's interest in and work in behalf of a canal is evaluated by Radke in two works, *John Tyler Morgan, An Expansionist Senator* (previously cited) and "Senator Morgan and the Nicaragua Canal," *Alabama History* 12 (Jan. 1959): 5–34; see also A. L. Venable, "John T. Morgan, Father of the Inter-Oceanic Canal," *Southwestern Social Science Quarterly* 19 (1939): 376–387.

CHAPTER 11: THE QUEST FOR A CANADIAN-AMERICAN CONSENSUS

Whether the proponents of Canadian annexation were serious or not, certainly Canada seemed to be a prime objective of the annexationist-minded politicians. Albert Weinberg's *Manifest Destiny* (Baltimore:

Johns Hopkins Press, 1935) explores this feeling. Contemporary accounts by legislators Ben Butler and John Sherman are interesting examples: Butler, *Should There Be a Union of the English-Speaking Peoples of the Earth?* . . . (Boston: Press of Rockwell & Churchill, 1889) and Sherman, *Recollections of Forty Years in the House, Senate and Cabinet*, 2 vols. (Chicago: Werner, 1895).

Several works treat the major aspects of Canadian-American relations: Donald F. Warner, *The Idea of Continental Union* (already cited), a reliable, solid work; Gerald M. Craig, *The United States and Canada* (Cambridge, Mass.: Harvard University Press, 1968), who feels there was generally little sincere motivation for closer ties; R. C. Brown, *Canada's National Policy, 1883–1900: A Study in Canadian-American Relations* (Princeton, N.J.: Princeton University Press, 1964); and the older works, L. B. Shippee, *Canadian-American Relations, 1849–1874* (New Haven, Conn.: Yale University Press, 1939) and Tansill, *Canadian-American Relations, 1875–1911* (New Haven, Conn.: Yale University Press, 1943).

If political interest in a union between the nations was slight, there was generally more feeling for closer commercial ties. See for example, in addition to the above, George S. Boutwell (later to be a leading anti-imperialist), *Reminiscences of Sixty Years in Public Affairs*, 2 vols. (New York: McClure, Phillips & Co., 1902); the works of Benjamin Butterworth and Erastus Wiman, figures who labored tirelessly for reciprocity. See for example, Butterworth, *Commercial Union between Canada and the United States* and Wiman, *The Advantages of Commercial Union to Canada and the United States in Canadian Club of New York, Canadian Leaves;* . . .; a series of new papers read before the Canadian Club of New York (New York: Thompson, 1887). Gary Pennanen, "American Interest in Commercial Union with Canada, 1854–1898," *Mid-America* 47 (Jan. 1965): 24–39 is a competent recent study.

The fisheries problem received due attention from Senator Henry C. Lodge, reacting to the feelings of his Massachusetts constituency. See "The Fisheries Question," *North American Review* 146 (Feb. 1888): 121–130. Warren, Tansill, and Craig should also be consulted. See too, Charles S. Campbell, Jr., "American Tariff Interests and the Northeastern Fisheries, 1883–1888," *Canadian Historical Review* 45 (Sept. 1964): 212–228. Campbell feels that the American fishing industry failed in their attempt to get Congress to grant them a monopoly of the American market by preventing the importation of Canadian fishery products into America. Cleveland and Bayard deserve credit for successfully resisting resort to the Retaliation Bill. Allan Nevins's *Cleveland* is still useful on this subject.

CHAPTER 12: ACROSS THE PACIFIC

An early statement on the potential the Pacific held for the United States is William E. F. Krause, *The Influence of the United States Abroad* (San Francisco: privately printed, 1868).

Still the best volumes on Samoa are George H. Ryden, *The Foreign Policy of the United States in Relation to Samoa* (New Haven, Conn.: Yale University Press, 1933) and Sylvia Masterman, *The Origins of International Rivalry in Samoa, 1845–1884* (Stanford, Cal.: Stanford University Press, 1934). Clara E. Schieber, *The Transformation of American Sentiment Toward Germany, 1870–1914* (Boston and New York: Cornhill, 1923) and Tyler's *Blaine* give information on Great Power rivalries. Robert L. Stevenson, *A Footnote to History, Eight Years of Trouble in Samoa* (New York: Scribner, 1892) provides contemporary color.

On Hawaii, see Sylvester K. Stevens, *American Expansion in Hawaii, 1842–1898* (New York: Russell & Russell, 1945), excellent on reciprocity; Merze Tate, *The United States and the Hawaiian Kingdom* (New Haven and London: Yale University Press, 1965), a competent general survey; Tate, *Hawaii: Reciprocity or Annexation* (East Lansing: Michigan State University Press, 1968); and Ralph S. Kuykendall, *The Hawaiian Kingdom: The Kalakaua Dynasty, 1874–1893* (Honolulu: University of Hawaii Press, 1967), a thorough, interesting volume, the last in a trilogy. Kuykendall points out the weaknesses of Kalakaua's government. The King's tour around the world which aroused American suspicions is interestingly portrayed in *Around the World with A King* (New York: F. A. Stokes, 1904) by William N. Armstrong. Two articles of value are Tate, "British Opposition to the Cession of Pearl Harbor," *Pacific Historical Review* 29 (Nov. 1960): 381–394 and Donald M. Dozer, "The Opposition to Hawaiian Reciprocity, 1876–1888," ibid. 14 (1945): 157–183.

Japanese-American cultural relations are treated in the very helpful volumes previously cited: Dulles, *Yankees and Samurai;* Neumann, *America Encounters Japan;* and Schwantes, *Japanese and Americans.* See also Payson Treat, *Diplomatic Relations between the United States and Japan, 1853–1895*, 2 vols. (Stanford, Cal.: Stanford University Press, 1932).

On American-Chinese affairs, see Kwang-Ching Liu, *Americans and Chinese* (Cambridge, Mass.: Harvard University Press, 1963); Mildred A. Preen, "Statistical Analysis of the Trade of the United States With

China," Master's thesis, Columbia University, 1941; and Tyler Dennett, *Americans in Eastern Asia* (New York: Macmillan, 1922), an old but still reliable volume. On the vexatious Chinese immigration issue, the following are sound interpretations: Mary R. Coolidge, *Chinese Immigration* (New York: Holt, 1909); Elmer C. Sandmeyer, *The Anti-Chinese Movement in California* (Urbana: University of Illinois Press, 1939); Gunther Barth, *Bitter Strength, A History of the Chinese in the United States, 1850–1870* (Cambridge, Mass.: Harvard University Press, 1964); and Stuart C. Miller, *The Unwelcome Immigrant. The American Image of the Chinese, 1785–1882* (Berkeley and Los Angeles: University of California Press, 1969). Gary Pennanen, "Public Opinion and the Chinese Question, 1876–1879," *Ohio History* 77 (1968): 139–148, 201–203 describes the Chinese immigration question in terms of its interest to the public and as a major diplomatic issue in the Hayes administration.

The "opening" of Korea is treated by Paullin in *The Opening of Korea by Commodore Shufeldt* and *Diplomatic Negotiations of American Naval Officers* (previously cited). Fred H. Harrington, *God, Mammon, and the Japanese: Dr. Horace Allen and Korean-American Relations, 1884–1905* is absolutely essential (cited). Other helpful sources are Dennett, "Early American Policy in Korea, 1883–1887," *Political Science Quarterly* 38 (1923): 83–103; H. J. Noble, "The United States and Sino-Korean Relations," *Pacific Historical Review* 2 (1933): 292–304; several items in the Horace N. Allen MSS; Albert Castel and Andrew C. Nahm, "Our Little War With the Heathen," *American Heritage* 19 (Apr. 1968): 19–23 f., a colorful popular account of the abortive 1871 expedition; and William M. Leary, Jr., "Our Other War in Korea," *United States Naval Institute Proceedings* 94 (June 1968): 47–53. This article stresses the fact that America's image in the Orient could not be easily sacrificed by attacks on the American fleet.

Two doctoral dissertations provided the information on American-Siamese relations: Chang Wook Moon, "American Relations with Siam: Diplomatic, Commercial, Religious and Educational," University of Southern California, 1935, and James V. Martin, Jr., "A History of the Diplomatic Relations between Siam and the United States of America, 1833–1929," Fletcher School of Law and Diplomacy, 1947.

American interests in the Pacific were increasing, so much so that other nations were becoming suspicious. This feeling is described in W. D. McIntyre, "Anglo-American Rivalry in the Pacific: The British Annexation of the Fiji Islands in 1874," *Pacific Historical Review* 29 (Nov. 1960): 361–380.

CHAPTER 13: EPILOGUE: OUT OF THE DOLDRUMS

On the surface, the United States took comfort in the fact that its foreign contacts were quite limited. For example, Seymour H. Fersh's analysis of Presidential "State of the Union" messages shows that in some cases, international news played a small part ("An Historical Analysis of the Changing Functions of the Presidential 'State of the Union' Messages," Ph.D. dissertation, New York University, 1955). This work was published as *The View from the White House; a Study of the Presidential State of the Union Messages* (Washington: Public Affairs Press, 1961). Bailey (*The Man in the Street*), Dulles (*The Imperial Years* [New York: Crowell, 1956]), and Dozer (*Anti-Imperialism in the United States*) document the seeming disdain for an aggressive foreign policy.

However, LaFeber, in *The New Empire*, and William A. Williams (*The Roots of the Modern American Empire* [New York: Random, 1969]) regard The Gilded Age as a time of preparation, a time when the impulse for empire was in a state of development. These authors emphasize commercial motivation—the need for overseas markets. The present volume is concerned with contemporary evidence that buttresses this point of view. One very provocative statement is that of John A. Kasson, "The Monroe Doctrine in 1881," *North American Review* 133 (Dec. 1881): 523–533. Admiral Mahan and Senator Morgan were also eloquent spokesmen for this point of view: Mahan, *From Sail to Steam, Recollection of Naval Life* (New York and London: Harper, 1906) and Radke, *John Tyler Morgan, An Expansionist Senator* (already cited). While every Secretary of State in this period had greater foreign interests than tradition has it, James G. Blaine did the most to keep expansionist thought viable. Winchester's doctoral dissertation, "James G. Blaine and the Ideology of American Expansionism" (already cited), convincingly argues that Blaine "bequeathed to the twentieth century a modern design for empire," emphasizing "selected reciprocity" and an "open door" philosophy. LaFeber's summary of the Secretaries in *The New Empire* is a penetrating analysis. James M. Callahan, *American Relations in the Pacific and the Far East, 1784–1900* (Baltimore: Johns Hopkins Press, 1901), writing at the time of the "Great Debate" over the territorial legacy of the Spanish-American War, describes America's expansive pioneer spirit, the sense of destiny that came to fruition after a time of gestation in the Gilded Age.

Index

Adams, Brooks, 14–16
Adams, Charles Francis, 39
Adams, Charles Kendall, 113
Adams, George J., 73
Adams, Henry, 61–62, 150; on travel overseas, 107, 110, 114–15
Adams, Herbert Baxter, 113–14
Adee, Alvey A., 148, 200–201, 232
Adler, Selig, 9
Africa, 119, 122, 228, 231, 235; American interest in, 23, 144; Arthur and, 148–49, 151; Belgium and, 151; Bismarck and, 152; expansionism and, 144–45, 147, 148, 150; forces accounting for American interest in, 145–47; France and, 147, 148, 150; Frelinghuysen and, 151–52; Germany and, 147, 152; liquor traffic in, 79, 84; missionary interest in, 78–79, 84, 144–45, 146, 153; Morgan's resolutions on, 148–49; official American interest in, 147–56; Shufeldt and, 87, 96, 99; slave trade involving, 144, 152; sub-Sahara in, 144

African Trade Society, 149
Agassiz, Louis, 120
Alaska: explorations of, 120–22; fisheries, 22; purchase of, 7, 115; Seward and, 233; travel to, 120
Alcott, Louisa May, 140
The Alhambra (Irving), 51
Allen, Dr. Horace N., 82
Alsace-Lorraine, 133
The Ambassadors (James), 56
The American (James), 56
American Atlantic Cable Telegraphic Company, 44
American Board of Commissioners for Foreign Missions, 74, 77, 85
American business. *See* Business, American
American Colonization Society, 144, 147, 150
American Copyright League, 142
American Exchange, 18
American Exporter, 18
American Geographical Society, 146
American Historical Association, 40, 114

American Machinist Publication Company, 18
American markets. *See* Markets
American Peace Society, 49
American Protective Association, 136
American Revolution, 182, 192
American Steamship Company, lines of, 93
American Typographical Union, 32
Amherst College, 114
Angell, James B., 40, 207, 216
Annexation, 7, 228; of Canada, 11, 12, 20–21, 65, 182, 196; forces opposing, of Canada, 186; of Cuba, 149, 171–72; of Hawaii, 64, 154, 205, 208; of Mexican territory, 11, 168; of Philippines, 149; of Santo Domingo, 7, 12
Anti-expansionism, 7, 9; business and, 16; Canada and, 186; evidences of, 228–29; the press on, 6–7; reasons for, 3–7; Samoa and, 199; Seward on, 5
Anti-immigration. *See* Immigration, concern over increasing
Arbitration, international, 49
Archer, Isabelle, 56
Arctic, 23, 120, 122
Armour and Company, 30
Army Signal Corps, 120, 121
Arnold, Matthew, 127
Arthur administration, 6, 40, 170
Arthur, Chester A., 23, 30, 42, 161, 166, 177, 179, 218; on Africa, 23, 148–49, 151; and Korea, 222–23; and naval renewal, 88, 99
"Asiatic Monroe Doctrine," 210, 225
Asiatic Turkey. *See* Palestine
Atkinson, Edward, 49, 194
Atlantis (Donnelly), 65
The Autobiography of Henry Adams, 61

Bailey, Thomas A., 4, 7, 8, 9
Bancroft, George, 39, 112
Barker, Wharton, 21, 189
Barrios, Justo Rufino, 161
Bates, George H., 201
Bayard-Chamberlain treaty, 21, 194–95

Bayard, Thomas F., 85, 155, 162, 179, 189, 223; assessment of, 235; displeasure with European policies, 130, 133–34; and the fisheries issue, 194–95, 196; and Hawaii, 208; and Samoa, 202; and the State Department, 39, 41
Bell, Alexander G., telephone of, 140
Bellamy, Edward, 65–66, 140
Belmont, Perry, 154, 159
Bemis, Samuel F., 152
Bennett, James Gordon, 121, 145
Berlin conference, 23, 151–52; debate over, 153–54; Kasson and, 152–53
Berlin University, 112, 114
Bern conference (1874), 47–48
Bernhardt, Sarah, 139
Berry, Dr. John C., 117
Bingham, John A., 220, 221
Birr, Kendall, 116
Bismarck, Otto von, 131–32, 159; and Africa, 152; and Samoa, 203
Blaine, James G., 22, 30, 37, 162, 168, 211; assessment of, 234–35; on Canadian relations, 187–88, 191; devises plan to aid the merchant marine, 94; displeasure with European expansionism, 130–31, 132; and Hawaii, 206–207; and an isthmian canal, 178–79; and Korea, 221–22; on Latin American policy, 157, 159; on naval bases, 160–62; and pan-Americanism, 19–20, 162, 163, 164–66; on protection of nationals, 68–69; and the War of the Pacific, 158, 159–60
Blaine, Walker, 160
Blake, William P., 116
Bland-Allison Act (1878), 48
Board of Trade and Transportation of New York, 24
Bolivia, and the War of the Pacific, 159, 160
Boston Board of Trade, 32
Boston Museum of Fine Arts, 213
Boulanger, Georges, 164
Boutwell, George S., 187

Bradshaw's Continental Railway Guide, 106

Brazil Steamship Company, 94

Britain: attitudes toward traveling Americans in, 126–27, 141; authors and, 52, 56–57, 59, 61, 63; and China, 214, 216; cultural exchanges with, 138–40, 142; fisheries issue affecting relations with, 192–96; Irish-Americans and relations with, 68–69; Isthmian relations, 172–73, 176, 178, 181; and Korea, 222–24; relations with, over Canada, 182–83, 190–91, 229; relations with, over Latin America, 162; relations with, over Liberia, 150; rival of U.S., 122, 133, 134, 228; rivalry over Hawaii, 205, 206–207, 208, 209; rivalry over Samoa, 200, 202–204; travel to, 109; union with U.S., 134, 138

Brooks, Van Wyck, 59

Browne, J. Ross, 81

Brussels conference, 48

Bryce, James, 141

Burgess, John W., 114

Burlingame, Anson D., 81

Burlingame treaty (1868), 217, 218

Burns, Robert, 61

Burnside, Ambrose, 181

Business, American, 8, 10, 24, 44; and anti-expansionism, 16; and Canada, 20; and China, 214–15; competition for markets, 17–18; and Cuba, 171–72; and expansionism, 229–30; and Hawaii, 205–206; and immigration, 136; interest in Africa, 144–45; interest in expositions, 45; interest in polar regions, 120, 122; and an isthmian canal, 176; and Latin America, 18–20; and Mexico, 19, 168–70; missionaries promote, 75; and the Navy, 96–97, 101; and reciprocity with Canada, 188–89; and Russia, 21–22; and the State Department, 18

Business, expansionism and. *See* Expansionism, business

Businessmen's Association of Buffalo, 189

Butler, Benjamin F., 183

Butler, Nicholas Murray, 103

Butterworth, Benjamin B., 189–90

Byron, George Gordon, Lord, 61

Cables, 19, 44, 48, 208

Caesar's Column (Donnelly), 65

Calkins, William Henry, 99

Canada: and the American market, 17; early attempts at annexation of, 182, 196; expansionism and, 182–85; and the fisheries question, 21, 192–96; forces advocating an americanized, 182–85; forces opposing an americanized, 186; markets and, 187, 190; raids into, 135; and reciprocity, 20–21, 32–33, 187–92, 196, 228; union with the United States, 11, 12, 20–21, 24, 65

Capron, Horace, 118

Carnegie, Andrew, 108, 127, 138, 165, 179

Cattle production, 27

Central Ontario Railroad, 20

Chamberlain, Joseph, 194–95

Chandler, William E., 98–99

Chile, and the War of the Pacific, 158–59, 160

Chimbote Bay, 160

China: American interest in, 214–19; immigration from, 217–19; and Korea, 221, 223–24; missionaries in, 81, 84, 86; opium and, 84, 134

Chinese Exclusion Act, 24

Chinese labor, 206–207, 217

Christiancy, Isaac D., 159

Church of the Messiah, 73

Clark, William Smith, 119

Clay, Henry, 163

Clayton-Bulwer treaty, 161, 173, 175, 178–79, 181, 235; abrogation of, 173, 177, 181

Cleveland administration, 9, 39, 49

Cleveland, Grover, 99, 166; and Africa, 150, 154; on anti-expansionism, 5; assessment of, 235; and the fisheries question, 21, 194–

Cleveland, Grover (cont.)
95, 196; on foreign service reforms, 41–44; and Hawaii, 208; and an isthmian canal, 173, 176, 177–78; and Samoa, 202–203
Cocos, 161
Cody, William "Buffalo Bill," 37, 109
Cogswell, Joseph G., 112
Colombia, Isthmian relations, 172, 173, 178–79
Columbia College Law School, 114
Columbia University, 114
Comly, James M., 206
Conferences, international, American participation in, 47–50
Congo region, 144–45, 149, 151–53, 154–56, 235
Conkling, Roscoe, 147, 169
A Connecticut Yankee in King Arthur's Court (Twain), 63
Consular reports, 28–29, 40, 42, 124, 130, 186, 200, 201–202
Consular services, 33, 35; and appropriations, 42; business demands reform in, 44; call for reforms in, 43; defects in, 43; expanded by Evarts, 28
Convention of 1818, 192
Cook and Ravel Company, 105
Coolies. *See* Chinese labor
Cooper, James Fenimore, 140
Copley, John Singleton, 111
Copyright, problem over, 141–42
Cornell University, 113
Cotton production, 15
Cox, Samuel S., 85, 115, 123, 180
Crapo, William J., 180
Crystal Palace Exhibition (1851), 45
Cuba: American interest in, 171–72; annexation of, 149, 171–72; business and, 171–72; expansionism and, 171–72; Grant and, 171; reciprocity with, 172; Seward on acquisition of, 11
Curti, Merle, 82, 116, 119

Dabney, Morgan and Company, 19
Daisy Miller (James), 56, 57

Daly, Charles P., 146
Damrosch, Leopold, 139
Danish West Indies, 11, 228
Dawes, Rufus R., 85
Dawson, Thomas M., 200
DeConde, Alexander, 9
De Lesseps, Ferdinand, 173, 175
DeLong, Lt. Comdr. George Washington, 120–21
Denny, Owen N., 224
Detroit Board of Trade, 188–89
Díaz, Porfirio, 19, 167, 168
Dickens, Charles, 142
Diplomatic and Consular Act, 224
Dole, Samuel B., 79
Donnelly, Ignatius, 65
Doshisha University, 117
Dual Alliance, 128

Eastman Kodak camera (1880), 105
Edison, Thomas A., incandescent lamp of, 140
Edmunds, George F., 42, 155–56, 180–81, 193–94
Edwards, Jonathan, 83
Eliot, Charles W., 103
Elgin-Marcy treaty, 187, 192
Ellesmere Island, 121
Ely, Richard T., 114–15
Emin Pasha, 145
Equitable Life Insurance Company, 21
The Europeans (James), 56
Evarts, William M., 69, 131, 150, 167, 178, 199, 211, 222; assessment of, 233–34; expands consular services, 28; and reciprocity, 20
Everett, Edward, 112
Exclusion Act (1879), 218
Exclusion. *See* Immigration, Chinese
Excursionist, 105
Expansionism, 3, 12–13, 14–15, 21–23, 133; in Africa, 144–45, 147, 148, 150; in the Arctic, 120, 121–22; business and, 8–10, 15–16, 17–20, 24; business and, into Canada, 20; business and, into Russia, 21–22; Brooks Adams on, 14; Cleveland and, 5; and Cuba, 171–72; European, 130–34, 144–45, 147,

148, 150, 158, 162; farmers and, 22, 26–28; forces advocating, into Canada, 182–85; forces inhibiting, 226–28; Grant and, 12; and Haiti, 170; and Hawaii, 205–10; historical assessments of, 3–9; into Latin America, 160–61; and Mexico, 167–70; missionary interest in, 24–25, 82–84; nature of post-Civil War, 228–30, 231, 232, 235–36; the press on, 10–11; and Samoa, 200–202; Seward on, 11
Expansionism, prevention of. *See* Anti-expansionism
Explorations. *See* Travel, overseas
Expositions, international, American involvement with, 45–47

Fairs. *See* Expositions, international
Farewell Address, of Washington, 159, 160
Farmers, 22, 26–28
Farragut, Adm. David C., 90
A Fearful Responsibility (Howells), 58
Federalist essays, 212
Fenians, 135
Fenollosa, Ernest, 213
Ferrell, Robert H., anti-expansionism, reason for, 9
Fiji Islands, 99, 225
Fillmore, Millard, 205
Fish, Hamilton, 4, 12; assessment of, 233
Fish, Nicholas, 41
Fisheries question, 21, 192–96; Cleveland-Bayard policy on, 194–96
Fogg, George G., 47
Foote, Lucius H., 223, 224
Ford, Worthington Chauncy, 194
A Foregone Conclusion (Howells), 58
Foreign commerce. *See* Markets
Foreign service. *See* State Department
Foster, John W., 69
Foulk, George C., 223
France: and authors, 52, 59–60; and China, 217; cultural exchanges

with, 139; relations with U.S. over Latin American matters, 158; relations with U.S. over Liberia, 150; rival of U.S., 133–34, 205; travel to, 110–11
Franco-Prussian War, 33, 124
Franklin, Benjamin, 112
Freer Gallery, 213
Frelinghuysen, Frederick T., 6, 30, 33, 43, 71, 131, 222; and Africa, 151–52; assessment of, 235; and Hawaii, 207–208; and an isthmian canal, 173, 179; and Latin American policy, 161, 169
Fujimaro, Tamaka, 117

Garfield administration, 6, 68
Garfield, James A., 30, 177
Geneva convention (1864), 47
George, Henry, 140
German-Americans, 124
Germany: cultural exchanges with, 139–40; exclusion of hog products, 29–31; relations with U.S. over Latin American matters, 159; rival of U.S., 131–33, 228; rivalry over Samoa, 200, 202–204; and Samoa, 99, 133; travel to, 111–15; universities of, 112–15
Gibbons, William G., 95
Gibson, Randall L., 183; on anti-expansionism, 6
Gilbert and Sullivan, 139, 198
Gilman, Daniel Coit, 113
Gladstone, William, 138
Glimpse of Unfamiliar Japan (Hearn), 60
Globe Express Company, 18
Godkin, E. L., 110, 176; anti-Blaine feeling of, 164–65, 166; on foreign service reforms, 37, 42
The Golden Bowl (James), 56
Good Neighbor Policy, early evidences of, 163
Göttingen University, 112
Goward, Gustavus, 201–202
Grant, Ulysses S., 4, 64, 118, 187, 228; assessment of, 233; and Cuba, 171; as an expansionist, 12, 199; and an isthmian canal, 173,

Grant, Ulysses S. (cont.)
177; and Santo Domingo, 7, 12, 170; world tour of, 109, 212
Great Northwestern Telegraph Company, 189
Great Western Steamship Company, 18
Great White Fleet, 160
Greely, Lt. Comdr. Adolphus Washington, 121–22
Grinnell, Henry W., 213
Guatemalan Central Railroad, 162
Guidebooks (travel), 105–106
Gulf of Mexico, 171
Gunckel, Lewis B., 123

Haiti: expansionism and, 170; U.S. relations with, 170
Hale, Eugene P., 89
Hall, Charles Francis, 120
Hall, George A. H., 119
Hamlin, Hannibal, 214
Handbook for Travelers in Europe and the East, 106
Harris, Townsend, 212
Harrison administration, 12, 165
Harrison, Benjamin, 15, 37, 41, 77, 101, 166, 191, 203, 219; assessment of, 234
Harte, Bret, 59, 140
Harvard University, 115
Hawaii: American interest in, 22, 204–10; annexation of, 64, 154, 205, 208; and authors, 63–64; Chinese labor and, 206–207; expansionism and, 205–10; missionaries in, 79–80; reciprocity with, 7, 63–64, 205, 206, 208, 209–10, 233, 235; 1875 reciprocity treaty with, 22, 206, 208, 209; Seward on acquisition of, 11
Hawaiian Commercial Company, 205
Hawaiian Evangelical Association, 79
Hawthorne, Nathaniel, 51
Hay, John, 107
Hayes administration, 160
Hayes, Rutherford B., 218, 219, 227, 234; on anti-expansionism,

5; and an isthmian canal, 173, 177, 178
Hearn, Lafcadio, 59–61
Hewitt, Abram S., 36, 46
Hitt, Robert R., 190
Hoar, George F., 42
Hog production, 29
Hokkaido, 118
Holman, William S., 91, 123
Holmes, Oliver Wendell, 109
Holy Land. *See* Palestine
Homestead Act, 118
Homer, Winslow, 110
Honshu, 118
House Resolution 63, 123–24
Howe, Samuel Gridley, 124
Howells, William Dean, 54–55, 57–59, 66, 107; on Italy, 57–58
Howgate, Capt. Henry W., 121
Hudson, Roderick, 55
Hudson's Bay Company, 121
Hunt, William M., 98–99
Hurlbut, Gen. Stephen J., 160

Immigration, 135–37; Chinese, 217–19; concern over increasing, 135–37; Irish, 135
Imperialism. *See* Expansionism
Imperial University, 117
Indian Summer (Howells), 58
Indo China, 211, 217
Industrialism, and expansionism, 229; and naval renewal, 88, 101
The Innocents Abroad (Twain), 62
Inter-American conference (1882), 163, 164
Inter-American conference (1889), 165–66
International African Association, 151, 153
International arbitration. *See* Arbitration, international
International conferences. *See* Conferences, international
International Copyright Association, 142
International expositions. *See* Expositions, international
International Exposition of Electricity (1881), 46

International Fishery Exhibition (1880), 46
International Polar Year, 121
International Postal Union, 48
International Red Cross, 47
Interoceanic Canal Commission, 173
Ionian Isles, 59
Ireland, emigration from, 68
Irish-Americans, 12, 124; affecting relations with Britain, 68–69, 135; protection abroad of, 68–69
Irving, Washington, 51
Israel Potter (Melville), 51
Isthmian canal, 12, 24, 208; Blaine and, 178–79; business and, 176; Cleveland and, 173, 176, 177–78; Colombian route, 172–73, 177, 180; Congress and, 180–81; desire for an, 10, 97–98, 149, 161, 172–81, 231, 232; Frelinghuysen and, 173, 179; Grant and, 173, 177; Hayes and, 173, 177, 178; Morgan and, 180; Nicaragua and an, 161; Nicaraguan route, 172–73, 177, 180
Isthmus of Panama, 130, 160
Isolationism. *See* Anti-expansionism
Italian Journeys (Howells), 58
Italy: Howells and, 57–58; travel to, 111, 127

James, Henry, 53–57, 59; compared with Howells, 58; expands national consciousness, 56–57; foreign themes of, 53–56; on travel overseas, 107, 110
James, William, 53, 54
Japan: American interest in, 211–13; authors and, 59–62; cultural exchange with, 212–13; and Korea, 221, 223–24; and missionaries, 80, 117, 212; technical missions to, 116–19; Westernization of, 210, 212–13
Jerusalem, 122
Jews: discrimination against Russian, 69; protection abroad of American, 70–73; protection in Turkey of American, 70–73

Johns Hopkins University, 113, 114, 115
Jordan River, 123
Josephson, Matthew, 62

Kalakaua, King, 132, 206–207
Kanakas, 204
Kasson, John A., 23, 157, 230; attendance at an international conference, 47; and Berlin conference, 23, 152–53; on the foreign service, 40
Kennan, George, 115–16
Kipling, Rudyard, 82
Korea: interest in, 220–24; missionaries in, 82, 84–85; Shufeldt's mission to, 22
Kurile Islands, 118

Labor, and naval renewal, 98
The Lady of the Aroostock (Howells), 58
Lady Franklin Bay, 121
LaFeber, Walter: on expansionism, 229; expansionism and business, 8
La Fortue, 170
Lake Nicaragua, 161
La Mamea, 199
LeGendre, Charles, 213
Leland, Dr. George A., 117
Leopold II, King, 151
Leopold, Richard W., 9
Li Hung-chang, 222
Lincoln, Abraham, 224
Lincoln, Robert Todd, 41
Literary journals, reflect European influence, 51–52
Literature, American, reflects European influence, 50–66
A Little Tour in France (James), 54
Liukiu Islands, 211
Livingstone, David, 145
Loans, 19
Lodge, Henry Cabot, 193, 232; on Canadian annexation, 183; on deplorable condition of U.S. Navy, 89
Logan, Cornelius A., 163
Longfellow, Henry Wadsworth, 53
Looking Backward (Bellamy), 65

Lowell, James Russell, 39, 178, 206; and Britain, 52, 141; on France, 52

Lynch, William F., 123

McCormick, Cyrus, 21

McFarland, Samuel G. M., 76

Mahan, Adm. Alfred T., 10; on expansionism, 231–32; on naval renewal, 97–98, 101–102

McKinley, William, 45

The Marble Faun (Hawthorne), 51

Marcy, William, 205

Maritime Canal Company of Nicaragua, 173

Markets, 10, 14, 27–28, 229, 231; American business competes for, 17–18; in the Arctic, 120, 122; Asian, 22, 198, 208, 209; with Canada, 17, 187; cattle production and, 27; cereal production and, 26–28; commercial journals and, 24; Congress and, 16–17; foreign restrictions on, 17; foreign restrictions on pork, 29–31; interest in Mexican, 168–70; Latin America, 18–20, 158, 164; and the Navy, 96, 98, 160–61; need for, 15–16; with Russia, 21–22

Mather, Cotton, 83

Maximilian, 158

May, Ernest R., 8

Meade, Richard W., 199

Meat Inspection Act (1890), 30–31

Melbourne, Australia Exposition (1880), 46

Melville, Herman, 51

Mendenhall, Thomas C., 117

Merchant marine, 87, 88; decline of, 93; government aid for, 93–94; and the Navy, 95–97, 98; reform of, 93–96; rivals of, 93, 94

Methodist, number of missionaries abroad, 74

Mexican War (1846–1848), 19

Mexico: American interest in, 167–70; annexation of territory of, 168; expansionism and, 167–70; French in, 158; interest of business in, 168–70; reciprocity with,

169; union with the United States, 11

Michigan State University, 119

Michigan University, 112, 113

Miller, Joaquin, 61

Missionaries, 24–26; in Africa, 78–79, 84; and anti-foreignism, 80, 81–82; in China, 81, 84, 86; as a civilizing force, 75–76, 78, 79, 80; in Hawaii, 79–80; interest in Africa, 144–45, 146, 153; interest in expansion, 24–25, 82–84; and Japan, 80, 117, 212; in Korea, 82, 84–85; in Latin America, 76; numbers of, abroad, 74; in Palestine, 77–78; periodicals on, 75, 76, 78–79, 83; Presbyterian, abroad, 76; promote American business, 75; protection abroad of American, 84–86; in Turkey, 85

Monroe Doctrine, 12, 19, 33, 37, 97, 131–32, 224, 230, 231, 234; interpretation of, 157–59; and an isthmian canal, 173, 174–75, 177, 179–81; and Pacific expansionism, 201, 205, 207

Montgomery Ward, 17–18

Moody, Dwight, 140

Moreno, Celso Caesar, 132

Morgan, Hank, 63

Morgan, John Tyler, 154; on Africa, 23, 148–49; on expansionism, 232; and an isthmian canal, 180

Morgan, Philip H., 168–69

Morris, E. Joy, 85

Morris, William, 139

Murchison episode (1888), 178

Murdock, J. N., 79

Napoleon III, 139, 158

National Civil Service Reform League, 43

National Geographic Society, 122

Nationals. *See* State Department, protection of

Naval Advisory Board, 98

Naval bases, 160–62, 231

Naval officers, serving as diplomats, 87–88, 97

Naval stations, Pacific, U.S. interest in, 198–99, 201, 202–203
Naval War College, 99–100
Navy Department, poor administration of, 92
Navy, U.S., 10, 213, 232; and business, 96–97, 101; deplorable condition of, 88–90, 96–97; expansion of, 10; and markets, 96, 160–61; and the merchant marine, 95–97, 98, 230; new developments and, 88–89; programs of renewal for, 98–100, 102; reasons for deplorable condition of, 90–93; renewal of, 88, 95–102; rivals of, 89–90, 98–99; sectional politics and, 91; size of, 89
Negroes, American, Africa and, 144, 149
Nellie Chapin, 73
Nevins, Allan, 3–4
New Granada treaty, 172, 178
Newman, Christopher, 56, 57
"New Navy." *See* Navy, U.S., renewal of
New Orleans Exposition, 60
New York Life Insurance Company, 18
New York State Chamber of Commerce, 24, 95, 124, 145, 151, 189, 219
New York Herald, and Africa, 145, 156
Nicaragua: and an isthmian canal, 161; Isthmian relations, 173
Nicaraguan Railroad Company, 161
Northwestern University, 115
Norton, Charles Eliot, 54

"Open door," early evidences of, 156
Otaru, 116
Ottoman Empire. *See* Turkey
Our Country (Strong), 26, 82–83
Outing, 107
Overseas markets. *See* Markets
Overseas travel. *See* Travel, overseas

Pago Pago, 7, 22, 199, 202, 203
Palestine Exploration Fund, 122–23
Palestine: missionaries and, 77–78; protection of Jews traveling to, 70–73
Pan-Americanism, 19–20, 162–66, 231
Paris conference (1867), 47
Paris conference (1878), 48
Paris conference (1881), 48
Paris Exposition (1867), 45
Paris Exposition (1878), 46
Pax Americana, 131
Pearl Harbor, 7, 22, 204, 209, 231
Peary, Robert Edwin, 122
Pendleton Act (1883), 38–39
Pennsylvania Railroad, 18, 93
Perkins, Dexter, 4
Peru, and the War of the Pacific, 158–60
Petroleum production, 44
Phelps, Capt. Seth L., 161
Philadelphia Centennial Exhibition, 213
Philippines, annexation of, 149
Pierce administration, 205
Pittsburgh Folding Chair Company, 18
Platt-Symonds bill, 142
A Pointer for the Tourist, 107
Point Four, 116
Polar explorations. *See* Travel, overseas
Polaris, 120
Polk, James K., 123
"Pork diplomacy." *See* Markets, foreign restrictions on
Poronai, 116
Port Arthur, 211
The Portrait of a Lady (James), 56
Portraits of Places (James), 54
Powell, Maj. John Wesley, 120
Pratt, Julius W., 4
Preemption Act, 118
Presbyterian Board of Foreign Missions, 74–75
Press, The, 140; on anti-expansionism, 6–7; on Canadian annexation, 184–85; on China, 214–15, 217; and Cuba, 171; on European problems, 128–30; on expansionism, 10–11, 133, 134–35; on the fisheries issue, 193, 194, 195–96;

Press, The (cont.)
and Hawaii, 208, 209–10; and immigration, 136, 218–19; interest in Africa, 145, 147–48, 153, 156; and an isthmian canal, 174–77, 181; and Korea, 223; and Mexico, 167, 169–70; on Pan-Americanism, 162–63, 165–66; and peace congresses, 49; on reciprocity with Canada, 187–88; and Samoa, 203–204; on the State Department, 38–40

Pumpelly, Raphael, 116
Pusey and Jones Company, 95

Ragnarok (Donnelly), 65
Rand McNally and Company, 18
Raouf Pasha, 72
Ray, Lt. Comdr. Patrick Henry, 122
Reciprocity, 19–21, 24, 32–33, 231; with Canada, 20–21, 32–33, 187–92, 196, 228; forces favoring Canadian, 187–90; forces opposing Canadian, 190–92; with Cuba, 172; with Hawaii, 7, 63–64, 205, 206, 208, 209–10, 233, 235; 1875 Hawaiian treaty on, 22; with Latin America, 164; with Mexico, 169
Redburn (Melville), 51
Reed, Thomas B., 229
Remington, Philo, typewriter of, 140
Restorationists, protection abroad of, 73
Ritchie, S. J., 20; on reciprocity with Canada, 189
Rives, G. L., 72–73
Roach, John, 93–94, 154
Robert, Christopher R., 76
Robert College, 76
Roderick Hudson (James), 56
Rodgers, Comdr. John, 221
Roosevelt, Franklin D., 103, 196
Roosevelt, Theodore, 10, 12, 167, 232
Royal College of the King of Siam, 76
Russia: cultural interest in, 139; future rival with U.S., 115; travel to, 107, 115–16; treatment of Jews affecting U.S. relations with, 69
Rutgers University, 117

Sakhalin, 118
Samana Bay, 97
Samoa, interest in: 22, 198–204, 205; German-American rivalry and, 133; Germany and, 99; tripartite protectorate, 202–204
Samoan treaty (1878), 199, 200–201
Sandwich Islands. *See* Hawaii
Sanford, Gen. Henry S., 151
San Francisco, Pacific interests of, 199, 208–210, 214
Sankey, Ira, 140
Santo Domingo: annexation to the United States, 7, 12; Grant and, 170
Saratoga (New York) agreement, 30
Sargent, Aaron A., 30, 131, 220, 222
Sargent, John Singer, 110
Sarmiento, Domingo F., 166
Schenck, Gen. Robert, 39
Schurman, Jacob G., 185
Schurz, Carl, on anti-expansionism, 6
Schwatka, Lt. Comdr. Frederick, 121
Seney, George W., 13
Seward, George F., 217–18, 219, 221
Seward, William H., 5, 12, 47, 73, 85, 109, 221, 229; acquisition of Cuba, 11; acquisition of Danish West Indies, 11; acquisition of Hawaii, 11; and Alaska, 228, 233; anti-expansionism, reasons for, 5; assessment of, 233; on expansionism, 11
Sherman, John, 156; on Canada, 183, 189
Shufeldt, Comdr. Robert W., 22, 97, 150, 156; and Africa, 23, 87, 96, 99; mission to Africa, 147–48; missions to Korea, 22, 147, 220–21, 221–24
Siam, interest in, 224–25
Sketchbook (Irving), 51
Smith, Goldwin, 183
Smith, Theodore Clarke, 4
Smith, V. V., 29
Spanish-American War, 7, 90, 204
Spanish Carolines, 133
Spencer, Herbert, 127, 141
Spiller, Robert E., 63

Spreckels, Claus, 205
Springer, William McKendree, 36
Standard Oil Company, 18–19, 44
Stanley, Henry M., 145, 155, 156
State Department: appropriations problems and, 42; call for professionalization in, 40–42; calls for reform in, 36, 39–42; critical views of, 35–39, 41; protection of nationals, 67–74, 84–86
Stimson, Henry L., 103
Stockdale, Thomas R., 181
Story, Joseph, 111
Story, William Wetmore, 111
Straus, Oscar S., 72
Strether, Lambert, 56
Strong, Josiah, 25–26
Strout, Cushing, 136
Stuart, Graham, 152
Students' Association, 111
Sudanese-Russian-French alliance, 130
Suez Canal, 173, 175, 176
Sumner, Charles, on Canadian annexation, 182–83
Sydney, Australia Exposition (1879), 46
Syrian-Protestant College, 76

Taft, William H., 10, 44, 192
Tappan, Henry P., 112
Tariff, 31–32, 93; Europeans adopt a high, 138
Ten Years' War (1868–1878), 171
Thompson, Richard W., 95, 161
Ticknor, George, 112
Tisdel, Willard P., African mission of, 154–55
Tokyo University, 119
Tourist companies, 105
Townsend-Harris treaty (1858), 80
Townshend, Richard W., 189, 214
Transatlantic Sketches (James), 54
Travel, 107
Travel, overseas: advances facilitating, 104–107; to Alaska, 120; American views concerning, 126, 127–28, 130, 140–41; to the Arctic, 120–22; authors and, 50–66; Birr on, 116; books on, 107; to Britain, 109; Curti on, 116; foreign attitude toward American, 126–27; to France, 110–11; to Germany, 111–15; influencing American scholarship, 112–15; to Italy, 111, 127; to Palestine, 122–23; passports for, 104; periodicals promoting, 107; reasons for, 103–109; to Russia, 107, 115–16; scholars and, 110–17; to South America, 124; technical missions and, 116–19; warnings about, 109–10
Traveler and the Ticket Agent, 107
Treaty of Washington, 192
Treitschke, Heinrich von, 131
Trescot, William H., 39–40, 160
Turkey: missionaries in, 85; treatment of American Jews affecting U.S. relations with, 70–73
Turner, Frederick Jackson, 127, 196
Tuscan Cities (Howells), 58
Twain, Mark, 38, 62–64, 107; on Britain, 63
Tyler-Webster doctrine (1842), 132

Union Pacific Central Railroad, 199
United States Coast and Geodetic Survey, 119–20
United States of Europe idea, 138
United States Naval Academy, 213
Universal Peace Union, 49
University of Berlin, 61

Venetian Life (Howells), 58
Verbeck, Rev. Guido F., 117
Vervain, Florida, 58
Vienna Exposition (1873), 45–46
Virginius crisis, 91
Von Bergen, Werner, 131

Wallace, Gen. Lew, 70–71
War of the Pacific (1879–1883), 89; U.S. as mediator during, 158, 159–60
Ward, William, 95
Washington Square (James), 56
Webb, William H., 199
Webster, Daniel, 205
West, Benjamin, 111

West Indies, 29, 134
Wheat production, 15, 26–27
Wheeler, James, 96
Whistler, James M., 110, 213
White, Andrew D., 39, 112–13, 131–32, 159
Whitney, William C., 99
Wilkes, Lt. Comdr. Charles, 199
Williams, George B., 116
Wiman, Erastus, 189

Wisconsin University, 115
Wise, George B., 88
World War I, 57, 102
Wyoming, 119

Yale University, 113
Yezo, 116
Young America movement, 186
Young, James Russell, 86
Young, John Russell, 214, 216–17

Plesur, Milton.
America's outward thrust; approaches to foreign affairs,
1865–1890. DeKalb, Northern Illinois University Press
₁1971₁

vii, 276 p. 25 cm.

Includes bibliographical references.

1. U. S.—Foreign relations—1865–1898. 2. U. S.—Relations (general) with foreign countries. I. Title.

E661.7.P55   327.73   76–137882
ISBN 0–87580–019–X   MARC